Surrendering the Task

Series Preface

Regnum Studies in Mission are born from the lived experience of Christians and Christian communities in mission, especially but not solely in the fast growing churches among the people of the developing world. These churches have more to tell than stories of growth. They are making significant impacts on their cultures in the cause of Christ They are producing 'cultural products' which express the reality of Christian faith, hope and love in their societies.

Regnum Studies in Mission are the fruit often of rigorous research to the highest international standards and always of authentic Christian engagement in the transformation of people and societies. These are for the world. The formation of Christian theology, missiology and practice in the twenty-first century will depend to a great extent on the active participation of growing churches contributing biblical and culturally appropriate expressions of Christian practice to inform World Christianity.

Surrendering the Task
British Baptists in China, 1937-1952

Audrey Salters

Edited by Clare Salters

First published 2024 by Regnum Books International

Regnum is an imprint of the Oxford Centre for Mission Studies
St. Philip and St. James Church
Woodstock Road
Oxford OX2 6HR, UK
www.regnumbooks.net

British Library Cataloguing in Publication Data
A catalogue record for this book is available from the British Library

ISBN: 979-8-8898-3887-6
eBook ISBN: 979-8-8898-3888-3

Cover design by Words by Design

Typeset by Words by Design

The publication of this book was funded by Regnum Books

Distributed by Fortress Press in the US, Canada, India, and Brazil

Acknowledgements

Editor's Note

This book is adapted from the doctoral thesis of my late mother, Audrey Salters (née Still), to whom full credit goes for the research.

It takes courage to embark upon a PhD in retirement. It takes even more to continue with it after being hospitalised (twice!) for a major stroke that paralysed her right side and, subsequently, resulted in two broken wrists. Thankfully, courage was something she possessed in abundance – as did her parents, whose work in China inspired her original research. Week after week we would meet in the early morning by video call for her to dictate and me to type then email the latest text to Dad to print and take to the hospital, to be painstakingly annotated by her heavily plastered, non-dominant hand ready for us to start again the next day. I learnt a lot from that experience – not just about mid-twentieth-century Chinese history, but about resilience and perseverance.

For readers interested in the personal dimension, you can see Audrey in the photo on page 52, seated in the front row beside her older sister, Rosemary (far left). In the middle of the back row are her parents, Ronald and Gwyneth Still, and her younger sister, Catherine.

The thesis benefited from input from a number of people, and the original acknowledgements are reproduced in full below, with renewed thanks for their input to the research.

In addition, there are others whose input has been instrumental in the final editorial stage of transforming the thesis manuscript into this book. I am most grateful to my father, Robin Salters, and sister, Judith Wilson, for putting their faith in me to edit the book to Mum's standards; and to my aunt, Rosemary Hollingworth, and my husband, Malcolm Thomas, for their encouragement and support throughout the process. My thanks also go to Christie Chow, for encouraging our family to pursue posthumous publication of the thesis; to the staff at Regnum Publishing, particularly Elizabete Santos and Tony Gray; to Rebecca Shuttleworth from the Angus Library, Oxford; to Edward Hood, archivist at the School of Oriental and Asian Studies; and to Qinghong Li for help accessing the Zibo City archives. Finally, the editing wisdom, support and encouragement of Elisabeth Okasha, family friend and professor emerita at University College Cork, have been invaluable throughout this process.

Clare Salters, 2023

Author's Acknowledgements, Reproduced from Original Thesis

I must first acknowledge, gladly and from my heart, the help of my daughter, Clare Salters, who undertook the latter stages of typing for this thesis when I was incapacitated following a stroke and two broken wrists, and without whose help I would not have been able to complete it. Her drive, technological skills and abundant willingness to put herself out on my behalf, have been of the highest possible order.

I am grateful for help from staff in the School of History, Classics and Archaeology at the University of Edinburgh and for the contribution of my supervisors. Trevor Griffith's eye for style and clarity in identifying a line of argument has been important and I have benefitted from Felix Boecking's keen attention to detail and thorough knowledge of this period of Chinese history. Adam Budd's enthusiasm and interest provided a stimulating introduction to this stage of university life and Stana Nenadic rescued me when lack of a supervisor threatened my initial progress.

Much of what follows was dependent on the Baptist Missionary Society Archives in the Angus Library, Oxford, and I value the generous access I was given to them. I am particularly grateful to Emily Burgoyne on the library staff there, who is always a pleasure to work with and who has been unfailingly energetic in helping me find particular items.

I am especially pleased to be able to thank the former China missionaries Vera Harrison and Peter J. Nelson, and the members of other former missionaries' families, who have shared information, letters and photographs: Sally Ball, Margaret Bennett, Derek Browne, Bill Clow, Peter Dart, Elizabeth Douglas, Elizabeth Fifer, Ian Flowers, Ruth Hingley, Eleanore Jamison, my sister Rosemary Hollingworth, Jean Houghton, Rosemary Pearson, Carol Redfern, Peter Richards, Margaret Roberts, Celly Rowe, David Seymour, Joan Wells, Dorothy Williamson, and Margaret Wyatt. Sheila and Steven Ball and Graham Little have also supplied information about missionary friends who formerly worked for the Baptist Missionary Society (BMS) in China.

I am grateful to Carole Comben and Elisabeth Okasha for much support and for reading early material. Very many individuals have helped me by sharing, locating, verifying or translating information. The long but possibly not exhaustive list includes David Coats, Chuan Gao, Gao Jian, Gao Lingjun, Gao Yan, Guo Jisheng, Brian Hollingworth, Sherman Xiaogang Lai, Joseph Lee, Sophie Lee, Sam Hallas, Han Jie, Michelle Huang, Lily Jackson, Andrew Kaiser, Rana Mitter, John Moffett, Marjory Park, Brian Stanley, Helen Stewart, Shenxiao Tong, Song Hong, Tian Daozheng and Wu Hongyi.

My husband, Robin, and both my daughters have been a great encouragement throughout. Clare's essential contribution has already been noted. From the outset, Judith has been an invaluable ally in practical difficulties and has supported me with much enjoyable hospitality in Edinburgh. Robin accompanied me through the long haul, and by his interest, sacrificial support and burgeoning cooking skills has helped me towards the conclusions. I dedicate this thesis to all three.

Audrey Salters, 2015

Contents

Introduction   1

1. The BMS and Its China Missionaries   19
    Origins, Early Influences and Founding Principles   19
    Organisational Structure, Terms of Service and Funding   24
    Profile of BMS China Missionaries, 1937   35
    The Development of BMS Work In China   37

2. Japanese Occupation in Shandong, 1937–1942   49
    The Impact of War   52
    BMS Missionaries as Third-Party Nationals During the Occupation   57
    The Chinese Baptist Church in Occupied Shandong   68

3. The BMS in Shaanxi, 1937–1945   81
    The Red Army in Shaanxi   82
    BMS Evangelical Work in Shaanxi before and During the War   88
    The Educational Work of the Mission   92
    Impact of the War in Europe, and the British Entry
        into the War against Japan   105
    Treaty Revision and International Relationships   108
    The BMS in Shaanxi by the End of the War   112

4. Planning and Recovery, August 1945 to July 1946   115
    Formation of BMS Policy   117
    Partnership with the Church of Christ in China   124
    Return to the Formerly Occupied Provinces   128
    Missionaries and Their Families   137
    SOS from Shandong   144

5. Civil War, July 1946 to December 1948   147
    The Civil War and Its Impact   147
    The Missionaries and their Chinese Co-Workers: The Case
        of Wang Juntang   160
    Rebuilding the Hospital in Xi'an: The Tilehouse Street Gift   169
    Policy with Regard to Mission Work under a Communist Regime   178

6. The BMS in China, 1949–1952   183
    Barriers to Understanding the BMS China Experience   185
    Communists Take Over Xi'an   189
    Shandong Churches under the CCP   194
    CCP Moves to Control the Chinese Church   199

Departure and Decisions about Subsequent Postings   205

Conclusions   211

Appendix 1: BMS China Missionaries   219
Appendix 2: The BMS In China: A Timeline   223
Bibliography   227
Index   253

List of Tables

1: BMS missionaries' income compared to UK-based counterparts   28

List of Figures

1: Extent of Japanese occupation, 1940   6
2: Shandong pastors and deacons, 1899   40
3: Key BMS locations in Shandong, Shanxi and Shaanxi   44
4: Baptist church workers in Shanxi, Shandong and Shaanxi, 1937   47
5: BMS missionaries before internment in Shanghai, Autumn 1942   52
6: Group of Shandong pastors, 1919   68
7: Zhang Sijing in 1937 (left) and 1947 (right)   78
8: Provincial origins of Zunde Girls' School pupils, Autumn 1943 97
9: Sources of funding, Zunde School, 1938–1942   100
10: Parental occupations of girls attending Zunde School, 1942–1943   101
11: Japanese- and Communist-controlled territories, August 1945 129
12: Transport challenges   151
13: Wang Juntang, Mrs Winifred Emmott and Wang's daughters   160
14: Memorial plaque in Tilehouse Street Church, Hitchin   178
15: BMS Missionaries in Shaanxi, June 1947   181
16: Location of BMS missionaries in China, June 1949   185
17: SBU Education Committee, June 1947   196
18: CCP moves leading to the departure of the BMS, 1948–1952   199
19: Location or Destination of ex-China missionaries, April 1952 208

List of Abbreviations

BMS	Baptist Missionary Society
BMSA	Baptist Missionary Society Archive
CBMS	Conference of British Missionary Societies
CBMSA	Conference of British Missionary Societies Archive
CWMA	Council for World Mission Archives
CCC	Church of Christ in China
CCP	Chinese Communist Party
CIM	China Inland Mission
CNC	Chinese National Currency
CNRRA	Chinese National Relief and Rehabilitation Administration
CPPCC	Chinese People's Political Consultative Conference
DRC	Development and Relief Committee
GMD	Guomindang (Wade Giles = Kuomintang)
HSBC	Hong Kong and Shanghai Banking Corporation
KMT	Kuomintang (pinyin = Guomindang)
LMS	London Missionary Society
MAB	Medical Advisory Board, a sub-committee of the CBMS
NCC	National Christian Council
PLA	People's Liberation Army
PRC	People's Republic of China
SBU	Shantung [Shandong] Baptist Union
SOAS	School of Oriental and African Studies
TSPM	Three-Self Patriotic Movement
UNRRA	United Nations Relief and Rehabilitation Administration
¥	Yuan
YMCA	Young Men's Christian Association
YWCA	Young Women's Christian Association

Abbreviated names are set out in full, with the relevant abbreviation in brackets, at the first mention in each chapter.

Note on Transliteration

Two systems have been developed over the past two centuries for transliterating Chinese calligraphic text into Roman script. The system familiar to Western readers for much of the twentieth century was the Wade Giles method. This was based on a system developed in the mid-nineteenth century by Thomas Francis Wade, and refined by Herbert A. Giles in his 1892 Chinese–English Dictionary.[1]

In 1958, the Hanyu Pinyin system (more commonly referred to simply as pinyin) was adopted by the Chinese government as the official system for transliteration. The International Organization for Standardization subsequently adopted this as the international transliteration standard for Mandarin Chinese in 1982.

Within this book, all Chinese personal and place names used in the text are written in pinyin, with the exception of Chiang Kai-shek, a name already familiar to Western readers in that form. Extracts from the archive are quoted using their original Wade Giles transliteration. The first time the name of a place or person occurs thus, the modern pinyin form is given in brackets. Thereafter it appears as in the original document.

In addition, Chinese characters are given in brackets for less-familiar personal and place names on the first usage, where these are known.

Note on Western Names

Missionaries and other individuals relevant to the narrative are named in full the first time they are mentioned in each chapter. Thereafter, they are referred to by surname only, unless the context or the need to differentiate between two individuals with the same surname means that it is clearer to use full names. Quoted authors and historians are referred to by their surnames throughout.

Note on Currency References

Just as today, the main unit of currency in China during the period covered by this book was the yuan. Following the establishment of the Republic of China in 1912, the Nationalist Government established the Chinese National Currency of which the primary unit was the silver yuan, sometimes translated as 'dollars' reflecting the similar specification between the silver yuan and the Spanish silver dollar. In 1935, the Nationalist Government made significant currency reforms, forbidding the circulation of silver dollar coins. The main unit of this new currency – the *fabi* (法幣), literally translated as 'legal tender' – was still called yuan, and still colloquially translated as 'dollar', the term commonly used by missionaries in correspondence with other English-speakers. The fabi was replaced by the current Chinese currency - the renminbi (人民币), literally translated as 'people's currency' - following the establishment of the People's Republic of China in 1948. Unless otherwise specified, throughout this book $ refers to yuan in pre-1948 fabi currency and not to American or other dollars; and ¥ refers to yuan in post-1948 renminbi currency.

---

[1] Herbert A. Giles, *A Chinese–English Dictionary*, (London: Kelly and Walsh, 1892).

Introduction

On the night of 9–10 September 1940, at the height of the London bombing, a high explosive bomb fell on 19 Furnival Street, headquarters of the Baptist Missionary Society (BMS). The library and several offices were destroyed and many mission records were lost.[1] News of the bombing reached missionaries in China some weeks later. Handley Stockley, a medical missionary based in the BMS hospital in Xi'an, wrote to the medical secretary in London, conveying his sympathy regarding this event, but saying he had 'very few regrets' about the loss of the mission records:

> [I]n many ways I'm glad they are gone beyond recall! I acknowledge we have great debts we owe to the past. But we live in a different era from our forefathers [...]. It may mean God wants us not to be anchored to the past, but to be free to sail into the unknown future with him.[2]

For Baptist missionaries working in China in 1941, the future must have seemed, more than ever, 'unknown'. Not only was Europe engulfed in a ferocious war, but since 1937 another war, the War of Resistance against Japan, had been tearing China apart. There were huge immediate practical consequences for missionary work in China, but there were also significant longer-term policy questions of which Stockley must have been aware when he wrote.

Since the late 1920s, the BMS had been engaged in painstaking discussions as to how it might wind down its missionary work in China. The early part of the century had seen unprecedented growth in missionary numbers and in the establishment of new missionary schools, colleges and hospitals. In the context of a growing Chinese anti-foreign movement, the scale and splendour of these new institutions seemed out of place. BMS Foreign Secretary C. E. Wilson, who toured China in 1929, expressed himself to be 'very sceptical and disquieted as to the effect of all this display of wealth to the Chinese'.[3] The 'display of wealth' must have seemed particularly incongruous to Wilson in view of the fact that the Missionary Society itself was heavily in debt. In July 1927, the Finance Committee had announced a gross deficit of over £41,000, equivalent to more

---

[1] Brian Stanley, *The History of the Baptist Missionary Society, 1792–1992* (Edinburgh: T & T Clark, 1992), p. 391.
[2] BMSA, CH/65, Stockley to Chesterman, 16 January 1941.
[3] Stanley, *History*, p. 315, citing BMSA, CH/12, Duplicate Book of C. E. Wilson, pp. 28–30 and 97; Diary of China Deputation Tour for April 1929.

than £2,500,000 in today's money, a daunting sum to a small organisation financed by voluntary contributions.[4]

The state of BMS finances and the political environment in China were not the only reasons for the society to be thinking about how it might disengage itself from its work there. The professed goal of the Baptist missionary movement had from the first been to achieve its own dissolution, to render itself unnecessary by building mature indigenous churches in countries overseas that were capable of maintaining and reproducing themselves without foreign support. The recognised formula for describing these mature indigenous churches was 'three-self churches': self-governing, self-supporting and self-propagating.[5]

It is a commonplace of missionary history that missionary societies, although supportive in theory of the three-self movement, were slow to adopt its principles in practice.[6] At the World Missionary Conference held in Edinburgh in 1910, it became clear that the goal of building independent self-supporting churches in Africa and Asia was a long way from realisation. Even in China, which had implemented the three-self principles to a greater extent than elsewhere, 'the confidence expressed [...] that Chinese Christianity was about to achieve complete financial and administrative independence was somewhat misplaced.'[7] Brian Stanley has drawn attention to the 'multiple ambiguities' that had occurred in attempts by missionary societies to implement the three-self principles, and suggests:

> What scholars have yet to attempt is a more comprehensive survey of how far, and with what regional or denominational variations, the three-self principle was translated into practice over a longer period of time.[8]

How well did British Baptists, working in China in the mid-twentieth century, translate these principles into practice?

The conventional narrative holds that missionaries were keen to stay in China as long as they could retain a foothold, and eventually left only because they were 'expelled' by the Communists after the establishment of the People's Republic of China (PRC).[9] On the contrary, the Baptist archive demonstrates that

---

[4] BMSA, General Committee Minutes, Vol. 25, 20 July 1927.

[5] C. Peter Williams, *The Ideal of the Self-Governing Church: A Study of Victorian Missionary Strategy*, (Leiden MA: Brill, 1990), p. 1.

[6] Williams, *The Ideal of the Self-Governing Church*; Paul W. Harris, *Nothing but Christ: Rufus Anderson and the Ideology of Protestant Foreign Missions*, (Oxford: Oxford University Press, 1999).

[7] Brian Stanley, *World Missionary Conference, Edinburgh 1910* (Grand Rapids MI and Cambridge: William B. Eerdmans, 2009), p. 149.

[8] Brian Stanley, 'The Church of the Three Selves: A Perspective from the World Missionary Conference, Edinburgh, 1910', *Journal of Imperial and Commonwealth History* 36.3 (September 2008), pp. 435–451 (p. 436).

[9] Missionaries 'were of course expelled from China by the Communists after 1949'. See Rana Mitter, 'Imperialism, Transnationalism, and the Reconstruction of Post-War China: UNRRA in China, 1944–7', *Past and Present*, Supplement 8, 2013, pp. 51–69 (p. 65).

the missionary departure was delayed by events in China, rather than brought on prematurely by them. In fact, the BMS plan for handing over all responsibility for church leadership, finance and growth to members of the Chinese church began to come undone in July 1937 when China was invaded by Japan.

A conference of all BMS missionaries in China, held in Qingzhou (青州) in February 1927, reiterated that the BMS had 'always regarded itself as a temporary organisation [...] prepared at any time to surrender its task'; devolution should be regarded 'as a practical working policy, towards the success of which every activity of the foreign missionary should be directed and adjusted'. Finding ways to bring their work in China to an end was to be the first priority for all missionaries working there: the task was to be surrendered 'as soon as an indigenous Chinese church [was] able and willing to assume the responsibility'.[10]

The BMS had initiated its China mission in Shandong province, where the earliest pioneers had settled in 1863. Leaders with exceptional energy and vision, including Timothy Richard and Alfred Jones, had established an indigenous Christian church in Shandong, which from the first had shown a character and vitality of its own. Work in two further provinces, Shanxi and Shaanxi, had come later, had taken off more slowly and had encountered several formidable setbacks. In the late 1920s, the BMS judged that only Shandong had a Chinese church 'able and willing to assume responsibility'.[11]

Chiang Kai-shek's (蔣介石; Jiang Jieshi) establishment of the unified Nationalist state led from Nanjing in 1928, and his conversion to Christianity in 1929, encouraged missionary societies to believe a climate might be created in which an indigenous Chinese church would thrive.[12] It seemed that here might be a man who could influence his country to an appreciation of the Christian message. Chiang's fight to extinguish the growing Communist threat led to three years of intense brutality and violence, but towards the end of 1931 China appeared to be entering a period of relative military and political stability during which plans for national reconstruction began to be formed.[13]

Accordingly, early in 1932 the BMS announced its decision to withdraw completely from Shandong. A conference of BMS missionaries working in China at the time requested a transitional period of fifteen years. The London-based General Committee felt this was too long and decided 'to reduce its allocation to Shandong by ten per cent annually, thus setting the goal of

---

[10] BMSA, CH/23, Secretariat Shantung, 1939–1946, Minutes of the English Baptist Mission Inter-Provincial Conference at Tsingchow (Qingzhou), 7–12 February 1927.
[11] Tsingchow Conference 1927.
[12] Jonathan Fenby, *Generalissimo: Chiang Kai-shek and the China He Lost* (London: Free Press, 2003), p. 191; BMSA, CH/68, A. K. Bryan, 'The status of the Missionary in the Chinese Church', 1943, p. 6; Daniel H. Bays, *A New History of Christianity in China* (Chichester, West Sussex: Wiley-Blackwell, 2012), p. 125; George A. Young, *The Living Christ in Modern China* (London: Carey-Kingsgate, 1947), p. 53.
[13] Hans J. van de Ven, *War and Nationalism in China 1925–1945* (London: Routledge, 2003), p. 130.

withdrawal by 1942'. This was later extended to 1947 in response to further input from missionaries in the field.[14]

Hopes for lasting peace in China were destroyed by the expansionist goals of Japan.[15] Between 1937 and 1948, members of the Chinese church in Shandong found themselves obliged on repeated occasions to seek additional help from the BMS in order to cope with the destruction occasioned first by the War of Resistance against Japan, and then by the Civil War. The BMS remained committed in principle to 'surrendering the task', to empowering Chinese Christians to take responsibility and control, but felt unable to do so in the face of these repeated requests.[16]

The focus of this book is not primarily on policies introduced and pursued by an organisation (the BMS), but on the experiences of individual men and women given the job of working out those policies in a challenging and rapidly changing environment, and the impact these experiences had on their relationships with Chinese Christians. Cavalcanti has noted the general disregard in sociological studies of religion of the way human agency contributes to the diffusion of religion:

> Religious organisations provide the structural component for diffusion: organisational resources, doctrinal boundaries, internal power structures, sanctioned recruiting strategies, and long-term goals. But it is the personal approach of missionaries that sets the fine print for the process of religious diffusion.[17]

Only by considering 'the personal approach' of the individuals involved can 'the fine print' of Baptist missionary activity in China be measured against the society's professed goals. What evidence is there that individual missionaries were really committed to enabling their Chinese colleagues to be given total responsibility for the work then being undertaken by the mission? To begin to unravel this question requires an understanding of the wider context of the missionaries' lives, the claims on them from their families, and their attitudes to what was happening both in China and on the 'home front'.

Missionaries, in China and elsewhere, often attracted hostile comment from their contemporaries. Pearl Buck shocked the members of the American Presbyterian Mission Board at the Astor Hotel in New York in 1932 by declaring that the missionaries she had encountered during many years in China were:

> so lacking in sympathy for the people they were supposed to be saving, so scornful of any civilization except their own, so harsh in their judgments upon one another,

---

[14] Stanley, *History*, p. 318, citing BMSA, General Committee Minutes, Vol. 25, 3 February 1932, 20 July 1932; Vol. 26, 6 February 1934.

[15] van de Ven, *War and Nationalism*, p. 197.

[16] Tsingchow Conference 1927.

[17] H. B. Cavalcanti, 'Human Agency in Mission Work: Missionary Styles and their Political Consequences', *Sociology of Religion* 66.4 (Winter, 2005), pp. 381–198 (p. 381).

> so coarse and insensitive among a sensitive and cultivated people that my heart has fairly bled with shame.[18]

Although the harshness of Buck's judgement caused general alarm and distress amongst her church-going audience, the sentiments she expressed had long been commonplace among observers outwith the church. Even one twentieth-century Baptist missionary recruit, Harry Wyatt, recalled that 'When I came out first there was one thing which I own I did dread a little, and that was the missionaries.' It should be noted that Wyatt went on to add, 'but I know now at first hand what homely, kind-hearted people they are, and I am not afraid of them any more'.[19] Bickers has shown that more realistic understandings and closer working relationships had gradually evolved between Chinese Christians and modernising missionaries in the years following the Nationalist revolution.[20]

'It is dangerous to sit in judgment,' declares Ling at the outset of her book on this phase of mission history, but she goes on to repeat many earlier criticisms of missionaries, without reference to Bickers' findings.[21] She is critical of missionaries' personal behaviour in their relations with the Chinese people: 'Missionary action was said to be motivated by the constraining love of Christ, but their love degenerated into condescending and patronising charity.'[22] This book offers a different perspective, giving examples that demonstrate the attitudes of individual BMS missionaries to their work and the ways in which they interacted with Chinese nationals, during this turbulent phase of Chinese history. These individual experiences make a major revisionist argument about the relationship between Baptist missionaries and the Chinese church, and about the approach of the Baptists, as an example of Protestant missionaries, to the China field as a whole.

During the period covered by this book, the BMS employed approximately one hundred missionaries in three provinces in northern China: Shandong, Shanxi and Shaanxi. Political and social conditions differed significantly between these provinces. In 1937 Shandong and Shanxi came under Japanese occupation, while Shaanxi, though under sustained attack right up to 1945, was never occupied (see Figure 1). After the war, Shandong was immediately affected by widespread and heavy fighting between Nationalists and Communists, whereas Shaanxi was less generally contested; parts of Shandong came under Chinese Communist Party (CCP) domination more than a year earlier than Shaanxi, and this also had a major impact on the foreign missionary societies. Information from and about Shanxi became almost non-existent from

---

[18] Cited in Hilary Spurling, *Burying the Bones* (London: Profile, 2011), p. 228.

[19] Ernest A. Payne, *Harry Wyatt of Shansi, 1895–1938* (London: Carey Press, 1939), p. 57.

[20] Robert A. Bickers, 'Changing British Attitudes to China and the Chinese, 1928–1931' (PhD thesis, University of London, 1992), pp. 225–45.

[21] Oi Ki Ling, *The Changing Role of the British Protestant Missionaries in China, 1945–1952* (London: Associated University Presses, 1999), p. 12.

[22] Ling, *Changing Role*, p. 320.

1939 to 1945, and again from 1947 onwards, and this makes comparisons with
that province more difficult.

Figure 1: Extent of Japanese occupation, 1940[23]

In addition to the geographical differences, the work undertaken by the BMS
fell into three broad areas: evangelical, educational and medical. Church
communities, schools and hospitals each encountered different problems. The
challenges involved in retaining a Christian ethos, responding to government
requirements, meeting financial demands and maintaining suitable staffing were
not the same in the three categories.

Recently released archival materials, and a greater openness to alternative
interpretations of twentieth-century Chinese history within the PRC, have given
fresh impetus to research amongst both Chinese and Western scholars into the
significance of the years in China from 1937 to 1952 and the transitions that took
place at that time. The period embraces the last years of the Nationalist
government, the social and military disruption of the War of Resistance against
Japan, the political uncertainties of the Civil War and the first years of the PRC,
each having generated its own substantial, and often controversial, literature.

Eastman's analysis of the achievements and limitations of the Nationalist
regime remains relevant, but has been succeeded by further examination of the

---

[23] Source: 'China Civil War, 1900-1949: Japanese Occupation, 1940', Department of
History, United States Military Academy, accessed 31 October 2014,
www.westpoint.edu/history/SiteAssets/SitePages/Chinese%20Civil%20War/ChineseCiv
ilWar05.gif.

extent of those achievements.[24] Mitter's account of the war with Japan explores the contributions of the three major Chinese players in the war – the Nationalists, the Communists and the collaborators – and points to continuities between their wartime and post-war roles.[25] Amongst the burgeoning literature on specialised or localised aspects of the war with Japan, the edited volumes by Barrett and Shyu, as well as Mackinnon and Lary's work, add new dimensions to the understanding of the meaning of the war to the Chinese people.[26] Only recently has interest been kindled in the difficulties experienced by those in occupied China, who had to find a morally acceptable means of self-preservation. Pepper and Westad's work on the Chinese Civil War 1946–1949 provides contextual understanding of the conditions with which missionaries and Chinese Christians were contending.[27]

'For the most part,' wrote Cohen in 1988, 'different people study the pre- and post-1949 periods. They ask different questions, rely on different sources, read different books and often attend different conferences.'[28] Historians in the 1980s and 1990s rejected the hitherto fixed barrier at 1949 and began to explore the continuities as well as the divide between the Republican and the Communist eras.[29] Ten years later, scholarly interest turned to the years immediately following 1949, when Cohen demonstrated that many of the changes introduced by the CCP had their roots in long-established Guomindang (GMD) or

---

[24] Lloyd Eastman, *The Abortive Revolution: China Under Nationalist Rule, 1927–1937* (Cambridge MA: Harvard University Press, 1974) and *The Seeds of Destruction: Nationalist China in War and Revolution, 1937–1949* (Stanford CA: Stanford University Press, 1984). For examples of more recent interpretations, see van de Ven, *War and Nationalism*; Felix Boecking, 'Republican China under the Nationalists, ca.1925–1945', in Naomi Standen (ed), *Demystifying China: New Understandings of Chinese History* (Lanham MD: Rowman and Littlefield, 2013), pp. 171–78.

[25] Rana Mitter, *China's War with Japan 1937–1945: The Struggle for Survival* (London: Allen Lane, 2013).

[26] David P. Barrett and Lawrence N. Shyu, *Chinese Collaboration with Japan, 1932–1945: The Limits of Accommodation* (Stanford CA: Stanford University Press, 2001); David P. Barrett and Lawrence N. Shyu, *China in the Anti-Japanese War, 1937–1945: Politics, Culture, and Society* (New York, Oxford: Peter Lang, 2001); Stephen R Mackinnon and Robert Capa, *Wuhan 1938: war, refugees and the making of modern China* (Berkeley: University of California Press, 2008); Diana Lary *The Chinese People at War: Human Suffering and Social Transformation, 1937–1945* (New York: Cambridge University Press, 2010).

[27] Suzanne Pepper, *Civil War in China: The Political Struggle 1945–1949* (Lanham MD and Oxford: Rowman and Littlefield, 1999); Odd Arne Westad, *Decisive Encounters: The Chinese Civil War, 1946–1950* (Stanford: Stanford University Press, 2003).

[28] Paul A. Cohen, 'The Post-Mao Reforms in Historical Perspective', *Journal of Asian Studies* 47.3 (August 1988), pp. 518–540 (p. 519).

[29] Philip C. C. Huang, *The Peasant Family and Rural Development in the Yangzi Delta, 1350–1988* (Stanford: Stanford University Press, 1990); Elizabeth J. Perry, *Shanghai on Strike: The Politics of Chinese Labor* (Stanford: Stanford University Press, 1993); Jeffrey N. Wasserstrom, *Student Protest in Twentieth-Century China: The View from Shanghai* (Stanford: Stanford University Press, 1991); William C. Kirby, *Germany and Republican China* (Stanford: Stanford University Press, 1984).

Nationalist objectives.[30] In this context, missionary expectations of continuity into the new PRC appear less far-fetched than earlier critics have claimed.[31]

Brown and Pickowicz's edited volume on the early years of the PRC throws light on the diversity and complexity of the years in China from 1949 to 1952, and on the reality that 'the era was many different things for different people in different places.'[32] Exploring this variety and fluidity helps to explain the conflicting reports from missionaries working in different parts of China during this period. Dikötter's analysis of post-war China reveals evidence from CCP archives of the terrible pressures brought to bear on large numbers of Chinese citizens in the first years of the Communist state.[33] Though Dikötter has been criticised for his 'moralistic and emotive language', and for some of the conclusions he draws, the factual basis of his material has not been disputed and is relevant for the evidence it gives of the gravity of situations faced by Chinese Christians at this time.[34]

The relationship between the British and Chinese governments played an important part in the experience of missionaries in China, and a number of publications that appeared towards the end of the twentieth century focus on the diplomatic and political history of the period.[35] China's wartime and post-war relations with the Western world are examined in Westad's broadly based study.[36] European and American scholars are also engaged in work on the colonial presence in China, illustrated, for example, in Bickers' examination of the growth of the foreign settlements during the late Qing Empire and their subsequent impact on Sino-foreign relations.[37]

The experience of British civilians in China during the eight-year war with Japan has escaped substantial historical analysis. Many memoirs recount the experience of occupation and internment, but few address the political or ethical

---

[30] Paul A. Cohen, 'Reflections on a Watershed Date: The 1949 Divide in Chinese History' in Jeffrey N. Wasserstrom (ed), *Twentieth-Century China: New Approaches* (London: Routledge, 2003), pp. 27–36 (p. 27).

[31] Ling, *Changing Role*, p. 145.

[32] Jeremy Brown and Paul G. Pickowicz, *Dilemmas of Victory: The Early Years of the People's Republic of China* (Cambridge MA and London: Harvard University Press, 2007), p. 8.

[33] Frank Dikötter, *The Tragedy of Liberation: A History of the Chinese Revolution, 1945–59* (London: Bloomsbury, 2013), pp. 40–184.

[34] Felix Wemheuer, 'The Chinese Revolution and "Liberation": Whose Tragedy?' in *The China Quarterly* 219 (September 2014), pp. 849–63.

[35] For example, Brian E. Porter, *Britain and the Rise of Communist China: A Study of British Attitudes, 1945–1954* (London: Oxford University Press, 1967); Guangsheng Liao, *Antiforeignism and Modernization in China, 1860–1980* (Hong Kong: Chinese University Press, 1986); Arthur Clegg, *Aid China, 1937–1949: A Memoir of a Forgotten Campaign* (Beijing: New World Press, 1989); Zhong-ping Feng, *The British Government's China Policy, 1945–1950* (Keele: Keele University Press, 1994).

[36] Odd Arne Westad, *Restless Empire: China and the World Since 1750* (London: Bodley Head, 2012), pp. 247–321.

[37] Robert Bickers, *The Scramble for China: Foreign Devils in the Qing Empire, 1832–1914* (London: Allen Lane, 2012).

questions involved. Chatterton's thesis on Protestant medical missionaries in Hubei province, 1937–1945, addresses the issues facing medical missions in the context of the war with Japan; some of these are also applicable to other aspects of missionary work.[38] She argues that the competence shown by Chinese medical staff during the war years called into question the need for Western governance of mission hospitals, and suggests that '[w]hat also became difficult to defend was the foreign medical missionary presence itself.'[39] This is in contrast to the findings of this book, and serves as a useful illustration of the significant variations in practice and experience in different parts of China and between missionary societies. Menzies Clow's experience of attempting to encourage Chinese staff to take over leadership of the BMS hospital in Xi'an in 1947–1948 (see Chapter Five) suggests there were many reasons for their reluctance to do so.

The apparently shamefaced departure of foreigners at the time of the establishment of the PRC has perhaps been a factor in the comparative lack of attention on the subject. Western firms were frozen out, and foreign businesses could no longer make money; missionaries had been discredited and were no longer welcome. There were plenty of nostalgic memoirs by those who had made China their home and now found themselves dispossessed, but little academic scrutiny of the fate of British businesses and commercial interests.[40] Hooper examines China's fresh stance with regard to the West, and Brady includes the early days of the PRC in her work on the way the CCP conducts its relationships with foreign bodies.[41] Bickers, and the chapters in the edited volume by Bickers and Henriot, both examine the interaction between personal and social issues and commercial and political ones, but neither are much concerned with the final years of the foreign presence.[42]

Howlett's research into the departure of foreign businesses from Shanghai has relevance for the end of the missionary era.[43] Using Chinese archives, he analyses the CCP approach to British businesses in the first months of the PRC, and demonstrates the mixture of pragmatism and ideological conviction with which the CCP went about dismembering them. This understanding of the CCP

---

[38] J. Chatterton, 'Protestant Medical Missionary Experience During the War in China 1937–1945: The Case of Hubei Province' (PhD thesis, University of London, 2010).
[39] Chatterton, 'Protestant Medical Missionary Experience', p. 146.
[40] William H. E. Thomas, *Vanished China: Far Eastern Banking Memories* (London: Thorsons, 1956); John Munro, *Beyond the Moon Gate: A China Odyssey, 1938–1950* (Vancouver: Douglas and McIntyre, 1990).
[41] Beverley Hooper, *China Stands Up: Ending the Western Presence, 1948–1950* (Sydney, London: Allen and Unwin, 1986); Anne-Marie Brady, *Making the Foreign Serve China: Managing Foreigners in the People's Republic* (Lanham MD: Rowman and Littlefield, 2003).
[42] Robert Bickers, *Britain in China: Community, Culture and Colonialism, 1900–1949* (Manchester: Manchester University Press, 1999); Robert Bickers and Christian Henriot, *New Frontiers: Imperialism's New Communities in East Asia, 1842–1953* (Manchester: Manchester University Press, 2000).
[43] Jonathan J. Howlett, 'Creating a New Shanghai: The End of the British Presence in China (1949–57)' (PhD thesis, University of Bristol, 2012).

approach to foreign commercial interests is helpful in trying to separate the issues of foreignness from issues of religious belief when considering the CCP attitude to the missionary presence.

It is time to take a fresh look at the missionary contribution in the light of the many new interpretations of twentieth-century Chinese history. Mitter has argued the case for bringing the imperial presence back into Chinese history, and suggests that intellectual originality is called for to make a fresh approach possible.

> The challenge for the new historiography of China has been to bring the imperial presence into the narrative of Chinese history, avoiding both a black-and-white condemnation of the imperial presence simply as depredation and plunder, and the complacent position that imperialism was essentially a 'helping hand' in bringing China to modernity.[44]

Just as there is a case for bringing back the imperial presence, so there is also a case for bringing missionaries back into Chinese history. Missionaries have a place, not simply as religious propagandists, misguided or otherwise – and not just as 'foreign devils', robbing China of its cultural heritage or standing in the way of its growth to independent nationhood – but as a formative influence on China's twentieth-century development. Many of China's political leaders, both during the Republican and Communist eras, received their education in Christian schools or colleges, and the influence of the Christian colleges on the development of modern sciences in China was seminal.[45] Mission hospitals cannot legitimately be omitted from a study of China's health provision.

Foundational to the secondary literature on the work of the BMS in China are the contributions of Williamson and Stanley.[46] The first of these is comprehensive in its account, from the viewpoint of the British Missionary Society, of all its activities and achievements in China from its beginnings in 1860 to the departure of the missionaries in 1952. The second puts the society's work in China into the context of its work worldwide, and of the practical and theological problems that it faced.

Studies written in the immediate aftermath of the withdrawal of foreign missionary societies in the late 1940s and early 1950s were greatly preoccupied with the significance of the missionary withdrawal and with the criticisms of the missions that were voiced at the time by leading Chinese Christians. The substantial generalist literature that was produced divided broadly into two main streams. There were writers who believed that criticisms of the missions could be explained by the CCP's manipulative use of the Chinese church as a political tool. They wrote that 'the facts should be made crystal clear' through the

---

[44] Rana Mitter, 'Modernity, Internationalization, and War in the History of Modern China', *The Historical Journal* 48.2 (June 2005), pp. 523–542 (p. 530).
[45] Deke Erh and Tess Johnston, *Hallowed Halls: Protestant Colleges in Old China* (Hong Kong: Old China Hands Press, 1998), p. 12.
[46] H. R. Williamson, *British Baptists in China, 1845–1952* (London: Carey Kingsgate Press, 1957); and Stanley, *History*.

'propaganda smokescreen which the Chinese authorities have ingeniously put up'.

> The missionary movement made many mistakes […] But these were not of deliberate or malicious intent. The motives of the Christian missionaries were from the first pure […] They were friends to all and offered their services in the realm of education and medicine with no ulterior motives whatever.[47]

Criticism from Chinese Christians, however, prompted many missionaries and ex-missionaries to harrowing self-examination about failures in the whole history of foreign missionary work in China, about relationships between missionaries and Chinese Christians, and about allegations of an integral association between missions and imperialism. This coincided with a period when scholars and churchmen were preoccupied with questions about the significance and validity of the missionary enterprise worldwide.[48] Along with a number of personal accounts, these concerns dominated the literature of the 1950s and 1960s. By the early 1970s the spate of personal memoirs, and accounts directed at a Christian readership, had died down.

In 1971 Lutz introduced fresh perspectives with her account of foreign missionary institutions caught up in the complexity of Chinese politics, from their beginnings in the mid-nineteenth century to the missionary withdrawal under the Communists a century later. This is relevant for its analysis of many of the issues that confronted the missionary movement in China in the mid-twentieth century.[49] While Lutz recognises the active and positive participation of the Christian Colleges in the Chinese Nationalist movements of the 1930s and 1940s, and the significant contribution the colleges made to the total number of college-educated Chinese, she argues that they 'became more important as contributors to the disintegration of the Chinese heritage than as agents of Christian evangelism'.[50] They were Western institutions transported to China and 'their Western administration, support and curricula, their general atmosphere made them mediators of Western civilization'.[51]

---

[47] Leslie Lyall, *Come Wind, Come Weather* (London: Hodder and Stoughton, 1961), pp. 6 and 25.

[48] See, for example, Victor E. W. Hayward, *'Ears to Hear': Lessons from the China Mission* (London: Edinburgh House Press, 1955) and *Christians and China* (Belfast: Christian Journals Ltd, 1974); Creighton Lacy, 'Protestant Missions in Communist China' (PhD thesis, Yale University, 1953); D. M. Paton, *Christian Missions and the Judgment of God* (London: SCM Press, 1953); Max Warren, *Challenge and Response: Six Studies in Missionary Opportunity* (London: SPCK, 1960); Norman Goodall, *Christian Missions and Social Ferment* (London: Epworth Press, 1964).

[49] Jessie G. Lutz, *China and the Christian Colleges, 1850–1950* (Ithaca and London: Cornell University Press, 1971).

[50] Lutz, *China and the Christian Colleges*, p. 494.

[51] Lutz, *China and the Christian Colleges*, p. 491.

Two academic works published in the 1990s focus on withdrawal of British Protestant missionaries from China after 1945.[52] Both Ling and Hood address the way in which the missionary societies dealt with changing political conditions in China and the circumstances leading to the eventual exodus of all foreign missionaries. Both also examine criticisms emanating from early PRC publications of missions as tools of imperialism.

Ling sets out to analyse whether Protestant missionaries working in China during those years adapted their style and practice in recognition of altered conditions in China and the developing independence of the Chinese church.[53] She concludes, somewhat contradictorily, both that they did not adapt and that they were naïve not to see that, even if they had adapted, there was no place for them in Communist China. She does not distinguish between different societies and different approaches. When the PRC was declared on 1 October 1949, 109 Western Protestant missionary bodies were active in China.[54] The Lutheran church alone was responsible for no less than twelve different missionary societies, each of which had its own organisational structure and theological perspective.[55] Fourteen of the societies active in 1949 were British.[56] Even within the different societies, individual missionaries experienced widely varying conditions and, at times, held conflicting views. Ling's undifferentiated approach to the distinctions between the different societies, and her dependence on such generalisations as 'missionaries were of the opinion', 'missionaries were appalled', 'missionaries found', 'missionaries realised', renders her conclusions less than convincing.[57]

Hood's perspective is that of the Mission Boards in London, Edinburgh, Belfast and Dublin, informed by their own, largely British, staff and supporters at home and in China. He differentiates between the various missionary bodies and the problems each encountered, takes account of the political and theological issues faced by the Mission Boards, and sets out in detail the way these were dealt with.[58] In an earlier work, Hood explores the extent to which missions reached their goal of handing over control to the Chinese church, concentrating on the English Presbyterian Mission in Lingtung (嶺東; Lingdong) from the beginnings of missionary work in China, including some observations on the years up to 1989 after missionaries had left.[59] Since Hood's accounts, there has

---

[52] Ling, *Changing Role*; George A. Hood, *Neither Bang Nor Whimper: The End of a Missionary Era in China* (Singapore: The Presbyterian Church in Singapore, 1991).
[53] Ling, *Changing Role*.
[54] Ling, *Changing Role*, p. 57.
[55] Jonas Jonson, 'Lutheran Missions in a Time of Revolution: The China Experience 1944–51'(PhD thesis, Uppsala University, 1972), p. 225.
[56] Hood, *Neither Bang Nor Whimper*, p. 57.
[57] Ling, *Changing Role*, pp. 54, 80, 112, 220.
[58] Hood, *Neither Bang Nor Whimper*.
[59] George A. Hood, *Mission Accomplished?: The English Presbyterian Mission in Lingtung, South China*, (Frankfurt am Main, Bern, New York: Verlag Peter Lang, 1986). Lingtung (now Lingdong) was in Guangdong province in the coastal area near Shantou (汕頭).

been little work on the history of foreign missionaries in China after 1937, and none that take account of the fresh understandings of the Chinese and international context generated by more recent research.

Among Western scholars of Christianity in China, there has been a new interest and emphasis on the development of Chinese Christianity: an area that, until recently, took a poor second place to studies of the missionary contribution. Charbonnier's substantial account covers mainly Catholic Chinese Christians, while Bays' book is predominantly, but not exclusively, concerned with Chinese Protestantism.[60] Bays' fine summary of the development of an indigenous Chinese church ranges from the Nestorian age to the early twenty-first century, and draws significantly on the work of Chinese scholars, both within and outwith the PRC, of the past twenty-five years.

Brook's chapter on Christianity under the Japanese occupation, in Bays' edited volume, argues that the Japanese approach to managing the Chinese church paved the way for the subsequent development of Christianity under Communism.[61] The almost complete absence of Westerners from occupied China during this period, and a shortage of Chinese documentary evidence, have meant that the experience of the Chinese church under occupation has remained largely uncharted territory. Other recent works that focus on Chinese Christianity are those of Wickeri and Lian Xi.[62] The former traces the development of Chinese Christianity through the life story of K. H. Ting (丁光训: Ding Guangxun), one-time Anglican Bishop of Zhejiang, who made it his life's work to achieve reform from within, rather than against, established political structures.[63] Lian Xi's focus is on the charismatic indigenous sects that, from the late nineteenth century, grew up outside the mission-led mainstream Protestant church. He argues that these are at the root of the phenomenal growth of Christianity in late-twentieth-century China.

The health of the missionary movement was bound up with the health of the British churches. Precise dating of the decline of Christianity remains a focus of scholarly debate. One view is that 'by the 1920s the principal intellectual (if not as yet social) orthodoxy was not any form of Christianity, but a confident agnosticism.'[64] Others suggest that the Second World War was a watershed moment for organised religion in the UK. Field's analysis of 'religious believing

---

[60] Jean-Pierre Charbonnier, *Christians in China A.D 600 to 2000*, M. N. L. Couve de Murville (trans), (San Francisco: Ignatius Press, 2007); Bays, *New History*.

[61] Timothy Brook, 'Toward Independence, Christianity in China under the Japanese Occupation, 1937–1945', in Daniel H. Bays (ed), *Christianity in China, from the Eighteenth Century to the Present* (Stanford: Stanford University Press, 1996), pp. 317–37.

[62] Philip L. Wickeri, *Reconstructing Christianity in China; K. H. Ting and the Chinese Church* (Maryknoll, NY: Orbis Books, 2007); Lian Xi, *Redeemed by Fire: The Rise of Popular Christianity in Modern China* (New Haven CT and London: Yale University Press, 2010).

[63] Wickeri, *Reconstructing Christianity*, p. 373.

[64] P. E. Dewey, *War and Progress: Britain 1914–1945* (London and New York: Longman, 1997), p. 188.

and belonging' during the war years remains one of the few studies that uses quantitative data derived from church statistics and social surveys to investigate whether the Second World War was a significant factor.[65] He argues that the war was not a major milestone in the UK's secularisation history. By the 1950s, however, the UK and the United States were deemed to be 'secular countries', 'where the place of religion was jeopardised by large-scale indifference to religion, significant hostility to the churches, and the declining institutional strength of religion in state and civil affairs'.[66] One consequence of the decline in the churches was the financial crises experienced by the missionary societies throughout the twentieth century, and these, in the case of post-war China, coincided with demands for substantial investment to make good the losses experienced during the war.

Like most studies of this period of British missionary history, this book draws on evidence from British parliamentary records, reports and papers from the Foreign Office, and records from the archives of the Hong Kong and Shanghai Banking Corporation (HSBC) and the British Red Cross. It also draws contextual information relating to the work of the BMS from contemporary newspapers and journals, including *The Chinese Recorder* and *Missionary Herald*, the monthly journal of the BMS. The former was an English-language ecumenical missionary magazine, published monthly in Shanghai from 1867. It ceased publication in 1941 but reflects the issues and activities that engaged missionaries in China over almost a hundred years.

Much of the evidence comes from the missionary societies' own archives – for example, those of the China Inland Mission (CIM), the Methodist Missionary Society, the Council for World Mission, the Conference of British Missionary Societies (CBMS), the International Missionary Council and the China Association, housed in the special collections reading room at the School of Oriental and African Studies (SOAS).

Given the particular focus of this book on the experience of the BMS, the research draws heavily on material from the BMS Archives (BMSA), held in the Angus Library at Regent's Park College, Oxford. In addition to the various committee minutes, the annual reports, the Baptist yearbooks, and the manual for missionaries, the archive holds substantial personal files for each individual missionary, which shed new light and bring a different perspective to more traditional studies of the period. These personal files mostly contain correspondence between the missionaries and the mission's home secretaries, with the occasional inclusion of minutes of meetings taking place in, or documents originating from, the mission field itself. It is unusual for details of

---

[65] Clive D. Field, 'Puzzled People Revisited: Religious Believing and Belonging in Wartime Britain, 1939–45', *Twentieth Century British History* 19.4, 2008, pp. 446–479 (p. 446).
[66] Callum G. Brown and Michael Snape, 'Conceptualising Secularisation 1974–2010: The Influence of Hugh McLeod', in Callum G. Brown and Michael Snape (eds), *Secularisation in the Christian World* (Farnham, Surrey and Burlington VT: Ashgate Publishers, 2010), p. 3.

personal circumstances to be included in the correspondence, though this does occur, and, occasionally, relationships between the missionaries and the home staff developed a level of intimacy that produce interchanges of a personal nature within the official correspondence.

Almost all the correspondence files contain examples of circular letters written in generalised terms to friends and supporters at home. These were one of the obligations of the missionary in the field, and the reader can sense different levels of enthusiasm for writing them in different missionaries' hands. One missionary hinted at the stereotypical style expected when she apologised for the inadequacy of her own early efforts:

> I fear my letters are very lacking those little mission anecdotes which delight the heart of missionary secretaries. But the life of a language student [...] just consists of language study from morning till night and I don't even seem to produce humorous language howlers.[67]

In addition to the content of the letters, the letter writers' style sometimes reveals information about the missionaries as individuals: the careful precision of one senior missionary, shown in his enthusiasm for formal reports, and numbered headings and subheadings; the exuberant thoroughness of another, his evident efficiency softened by his humour and enthusiasm for his work; and the cheerful individualism of a third, with her readiness to say the bold and unorthodox. The use of different typewriters, different types of paper, different forms of address and different ways of signing off are also illuminating: one sending typewritten accounts on elegantly illustrated and transparent Chinese writing paper; another writing page after page, apparently hastily in a liberal and almost indecipherable scrawl.

Some of the letters in the correspondence files that reveal the most about the personal problems faced by the missionaries are those to the members of the Home Board from members of missionaries' families in the UK, seeking help with a difficulty caused by the absence of a spouse, parent, son or daughter overseas; pleading a relative's case; or passing on urgent information they were unable to send directly to their family member abroad. The mother and sister of a prospective missionary bride sent poignant letters expressing their concern at the insistence of the Mission Board that the wedding be postponed for a year or more until her prospective husband had completed his language studies.[68] One schoolboy wrote anxiously to request assistance in arranging for his exam results to be sent to his guardian in England rather than to his parents in China, as the examination board required.[69] Had the results been sent to China in the summer of 1940, it would have been many months, if not years, before the results reached the boy himself. A missionary's sister asked the secretaries how she could let her sister in China know about the death of their thirteen-year-old niece in a cycling

---

[67] BMSA, CH/74, Gladys Seymour to friends, 20 September 1948.
[68] BMSA, CH/63, Cheshire to Wilson, 11 September 1927.
[69] BMSA, CH/62, Mudd to Wilson, 25 July 1940.

accident, when normal correspondence was impossible because of Communist restrictions.[70]

Although much recent scholarship dealing with China's modern history is being informed by access to previously inaccessible Chinese archives, material relating to the missionary presence may be less likely to come to light in this way. Systematic destruction of such documents took place first in the early 1950s and then again during the Cultural Revolution, when evidence of association with the foreign presence was likely to prove grounds for persecution. When interviewed in 2010, Peter J. Nelson, one of the last British Baptist missionaries to leave Shandong in 1951, emphasised more than once that before his departure he was urgently charged with destroying all the BMS records held in Jinan, including 'much interesting material relating to the local workings of the mission, its missionaries, Chinese staff and congregations':

> On the advice of local church leaders, we did not wish to leave papers which might count against them in the eyes of the new regime, so I also destroyed them.[71]

Likewise, Gao Yan (高艳), the daughter of a Chinese doctor who received his medical training under the auspices of BMS missionaries at Qilu University (齐鲁大学) in the late 1940s, recalled the hasty preparations her family made for the visit of a group of Red Guards to their home in 1967. Any papers written in English, and any photographs that might have associated them with foreigners, were burned, including her parents' wedding photos where they were wearing Western dress. She had been eight years old in 1967, but the memory was a powerful one.[72]

Large quantities of private and institutional records are likely to have been lost in this way. Although CCP municipal records of foreigners living within their areas are likely to have been preserved within Chinese local archives, the language barrier renders them inaccessible to many Western researchers. However, with assistance from contacts in China (Gao Yan and Han Jie (韩结)), it was possible to gain some oral evidence for this research from individuals in China with direct experience of the work of the BMS and its legacy. These, together with a small number of Chinese letters and private publications, the translated writings of Mao Zedong and Zhou Enlai about the Chinese church, the *Documents of the Three-Self Movement: Source Materials for the Study of the Protestant Church in Communist China* and the *Collected Writings of K. H. Ting* bring a very welcome Chinese perspective and a triangulation point for the missionaries' story.

Many institutions founded by British missionary societies have recently reached or are currently reaching anniversaries of one hundred years old or more. Keen to take advantage of the prestige associated with such early foundations,

---

[70] BMSA, CH/62/3, Down to Clow, 12 June 1950.
[71] Peter J. Nelson, interviewed by Audrey Salters at Dalgety Bay, 13 May 2010. See also Nelson's unpublished memoir.
[72] Gao Yan, (高艳), in conversation with Audrey Salters in Jinan, 16-19 April 2013.

many have engaged in centenary celebrations or have published histories. In the current 'less heated political climate',[73] it has become acceptable and even desirable to acknowledge the foreign origins of their institutions, and it is now common for Chinese researchers interested in the history of the missionary presence to come to the UK to access the archives held in British libraries. A recent short film, shown on a Shandong television network, described an incident that occurred while setting up an exhibition to celebrate the centenary of the Guangbei School (广北学校) in Zhoucun (周村), founded by the BMS in 1910.[74] A photograph was discovered of the school governors, taken in 1947, but no one in Zhoucun knew the names or designation of anyone pictured. By coincidence a copy of the same photo was sent from the UK as a contribution to the exhibition. It had been in the private collection of a former BMS missionary, and, to the delight of the Zhoucun staff, the missionary had carefully recorded on the back the names and designations of everyone in the picture when it was taken in 1947.

One hundred BMS missionaries, working in mission stations, schools, colleges and hospitals in three different provinces, were engaged in diverse and multiple activities in China between 1937 and 1952. It is not possible to reflect all their different concerns, styles and attitudes but the case studies covered by this book are representative of the collective experience and are told through the missionaries' own words. Through them, we can see the different experiences of the three BMS provinces – Shandong, Shanxi and Shaanxi – two of which were occupied by the Japanese while one remained in Free China. We see the challenges experienced in running a school and a hospital, and the tension created by, on the one hand, the enthusiasm of the missionaries to rebuild the damage caused to the church and medical work in Shandong and Shanxi during the occupation and, on the other hand, their commitment to the goal of withdrawal.

We also see the changes in China and the UK brought about by world war and subsequent civil war, which affected both the practicalities of continued missionary work in China and also the understanding – of field staff and those at home in London or in congregations around the country – of evolving Chinese attitudes to their relationships with foreign colleagues.

---

[73] Boecking, 'Republican China', p. 177.

[74] Stories about an English missionary in Zhoucun 英国传教士在周村 (*Yingguo chuan jiao shi zai zhou cun*) from 山东往事 (*Shandong wang shi*) section by 齐鲁网 （*Qilu wang*） of 山东网络台 (*Shandong wang luo tai*) (v.iqilu.com), accessed 10.September.2013,
First Part: (上 shang) http://v.iqilu.com/2013/09/09/3941353.shtml
Second Part: (下 xia) http://v.iqilu.com/2013/09/10/3941889.shtml.

1. The BMS and Its China Missionaries

> I shall never rest until I see the native church self-governing, self-supporting and free from every kind of foreign influence which tends to hinder its free native natural development and extension.[1]

The activities and expectations of British Missionary Society (BMS) missionaries working in China in the mid-twentieth century were shaped by many factors: historical, political, geographical, financial, theological and personal. There was a strong drive from BMS pioneers towards building an independent indigenous church and, particularly in Shandong, Chinese Christians responded with initiative and enthusiasm to this way of working.

Origins, Early Influences and Founding Principles

The primary purpose of the Baptist missionary movement was 'the diffusion of the knowledge of the religion of Jesus Christ throughout the whole world beyond the British Isles'.[2] The early pioneers were concerned that, without their personal endeavours, millions of men and women all over the world would die without having had the opportunity to hear the Christian message. Following its formation in 1792, the BMS first sent missionaries to India, and then to the West Indies and what was then Ceylon.

One of the founders of the society, and its first missionary, William Carey, arrived in Bengal in November 1793.[3] He and his colleague were faced immediately with questions as to how to organise their work and their living arrangements, questions that had taken second place to theological debate when the society was set up in England. Carey decided that the ideal would be to create a 'colony of seven or eight families, supporting itself by agriculture, and living according to a common rule'. He hoped that 'converted Indians would join the community, and be treated on the same basis as European missionaries'.[4] It was a plan that envisaged local converts and foreign missionaries living and working together on a completely equal basis, supporting themselves by the labours of their own hands. There was no expectation of financial support from elsewhere.

---

[1] Williamson, *British Baptists*, p. 31, citing Rev Richard Laughton, BMS missionary to China 1862-70.

[2] Baptist Missionary Society. *Manual of the Baptist Missionary Society for India, Ceylon, China, Congo and the West Indies, revised edition.* (London: Carey Press, 1939), paragraph 1.1.

[3] Stanley, *History*, p. 36.

[4] Stanley, *History*, p. 39, quoting Carey to Fuller, 16 November 1796 (BMSA, IN/13).

With the benefit of hindsight, this seemingly attractive plan did not take sufficient account of practical realities or social and cultural differences. Although, for a number of reasons, the plan in its pure form foundered quite quickly, Carey's vision still exerted 'a consistent and profound influence' on the policy of the society's first pioneers in India.[5] The influence was also felt profoundly in China, for example in the proposals for a Christian service centre, set up in the Shandong town of Zhoucun to co-ordinate Christian activities after the introduction of the Communist regime in 1949 (see Chapter Six).

William Ward followed Carey to Bengal in 1799.[6] In 1802, he recorded in his personal journal the conviction that he was 'ready to doubt whether Europeans will ever be extensively useful in converting souls by preaching in this country'.[7] He believed that fundamental linguistic and cultural barriers stood between him and his would-be converts. Evangelism was likely to be most effective, he considered, when carried out by local evangelists rather than by foreign missionaries. This had an immediate and lasting impact on BMS policy. A pattern of work developed that relied on responsibility being handed over at the earliest opportunity to local Christians. The concept of 'self-propagation' was regarded as fundamental.

As well as establishing the practice of depending on the efforts of local evangelists, this belief had other consequences for mission policy. If local Christians were to take a key role in evangelism, it was essential that they should be able to read and understand the Bible in their own language. The efforts made by early missionaries to translate the Bible into local languages were remarkable: William Carey himself completed six entire and twenty-nine partial translations of the Bible.[8] By 1823, another BMS missionary based in India, Joshua Marshman – confident that missionary work would eventually be initiated in China – had completed a translation of the whole Bible into Chinese.[9] In due course, the society made a practice of opening schools to teach children to read, and adult classes to introduce biblical studies.

BMS policy was also influenced by Ward's views on the importance of foreign missionaries not interfering with personal habits or lifestyles of the local communities they served. He realised that social habits practised in England were not necessarily considered desirable in other parts of the world. In fact, elsewhere they might be thought impolite or even repulsive. He made it clear that it was not the job of the missionary to change habits that could be regarded as 'the innocent usages of mankind'.[10] The essential Christian message, he

---

[5] Stanley, *History*, p. 40.

[6] Stanley, *History*, p. 37.

[7] Stanley, *History*, p. 48, quoting BMSA, William Ward's Journal, 13 [in fact 15] November 1802.

[8] Stanley, *History*, p. 49.

[9] Williamson, *British Baptists*, p. 9.

[10] Stanley, *History*, p. 48, citing BMSA, Periodical Accounts Relative to the Baptist Missionary Society, 'Form of Agreement', pp. iii, 200 and 208.

declared, was not about manners, personal habits or lifestyle, and it was not the business of the missionary to intervene in such matters.

This last point distinguished the BMS missionaries from many other groups of Western missionaries. Two eminent scholars of the missionary movement in China, Stanley and Bays, have both expressed the view that the great majority of Western missionaries believed, whether consciously or unconsciously, that the gospel and civilisation were necessarily linked. With Christianity, most missionaries took to Africa and Asia the trappings of the West: Western values and culture, Western organisational structures, Western forms of worship and Westernised church buildings. Stanley considers that 'with very few exceptions, British Christians accepted that non-Christian societies stood in need of comprehensive regeneration.'[11] Bays, like Stanley, allows for rare exceptions, but maintained that the 'Protestant mission community' throughout the nineteenth century was united in its conviction 'that China needed not only Christ, but the norms of Western culture as well'.[12] Ward's realisation that this was not only unnecessary but undesirable – even positively harmful – was strongly echoed in the thinking of the first British Baptists working in China.

Missionary interest in China was widely stimulated following the treaties that concluded the two Opium Wars of 1839–1842 and 1856–1860. Under the first of these, British subjects were allowed to live and trade in a number of Chinese ports. Under the second series of treaties, foreigners were allowed to travel inland, and to preach Christianity throughout the Chinese Empire. The treaties guaranteed official protection to foreign missionaries and to Chinese Christians. The BMS was one of thirty missionary societies to take advantage of the new opportunity, and from 1860 to 1905 missions in China experienced a period of outstanding growth. By 1905 there were 3,445 Protestant missionaries, including wives and 300 medical specialists, in China.[13]

The same treaties that opened the door for the spread of Christianity also legalised the trade in opium, and were the result of aggressive military action and humiliating Chinese defeats. Some Christians in the UK strongly disapproved of the opium trade and had been unhappy about taking advantage of the treaties. Their scruples were overridden by the conviction of a majority of British churchgoers that this was a God-given opportunity to preach the gospel in China. Baptists generally supported this view. The BMS General Committee, meeting on 20 April 1859, referred to 'the great providential fact' that China was now 'open to the instruction of the gospel', and that this constituted 'an urgent call

---

[11] Brian Stanley, *The Bible and the Flag: Protestant Missions and British Imperialism in the Nineteenth and Twentieth Centuries* (Leicester: Apollos, 1990), p. 171.

[12] Bays, *New History*, p. 71.

[13] Donald MacGillivray, *A Century of Protestant Missions in China (1807–1907): Being the Centenary Conference Historical Volume* (Shanghai: American Presbyterian Mission Press, 1907), Appendix II, p. 1.

upon the churches of Christ to send missionaries to that great country'.[14] Dr Edward Steane wrote in *The Baptist Magazine*:

> It is the prerogative of God, out of evils which nations inflict upon another, to bring forth their greater good…In the present instance, the issue to which events have led exhibits unmistakable evidence of His over-ruling hand, nor less clearly indicates His will.[15]

From the very beginning, therefore, a connection was firmly cemented in the minds of many Chinese people between Christianity, foreign aggression and the opium trade. Later, some missionaries reported 'occasions when they attempted to preach only to be shouted down by cries of "Who brought opium to China?"'[16] This was a difficult beginning that had far-reaching implications for the future of foreign missions in China (discussed further in Chapter Three).

Between 1840 and 1870, and at much the same time as missionaries first settled in China, Henry Venn of the Church Missionary Society and Rufus Anderson, Secretary of the American Board of Commissioners for Foreign Missions, were developing the concept of 'three-self' churches on the mission field: churches that were self-governing, self-supporting and self-propagating.[17] The earliest proponents of the ideas were members of the BMS mission in Serampore – Carey, Marshman and Ward – and the principles were adopted with enthusiasm by Rev. Richard Laughton, one of the first BMS missionaries to China. In a letter home in 1869, Laughton wrote:

> I shall never rest until I see the native church self-governing, self-supporting and free from every kind of foreign influence which tends to hinder its free native natural development and extension.[18]

Laughton had established an ideal for Baptist work in China that aimed to be consistent with local cultural norms and in keeping with indigenous styles of expression. Realisation of the ideal in practice was a continuing challenge.

All Baptist missionaries, and all those responsible for leading the BMS in the UK, were expected to be members of the Baptist denomination, admitted to membership by profession of faith and through the practice of believers' baptism. Two fundamental Baptist principles had a direct bearing on the thinking of individual missionaries and on the nature of the church that the BMS established overseas.

---

[14] Williamson, *British Baptists,* p. 20; BMSA, General Committee Minutes, Vol. N, 20 April 1859.

[15] *The Baptist Magazine*, June 1859, cited in Williamson, *British Baptists*, p. 21.

[16] Kathleen Lodwick, 'Missionaries and Opium' in R. Gary Tiedemann (ed), *Handbook of Christianity in China, Volume Two, 1800–Present* (Leiden MA: Brill, 2010), pp. 354–360 (p. 354).

[17] Williams, *The Ideal of the Self-Governing Church*, p. 1.

[18] Williamson, *British Baptists*, p. 31.

The first was that there is no hierarchy of membership within the denomination:

> The Church is one Body in Christ, and all its members occupy the same relation to Him, whatever their special gift or office…There are no priests as distinct from people; all alike, in fact, are priests.[19]

The principle extended to all baptised believers, whether members of the missionary society or of the native Christian church. Andrew Fuller, the first secretary of the BMS, set the tone for the mission when he wrote, 'We do not consider ourselves as legislators for our brethren; but merely as co-workers with them.'[20] While the society consisted on the home front of a variety of organisers and committees, and on the mission field of missionaries with administrative responsibilities or long years of experience, and of newly converted Chinese Christians, in the eyes of the Baptist membership the contribution of all was equally valid and equally valuable.

The second, closely related, principle was that of freedom of belief. In their history of the Free Churches, Skeats and Miall wrote:

> It is the singular and distinguished honour of the Baptists to have repudiated from their earliest history, all coercive power over the consciences and the actions of men with reference to religion.[21]

The principle was reiterated in the declaration of the Baptist World Congress held at Atlanta, Georgia, in 1939:

> In continuance of our consistent Baptist practice, we are imperatively constrained to insist upon the full maintenance of absolute religious liberty for every man of every faith and no faith.[22]

The responsibility of the missionary was to make the Christian message known to those who had not heard it. Having made every effort to do so, however, it was not the duty of the missionary to cajole or exert pressure on those who did not choose to accept it. On the contrary, missionaries should accept the views of those who, having understood the options, elected to live with no religious faith. This is a principle that played itself out in the way BMS missionaries related to members of the People's Liberation Army (PLA) and Chinese Communist Party (CCP) in their early encounters with them in the 1940s.

---

[19] Henry Cook, *What Baptists Stand For* (London: Carey Kingsgate Press, 1947), p. 76.

[20] Stanley, *History*, p. 34, citing BMSA, H/1/1, Fuller to Ward, 05 March 1813.

[21] H. S. Skeats and C. S. Miall, *History of the Free Churches of England, 1688–1891: From the Reformation to 1851* (London: Alexander and Shepheard, 1891), p. 19.

[22] Cook, *Baptists*, p. 135, quoting from the 'Declaration on Religious Liberty adopted unanimously by the Baptist World Congress in Atlanta, Georgia, on July 27, 1939, as Expressing the General Conviction and Position of Baptists throughout the World.'

Difficult decisions on matters of conscience confronted every individual missionary working in China in the mid-twentieth century – not just questions about the freedom of the Chinese people to choose or reject Christianity, but about the missionaries' own freedom of action. In Lord Acton's opinion, liberty meant 'that every man shall be protected in doing what he believes his duty against the influence of authority, and majorities, custom, and opinion'.[23] For missionaries, these matters of conscience included whether to continue working under Japanese occupation in 1937; how to respond to the national call-up to military service in Europe in 1939; and whether to remain in China working under the Communist government after 1949. Besides such general questions, individual missionaries were frequently called upon to exercise their consciences in resolving matters of a personal nature, including particularly how to balance the needs of their families against the needs of the missionary society. Meanwhile, members of the London-based BMS Home Committees had to find an appropriate line to tread between allowing for freedom of conscience and exercising proper managerial control of the staff they were employing to work overseas.

Baptist beliefs about church organisation and church government were also important factors in determining the nature of governance in newly established churches in China. Baptists believe that every local church has the right to be self-governing, answerable to no authority but Jesus Christ. There is, therefore, no formal centralised linking of congregations. From the outset, the congregations of Christian converts overseas were expected to be independent and to take responsibility for their own affairs, accountable neither to individual missionaries nor to the BMS. This belief lent itself well to the development of self-governed churches on the mission field and was a fundamental principle of the churches founded by the BMS in the 1880s. By 1910, the Shantung [Shandong] Baptist Union (SBU), a union of Chinese Baptist congregations within Shandong province, was 'in full operation', administratively independent of the missionary society.[24]

Organisational Structure, Terms of Service and Funding

The BMS was separate from the Baptist Unions of England, Scotland and Wales. It consisted of a central organisation with a secretariat and network of committees in London; a body of missionaries working overseas for whom it was responsible; and supporters from amongst the churches or the individual church members who were committed to missionary work. All regular subscribers to the BMS theoretically had both the authority and opportunity to contribute to its policy formation and decision-making by means of the week-long annual general meeting, when the annual report, including the statement of

---

[23] Cook, *Baptists*, p. 131, citing J. E. E. Dalberg-Acton, *The History of Freedom and Other Essays* (London: Macmillan, 1907), p. 3.
[24] Williamson, *British Baptists*, p. 77.

accounts, was made public. In practice, from the late nineteenth century these events chiefly provided opportunities for enthusiastic members of the denomination 'to socialise and engage publicly in conspicuous religious activity'. [25] Nevertheless the fact that the central organisation and the missionaries themselves were accountable to a substantial body of individual members had a continuing influence on policy formation and on the decisions of missionaries.

The permanent staff at the mission headquarters in London undertook the essential work of planning and organisation, acting under the authority of a hierarchy of sometimes overlapping committees. Three members of staff oversaw the work in China during the years covered by this research: the women's secretary, Eleanor Bowser (from 1925); the medical secretary, Clement Chesterman (from 1936); and the foreign secretary, Raymond (H. R.) Williamson (from 1939). Two had first-hand experience of working as missionaries overseas: Williamson in China from 1908 to 1939, and Chesterman, a qualified doctor, in Congo from 1920 to 1936. Ellen Clow and Victor Hayward, both with experience of working in China, succeeded Williamson as foreign secretary from 1948 and 1951 respectively. The division of responsibility between the three staff members with particular responsibility for China cannot always have been straightforward.

The BMS General Committee had overall responsibility for work in all the countries where the society was active: in 1937, India and Ceylon, the West Indies, China and Congo. All matters involving China also came before the China Subcommittee, but might additionally have been considered by the Finance Committee, Women's Committee, the General Purposes Subcommittee, the Staffing Subcommittee, the Medical Subcommittee, or any of a number of special subcommittees convened to consider particular issues. The committees were made up of ministers or retired missionaries and members of the denomination with a particular interest in missionary work. Membership of most of the committees was very large, and it was not uncommon for thirty-five or more members to be present at the quarterly meetings of the China Subcommittee.

Each committee and subcommittee generated voluminous minute books in which all official decisions were recorded, carefully but 'in brief, factual language sheared of most illuminating explanatory detail'.[26] Not only were the records brief but, as Maughan observed, 'differences of opinion and scandals in committee were generally disguised and concealed as much as possible', lest any publicly aired conflict should undermine the society's basis of community support.[27] Within the denomination it was expected that those who were involved

---

[25] Steven Maughan, '"Mighty England do Good": The Major English Denominations and Organisation for the Support of Foreign Missions in the 19th Century', in Robert A. Bickers and Rosemary Seton (eds), *Missionary Encounters: Sources and Issues* (Richmond, Surrey: Curzon Press, 1996), pp. 11–37 (p. 18).
[26] Maughan, 'Mighty England Do Good', p. 11.
[27] Maughan, 'Mighty England Do Good', p. 11.

in the missionary movement were Christian colleagues who would behave with tolerance and generosity towards each other. This expectation is neatly, if not entirely realistically, encapsulated in one comment by a member of the committee set up to review working relationships between the committees:

> The Society is a living fellowship, delicately constructed, with traditions and habits of working slowly formed and not easily answered…[O]ur task was not so much the drawing of the neat blue-print of an efficient machine, as the suggesting of ways in which a group of friends may happily and effectively discharge their common tasks.[28]

The correspondence between the mission secretaries at home and missionaries on the field tends at first sight to confirm this impression of 'a group of friends' discharging common tasks. There are many expressions indicating warmth and personal familiarity on the part of the letter writers. During the years when Bowser was women's secretary, the correspondence between her and the single women who became missionaries, or were preparing for marriage to a missionary, contains words and phrases that today would be considered excessively affectionate, and inadvisable.[29] She habitually addressed them as 'dearest' and signed off 'with love and best wishes, yours affectionately'.[30]

In practice, the warm tone of the letters did not detract from the fact that staff in the mission house exercised a formidable degree of control over the lives of missionaries in the field. Edward Phillips went out to China in 1924, anticipating that his fiancée would follow him there. When the time came for their marriage, the BMS China secretary had other ideas:

> It is not practicable to send your bride to China, you should arrange to meet her in Ceylon…your marriage should take place […] at Colombo […] and, as your 'honeymoon' you should proceed to temporary service in Bengal.[31]

The daughter of another China missionary recalled that when her father proposed marriage, her mother (already an employee of the BMS in her own right) responded at once by asking, 'What would Miss Bowser say?' She was half-joking, but was aware that the approval of the women's secretary at the mission house was a *sine qua non*.[32] At other times, the genial tone of the correspondence did little to conceal a hard-hitting message. One woman at home in England wrote to the London-based China secretary to ask that her missionary husband might be given leave to return from China, during the anxious days shortly after the Communist takeover. She received a flinty response:

---

[28] BMSA, General Committee Minutes, Vol. 44, November 1946, Report of the Staffing Sub-Committee, p. 193.
[29] See for example BMSA, CH/61, Bowser to Lloyd, 10 December 1936.
[30] BMSA, CH/61, Bowser to Lloyd, 14 May 1937.
[31] BMSA, CH/63, Wilson to Phillips, 7 July 1927.
[32] Margaret Bennett, interviewed by Audrey Salters, London, 22 June 2011.

> I do feel very sincere sympathy with all China missionaries today, but, as you are fully aware there are a number of missionaries [*sic*] wives who have been managing without their husbands and perhaps I may say that no real harm has befallen them!![33]

Manktelow's study of missionary families traces the ad hoc way the London Missionary Society (LMS) was forced to develop policies to meet the personal needs of missionaries and their families.[34] Her careful analysis of the records and correspondence of the society's early work in the South Seas and South African missions uncovers a long-drawn-out process of protest and plea from the families, and painful experimentation by the mission, which together transformed the administrative practice and organisational goals of the society. By the mid-nineteenth century, the LMS had become 'a professional institution', providing for the welfare of missionary families, 'including financial security in the face of death, investment in the future careers of missionary children, and ultimately expensive "homeland" education'.[35]

The BMS, like the LMS, found itself obliged to put arrangements in place to cater for many of the practical needs of missionaries and their families. Every missionary was issued on appointment with *The Manual of the Baptist Missionary Society for India, Ceylon, China, Congo and the West Indies*, with the requirement that he or she 'accept and abide by these regulations'.[36] The manual contained very detailed information about missionaries' salaries, allowances, furloughs and pensions, as well as regulations about language-learning requirements, when and under what circumstances missionaries might marry, what they must do with any additional earnings and where they should make their homes.

It seems very unlikely that those opting for missionary service, especially those with professional qualifications, were attracted by monetary gain. BMS missionary salaries were remarkably low compared to equivalents back in the UK. Before the Second World War, an annual income of '£250 was commonly regarded as the social dividing line marking off the working classes from the rest of society'.[37] Many BMS missionaries earned considerably less than this (see Table 1), irrespective of professional qualifications; and regulations stipulated that any additional earnings (for example from professional work done in their own time overseas, or as locums while on furlough) must be remitted to the BMS.

---

[33] BMSA, CH/54, Clow to Bastable, 10 June 1949.

[34] Emily Manktelow, *Missionary Families: Race, Gender and Generation on the Spiritual Frontier* (Manchester: Manchester University Press, 2013).

[35] Mankeltow, *Missionary Families*, p. 14.

[36] Baptist Missionary Society, *The Manual of the Baptist Missionary Society for India, Ceylon, China, Congo and the West Indies* (1939).

[37] Sue Bowden, 'The New Consumerism', in Paul Johnson, *Twentieth Century Britain: Economic, Social, and Cultural Change* (London and New York: Longman, 1994), p.256.

Table 1: BMS missionaries' income compared to UK-based counterparts

	Average UK-based annual earnings 1935-37[38]	Annual salaries for BMS missionaries working in China, 1939[39]	
		Single men & women	Married men
Male GP	£1,094	£120 for first 3 years £140 for next 17 years £160 thereafter	£240 for first 3 years £270 for next 7 years £300 thereafter
Male clergy	£370		Additional payments of £30 to £65 per child depending on age

There was also an impact on the difficult question of pay for local staff working for the society. It was often the case that Chinese doctors, teachers and pastors left jobs with the BMS because they could earn more working for non-mission organisations. In June 1946, Handley Stockley wrote to the mission house asking how he should respond to a Chinese doctor in Taiyuan who had formerly worked for the BMS but said he could not afford to return.[40] He would only return, he said, if, after working for one year in Taiyuan, he could be sent to England for one year of postgraduate work while his family remained in China, housed and cared for, all at BMS expense. 'On return, he would definitely like to come back to the BMS.' Writing, eventually, in October, Chesterman commented:

> If you and Nellie both consider him as indispensable we must engage him and get a supplementary estimate on the budget for Chinese staff replacing European staff, as we do for India. I should be willing to support a claim for salary and allowances which will not be more than what you yourself are drawing. Beyond that I feel we ought not to go [...] though we have actually given way in the case of some Indian women doctors who are getting more than our single lady mish [*sic*] doctors.[41]

BMS missionaries accepted sacrificial working conditions as part of their commitment to the cause. Chesterman's comments suggest that some also considered that indigenous professional staff should be expected to accept a comparable loss of income and status.

The BMS expected that each missionary would serve abroad for seven years before becoming eligible for one year's furlough. The long periods between

---

[38] Guy Routh, *Occupation and Pay in Great Britain 1906–79* (London: Macmillan, 1980), p. 63.

[39] *Manual*, paragraph 34.

[40] BMSA, CH/65, Stockley to Chesterman, 18 June 1946.

[41] BMSA, CH/65, Chesterman to Stockley, 9 October 1946.

furloughs had other implications for family life. Missionaries in their fifties or sixties had to take into consideration the wellbeing of their parents and other older family members. It was one thing to leave home in one's twenties or thirties with the blessing of parents still active and fit in their middle years, but another thing to commit to several years abroad knowing that those same parents were becoming frail and in need of care and the companionship of family members. In the event of a sudden death or other emergencies in the family, it was impossible to organise a speedy return home. Travelling from a mission station in inland China could take days or weeks to reach the coast, and the sea journey from Shanghai would take another six or seven weeks.

In rural areas there were very limited opportunities for educating the children of missionaries, and making arrangements for schooling was a serious consideration for missionaries with young children. Many Baptist missionaries sent their children from the age of six to the China Inland Mission boarding school in Chefoo (芝罘; Yantai) for their early schooling, and then transferred them for their later school years to one of the boarding schools in England that catered specially for the children of missionaries. There was no prospect for the children of missionaries to be reunited with their parents during school holidays, and the children spent their holidays with guardians, with whom they sometimes had little in common.

Accommodation on the field was provided by the society, and an additional annual rent allowance of £75 was payable during furloughs when missionaries had to find their own accommodation in the UK. Male missionaries' wives remaining in the UK while their husbands were abroad were paid a 'special rent allowance' of £25 'for a period not exceeding a year'.[42] The time limit on the payment of this additional rent allowance reflected the importance the society attached to their 'policy that wives should cooperate with their husbands throughout their service on the field. Only in exceptional circumstances will permission be given for them to remain in this country.'[43]

Just as Baptist missionaries were kept on a tight rein financially, arrangements for the direction of work on the mission field were also firmly controlled from London, as with many other British missionary societies of the period. The BMS's Home Committee appointed field secretaries as 'the direct and legal representatives on the foreign field of the Home Committee'. These people had responsibility for reporting to the Home Committee on all mission activity in their area and for ensuring that the decisions of the Home Committee were implemented. They were only empowered to act on their own initiative 'in cases of emergency calling for immediate action', and to sanction expenditure up to £100, before duly reporting any such action to the Home Committee.[44] In China each province had its own field secretary, and in addition an interprovincial secretary, all appointed by the Home Committee, where possible on the

---

[42] *Manual*, paragraphs 86 and 97, 19, 21.

[43] *Manual*, paragraph 34 (iii).

[44] *Manual*, paragraph 25.

nomination of the Interprovincial Conference, a gathering of representatives of the whole missionary body.[45]

As the independence and influence of the Chinese church members developed, particularly in Shandong, under the leadership of the able and charismatic Zhang Sijing (张思敬), president of the SBU, it became necessary to make decisions about representation of Chinese Christians on missionary committees. The General Committee considered the matter in February 1934 and resolved that 'the Interprovincial Council be retained and regarded as the representative of the Home Committee to deal with all matters connected with the Chinese church, but that, as occasion requires, it should be empowered to invite Chinese representatives for consultation on important matters of policy.' However, provincial executives – dealing with the detailed administration of 'the portion of the Allocation [of funds] devoted to evangelistic, educational or medical work' – should include Chinese members.[46] It is not always clear from the records of these meetings who was present at each meeting, and therefore how strongly the voice of Chinese church members had been heard.

Perhaps not surprisingly in such a complex management structure that had evolved over time, the dividing line between the responsibilities of those in London and those in the field was not always clear. The manual specified that 'the Home Committee desires to leave the administration on the fields largely under the control of the Conferences or Church Councils', who were empowered to act executively 'in all matters in which autonomy has been given by the Home Committee', and to send recommendations to the Home Committee 'in all matters in which control must be left with London'. Power to decide on the location of each missionary within China rested with the Home Committee, but only after careful consideration of 'any recommendation of Field Conference or Church Councils'.[47] Tensions quite often arose concerning the placement of missionaries within China, when staff in one province thought that another province was being favoured regarding much needed additional or specially qualified missionaries. For example, in late 1946, Stockley wrote indignantly to the medical secretary in London, complaining that the Xi'an hospital's needs for medical reinforcements were not being met:

> I must say the way you give CheeLoo [Qilu] precedence over every other place whatever their needs makes me 'fed-up'…It looks as though Sian [Xi'an], in spite of all its work has no real standing except to take the 'left-overs' when CheeLoo's voracious appetite is satisfied. CheeLoo is not doing at the moment a fifth of the work of Sian.[48]

These arrangements ensured that executive power over the work of missionaries remained firmly in the hands of the London Committees and the

---

[45] *Manual*, paragraph 27.
[46] BMSA General Committee Minutes, Vol.26, February 1934.
[47] *Manual*, paragraph 31.
[48] BMSA, CH/65, Stockley to Chesterman, 29 November 1946.

senior staff based there. They reflected the society's desire to present a united front and consistent message in its work overseas, and also its need to keep reins on the budget. They also disempowered individual missionaries and mission teams, as an editorial in *The Chinese Recorder* of January 1927 suggests:

> If the mission boards would transfer nine tenths of the details of administration of mission affairs to the mission fields it would make mightily for the strengthening of missionary morale.[49]

The regulations required close communication between London and China, and willingness on the part of the missionaries on the field to abide by the decisions of others who might have no experience of life as a missionary and limited knowledge of what was happening in China. During the 1940s, when communications were severely restricted, it was not always possible to comply with these expectations. More fundamentally, as we will see in Chapter Two, they could become cumbersome in the context of increased expectations regarding joint work with Chinese church leaders and devolution of responsibility to the Chinese church.

The eighteenth-century founders of the BMS had made it a principle that missionaries working abroad would not have direct personal responsibility for raising the funds necessary to support their work. Within Baptist churches in the UK, corresponding societies, later known as assistant societies, were formed to raise money to support the work overseas.[50] This was in contrast to the North American faith missions, which grew up in the late nineteenth and early twentieth centuries financed on the basis of personal support; that is through the pledged support of the individual missionary's network of friends and sympathetic churches.[51] It was also a different, arguably more worldly, approach than that of the China Inland Mission that held, as two of its five founding faith principles, 'no solicitation of funds or missionaries' and 'faith in God alone to supply one's needs' (the other three being no guaranteed salary, no debt and non-denominational membership).[52]

Occasionally the BMS benefitted from substantial legacies, such as the significant sum of more than £466,926 from the estate of Robert Arthington in 1910, worth more than £70 million in 2023.[53] From time to time the society also held special fundraising drives: the Ter-Jubilee Fund, launched in spring 1942 stood at £157,677 by the end of 1943 (equivalent to £9.57 million in 2023).[54]

---

[49] *The Chinese Recorder*, Vol. lviii (58) January 1927, editorial, p. 18.

[50] See Stanley, *History*, pp. 16–20.

[51] Robert T. Coote, 'A Boon or a Drag? How North American Evangelical Missionaries Experience Home Furloughs', *International Bulletin of Missionary Research*, 15.1 (January 1991), pp. 17–23.

[52] Alvyn Austin, China's Millions, *The China Inland Mission and Late Qing Society, 1832–1905* (Cambridge: W. B. Eerdmans, 2007), p. 18.

[53] Stanley, *History*, pp. 381–82; Brian Stanley, 'The Legacy of Robert Arthington', *International Bulletin of Missionary Research* 22.4 (October 1998), pp. 166–71 (p. 166).

[54] Stanley, *History*, p. 392.

However, the modest everyday contributions of individual church members were always the bedrock of the society's funding, and these were diligently solicited through national publicity and through local appeals. In the mid-nineteenth century, missionary societies 'stumbled upon an enormously effective rhetorical tool, the missionary box, placed in individual households'.[55] This tool remained an important part of mission fundraising well into the twentieth century, as one witness recalled: 'every household I visited in Burnley in the 1940s and 1950s had its missionary box.'[56]

Such personalised and often sacrificial giving by individual supporters created a sense of obligation, even guilt, on the part of some missionaries and of ownership on the part of some donors, who often kept a careful, occasionally jealous, eye on the way it was spent. When Bill Upchurch left China in December 1951, he purchased a tax-free Morris Minor in Hong Kong on his way home. At the time, only two members in his home congregation in Hitchin were able to afford car ownership. 'We heard people express amazement that a missionary could even afford [a car]; was he not supported by our pennies?'[57]

By the mid-1920s, depression and unemployment in the UK meant that the BMS was having serious difficulty raising the funds necessary to resource its greatly increased expenditure. This was not primarily because of declining church membership. Church membership overall was at a twentieth-century peak in the late 1920s, though nonconformist membership had reached its peak slightly earlier in 1906.[58] Rather it was the result of the growth in missionary numbers, which had risen from 311 in 1900 to 515 in 1921, and of the increase in institutional work that had taken place, mainly as a consequence of the Arthington bequest.[59] A deficit of £23,000 was recorded for the financial year 1924–1925 (equivalent to around £1.8m in 2023), and by the following year this had increased to £34,565 (over £2.7 million in 2023).[60] For a relatively small and modestly resourced organisation, such sums were alarming. Commissions of enquiry were set up in 1924 and 1925, resulting in plans for increasing income and reducing expenditure.

These plans included simplifying the committee structure, reducing missionary numbers and making cuts in overseas expenditure. The cuts were to be achieved by withdrawing missionaries from some mission stations, mostly in India, reducing missionary allowances by 5% and putting more responsibility for costs on to indigenous Christian communities. It was also agreed that in future BMS hospitals would be expected to raise at least 80% of their running costs

---

[55] Jeffrey Cox, *The British Missionary Enterprise Since 1700* (New York, London: Routledge, 2008), p. 96.
[56] Brian Hollingworth in conversation with Audrey Salters, Edinburgh, 30 July 2012.
[57] William S. Upchurch, *A Prevailing Wind* (Peterborough, 2007), p. 236.
[58] Peter Brierley, 'Religion', in A. H. Halsey (ed), *British Social Trends Since 1900*, p.524; Robert Currie et al, *Churches and Churchgoers: Patterns of Church Growth in the British Isles Since 1700* (Oxford: Clarendon Press, 1977), pp. 31 and 34.
[59] BMSA, H/96-97, Details of Missionary Staff 1900–1949.
[60] BMSA, General Committee Minutes, 13 May 1925 and 28 April 1926.

locally.[61] Implementing plans to reduce missionary allowances, to depend more on money raised by overseas Christians, and to attempt to raise money by charging for hospital services, all gave rise to practical difficulties as well as raising matters of principle.

Recommendations for reducing missionary allowances carried a strong risk that missionaries would be driven by practical necessity to abandon missionary service. As we have seen, Baptist missionary salaries were low, compared to those of professionals in similar jobs at home, and there is evidence that many missionaries in China during the 1940s found it impossible to provide, even at a minimal level, for the needs of their families without having to rely on family and friends for help.[62]

Putting more responsibility on to local Christians raised fundamental questions about the whole structure of mission finances. How should decisions be made about what part local church members should play in supporting evangelical and welfare work being undertaken in their communities? To what extent should responsibility for control of any given activity be dependent on who held the purse strings? Should salaries for workers locally employed by the BMS be on the same scale as for the foreign staff? Or, if not on the same scale as foreign staff, at a rate comparable to the amount they would receive if working at the same job in a secular organisation? Was it appropriate to charge fees to those using medical and educational services provided by the mission or the local church? And in doing so should there be any differentiation between Christian and non-Christian service users?

This subject exercised missionary organisations from their earliest days and reappeared frequently in the pages of *The Chinese Recorder*. An editorial in 1928 declared, 'the relation of western money to Christian work in China is one of the most difficult problems facing Christians in China.'[63] It then set out a number of possible solutions, all of them problematic: using 'western money' only for the support of missionaries, rather than also for supporting Chinese church workers; turning over all the Christian institutional work in schools and hospitals to the Chinese church, and using missionaries for evangelical work only; or using 'western money' exclusively for the development of institutional work and no longer providing Western financial aid to the Chinese churches. In a subsequent issue, the virtues of limiting support were discussed with passion in an article quoting from a National Christian Council (NCC) pamphlet by H. C. Chang:

> The missions, since they came to China, have out of the benevolence of their hearts made a gift to the church of two great stones – and crushed the tender sprouts of initiative and independence of our country church. These stones were the free gift of leaders and the free gift of funds. If we still have hopes that the first sprouts of

---

[61] Stanley, *History*, pp. 384–85, citing BMSA, General Committee Minutes, Vol. 24, 27 May 1926.

[62] For example: BMSA, CH/66/2, Smith to Williamson, 19 June 1943; CH/64/7/1, Spillett to Williamson, 7 October 1946; CH/57, Drake to Rowley, 28 November 1947.

[63] *The Chinese Recorder* 59.6 (June 1928), pp. 335–38.

initiative and independence will somehow grow out around these great stones – it's a difficult thing to expect![64]

Many people believed that financial issues presented the main obstacle to the churches achieving independence. The report of Commission II on 'The Church in the Mission Field' at the World Missionary Conference at Edinburgh in 1910 asserted optimistically that the church overseas, founded by missionaries, 'is now both fitted and willing [...] to take upon itself its full burden of responsibility and service'.[65] That claim ignored the importance of wider questions about funding. One delegate, Herbert Anderson, BMS India secretary, suggested that the goal of self-government was already in place in Baptist churches in India, since 'in accordance with Baptist ecclesiological principle, the society possessed "no authority" over local churches.' In his discussion of the conference, Stanley observes that, at that time, all 500–600 Indian evangelists and other staff were paid by the London committee, and Anderson's claim 'disguised the extraordinary influence which the power of the purse still exercised'.[66]

Many missionaries undoubtedly remained unaware of the impact of this interplay between cash and power, but nevertheless they may have wielded power without realising it. In his retrospective review of how the missions functioned, Hayward describes how this power could be exerted, even in seemingly unobtrusive ways:

> One missionary could sit silent at the back of a room while his Chinese colleagues debated a matter. He congratulated himself on his self-restraint, and on not even participating (as he thought) in the discussion. Yet all the time, with an innate sensitivity to personal relationships and unspoken factors, the Chinese were not only aware of his presence, but of his unexpressed attitudes. They deemed it advisable that the outcome of the discussion should please those who, after all, were going to provide the finances.[67]

These subtle influences are important factors to consider when seeking to reconstruct the decision-making processes behind both the Chinese church's desire for independence, and the BMS's commitment to 'surrendering the task'.

---

[64] Lewis F. Havermale, 'Western Money and the Chinese Church', in *The Chinese Recorder*, Vol. LIX, July 1928, p. 427, citing H. C. Chang, 'The Rural Church of China Today', NCC pamphlet, p. 24.

[65] World Missionary Conference, 1910, Report of Commission II, the History and Records of the Conference Together with Addresses Delivered at the Evening Meetings, p. 3, cited in Stanley, *World Missionary Conference*, p. 133.

[66] Stanley, *World Missionary Conference*, p. 145.

[67] Hayward, *Christians and China*, pp. 31–32.

Profile of BMS China Missionaries, 1937

In the late nineteenth century, missionaries were viewed as 'commonplace persons, not very well educated, not quite gentlemen [...] with not much learning and still less knowledge of mankind'.[68] Writing more than half a century later, Joan Williamson reflected a similar self-deprecatory view in a private letter to Bowser:

> In ordinary missionary life, there isn't much place for brilliance. We are mostly oxen or cows and we plod along a given way, goaded by Hell behind and coaxed by Heaven before…We are, to use an exaggeration, sows' ears, most, if not all of us; brought up in ordinary Baptist churches; [...] and with all the faults, virtues and glories of little people. Therefore we make good missionaries. Set us down in a foreign land and we will remain there, year in year out, plodding away at what we fondly hope is the Kingdom…Well, it may be, but again it may be that we are not quite on the right lines – but you mustn't tell us, [...] we have to find it out in blood and tears.[69]

This was not strictly true. Of the 101 BMS missionaries designated as 'China staff' in 1937, thirty-one of the 'ministerial staff' were university-educated and ordained, working primarily in evangelism, pastoral care and church organisation.[70] Of the others, fourteen were qualified teachers, fifteen were nurses, fourteen were doctors, and nine had other professional qualifications, including pharmacy, business management, banking and accountancy. Among the graduates was one with a first-class degree in mathematics and astronomy from Cambridge, and another who had qualified simultaneously in classics and medicine at Cambridge. There were, of course, others who had had to return to education to acquire, often painfully, the educational requirements to qualify for missionary service.

What united these twentieth-century missionaries with their less-educated counterparts from the previous century was their combination of a Christian upbringing and a dogged sense of commitment to the church and to their work in China, reflected in Joan Williamson's observation. This commitment was to become essential during the uncertain and difficult years between 1937 and 1952.

The 1937 cadre of missionaries were not wet-behind-the-ears new recruits, unfamiliar with mission life. Six had already completed more than thirty years' service with the mission, and a further seven had been in post since before 1910.[71] Twenty had been appointed within the previous five years. The majority had come to China during the 1920s. Nine had been born in China to missionary parents.[72] One was a member of the third generation of his family to serve with

---

[68] Bickers, *Scramble for China*, p. 240, citing *The Times* editorials, 3 December 1868, 11 January 1869, 10 March 1869.

[69] BMSA, CH/78, Williamson to Bowser, 21 July 1946.

[70] BMSA, BMS Annual Report, 1938.

[71] Williamson, *British Baptists*, pp. 363–72.

[72] BMSA, Candidate Papers of individual missionaries.

the BMS in China. His grandfather had gone to China with the China Inland Mission in 1876, transferring to work with the BMS in 1883 and remaining in China until his death in 1937. His father, a doctor like himself, had died of typhus in 1916, but his mother had continued her appointment as a missionary in her own right after his father's death, and was still on active mission service in 1937.

As nonconformists and members of a small denomination, Baptists were accustomed to being placed on the margins of society. In 1939, the combined membership of the Baptist Unions of England, Scotland and Wales was a little over 380,000, compared to more than 3.7 million Anglicans, 1.5 million Presbyterians and 800,000 Methodists. [73] Although this is not a direct comparison, since the (Anglican) Church of England and (Presbyterian) Church of Scotland do not have the same concept of church membership as the nonconformists, nevertheless, as the label 'nonconformist' implies, members of the Baptist church were often regarded as somehow outside societal norms. Ordained Baptist ministers numbered fewer than 2,000.[74] There were only five recognised Baptist institutions specifically designed for training prospective ministers and missionaries, many of whom followed their parents into the ministry or missionary service. People tended to know, or know of, each other. A majority of the children of missionaries at one time or another attended one of the two boarding schools founded for their benefit: Eltham College for boys and Walthamstow Hall for girls. Friendships, or enmities, formed in the claustrophobic atmosphere of a small boarding school tended to last for life.

It was not until after 1854 that nonconformists were permitted to study at and graduate from the universities of Oxford and Cambridge. The social dominance of the Church of England continued to play a part in community attitudes and expectations well into the twentieth century. A school friend refers to this in his account of the Worcester boyhood of Harry Wyatt, who worked as a doctor with the BMS in Shanxi province:

> Educated as we were in a cathedral city, the fact of our nonconformity was, in those days, brought home to us both by schoolmasters and boys in a way which would probably be unheard of now. Harry cheerfully bore the double burden of being not only the son of a parson, but of a Baptist minister at that.[75]

Baptists often had experience of standing out from the crowd, where necessary, or of being penalised for their beliefs. When the 1902 Education Act integrated denominational schools into the state system, forty-eight Baptists were amongst more than 170 nonconformists who had gone to prison for refusing to pay school taxes, which they believed went towards the provision of a particular form of religious education in schools with which they were not in

---

[73] Field, 'Puzzled People', p. 477.
[74] A. H. Halsey (ed), *British Social Trends since 1900* (Basingstoke: Macmillan, 1988), p. 530.
[75] Payne, *Harry Wyatt*, p. 28.

agreement.[76] Such capacity to think and act independently fitted them well for situations on the mission field where difficult ethical issues needed to be addressed, or where they might find themselves endangered by their beliefs, but arguably must have left many frustrated at the degree of central control from London.

The Development of BMS Work in China

Was Laughton's early goal to build an independent self-supporting Chinese church fulfilled in the way the BMS developed its work in Shandong, the province in which the society first took up work in China? Laughton was followed in the province by two enormously influential pioneers: Timothy Richard (known to the Chinese as Li Ti-mo-tai 李提摩太), who arrived in China in 1869; and Alfred G. Jones (known as Zhong Jun'an 仲鈞安), who joined him in 1876. Although Richard has become much more widely known outside the Baptist denomination, Jones's influence on the nature of the Shandong Baptist church was pivotal. A colleague, who worked with them both, wrote of Jones that he was:

> every whit as great a missionary [as Richard…], always looked up to by the Chinese and his colleagues as the uncrowned king of the mission, to whom they turned in every crisis for help and counsel. The organisation of the Chinese church in Shandong owes more to A. G. Jones than to any other man.[77]

Jones was killed in 1905 in a landslide caused by a cloudburst on the sacred mountain of Tai Shan (泰山), where he went periodically for relaxation and study. His premature death at the age of 59 was considered a great loss to the BMS.[78]

In an important and influential document published in 1883, Jones described China as 'an ancient, highly civilised Empire, with a vast literature, and most complex social constitution', and set down the principles that he believed should govern the work of the BMS in the country.[79] He set out his model for relationships between missionaries and Chinese, the place of the Christian church within Chinese society, and the stance he believed missionaries should adopt in relation to political issues. He also described the attitudes resulting from local institutions and traditions, and the difference between the essential Christian message and aspects of local culture.

---

[76] David W. Bebbington, *The Nonconformist Conscience: Chapel and Politics, 1870–1914* (London: Routledge, 2010), p. 147.
[77] E. W. Burt, *After Sixty Years: The Story of the Church Founded by the Baptist Missionary Society in North China* (London: Carey Press, 1937), p. 78.
[78] E. W. Burt, *Alfred George Jones: Layman, Pioneer Missionary and Theologian* (Brief Biographies of Leading Laymen, No. 8, London: Carey Press, 1944), p. 13.
[79] BMSA, CH/6, Alfred G. Jones, 'Past and Present Principles and Policy in China', 1883.

Jones's view was that missionaries should encourage outward expressions of Christianity that were consistent with Chinese styles, buildings and language, and should enable Chinese Christians to take ownership of the church and its organisation:

We abstain from denationalising our converts. We have abstained from constraining our converts to support the institutions [...] in a distinctively Western style (e.g. by building chapels, building in Gothic style)...

We have recognised that the Christian religion may naturally take different expression and form in various countries, while maintaining its essence pure and intact. So far as in us lay, we have tried to conform to the manners and customs of the people.

We have always viewed the Chinese and treated them as if the church and its organisation were to be theirs, the force for working and supporting it latent in and to come from them.

We have tried in our ministry to apply the teachings of scripture to Chinese circumstances in Chinese forms of thought and language [...] without coining terms barbarous to them, or rejecting their old thought moulds.

We neither feel, show nor teach anything that could be construed into disrespect of the government, priesthood, rites, manners or notions of the people.'[80]

A personal incident illustrates Jones's sensitivity on the importance of observing local traditions. He was greatly distressed when, shortly before his marriage in 1881, his prospective parents-in-law made it a condition of the marriage that he should wear his hair 'in European style, and dress foreignly [*sic*] at the ports'.[81] This meant cutting his 'queue', which he thought would make him become 'an insult to the Chinese'. 'I actually felt I would have to go back to England for change so low did I feel; but I couldn't do that.'

Jones was a firm advocate of self-propagation; of allowing local converts to take a key role in passing on their new faith to others. One of his early reports described the process:

Stations are springing up and adherents are multiplying at a rate out of all proportion to the foreign influence brought to bear on the work. That *one fact* is precious, almost above every other. How is it done? By me? No. By paid helpers? No. By office bearers of the church? No, in no way. It is just this. So-and-so in such a village had friends in the adjoining county and persuaded them. Such a man had [his] wife's relations in the next village. They wanted books and teaching. This man keeps a shop twenty miles from his native village, and when he goes home he exhorts his friends, of course. The leader at another village wants to collect some accounts...[82]

---

[80] Jones, 'Past and Present Principles'.
[81] BMSA, CH/5, Jones to Baynes, Letter 1,663, 25 July 1881.
[82] Burt, *Alfred George Jones*, pp. 10–11, citing Jones.

Raymond Williamson described the methodical way Jones engaged Chinese Christians in building and taking responsibility for their own church communities:

> The Christians of each locality were organised into groups, and given a leader, selected for his general intelligence and spiritual qualities. Catechisms, collections of hymns, addresses and sermons were printed and distributed to the leaders for their use… And at intervals the local leaders were called in to Ch'ing-Chou-fu [Qingzhou] for a period of instruction and training. The local churches were then grouped together to form district Associations, which gradually developed into the Baptist Union of Shantung.[83]

When Jones went home for furlough in 1883, 'he left behind forty-two churches, all self-supporting and with their own Chinese pastors, with an aggregate membership of over 800.'[84]

In January 1885, the General Committee drew up regulations 'for the future conduct of the China Mission'.[85] They stipulated that 'all European missionaries shall be *ex officio* members of Field Committees,' and added that 'such other Brethren as may be deemed suitable, being recommended by the Missionaries in China, and appointed by the Executive in England, may become full members of these Committees.' This was a significant acknowledgment of the recognition that Chinese Christians were expected to play a full part in local decision-making.

Deputation tours were periodically organised to give the Home Committee an up-to-date understanding of the situation in the field. Accounts of W. Y. Fullerton and C. E. Wilson's deputation in 1907, and R. F. Moorshead and A. C. Ingle's medical deputation in 1919, include details of increasing numbers of pastors wholly supported by church funds and of initiatives taken by Chinese Christians. Despite the loss of over 120 church members killed during the Boxer Rebellion of 1900 (in which all the BMS missionaries in Shanxi were also executed), within three years the number of pastors wholly supported by church funds increased from seven to eighteen.[86] Fullerton and Wilson concluded their published account of their tour by asserting that 'the rapid increase of the Christian Church in China is mainly due […] to the evangelistic fervour and consistent character of the Christian converts.'[87]

---

[83] Williamson, *British Baptists*, p. 39.

[84] Stanley, *History*, p. 187.

[85] BMSA General Committee minutes, 21 January 1885.

[86] W. Y. Fullerton and C. E. Wilson, 'Report on the China Mission of the Baptist Missionary Society (1908)', pp. 48 and 63, cited in Stanley, *History*, p. 203; A. C. Ingle and R. F. Moorshead, *The Challenge of China: Being the Report of a Deputation Sent Out to Visit the China Mission Fields of the BMS, 1919–1920* (London: Carey Press, 1920).

[87] W. Y. Fullerton and C. E. Wilson, *New China: A Story of Modern Travel* (London: Morgan and Scott, 1909), p. 249.

The members of the medical deputation in 1919 were approached by a group of women from Peichen (now Binzhou 滨州, Shandong province), requesting that 'ere long we may have not only a hospital in Peichen, but a lady doctor to attend especially to the needs of sick women.'[88] The women also urged the need for a girls' school, and indicated that they had already collected funds amongst themselves towards financing these two projects. The petition was signed by twenty-one Chinese women, ten designating themselves as village school teachers, four as evangelists, three as Bible women, and four simply as 'Christians'. The thoughtful analysis presented, and the appreciation of the need to contribute to the funding of the project, demonstrated the well-established nature of the local Christian community and the authority of its leaders, as well as the priority they gave to strengthening the provision of women's health and education services.

The photograph albums of Rev. Ernest Greening, missionary in Shandong from 1897 to 1936, depict the significant numbers of Chinese leaders in post in the early part of the twentieth century (for example, see Figure 2). The albums contain numerous pictures of small groups of Chinese, the groups being identified variously as 'pastors', 'evangelists' or 'teachers' and showing the name of each individual within the group.[89]

Figure 2: Shandong pastors and deacons, 1899

---

[88] BMSA, CH/23, Secretariat Shantung, 'Petition for the early establishment of a Hospital and a Girls' Higher Primary School, in order that the work of the Church may prosper in this District', Peichen, 24 September 1919.
[89] Photographs in private collection of Celly Rowe, viewed in St Andrews on 27–28 October 2009.

The way in which BMS work expanded into other provinces demonstrates both the significance of local history for the development of the mission, and the extent to which the three-self principles had been successfully applied in Shandong. In the autumn of 1877 the International Famine Relief Commission in Shanghai invited Richard to undertake relief work in Shanxi, one of the five provinces most severely affected by the acute famine conditions that devastated much of northern China at the time. Working along with Jones and others in horrific conditions, Richard is estimated to have saved 100,000 families from starvation and death.[90] The opening of the first Baptist church in Taiyuan, Shanxi, was a direct result of this work.

Some saw this as an unconvincing start to the church in Shanxi: Chinese Christian converts were sometimes disparagingly labelled 'rice Christians', implying that they 'converted' for what they could get out of it.[91] Possible advantages afforded by 'treaty protection', the promise of access to famine relief, or protection from the Japanese in occupied China between 1937 and 1945 might all have been attractions. On the other hand, it may be that the involvement of missionaries in humanitarian relief 'created a climate conducive to conversion', which 'made it possible for members of rural society interested in Christianity to come forward without immediate fear of persecution'.[92] Whatever the reality, records suggest that the number of converts increased significantly 'during and immediately after severe subsistence crises'.[93]

Richard remained in Shanxi for ten years after the worst of the famine abated, but 'was not privileged to see any spectacular spiritual results'.[94] Fifteen BMS missionaries succeeded him there, thirteen of whom, with their children, were killed during the Boxer Rebellion of the late nineteenth and early twentieth centuries. 125 Chinese Christians connected to the BMS were also killed, and mission and church property was extensively damaged. The church recovered very slowly, and Chinese leadership was fundamentally undermined by fears of a recurrence of the Boxer events, compromising Shanxi's progress towards the goal of self-governance. It was reported that 'Chinese evangelists were very few, and widely dispersed.'[95] However, Baptist missionaries gained the support of the provincial governor, Yan Xishan (阎锡山), as they were instrumental in stamping out an epidemic of pneumonic plague in northern Shanxi during the winter of 1917–1918. Claiming to have been influenced by the missionaries' philanthropic behaviour, Yan instituted a wide-ranging programme of social

---

[90] P. R. Bohr, *Famine in China and the Missionary: Timothy Richard as Relief Administrator and Advocate of National Reform, 1876–1884* (Cambridge MA: East Asian Research Center, Harvard University, 1972), p. 114, citing 'Report of the Committee of the China Famine Relief Fund' (Shanghai, 1879), p. 22.
[91] Tiedemann, *Handbook*, p. 323.
[92] Tiedemann, *Handbook*, p. 323.
[93] Tiedemann, *Handbook*, p. 323.
[94] Williamson, *British Baptists*, p. 50.
[95] Williamson, *British Baptists*, p. 81.

reform in the province that earned him the title 'the Model Governor'.[96] During this period, Yan formed a strong relationship with H. R. Williamson, who worked with the BMS for many years in the province and became a strong influence on BMS China policy in the 1940s.

Shaanxi was the third province in which the BMS undertook work towards the end of the nineteenth century. The Baptist church there had been founded, not by foreign missionaries, but by forty Chinese Baptists from Shandong. These Christians had migrated to Shaanxi in the late 1880s to take advantage of an offer of cheap land by the Shaanxi provincial government. The offer was designed to encourage immigration at a time when the population had been seriously reduced by rebellion and famine. The Baptist immigrants from Shandong travelled as a group and, on arrival, established their own village community, Fuyincun, or 'Gospel Village' (幅音村), some seventy kilometres north of Xi'an. There they built a small church and organised church life along the model already established in Shandong, effectively self-supporting, self-governing and self-propagating. Two years later, they invited the BMS to send missionaries to assist in the work of expanding the church into the surrounding areas. After initial hesitation on the part of the BMS Home Committee, which was reluctant to undermine the Shaanxi church's self-supporting status, in 1891 the committee assigned two missionaries and their wives to work in Fuyincun.[97] In the first ten years, the membership of the Fuyincun church grew only slowly, from forty-eight at the outset to 135 in 1897, practically all the additional members being immigrants from Shandong.[98]

It is possible that these early difficulties reflected suspicions of the rapid influx of outsiders, similar to those seen in Sichuan province in the eighteenth century, when the Qing government attempted to repopulate the province by introducing generous land reclamation policies. During the last two decades of the nineteenth century, Sichuan experienced 'the highest incidence of attacks on Westerners and Chinese Christians in all of China'.[99] In her study of relations between foreign and Chinese communities in Chongqing, Judith Wyman questions the conventional explanation that these attacks were grounded in anti-imperialism and xenophobia. Rather, she suggests that the rapid population growth, from an estimated 2 million at the end of the seventeenth century, to approximately 40 million by the late nineteenth, generated latent hostility towards all incomers. Attacks on members of the Christian community, Chinese and foreign, were, she suggests, 'part of a larger process, that of dealing with

---

[96] Williamson, *British Baptists*, pp. 103–4.
[97] Fullerton and Wilson, *New China*, pp. 49–50.
[98] Williamson, *British Baptists*, pp. 54–55.
[99] Judith Wyman, 'Foreigners or Outsiders? Westerners and Chinese Christians in Chongqing 1870s–1900', in Robert A. Bickers and Christian Henriot (eds), *New Frontiers: Imperialism's New Communities in East Asia, 1842–1953* (Manchester: Manchester University Press, 2000), pp. 75–87 (pp. 75–76).

other outsiders, Chinese ones, who had been arriving for more than two centuries'.[100]

The three provinces, Shandong, Shanxi and Shaanxi (see Figure 3), remained the primary focus of the work of the BMS in China until the departure of foreign missionaries in 1952. While the geographical boundaries of the work remained settled, however, the development of medical and educational work in the late nineteenth and early twentieth centuries was greatly extended. This was partly the result of the increasing emphasis on the 'social gospel', 'the idea of Jesus as a social reformer and the Christian responsibility to confront social ills', which prompted ever-growing missionary involvement in a range of social welfare activities.[101] For the BMS, ambitious schemes for expansion were encouraged by the Arthington bequest, which came with the condition that the funds should be used for 'forward work' and spent within twenty-five years.[102] At the same time, the fall of the Qing dynasty and the founding of the Republic of China in 1912 encouraged missionaries to believe that contributions from Westerners and from the Christian church would be received more positively than previously. One missionary described the change in public attitudes to missionaries as 'a moral miracle of the first magnitude'.[103]

By the beginning of the twentieth century, the BMS was making a significant contribution to the provision of Western medicine in northern China. The society established three hospitals in Shandong province (Qingzhou, 1889; Zhouping (周平), 1903; and Zhoucun, 1915) and was contributing to Qilu University Hospital in Jinan, an ambitious joint venture involving eleven Protestant missionary societies: five American, five English and one Canadian.[104] By 1937, the medical school attached to Qilu was offering full medical courses to over a hundred students, including twenty-five women, and also courses in pharmacy, physiotherapy and radiotherapy.[105] The nursing school had fifty-eight nurses in training. BMS staff had run a dispensary and a refuge for opium addicts in Taiyuan, Shanxi, from the mid 1880s. A men's hospital

---

[100] Judith Wyman, 'Foreigners or Outsiders?'.

[101] Dan Cui, 'British Protestant Educational Activities and the Nationalization of Chinese Education in the 1920s' in G. Peterson, R. Hayhoe, Y. Lu (eds), *Education, Culture and Identity in Twentieth-Century China* (Ann Arbor MI: University of Michigan Press, 2001), pp. 137-159 (p. 137). For further information on the origins of the social gospel movement, see Alan D. Gilbert, *Religion and Society in Industrial England: Church, Chapel and Social Change, 1740–1914* (London: Longman, 1976).

[102] Williamson, *British Baptists*, p. 81.

[103] E. W. Burt, 'China's Second Revolution', *Missionary Herald*, September 1916, pp. 197–200 (p. 199).

[104] Women's Foreign Missionary Society of the Methodist Episcopal Church; Methodist Missionary Society; American Presbyterians (North); American Presbyterians (South); Lutheran United Missions; Canadian Presbyterian (later United Church of Canada); Church Missionary Society; English Baptist Missionary Society; London Missionary Society; Society for the Propagation of the Gospel in Foreign Parts; Wesleyan Methodist Missionary Society.

[105] C. H. Corbett, *Shantung Christian University (Cheeloo)* (New York: United Board for Christian Colleges in China, 1955), pp. 98–103 and 185–88.

(1905) and a women's hospital (1910) were built on adjoining sites in Taiyuan. In 1905, a hospital was also established in Xi'an, Shaanxi, and a small hospital in Sanyuan.

Figure 3: Key BMS locations in Shandong, Shanxi and Shaanxi[106]

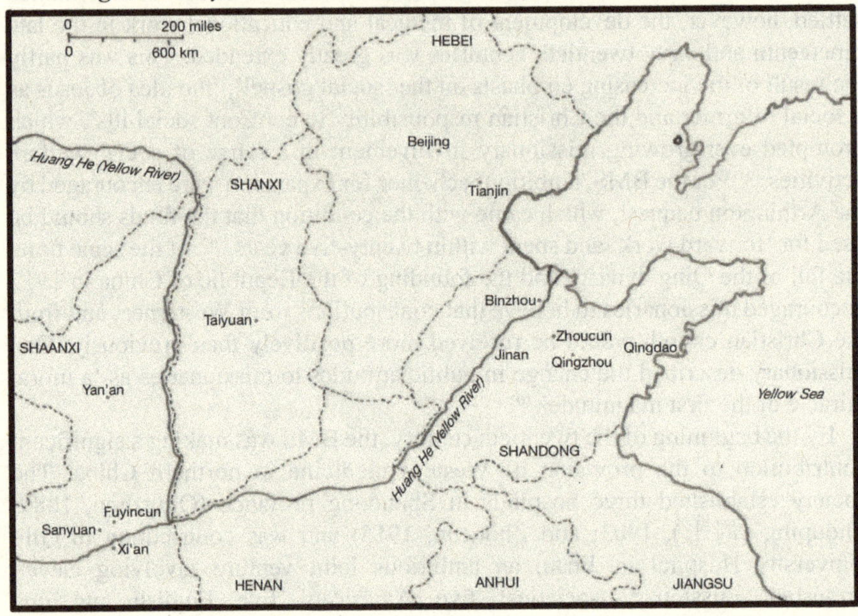

This map shows the course of the Huang He as it was before 1938, when its course was deliberately diverted in an attempt to foil the Japanese military advance.

In schools, too, the influence of missionary societies was evident. By 1915 there were almost 170,000 Chinese children and young people being educated in schools run by missionary societies; in the mid 1920s the figure rose to almost a quarter of a million.[107] Of these, the BMS was responsible for more than 7,200 boys and girls at primary and secondary schools. Ninety-five students were also attending BMS Bible schools and colleges, of whom eleven were girls.[108] The abolition of the traditional examination system in China in 1905 was the spur to the creation of many new government schools.

The missionary societies' energetic expansion in the field of education received a serious setback when mission schools and colleges found themselves bitterly attacked as instruments of cultural aggression, during the anti-foreign and anti-Christian movement of the 1920s. 'For the first time, Christian missions

---

[106] Map by Clare Salters, January 2015.
[107] Bays, *New History*, p. 94.
[108] Williamson, *British Baptists*, p. 230.

were denounced, not just as tools of foreign influence, but in specifically Marxist-Leninist terms as handmaidens of the forces of capitalist imperialism.'[109]

This anti-foreign sentiment had its roots in the unequal nineteenth-century treaties that granted foreign citizens and companies extraterritorial rights and privileges within China, leading to resentment among the Chinese population.[110] While the resentment was not new, it was fuelled in the 1920s by yet another treaty: the Treaty of Versailles negotiated in the Paris Peace Conference following the First World War. Chinese priorities in the negotations had been to find a satisfactory resolution to the so-called 'Shandong Problem' allowing China to regain sovereignty over Qingdao and the surrounding area.[111] This territory had formed part of the German concession under earlier treaties but was 'liberated' in 1914 by the Japanese, who retained occupation through the First World War. The decision to hand Qingdao to the Japanese – honouring a 1917 secret agreement between the British and Japanese – was bitterly resented, to the extent that China refused to sign the Treaty of Versailles. Opposition to the treaty within China was widespread, with protests from students and workers in many major cities, including at Beijing's Tiananmen Gate on 4 May 1919, a date that was to become iconic in Chinese political history as the inspiration for the 'May Fourth Movement'. Although Qingdao was formally restored to Chinese sovereignty in 1922, Japan maintained a significant presence in Shandong, and the impact of what was seen as betrayal by the Western powers, especially the British, was firmly established in China.

The anti-Western feelings received further impetus following the deaths of Chinese workers at the hands of the Shanghai Municipal Police in the International Settlement on 30 May 1925. Anti-British and anti-foreign demonstrations were staged by students and workers throughout China; British as well as Japanese goods were boycotted; and slogans were posted everywhere, demanding 'down with imperialism', 'down with the religion of Jesus' and 'kill all British and Japanese'.[112] In many parts of the country, serious damage was sustained by mission and church property, and many missionaries and Chinese Christians were attacked by mobs. The foreign authorities at Peking (Beijing) strongly advised all their nationals, including missionaries to move to the coast. By July 1927, about 5,000 of the total force of more than 8,000 Protestant missionaries in China left for either the coastal ports or home.[113]

It was during this political upheaval that the BMS faced its most difficult problems on the financial front. Assessing their work in the three provinces, it was clear that it was the church in Shandong that had progressed most decisively towards devolution. This led the London-based General Committee to decide in

---

[109] Stanley, *History*, p. 309.

[110] Rana Mitter, *A Bitter Revolution: China's Struggle with the Modern World* (Oxford: Oxford University Press, 2004), p. 32.

[111] Margaret MacMillan, *Paris 1919: Six Months that Changed the World*. (London: John Murray, 2001) pp. 322–44; Mitter, *Bitter Revolution*, pp. 3–40.

[112] See *The Times*, 4 June 1925, p. 13.

[113] Williamson, *British Baptists*, p. 127.

late 1931 that the time had come for the BMS to withdraw from Shandong, while continuing work on a similar scale as before in Shanxi and Shaanxi. Missionaries working in Shandong at the time assessed that a transitional period of fifteen years would be needed to ensure a smooth transfer. The committee felt this was too long, and in July 1932 decided 'to reduce its allocation to Shandong by ten per cent annually, thus setting the goal of withdrawal by 1942'. Missionaries on the field continued to argue that this timescale was too short, and as a consequence the period of devolution was extended to fifteen years, taking the end date to 1947.[114]

As part of the devolution process, a considerable amount of BMS property in the town of Zhoucun in Shandong had transferred to the ownership of the Chinese church in 1934 and again in 1936. This was used to set up administrative accommodation for the SBU, for church meeting rooms, orchards and rented property used to generate income for the church.[115] A letter received by the General Committee from Zhang Sijing of the SBU, thanking the committee for making these arrangements regarding mission property also appealed for reinforcements to the missionary staff and for the maintenance of the financial grant to the SBU at a fixed figure without reduction for the next five years.[116]

In 1937, a committee was set up by the Shandong Provincial Conference to assess the effects of the devolution scheme on church work in the province, constituted in a way that ensured provision for Chinese members to contribute.[117] The committee reported that numbers of foreign staff engaged in evangelistic work had dropped from twelve in 1931 to six in 1937. As a result of the reduction in mission grants, the number of Chinese staff engaged in evangelism had also dropped substantially, from forty-seven to thirty-six. Some of the most able men had left, and others were reduced almost to destitution. The report considered the reduction in numbers had been too fast, and detrimental to the work of the church.[118]

Figure 4 shows the number of Baptist church workers in the three provinces – Shanxi, Shandong and Shaanxi – in 1937, broken down by nationality, sex and method of payment. It includes only church workers, not staff in mission schools or hospitals.

It is clear that a very large proportion of leadership positions in Shandong (91%) and Shaanxi (93%) were filled by Chinese men and women, suggesting a strong movement towards self-government and self-propagation. However, the chart calls into question, somewhat starkly, the contention that the churches were moving towards self-support. In both of those provinces, only a very small number of men (around 6% of the total workforce) and no women were

---

[114] Stanley, *History*, p. 318, citing BMSA, General Committee Minutes, Vol. 25, 3 February 1932, 20 July 1932; Vol. 26, 6 February 1934.
[115] BMSA, General Committee Minutes, Vol. 34, 24 April 1936.
[116] BMSA, General Committee Minutes, Vol. 34, 3 November 1936.
[117] BMSA, General Committee Minutes, Vol. 34, 21 January 1885.
[118] BMSA, CH/23, Secretariat Shantung, 1936–1949, Report of Committee Appointed to Prepare Statement on the Effects of the Devolution Scheme in Shantung, 1937.

supported by Chinese church funds. A few Chinese men and women were paid by the mission, but most were working on an entirely voluntary basis. This suggests that, in times of hardship, the ability of Chinese church workers to maintain the same level of commitment to their work for the church would be much reduced. In contrast to Shandong and Shaanxi, church work in Shanxi was almost entirely dependent on foreign funds. Withdrawal of foreign funds, therefore, would have the most significant financial implications for Baptist church leadership in Shanxi, though the large number of Chinese men in Shaanxi paid from foreign funds would also be disadvantaged. This suggests that a policy of devolution was likely to have the most disturbing effect in Shanxi, where the church in its present form was very much mission-dominated.

Figure 4: Baptist church workers in Shanxi, Shandong and Shaanxi, 1937[119]

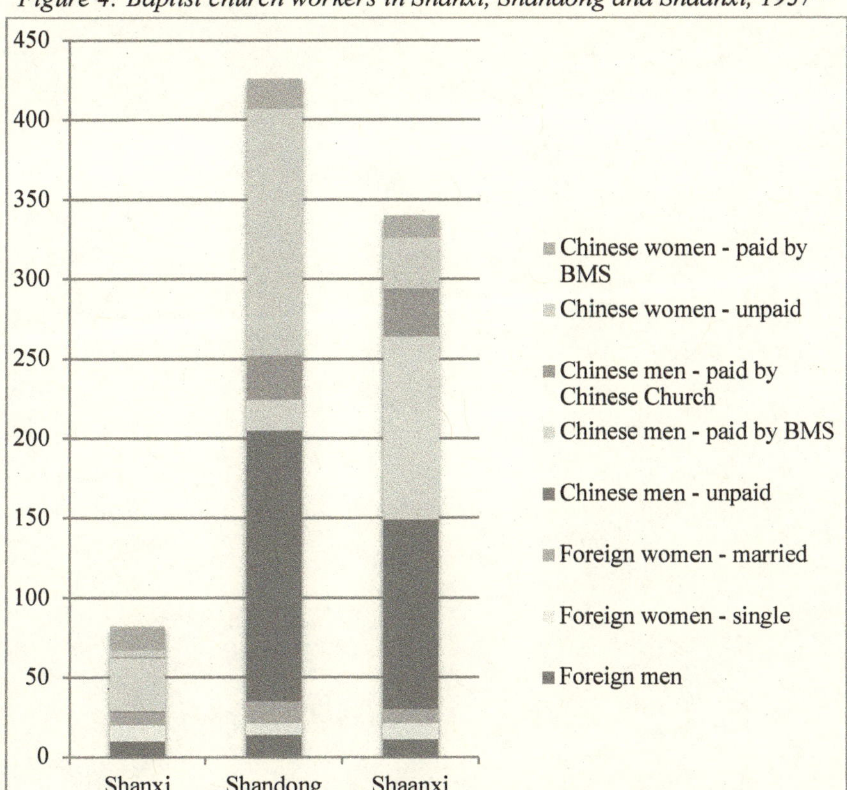

While progress towards achieving the self-governing, self-propagating and self-supporting principles was relatively modest in Shanxi and Shaanxi, by 1937, the Chinese Baptist Church in Shandong was flourishing. The decision of the BMS to withdraw from Shandong was based on the conviction that withdrawal

---

[119] Source: BMSA, Baptist Missionary Society, Directory of Missionaries, Financial Statement and 146th Annual report, 1938, p. 110.

was both possible and necessary, although there were questions about the appropriate speed of implementation. The fragile nature of arrangements for financing the work of the church, even in Shandong, suggested that without foreign assistance the church would be hard-pressed to survive. At the same time, the society itself was operating at the very edge of its financial resources. As well as the risks and restraints this introduced, it had the potential to have significant influence on decision-making.

What could not have been anticipated, at that juncture, was the impact of external events. The mission, and the close-knit community of individual missionaries working for it who had already surrendered to austere conditions and tight controls over their personal lives, were about to face a formidable test: life under occupation.

2. Japanese Occupation in Shandong, 1937–1942

> 'Truly one sympathises with the folk who say "the Honourable one in the Heavens has forgotten this land."'[1]

By the end of December 1937, Shandong and Shanxi had fallen to the Japanese, and an army of occupation was in place throughout the two provinces. Shaanxi, however, escaped Japanese occupation.

Some historians have argued that both these new situations had the effect of weaning Chinese Christians from dependence on missionary support.[2] Brook argues that before the war the indigenous Chinese church was still largely controlled and dominated by foreign missionary societies, but that the experience of Japanese occupation had the effect of assisting it towards its long-stated aim of independence.

> [T]he occupation pushed Protestant Christianity [...] from a church that in 1937 was externally dependent, mission oriented, and mission dominated, to a church that in 1945 was moving in the direction of independence, union and Chinese control.[3]

On the other hand, Ling contends that at the end of the war the Chinese Protestant churches were still mission dominated. '[M]issionaries were still arbiters of doctrine, the source of power, and paymasters of the Chinese Christians.'[4]

In fact, the position was more nuanced: BMS records, including correspondence from the Chinese Baptist church leadership, show that neither Brook nor Ling provide a sufficiently granular picture of the effect of occupation on the relationship between missionary societies and the indigenous Chinese. Rather than finding that the war provided an opportunity for liberation from Western mission control, Chinese Christians in the Shandong Baptist church found themselves more reliant on foreign staff and funds than they were before the outbreak of the Japanese war.

There are obvious challenges in reconstructing the missionary experience in this period. The impact of censorship on mail in both China and the UK has restricted the material within the BMS archive. After 1937, any mail within China, or leaving China, was subject to strict censorship by the Japanese military. References to anything considered derogatory to the Japanese was excised by the

---

[1] BMSA, CH/76, Thomas to Bowser, 14 July 1939.
[2] Brook, 'Toward Independence'.
[3] Brook, 'Toward Independence', p. 318.
[4] Ling, *Changing Role*, p. 51.

censors and might put at risk anyone it referred to. In December 1937, BMS officials in London wrote 'to the relatives and friends of BMS missionaries in China':

> Our people in China write with the knowledge that any criticism or information that the Japs [*sic*] do not care to be known will only cause the letter to be burnt by their censor. So there is a good deal we are not being told.[5]

Later, after the onset of war in Europe, mail entering or leaving the UK was also subject to British censorship, and writers in both the UK and China adopted a habit of self-censorship to avoid attracting unwelcome attention from officialdom.

Enemy occupation introduced changes in the relative power of different groups and individuals within an occupied area, and in the way in which they regarded and dealt with each other. During the Japanese occupation of China from 1937, the Chinese in the occupied areas were faced with a daily fight for physical survival. Some also found themselves having to make decisions about matters of principle – for example, where to position themselves in relation to the main players in the war: the Japanese, the local Chinese puppet government, and the Communist and Nationalist guerrilla forces. One witness described how her father, one of three brothers, remained in his pre-war employment with the postal service, thus in effect supporting the occupation, but thereby remaining able to provide for his elderly parents. Of his two brothers, one joined the Communist guerrillas, the other the Nationalist guerrillas in the fight against the Japanese.[6] Chinese Christians needed to make decisions about where to place themselves in relation to the Japanese Christian church and the foreign missionaries with whom they had formerly been associated. Chinese church leaders also needed to decide whether to attempt to work for the growth and development of the church during the occupation, or to accept that they were living through exceptional times and so concentrate their energies simply on maintaining the status quo.

The Japanese occupation introduced new dilemmas for British missionaries as foreign nationals. BMS missionaries had to decide whether to stay or to evacuate. They had to consider what impact staying or leaving would have on their Chinese friends and colleagues, on themselves and their families and on the continuation of BMS work. They had to consider how much freedom they would have to pursue the goals of the mission if they remained. They had to weigh up whether the plan to withdraw material support from the Chinese church continued to be appropriate in the prevailing conditions, or whether the plan to devolve responsibility should be shelved until times were more peaceful. Like the Chinese, they had to decide how to position themselves in relation to the occupiers, and what behaviour on their part was appropriate to their role as third-

---

[5] BMSA, CH/65, Chesterman 'To the relatives and friends of BMS missionaries in China', 29 December 1937.
[6] Gao Lingjun (高令俊), interviewed by Audrey Salters in Beijing, 15 April 2013.

party nationals. They had to decide how to reconcile their personal convictions with their national and civic duties, and how to deal with the moral choices arising as a result.

The Japanese occupation had consequences for relationships between Baptist missionaries and members of the Chinese church, and for the plans to devolve responsibility and authority from the BMS to Chinese Christians, although not always in the way that might be assumed. For example, did the shared experience of occupation bring a closer understanding between missionaries and their Chinese colleagues, or were their experiences of occupation so different that this emphasised the gulf between them rather than their common concerns? Similarly, in relation to devolution, was the outcome of occupation a stronger and more independent Chinese church, or one that was no less dependent on foreign missions than previously, or one that had reverted to greater dependence?

Missionaries in Shandong and Shanxi remained at their posts until July 1939, when the BMS hospitals were forced to close down and the Japanese-inspired, anti-British campaign caused the foreigners to relinquish their work in schools and churches.[7] In Shandong, the hospitals reopened in December 1939, and missionaries also resumed church and educational work, in increasingly oppressive conditions. This continued until the UK and the United States entered the war against Japan in December 1941, when mission staff were placed under house arrest. In March 1942, all BMS mission institutions in occupied territory were closed by the Japanese military, and in August, all foreigners were transferred to Shanghai for internment.

Shanxi was also occupied in 1937. However, the ferocity of the anti-British campaign there was accompanied by sustained intimidation of Chinese Christians and anyone connected with the mission. In August 1939, all Shanxi missionaries were evacuated from the province. They did not return until late 1945.[8]

The BMS missionaries from Shandong and Shanxi were assembled initially in the former Columbia Country Club (see Figure 5) before being allocated to one of the internment camps in and around Shanghai, where they remained until August 1945.

---

[7] BMSA, CH/22, Secretariat Shansi, Report on the Evacuation of Baptist Mission Stations in Shansi, North China, June–August 1939; CH/22, Secretariat Shansi, Price to Williamson, 18 September 1940.

[8] See, for example, the chapters by Annie Rossiter and Fred Price in *Through Toil and Tribulation: Missionary Experiences in China During the War of 1937-1945* (London: Cary Press, 1947).

Figure 5: BMS missionaries before internment in Shanghai, Autumn 1942[9]

Front Row, L to R: *R. Still, A. Still (Audrey Salters), P. Dart, A. Bloom, R. Phillips,
R. Phillips, D. Scott, S. Scott, N. Phillips, H. Bloom, R. Bloom.*
Second Row, seated, L to R: *G. and A. Lewis, J. L. and R. Lewis, [unknown],
W. P. Pailing, M. Pailing, A. Black?, M. I. Thomas, F. W. Price, [unknown],
H. Payne, E. J. Payne, A. B. Light, C. and J. Light;*
Third Row, standing, L to R: *[unknown], E. Smith, C. Scott, J. C. and I. Scott,
E. Pentelow, A. Smurthwaite, R. H. P. Dart, F. E. Dart, T. W. Allen, [unknown];*
Back Row, L to R: *E. S. A. Wheal, B. H. Bloom, C. V. Bloom, G. M. and C. Still,
R. J. Still, E. L. Phillips, E. Phillips, J. C. Newton, M. Newton, A. Jagger.*

The Impact of War

All this activity took place in the context of a brutal war that affected the whole
of China, and for which the Chinese people paid a very heavy price.

The Japanese occupation had a momentous effect on China. The publication
of Iris Chang's bestselling account of the December 1937 capture of Nanjing by
the Japanese military stimulated a stream of publications concerning this
catastrophic event; the exact scale of the massacre remains a matter of
controversy to this day.[10] For many years, however, neither Chinese nor Western
writers had much to say about the more widespread human suffering and

---

[9] Private collection of Audrey Salters.

[10] Iris Chang, *The Rape of Nanking: The Hidden Holocaust of World War II* (London:
Penguin, 1998); Zhang Kaiyuan (ed), *Eyewitnesses to Massacre: American
Missionaries Bear Witness to Atrocities in Nanjing* (New York: M. E. Sharpe, 2001);
Joshua A. Fogel, *The Nanjing Massacre in History and Historiography* (Berkeley,
London: University of California Press, 2000); Erwin Wickert (ed), *The Good Man of
Nanking: the Diaries of John Rabe*, trans. John E. Woods (New York: A. A. Knopf,
2000); Bob Tadashi Wakabayashi (ed), *The Nanking Atrocity 1937–1938: Complicating
the Pictur*e (New York and Oxford: Berghahn Books, 2007).

physical devastation that occurred during the whole period of Japan's war against China, 1937–1945. In the immediate aftermath of the Second World War, attention in the West was drawn primarily to recent events in Europe, and to pressures for change within the British Empire. On the Chinese side, political constraints and suppression by survivors of painful memories ensured that the subject was generally avoided.

Recent work has served to make the harrowing details more widely known. Lary and Mackinnon write of 'suffering [...] so great that it *does* almost defy description', 'the nadir of civilian suffering in modern China'.[11] In *The Chinese People at War*, Lary traces the long-term social effects of wartime trauma and dislocation. She writes of 'a grim equality to suffering [...], the destruction of property, the loss of income and the death of family members'.[12] She presents her readers with a powerful picture of havoc and desolation: millions of people forced to flee from their homes; crops and means of production destroyed; and businesses uprooted or at a standstill. Mitter, in the first recent comprehensive history that draws on both Chinese and Western sources, describes it as 'one of the bloodiest wars in history'.[13]

The war transformed vast sections of the population into refugees. During July and August 1937, as a consequence of the Japanese occupation of Beijing and Tianjin, a flood of refugees travelled from the North China Plain to Shandong, causing the population of Jinan (the largest centre of BMS activities within the province) to mushroom from 300,000 to 600,000. When, in October 1937, the provincial governor Han Fuju (韩复榘) abandoned the city, leaving it defenceless before the Japanese advance, half a million people from the town fled into the countryside and the population dropped to less than 100,000. During the whole course of the war, more than 11.5 million of the Shandong population (just over 30% of the population) became refugees or homeless.[14]

There was 'almost no government relief and no compensation for deaths, injuries, lost income or property', an almost complete lack of public provision for the poor and dispossessed. 'There were no state pensions for the injured or for the dependents [*sic*] of the dead. There was no insurance to cover property loss.'[15] All over Shandong, villages were burned down by the Japanese forces in reprisal for guerrilla activities, and any survivors were left completely destitute. In the first months of 1938, more than 150 villages between Jinan and Qingdao were burned down by the Japanese forces, and the inhabitants shot or incinerated.[16] Those families with fathers and sons in Free China serving with

---

[11] Diana Lary and Stephen MacKinnon, *Scars of War: The Impact of Warfare on Modern China* (Vancouver: University of British Columbia Press, 2001) p. 5.

[12] Lary, *The Chinese People at War*, p. 32.

[13] Mitter, *China's War*, p. 17.

[14] Stephen R. MacKinnon, 'Refugee Flight at the Outset of the Anti-Japanese War', in Diana Lary and Stephen R. MacKinnon, *Scars of War: The Impact of Warfare on Modern China* (Vancouver: University of British Columbia Press), pp. 118–134 (p. 122).

[15] Lary and MacKinnon, *Scars of War*, p. 5.

[16] BMSA, CH/63/1, Emmott to friends, June 1938.

the military had no access to their earnings, since 'there was no effective system for paying allowances to soldiers' dependents [*sic*]'.[17]

Both Lary and Mitter underline the fear induced by Japanese aerial bombardment, a new and unfamiliar weapon of war. Mitter cites a contemporary report by the journalist Du Zhongyuan on the assault on Taiyuan on 8 November 1937, which includes the detail that even those taking shelter from the bombs in underground tunnels 'did not dare to talk in a loud voice as they were afraid they could still be heard by the planes'.[18] In April 2013, two Chinese octogenarians, recalling their memories of the war, both independently referred first to the falling bombs and the terrible sense of vulnerability to which they gave rise.[19]

The threat to the Chinese people came not only from the Japanese invaders but also from China's own military actions. The Guomindang's (GMD's) strategic decision, in June 1938, to divert the Yellow River from its traditional course through Shandong province – so that its floodwaters held back advancing Japanese troops – led to the flooding of much of the Henan, Anhui and Jiangsu provinces.[20] Although the strategic benefit of the action was minimal, the consequences for the Chinese people were devastating, with casualty estimates ranging from 300,000 to 800,000 dead and 500,000 to 10 million refugees.[21] Even at the most conservative end of these estimates, the scale of the devastation was enormous.

The impact of war was not solely physical. There was a significant psychological cost too in terms of the impact on community relations under occupation. Lary draws attention to the occupiers' insistence, in Japanese occupied areas, on humiliating the local people, reducing them to 'a state of uncertainty and insecurity that gradually distorted their lives'.[22] The consequence, as a contemporary observer noted, was that 'men fear to be noticed, walk carefully with a backward glance over their shoulder, suspect everyone'.[23]

From the moment in July 1937 when Chiang Kai-shek, in an impassioned address to the nation, announced that China had reached the last limits of endurance and must fight the Japanese aggressor to the end, there was an expectation that every patriotic Chinese citizen had a duty of resistance:

---

[17] Lary and MacKinnon, *Scars of War*, p. 10.

[18] Du Zhongyuan, 'You Taiyuan dao Fengzhen' ['From Taiyuan to Fengzhen'], 26 September 1937, *Return Our Rivers and Mountains: The Collected Essays of Du Zhongyuan* (Shanghai, 1998), p. 260, cited in Mitter, *China's War*, p. 108.

[19] Gao Lingjun (高令俊) and Tian Daozheng (田道正), interviewed by Audrey Salters in Beijing and Jinan, 15 and 17 April 2013 respectively.

[20] Diana Lary, 'Drowned Earth: The Strategic Breaching of the Yellow River Dyke, 1938', *War in History* 2001 8.2, pp. 191–207.

[21] Lary, 'Drowned Earth'.

[22] Lary, *The Chinese People at War*, p. 65.

[23] Winifred Galbraith, *In China Now* (New York, 1941), 255, cited in Lary, *The Chinese People at War*, p. 65.

If we allow one more inch of our territory to be lost, we shall be guilty of an unpardonable crime against our race.[24]

Where resistance failed, and Japanese occupation threatened, the GMD demanded that all assets that could be used by the enemy should be destroyed or removed. Every true patriot would also remove himself so that he could continue the fight against the aggressor in Free China. Those who remained within the occupied areas were considered to be working with the enemy and labelled traitors, *hanjian*, 汉奸.[25] In January 1939, a journalist in China noted that 'Even children under the age of four or five are, consciously or unconsciously, familiar with the subject of a war of resistance.'[26]

Thus began the myth that still dominates the popular narrative of the Chinese War of Resistance against Japan, a myth that promotes a dismissive, even contemptuous, attitude towards those who failed to 'resist' the Japanese. More than that, claims Brook, 'the myth of resistance has been a powerful moral weapon in the arsenals that political elites on both sides of the Taiwan Strait have used to sustain their post-war dictatorships.' Little wonder that 'the moral landscape of the Japanese occupation has remained unassailable in the Chinese historiography of the war.'[27]

This long-held interpretation of allegiances during the war against Japan has been challenged by recent scholarship in the West and, more tentatively, in China. A growing literature has begun to address the complex continuum of behaviours, and the underlying ethical issues, between collaboration, compliance and resistance.[28] The need of those left behind in occupied China to balance the human drive towards self-preservation with an acceptable moral cost has been acknowledged and, at least in scholarly analysis, given legitimacy independent of moral judgment. Those who were unable, for whatever reason, to travel West and re-establish themselves in Free China, had to find a way to survive the occupation without betraying their country or themselves, to make an honourable choice between personal safety and patriotic commitment. This is the theme explored by Poshek Fu in his study of the painful moral dilemmas faced by three

---

[24] Jonathan D. Spence, *The Search for Modern China* (New York and London: Norton, 1990), p. 445.

[25] Lary, *The Chinese People at War*, p. 38.

[26] *The Chinese Recorder*, Vol. 70, January 1939, p. 13.

[27] Timothy Brook, *Collaboration: Japanese Agents and Local Elites in Wartime China* (Cambridge MA: Harvard University Press, 2005), p. 7.

[28] For example, Barrett and Shyu, *Chinese Collaboration*; John H. Boyle, *China and Japan at War, 1935–1945: The Politics of Collaboration* (Stanford CA: Stanford University Press, 1972); Brook, *Collaboration*; Poshek Fu, *Passivity, Resistance and Collaboration: Intellectual Choices in Occupied Shanghai, 1937–1945* (Stanford, CA: Stanford University Press, 1993); John W. Treat, 'Choosing to Collaborate: Yi Kwang-su and the Moral Subject in Colonial Korea', *Journal of Asian Studies* 71.1, (February 2012), pp. 81–102; Timothy Brook, 'Hesitating before the Judgment of History' *Journal of Asian Studies* 71.1, (February 2012), pp. 103–114; and Michael D. Shin, 'Yi Kwang-su: The Collaborator as Modernist against Modernity', *Journal of Asian Studies* 71.1, (February 2012), pp. 115–120.

Chinese intellectuals during the Japanese occupation: poet and novelist Wang Tongzhao (王 统 照), university teacher and dramatist Li Jianwu (李健吾) and journalist Zhou Fohai (周佛海), who each made, or were steered into, a different choice.[29]

Brook suggests that it is the association of the word 'collaboration' with moral failure, and the judgment this implies, that interferes with productive historical analysis.[30] 'The very word is loaded with moral failure.'[31] He suggests the wide span of definitions of the concept also make it problematic. The word is used, at one extreme, to cover 'all manner of cooperation, active or passive, shown to the occupier; anything that enables the occupation to continue'. At the other end of the spectrum, it has been narrowed to the much more specific 'supportive engagement in the tasks and ideology of the occupier'.[32]

Such widely diverse definitions make it possible for different people to reach sharply divergent conclusions about the significance of the same set of human interactions. 'Passive cooperation' does not speak of perfidiousness, whereas 'engagement in the tasks and ideology of the occupier' immediately conveys the idea of informed treachery. For this reason, Brook suggests that historians should suspend judgement, except in cases where there is evidence of 'self-advancement won at the blatant cost of the lives and dignity of others'.[33] For historians, this may be a useful path. For civilians seeking to interpret events in which they are engaged, and to find a way forward that enables them to preserve their self-respect, suspending judgement may not be an option.

Brook's exploration of the link between the recognition of collaboration as a feature of war and the growth of twentieth-century nationalism brings us to the fringes of the complex situation in which British nationals found themselves at the outset of the war against Japan.[34] The peculiarly modern application of the term 'collaboration', writes Brook, is intrinsically bound up with nationalism's premise 'that everyone should have a nation, and each individual only one'. Further, along with the conviction that 'nationalism supposed absolute loyalty', came the 'invention of collaboration between the individual and the nation to which [under occupation] he had now been made to belong'.[35] These are useful considerations when exploring the role of third-party nationals in China during the Japanese hostilities. As members of non-participant nations, there was no call for Britons to defend their own nation in the Asian conflict, nor any need for them to feel they had been 'made to belong' to another nation.

Patriotic Chinese Christians remaining in the occupied areas were burdened with a particularly problematic dilemma. As patriots, it was natural for them to support their fellow countrymen in resisting the Japanese occupation. As

---

[29] Fu, *Passivity, Resistance and Collaboration.*
[30] Brook, *Collaboration,* pp. 9–11.
[31] Brook, 'Hesitating', p. 104.
[32] Brook, *Collaboration,* p. 10.
[33] Brook, *Collaboration,* p. 13.
[34] Brook, 'Hesitating', p. 105.
[35] Brook, 'Hesitating', p. 105.

Christians, they were encouraged to 'love their enemy'. Ronald Still, working in the BMS hospital in Zhoucun, indicated on at least two occasions in letters to his parents his admiration for Chinese hospital staff who acted with generosity and forbearance towards Japanese patients and towards Chinese patients who were recognisable as collaborators:

> One of the things that has struck me most about [our Chinese colleagues'] attitude through all the fighting has been their freedom from hatred and resentment, and I can't help admiring them very much for it. Their whole attitude seems to have been one of sorrow because their country has been forced into this war…[36]

> A few days ago we took in a Chinese soldier who, while acting as a J [*sic*] guard, was shot by Chinese guerrillas. He had a bullet through both his lungs…I've been impressed with the kindly treatment that he has received at the hands of all our nurses and coolies since he might easily be regarded as a traitor to their country.[37]

Still chose to interpret the behaviour of the Chinese staff members as an expression of Christian love, but it is impossible to know whether they felt compromised in these situations, or how they were regarded by their fellow Chinese as a consequence.

Certainly the tone of Still's letters is in contrast to an incident described by Chatterton of a Japanese civilian being brought to a London Missionary Society (LMS) hospital in Wuxi (无锡) for an emergency operation.[38] Having agreed to operate, the missionary doctor, John Roberts, found himself at odds with his Chinese staff: 'they said she was the enemy of the country. And I said, "Well, we are going to do it anyway." So we operated on her.' Chatterton asks, 'Did Roberts, by his authority, place his colleagues in a position where they felt they were collaborating with the enemy? It seems he did.'[39] There is no evidence of such unease within the BMS archive. Whatever the undisclosed misgivings, any indications there are, such as those in Still's letter above, suggest an outwardly united approach from Chinese and British medical staff and there is no suggestion that the Chinese staff were regarded by other Chinese as showing a less than properly patriotic attitude.

BMS Missionaries as Third-party Nationals during the Occupation

Missionary attitudes to the occupation need to be understood in the context of their pre-existing relationships with both the Chinese and Japanese. The presence of foreigners resident in China under the treaty provisions was itself regarded by many Chinese as a form of occupation. Occupation by the Japanese thus

---

[36] Private collection of Audrey Salters, Still to parents, 14 November 1937.
[37] Private collection of Audrey Salters, Still to parents, 12 February 1939.
[38] Chatterton, 'Protestant Medical Missionary Experience', p. 126.
[39] Chatterton, 'Protestant Medical Missionary Experience', p. 126.

constituted 'a foreign occupation of a foreign occupation'.[40] This delicate situation was made more complex by the history of pre-war relationships between the UK and Japan.

The rights of the British to reside and trade in China, under the terms of the nineteenth-century Treaties of Nanjing and Tianjin were mirrored by those granted to Japan under the 1895 Treaty of Shimonoseki and the 1896 Protocols that followed. These included, significantly, the right under the Boxer Protocol of 1901 to allow both countries to station troops on Chinese soil.[41] The 'most favoured nation' clause in the treaty agreements meant that any privilege granted to one of the powers would automatically be enjoyed by all. The British had therefore benefitted from expanded treaty rights negotiated by Japan, including steam navigation rights on the river Yangtze, and the right to manufacture goods in the treaty ports, such goods being exempt from tariff duties.[42]

The UK's relationship with Japan had been coloured by this enforced interdependence since the end of the nineteenth century. The two countries had been allies both before and during the First World War, but the UK had been discouraged from developing the alliance during the 1920s because of opposition from the United States and Canada.[43] By the mid-1930s, however, with economic depression, ideological conflicts at home, increasing difficulties in maintaining the UK's position as a world power overseas and the growing threat of Germany, the British government was under pressure 'to try to get on better terms with Japan'.[44]

British missionaries were accustomed to dealing with Japanese civilians, especially in Shandong. Despite sovereignty of Qingdao and the surrounding area being returned to China in 1922, there remained a significant Japanese civilian population in China in addition to the troops permitted by the Boxer Protocol. By 1935, there were more than 14,000 Japanese residents in Qingdao alone.[45] Qingdao was a popular holiday destination for missionaries in northern China, with BMS missionaries in particular making frequent use of two holiday cottages there, owned by their colleague Jessie Manger.[46] They got to know the proprietors of the Japanese shops that lined the streets, saved their dental problems for the attention of the Japanese dentists who practised there, and did

---

[40] Lawson, 'Wartime Atrocities and the Politics of Treason in the Ruins of the Japanese Empire, 1937–1953' (PhD thesis, Harvard University, 2012), p. 7.
[41] Spence, *The Search for Modern China*, p. 235.
[42] Peter Duus, Raymond Myers and Mark Peattie (eds), *The Japanese Informal Empire in China, 1895–1937* (Princeton NJ: Princeton University Press, 1989), p. xix.
[43] Bradford Lee, *Britain and the Sino-Japanese War, 1937–1939: A Study in the Dilemmas of British Decline* (Stanford and London: Stanford University Press and Oxford University Press, 1973), pp. 2–5.
[44] Lee, *Britain and the Sino-Japanese War*, p. 8.
[45] Mark Peattie, 'Japanese Treaty Port Settlements in China, 1895–1937' in Peter Duus, Raymond Myers and Mark Peattie (eds), *The Japanese Informal Empire in China, 1895–1937* (Princeton NJ: Princeton University Press, 1989), pp. 166–205 (p. 170).
[46] Williamson, *British Baptists*, 367; BMSA, Finance Sub-Committee Minutes, Vol. 52, 23 May 1946.

business with the Japanese employees in banking and shipping firms. At the same time, Japanese patients took advantage of the facilities provided by the missionary hospitals: in early 1937, one BMS doctor described operating in the hospital in Taiyuan on a young Japanese man with 'a bad case of appendicitis'.

> It was the worst I have had to do and, to add to my embarrassment, the patient's Japanese doctor, himself a surgeon, had flown over from Peiping [Beijing] that morning to see me do it![47]

In the context of such social and everyday interactions, gestures of friendship between missionaries and Japanese would have been a natural enough occurrence.

The missionaries' status as foreigners under the treaty provisions had always been a prominent part of their identity in China. In all their communications, missionaries habitually referred to themselves as the 'foreign' staff, rather than the 'British' or 'missionary' staff, using the Chinese term for foreigners: 'waiguoren' (外国人), literally 'outside people'. Does this suggest that to some extent they understood and accepted their position as aliens or even misfits? The distinction was deeply felt by Chinese people. Writing about early twentieth-century government textbooks used for first-year primary-level pupils, Harrison comments, 'An early lesson shows the difference between "Chinese people" and "foreign people."'[48] British missionaries' role as outsiders in Chinese society was underlined by their role as non-participants in China's war with Japan.

At the outbreak of war in July 1937, British residents in China were faced with the decision whether or not to evacuate. Under extraterritoriality legislation, Britons living in the concession areas were governed and protected not by Chinese but by British courts and legal framework, and at first it seemed possible that life there might go on as normal even though fighting raged around them. Some chose to go; others dared not leave their jobs or businesses; others, living within the concession areas, could not conceive that war would affect them personally. 3,000 British women and children were evacuated from Shanghai to Hong Kong before August 1937 but had returned by Christmas.[49] The United States government encouraged its citizens to leave: 1,400 Americans left Shanghai in August and September 1937.[50]

The knowledge that the British government would assume some responsibility for their welfare was a factor that may have governed the decision of missionaries and their families of whether to stay or evacuate. When war first broke out in July 1937, many missionaries were taking holidays at the coast, in

---

[47] Private collection of Audrey Salters, Still to parents, 20 April 1937.
[48] Henrietta Harrison, *China: Inventing the Nation* (London and New York: Arnold with Oxford University Press, 2001), p. 93.
[49] Bickers, *Britain in China*, p. 155.
[50] Mark F. Wilkinson, 'The Shanghai American Community, 1937–1949', in Robert A. Bickers and Christian Henriot (eds), *New Frontiers: Imperialism's New Communities in East Asia 1842–1953* (Manchester: Manchester University Press, 2000), pp. 231–249 (p. 237).

Beidaihe or Qingdao. In early August, Gwyneth Still wrote to tell her parents in Cambridge that her husband, Ronald, had returned to his post at the Foster Hospital (復育醫院), Zhoucun, to ensure the safety of the hospital, but she was staying in Qingdao without him. She reassured her parents:

> Don't be alarmed – this is one of the safest spots – and the British Consul is constantly in touch with us. We are all registered and if any need arose we should be got out of the way – there are British ships in port.[51]

As the cities in northern China began to fall to the Japanese, the knowledge of communications between the British and Japanese authorities continued to give missionaries a measure of security.[52] Taiyuan, in Shanxi province, fell on 8 November 1937. Two days later, Fred Price, senior BMS missionary in the province, wrote to the mission house in London, 'this morning an officer [Japanese] came to see if we were all safe, in order to send a message to our Consul at Tientsin [Tianjin]'. In the afternoon, two more Japanese came to the door. 'We brought them in and had tea together, and they went off with the names of all of us.'[53] A week later Price expressed satisfaction when he learned 'that the British authorities have been making enquiries at the Japanese headquarters and we think that a telegraphic message has been sent to them and through them to all our enquiring friends'.[54]

As the war progressed, most British missionaries and their families in rural northern China chose to remain at their posts, doing, as one missionary wrote, 'what they feel they came out to do – namely giving support and comfort to their Chinese friends and associates just when they are most needed'.[55] They took risks in doing so. In 1938, two BMS missionaries, Harry Wyatt and Beulah Glasby, and their Chinese driver were killed by Chinese guerrillas, who mistook them for Japanese.[56] At times, Japanese controls over banking meant that they were without funds. However, until December 1941, they were able to continue to take holidays in the Chinese resorts, and to order supplies of foreign goods from the coast to supplement products available locally. More importantly, they had the knowledge that their government knew of their whereabouts and was prepared to accept a measure of responsibility for them. This gave them a level of security unknown to the Chinese with whom they worked.

Given these inequalities, was their continued presence universally welcomed by the Chinese? Could it be that their very presence in occupied China, carrying on with their usual activities, gave the occupation a veneer of legitimacy that was abhorred by the Chinese and categorised as an act of collaboration?

---

[51] Private collection of Audrey Salters, Still to parents, 2 August 1937.
[52] Brook, 'Toward Independence', p. 324.
[53] BMSA, CH/22, Secretariat Shansi, Price to Wilson, 10 November 1937.
[54] BMSA, CH/22, Secretariat Shansi, Price to Wilson, 19 November 1937.
[55] BMSA, CH/60, Hickson to Bowser, 13 November 1937.
[56] Williamson, *British Baptists*, p. 162.

The delicate position of foreign residents in choosing a legitimate role for themselves during hostilities is illustrated by the experiences of the small group of foreigners, led by the German businessman John Rabe, who put forward the idea of establishing an International Safety Zone in Nanjing in October 1937. Initially, Rabe and his colleagues were suspected by the Japanese of creating a hiding place for Chinese soldiers defending the city.[57] Over the six weeks of violence that followed the Japanese assault on Nanjing, the Safety Zone provided protection for many civilians. However, the Safety Zone was unable to provide complete protection. Gao Xingzu claims that 'several thousand' of those who had sought shelter there 'were taken out by the Japanese and executed in defiance of the zone's neutrality'.[58]

Other activity that so-called neutral third parties might engage in, with innocent intent, was less easy to justify. Rabe might have been accused by Chinese partisans of assisting the enemy when he acceded to a Japanese request to organise a Chinese workforce to help restart supplies of electricity.[59] His action was in the interests of preserving order but enabling an occupying force to preserve order, and thus to gain control, may arguably constitute an unacceptable deviation from the narrow path of neutrality. The decision of members of the Shanghai Municipal Council to continue running public utilities in Shanghai after war had been declared between Japan and the Western allies in December 1941, 'for the welfare of the Settlement', provoked an angry reaction in London. An official telegram, explicitly ordering them not to do so, was sent (6 December 1941) too late to be acted on in Shanghai. However, the foreign secretary Anthony Eden later minuted that British subjects must themselves decide whether it would 'embarrass the enemy war effort most' if they remained at their posts or resigned.[60]

Missionaries in occupied China understood that, as third-party nationals living within an enemy zone, they were explicitly disallowed from participating in the conflict. To preserve their protected status, they had a duty to conduct themselves in a way that would not compromise their government's interests, or risk sparking off international incidents. As the Japanese army advanced through northern China, one of the BMS medical missionaries in Shandong asked the British consular authorities whether it would be legitimate to give medical assistance to wounded Chinese. The consul checked with the ambassador who, in return, advised opaquely that 'formalities [...] should be observed'.[61] The doctor was clearly concerned to know whether treating Chinese wounded would

---

[57] Mitter, *China's War*, p. 123, citing John Rabe, *The Good Man*, pp. 46–48.
[58] Brook, 'Toward Independence', p. 320, citing Gao Xingzu, *Rijun qin Hua baoxing: Nanjing datusha* (*Japanese Army Atrocities During its Occupation of China: The Nanjing Massacre*) (Shanghai: Shanghai Renmin Chubanshe, 1985), pp. 6–11, 38–42 and 66.
[59] Mitter, *China's War*, pp. 130.
[60] Christian Henriot and Wen-Hsin Yeh, *In the Shadow of the Rising Sun*, (Cambridge: Cambridge University Press, 2004) p. 246.
[61] BMSA, General Committee Minutes, Vol. 35, 2 November 1937.

be considered as assisting the enemy. The question was discussed at the BMS General Committee meeting early in November 1937, and members present registered their agreement with the advice of the society's medical secretary: 'BMS doctors should treat any wounded who are brought to the hospital, without any question of formal proceedings being raised.'[62] BMS doctors were thus assured that their responsibility was to treat the sick and injured, without resorting to formal notifications or negotiations. There are no recorded discussions about what the medical missionaries would have done if the instructions had been not to treat all casualties equally.

Non-medical missionaries also needed to know how to ensure that they did not compromise their government's interests. Early in 1938, the British consul general in Hankou (now part of Wuhan), George Moss, gave this advice to Fred Russell, senior Baptist missionary in Xi'an:

> Should the Japanese arrive in Sian [Xi'an] you must be guided by circumstances, and act with prudence and common sense. Keep indoors and try to avoid contact with any parties of troops without officers of apparent discipline…Do not attempt any quixotic protection of people you cannot protect…Don't be obstinate and do not add avoidable international incidents to the difficulties we already have if you can possibly help it.[63]

Moss's caution in tendering this advice was well suited to the delicate position in which the UK found itself on the international stage at the time. It could be argued, however, that 'quixotic protection' was exactly what a Christian was called to offer.

It was relatively easy to abide by Moss's advice during initial encounters with Japanese troops, especially as most missionaries were accommodated in compounds separated from the areas lived in by Chinese people, often outside the city walls. This did not mean they were not at risk, however, as bombing was indiscriminate. The location of mission compounds was not always immediately obvious to incoming troops, and not all Japanese troops were concerned about the finer points of international law. When twenty-two bombs fell on the BMS compound in Zhoucun during the bombing on 24 December 1937, Wilfred Flowers reported:

> There is no doubt that they were aiming to hit us. The Chinese thought they were trying to hit the Union Jack. The APC [Asiatic Petroleum Company], also flying Union Jacks, had ten just around them.[64]

It appears, however, that in the early stages of the war the Japanese generally took notice of the special status of British and American nationals, and the foreign community was not exposed to direct confrontations with the Japanese

---

[62] BMSA, General Committee Minutes, Vol. 35, 2 November 1937.
[63] BMSA, CH/64/2/1, Moss to Russell, 10 March 1938.
[64] BMSA, CH/58, Flowers to Williamson, 6 January 1938.

invading army. Harry Wyatt, one of the doctors at the BMS men's hospital in Taiyuan, reporting on the fall of the city, commented:

> At an early date we were visited by an English-speaking Japanese who had official instructions to enquire after our well-being, and to make sure we had some food to eat. He obtained notices for us to place on doors forbidding the entry of soldiers.[65]

The British government's anxiety that its citizens should do nothing to compromise national interests, and the advantages that could accrue from smooth relationships with the occupiers, had the potential to expose missionaries to the accusation that they were too friendly, or even collaborating, with the Japanese. This is the question posed by Chatterton, in her thesis: 'whether it was accurate to accuse those [missionaries] who remained in occupied China of collaboration'.[66]

There are one or two letters in the BMS archive that give the impression that some missionaries regarded the occupation with something approaching equanimity. One such letter was sent by Christina Smith to mission headquarters in London, at the time of the capture of Qingzhou, Shandong, on 8 January 1938. No resistance was offered and the town fell without a battle. Smith's letter makes it hard to believe that an enemy assault had taken place:

> You know, I presume, that the city was occupied by the Japanese forces on the afternoon of January 8th. They were welcomed by responsible men in the city and arrangements made for their comfort. From that time, troops have been coming and going and many have been quartered in the homes of the people.[67]

The tone of the letter suggests that Smith did not consider herself to be in danger, and had little personal investment in the outcome of the conflict. It is almost as if she was opening her home to welcome guests. Was this really how she viewed the occupation? Was her apparent sense of detachment from the hostilities an indication of an underlying assumption that as a foreigner she was entitled to a different – and better – fate than the Chinese? Or was she thinking, as she wrote, of the Japanese censors who would examine her letter? The latter is almost certainly the case when another missionary, returning to Dai Xian (代縣) from Taiyuan, wrote, doubtless ironically, that 'our friends the Japanese were in occupation'.[68]

Smith goes on to say that there had been no difficulty getting supplies and 'we have indeed much cause for thanksgiving'.[69] The reference to 'much cause for thanksgiving' was a common refrain in missionary letters home. It did not by any means signify a straightforward or pleasant experience but, rather, was a

---

[65] Brook, 'Toward Independence', pp. 323–24; BMSA, CH/78, Wyatt, Report on the Fall of Taiyuan, undated.

[66] Chatterton, 'Protestant Medical Missionary Experience', p. 79.

[67] BMSA, CH/66, Smith to Bowser, 25 January 1938.

[68] BMSA, CH/62/3, Madge to friends from Taichow, 24 April 1938.

[69] BMSA, CH/66, Smith to Bowser, 25 January 1938.

form of shorthand indicating 'we are still alive and our faith has not wavered'. Smith's colleague, Hubert Emmott, writing five months later, when the nature of the Japanese occupation was more apparent, presents a more graphic picture: 'Nearly every house in the city was looted and the occupants often treated to indignities.'[70]

While missionaries ran the risk of the Chinese accusing them of collaborating with the occupiers, they were also in danger of being accused by the Japanese of providing inappropriate help to the Chinese. Mission compounds across the country were crowded with refugees. Many Chinese people who had no previous connections with missions were eager to avail themselves of the protection afforded. An incident that occurred at the time of the capture of Taiyuan on 8 November 1937, recounted by BMS doctor Wyatt, gives an idea of some of the difficulties of the situation.

> After we had retired for the night we received a call to the Boys' School where we had some seventy-five refugees. A group of twenty Chinese soldiers had come over the back wall to seek our protection. They had mostly been able to steal civilian clothes. They knelt and pleaded with us, saying that their lives were in our hands. We pointed out to them that we were quite unable to give protection from [the] Japanese, and were unwilling to conceal the fact that they were soldiers. After taking two pistols from them, we escorted them through the break in the wall, advising them to get out of the city at all costs.[71]

Wyatt must have been aware that sheltering the soldiers would put at risk the lives of the refugees already sheltering in the compound. Making concessions in this instance might also have opened the floodgates to many other Chinese soldiers who were equally desperate. It cannot have made for a comfortable decision in the face of the soldiers' pleas, and no doubt seemed an act of betrayal to the men concerned.

A more complicated example occurs in the case of the gateman at the BMS Whitewright Institute in Jinan, who was arrested by the Japanese on 27 May 1939.[72] Soldiers from the gendarmerie, the Japanese military police, visited the mission hospital, wanting to question one of the lab technicians, Tian Xuelin. The technician was missing but was thought to have gone to his home in the grounds of the institute, where his father was gateman. When the gendarmes discovered that Tian was not there, they arrested his father for questioning. On hearing this, Edward Phillips, the BMS missionary in charge of the institute, went to the gendarmerie headquarters and managed to see the sergeant handling the case. Phillips was advised that the military believed that young Tian was carrying mail on behalf of an important guerrilla leader, and they needed to get hold of him in order to catch the leader. They believed Tian Senior knew where his son was, but had not revealed this information.

---

[70] BMSA, CH/58, Emmott to friends, June 1938.
[71] BMSA, CH/78, Wyatt, Report on the fall of Taiyuan, undated.
[72] BMSA, CH/23, Secretariat Shantung, Phillips to Williamson, 11 June 1939.

The issue for Phillips was 'whether, or no, I should have started waving the Union Jack right away', with a view to rescuing his staff member, the gateman, from Japanese custody, interrogation and almost certain ill treatment. It would have been perfectly proper for Phillips to claim that the Japanese were exceeding their powers in removing the gateman from British property, but 'I had good reason to believe that there were one or two individuals on the Medical School premises who were not obeying the law as those in power here understand it'. Rather than risk public charges, and possibly provoke international complications, Phillips did not directly report the removal of the gateman to the British consul, although he arranged for the information to reach the consul informally via the American consulate in Jinan.[73] Meanwhile, Phillips sought advice from the local civil adviser to the Japanese, Nishida, with whom he had had constructive dealings in the past. Despite persistent enquiries from Phillips and Nishida, the gateman was never heard of again.

Phillips was later able to send a hand-delivered letter to the mission house in London.

> I do not think it quite wise to put down absolutely *all* the little bits of information I have even in this letter, but they are, I fear, sufficient to make me believe that our gatekeeper's son (who I believe has managed to escape) had involved his father in the games he was up to.[74]

Phillips's use of the word 'games' might appear to patronise or trivialise Chinese guerrilla activities. If taken in the context of his other correspondence, it seems more likely to be a reflection of his personal style and a product of his public-school education, where it was customary to make light of serious or painful issues. For example, under fire during the siege of Xi'an in 1926, he wrote a seemingly light-hearted letter, describing the heavy bombardment as 'the crumps'.[75] On his post-war return to Jinan in late 1945, he wrote that both the provincial governor and his chief secretary had been active in the guerrilla forces in Shandong during the Japanese occupation, 'and can tell good stories of hazards and escapes'.[76] The final lines of his report of the gateman's arrest suggest that he was by no means taking the incident lightly: 'It makes me sick to think of what has happened, and I will not try to put my feelings into words.'[77] It is likely that missionaries in occupied China were faced with many incidents of this nature, which tested the clarity of their judgement, set their loyalty to British national interest against their allegiance to their Chinese colleagues and tested their moral compass.

---

[73] BMSA, CH/23, Secretariat Shantung, 1939–1946, Drake to Williamson, 10 June 1939.

[74] BMSA, CH/23, Secretariat Shantung, 1939–1946, Phillips to Williamson, 11 June 1939.

[75] BMSA, CH/63, Phillips to Wilson, 25 April 1926.

[76] BMSA, CH/63, Phillips to friends, 5 January 1946.

[77] BMSA, CH/23, Secretariat Shantung, 1939–1946, Phillips to Williamson, 11 June 1939.

The only other direct reference to suspicions of collaboration appears in the minutes of a post-war meeting of the China subcommittee:

> The Committee heard with deep relief and gratification the evidence now produced which clears the character of Pastor Meng Lo San. We are making this finding as public as possible as rumours had even reached this country that he had been an instance of failure to maintain his patriotic and Christian principles.[78]

No other reference to the incident concerning Pastor Meng could be found in the archive. This is consistent with the understanding that many of the tensions and difficulties of this period were never documented. It is noteworthy that, in this instance, 'patriotic and Christian principles' are given equal weight by the committee members.

By September 1939, Ronald Still was the only BMS doctor working in occupied China. When the Zhoucun hospital was forced to close as a result of the anti-British campaign, Still arranged a meeting with the British consul in Qingdao. The consul told him that he had been informed by the Japanese military that the hospital was known to be 'assisting the guerillas', and that as long as this continued, he 'must expect to have trouble'. The consul had challenged the Japanese, saying that he regarded it as a grave allegation, and asking for substantiation or withdrawal, but neither had been forthcoming. Still was confident in reporting to the mission house that he was completely innocent of the charges against him:

> Although of course we treat any wounded who present themselves, there is no truth at all in the allegation that we take sides in the political struggle, and we cooperate in whatever ways we can with the Japanese authorities in their investigations and examinations.[79]

It is possible that 'cooperating' with the Japanese authorities in their investigations may have involved allowing the Japanese military to remove from the hospital any patients or staff members who were under suspicion. Although Still was no doubt acting under the belief that this was his duty as a third-party neutral, it cannot have been regarded with equanimity by resistance fighters, especially given the grim fate of any who were thought to have acted against the regime. Elsewhere Still writes of accompanying a patient who the authorities were taking away for questioning, and it seems likely that this was in order to protect the patient from ill treatment at the hands of the Japanese soldiers during questioning.[80]

Missionaries also found themselves in a difficult position in attempting to decide how to relate to the Japanese they encountered who were not personally connected with military activity. A BMS account, detailing missionary

---

[78] BMSA, China Sub-Committee Minutes, Vol. 11, 19 July 1946.
[79] BMSA, CH/64, Still to Chesterman, 28 September 1939.
[80] Private collection of Audrey Salters, Still to father, 15 March 1938.

experience, records that 'Christians among the Japanese also visited and prayed with us, as we with them.'[81] Those missionaries who had come to China as evangelists believed they had a responsibility to 'preach the gospel' to everyone they encountered, including the Japanese. They considered it appropriate, if not a duty, to look for ways to extend the audience for their message. The minutes of the General Committee in London for January 1938 record a request from Nellie Lewis of Shanxi for 'time and opportunity to study Japanese', and in 1939, Price wrote, also from Shanxi, suggesting to the BMS that they should send some of their China missionaries to Japan to learn the language in order to facilitate work in China.[82] It is not clear whether the incentive to learn Japanese arose from a wish to evangelise the Japanese or with the intention of improving communication with the occupying forces, but the committee appeared to assume the latter and responded by encouraging more effective use of interpreters.[83]

Williamson's emphasis is clear, however, when he describes the friendly and considerate manner in which the Japanese occupiers dealt with foreigners in the early days of their occupation of Jinan.

> Large numbers of Japanese troops visited the Whitewright Institute, listened attentively to short evangelistic addresses, and accepted copies of the Gospels in Japanese. Quite a few soldiers are Christian and some attended Chinese church services. On one memorable Sunday two stayed behind for Communion...[84]

Yenching University (Yanjing Daxue, 燕京大学) was one of only two missionary-run universities to stay open in Beijing throughout the occupation.[85] In February 1938, the president, John Leighton Stuart, raised with a Japanese embassy official in Beijing the possibility of adding courses in Japanese history and literature to the curriculum, taught by Japanese professors and funded through the Boxer indemnity: funding committed by the Qing Empire in 1901 to countries, including the UK, USA and Japan, for damages incurred in the Boxer uprising. 'The president even suggested a spring visit to Japan for Yenching's Class of 1938' and suggested it 'would be a beautifully Christian attempt at helping toward peace and constructive goodwill'.[86]

In all, foreign missionaries in occupied China trod a delicate line between their duty as British or American citizens and compassionate concern for the suffering Chinese people. The absence of more detailed accounts of particular

---

[81] BMSA, CH/45, J. Payne and L. N. Lewis, 'Unbroken China: Some Account of the Church and Mission in Shantung and Shansi during the Japanese Occupation, 1937–1945', p. 4.

[82] BMSA, General Committee Minutes, Vol. 36, 19 January 1938; CH/63/6, Price to Williamson, 5 May 1939.

[83] BMSA, General Committee Minutes, Vol. 37, 4 July 1939.

[84] Williamson, *British Baptists*, p. 158.

[85] Lutz, *China and the Christian Colleges*, p. 366.

[86] Sophia Lee, 'Yenching University and the Japanese Occupation, 1937–1941' (Unpublished paper, California State University, 2011), p. 20.

issues that they faced makes analysis of their attitudes problematic. It would certainly have impacted Chinese Christians' perceptions of the missionaries' loyalties.

The Chinese Baptist Church in Occupied Shandong

If the occupation impacted the lives of BMS missionaries, what of its impact on the members of the Chinese church in Shandong? The BMS had settled on 1942 as the year for withdrawing from Shandong.[87] How well had the mission and the Shantung [Shandong] Baptist Union (SBU) been able to use the first five years of the Japanese war to make progress towards 'surrendering the task'?[88]

In 1937, the SBU was made up of 300 separate congregations. The care of these congregations was in the hands of 217 Chinese men and 174 Chinese women, the majority of them unpaid (see Figure 14, page 47). In a further 212 villages where there was no settled church, church services were held at least once a week. It is an indication of the extent to which the churches had already moved towards independence that in 1937 only a small number of more than 500 centres of Christian teaching had any financial support from the BMS.[89]

Central to the survival of the Shandong church in the 1940s were people such as Zhang Sijing, seen here (Figure 6, bottom right) among a group of pastors photographed by Greening in 1919.

Figure 6: Group of Shandong pastors, 1919[90]

---

[87] Stanley, *History*, p. 318, citing BMSA, General Committee Minutes, Vol. 25, 20 July 1932.
[88] Tsingchow Conference 1927.
[89] BMSA, data obtained from 146th Annual Report for year ended 31 March 1938, pp. 110–11.
[90] From the private collection of Celly Rowe.

The picture shows a relaxed group, at ease in their relationship with the foreign cameraman, and comfortable in the ordinary dress of a Chinese teacher. The photograph was taken at a time when many people in rural China were fearful of having their photos taken, believing that in some way the process detracted from their life chances. The young Zhang Sijing looks eager and enthusiastic as he embarks on a future clearly linked to that of the foreign missionaries. In 1937, Zhang was secretary of the SBU, and had overall administrative responsibility for its work. It was his job to keep in touch with these scattered churches, to provide support and training for their pastors and to plan developmental work. His responsibilities far outreached the work of the mission. At the time, there were a mere thirty-five foreign missionaries in Shandong, including wives and university, medical and administrative staff, based in the mission stations at Jinan, Zhoucun and Qingzhou.[91]

Between the early months of the war with Japan and the end of 1940, Zhang wrote several times, in Chinese, to Raymond Williamson, Foreign Secretary in the mission house, reporting on conditions in the church. Of the letters retained in the BMS archive, some are accompanied by an English translation.[92] The fact that some appear without an English translation is a reflection of Williamson's easy fluency in Chinese and his close relationship with Zhang. The letters that were translated into English are likely to have been those that Williamson judged needed to be considered in full by the committees. The letters provide a rare glimpse of the work of the Chinese Baptist community since the greater part of the church records held in China were destroyed when the foreigners left in 1951. Here was a Chinese church leader writing as a colleague direct to mission headquarters in London. Although occasional letters or petitions were sent to the BMS in London by groups of Chinese church leaders, only one other Chinese employee of the mission appears to have reported to London regularly in this way: Dr Jing Yihui (景以惠), who had been medical superintendent of the BMS hospital in Qingzhou since 1928.

Zhang had worked with Williamson in Shandong between 1926 and 1938 and this close working relationship informs their correspondence. Despite the precarious conditions in which church members were living, the letters are remarkable for the evidence they provide of Zhang's continuing focus on the three aspects of devolution: self-support, self-propagation and self-government. It appears that Zhang made strenuous efforts to refrain from asking the BMS for additional staff or funds, and made it a priority to find ways to build up the independent leadership and financial resources of the Chinese church. His attempts to do this were regularly undermined by war conditions and by natural disasters. Circumstances were much more difficult than those identified in 1937 by the committee assessing plans for devolution.

---

[91] BMSA, data obtained from 146th Annual Report for year ended 31 March 1938, pp. 110–11.

[92] BMSA, CH/23, Secretariat Shantung, 1939–1946.

The first major wartime challenge to the progress of the Chinese church towards self-support occurred within two months of the outbreak of war. In September 1937, the dykes burst on the Yellow River (黃河, Huang He) and caused extensive flooding in north-west Shandong, around Binzhou.[93] In Zhoucun, some sixty kilometres south, the BMS compounds were inundated with around 400 refugees, and church and mission members attempted to provide them with food and shelter.[94] Zhang himself led a party of 3,000 men who worked for twenty days to repair the burst river dykes.[95]

On 24 and 25 December 1937, Zhoucun itself, where Zhang was based in the SBU headquarters, came under aerial and artillery attack by the Japanese, causing large numbers of townspeople to evacuate, either for temporary shelter in the nearby hills or to begin a flight west, in pursuance of the Nationalist government's scorched earth policy of destroying or removing anything or anyone that might be of assistance to the enemy.

By this stage, the majority of the trained nurses in Zhoucun's BMS hospital, the Foster Hospital, had left to volunteer for work with government troops engaged in battle further south.[96] It was common for professionally trained staff to leave mission hospitals for better-paid posts elsewhere.[97] Chatterton has argued that one incentive for the exodus of nurses from the mission hospitals during the early part of the Japanese attack might have been the higher salaries paid by the government hospitals. There is nothing in Still's correspondence or in the Zhoucun records to suggest that this was the case in this instance. All the indications are that the nurses were acting from a sense of patriotic duty. As it turned out, the nurses returned two days later, finding the government hospitals had transferred from Nanjing to Hankou and being unable to secure transport there. Four nurses later set off by rail for Hankou but the others remained in Zhoucun.

During January 1938, Henry Payne, BMS Provincial Secretary and a veteran of more than thirty years' work in Jinan, notified the BMS General Committee in London that the aid for flood victims had exhausted church funds, and appealed for help from home. The finance committee recommended a gift of $6,000, 'from special funds left to the Society with the express intention that they may be employed for work in which Mr Henry Payne is engaged'.[98] A number of such special funds were held by the BMS and some donors asked for their gifts to be earmarked for the work of missionaries whom they particularly wanted to support. Using money that had been ring-fenced for Payne's work

---

[93] Mitter, *China's War*, pp. 157–62.

[94] BMSA, CH/23, Secretariat Shantung, 1939–1946, Smurthwaite to Bowser, 30 January 1938.

[95] BMSA, Annual Report for year ending 31 March 1938, p. 15.

[96] Private collection of Audrey Salters, Still to parents, 29 November 1937.

[97] Bickers, 'Changing British Attitudes', p. 238; Chatterton, 'Protestant Medical Missionary Experience', p. 130.

[98] BMSA, General Committee Minutes, Vol. 36, 19 January 1938, p. 10.

enabled the society to take action without increasing regular financial support for Shandong, thus not jeopardising the devolution plan.

By 1939, the finances of the BMS itself were in an unhealthy state: receipts for all the society's work during the previous year fell more than £17,000 short of expenditure.[99] Total expenditure for the year, including work on all mission fields and work at home, came to £144,391 whereas receipts were only £127,247. Expenditure on China amounted to £28,232. In India, the most costly mission field, expenditure was in excess of £64,600. In 2023, this would translate to a shortfall of more than £1.4 million on the total expenditure of £12.1 million, of which £2.4 million was spent in China and £5.4 million in India; income was £10.6 million.

Nevertheless, two additional grants were made for work in Shandong. Failed harvests in 1938 and 1939, and looting by soldiers, guerrillas and bandits, further reduced almost the whole rural population of Shandong to destitution.[100] It became clear that Chinese church workers could not continue without supplementing their very modest wages. A bonus of 25% was added to the salaries of Chinese workers, initially for six months to 31 December 1939 but was later extended for a further six months to 30 June 1940, to enable these Chinese staff to maintain a barely sufficient lifestyle.[101]

The seriousness of the BMS's concern about its own financial position, and its anxiety not to set back the programme for devolution, is reflected in the letter from Williamson to Fred Drake, who had taken over as provincial secretary during Payne's absence on furlough:

> It is to be made perfectly clear to all concerned that this is a bonus, granted as a temporary measure, to meet the exigencies of the times, and carries with it no guarantee that at the termination of six months the bonus may be continued.[102]

Drake asked, in response, whether the bonus was to include pastors and evangelists paid by the Chinese church, or mission-paid workers only?[103] The question highlights the complexities involved in trying to separate mission and church finances, and the potential for inequalities resulting from such an attempt. Arrangements that had grown in an *ad hoc* way over many years could become invidious or unfair, particularly in conditions where they became, literally, matters of life or death.

---

[99] BMSA, Baptist Missionary Society, Directory of Missionaries, Financial Statement and 148th Annual report, 1939, pp. 215-17.

[100] Private collection of Audrey Salters, Still to parents, 24 May 1939; Still to father, 17 April 1940.

[101] BMSA, Finance Committee Minutes, 13 July 1939; General Committee Minutes, Vol. 38, 17 January 1940, pp. 7 and 12.

[102] BMSA, CH/23, Secretariat Shantung, 1939–1946, Williamson to Drake, 14 July 1939.

[103] BMSA, CH/23, Secretariat Shantung, 1939–1946, Drake to Williamson, 8 August 1939.

At this time of national crisis, Zhang was far-sighted enough to be concerned about the education of future church leaders. Formerly, an 'educational ladder' had allowed children in Shandong to progress within the Baptist school system from primary school to school-leaving age. This was considered essential if enough candidates were to be prepared for Christian leadership in the long term, but had been disrupted in 1929 as a result of government registration requirements (see Chapter Three). The urgent need to reopen a BMS junior middle school in the province became an important focus of Zhang's letters during 1939. He and Drake formulated detailed plans to restart the middle school in Zhoucun and asked the BMS to contribute $25,000, the sum they calculated was needed. This was agreed by the finance committee in May 1939.[104]

Once again, Williamson's concern not to allow any dissipation or deviation of funds comes across in his letter to Drake:

> Of course you will make it perfectly clear to our Chinese friends that this money is to be held in Shanghai in a special suspense account earmarked for the purpose until such time as the school is begun, or definite plans made for the beginning of the work.[105]

This rather heavy-handed warning is redolent of the patronising oversight for which Westerners were criticised when delegating responsibilities to their Chinese colleagues.[106] However, from the society's perspective, given the other claims on its already-stretched resources, it might have seemed remiss not to make such a stipulation when handing over a substantial sum. Subsequent correspondence indicates that the school was successfully reopened and did well up to the middle of 1941.[107] The school's centenary history, published in 2007, has no information covering the years from 1942 to 1946, but records that, after a brief post-war relocation to Jinan, it reopened in Zhoucun in September 1949.[108]

From early in the occupation, Japanese pastors had infiltrated all the activities of the Chinese church, and it fell upon Zhang to front negotiations between the church and the occupiers.[109] In November 1938, in order to legitimise the occupation and eliminate foreign influence, Prime Minister Fumimaro Konoe

---

[104] BMSA, Finance Subcommittee Minutes, Vol. 49, 11 May 1939.

[105] BMSA, CH/23, Secretariat Shantung, 1939–1946, Williamson to Drake, 16 May 1939.

[106] Bickers, 'Changing British Attitudes', p. 215.

[107] BMSA, CH/23, Secretariat Shantung, 1939–1946: Payne to Williamson, 20 September 1940; SBU Report by Rev. Chang Ssu Ching [Zhang Sijing], 1 February 1941; Price to Williamson, 7 May 1941.

[108] Mu Feng 牟峰, Lu Chengliang 呂承良, Gao Xilu 高希祿, Liu Yuwah 劉玉華, and Zhang Jun 張軍 (eds), *Bainian Guangbei: Shandong Sheng Zibo Diliu Zhongxue 1897–2005* (百年光被: 山東省淄博第六中學 1897–2005) (*A Hundred Years of the Sixth Middle School in Zibo, Shandong Province, 1897–2005*) (Shandong 山東: privately published, 2005), p. 38.

[109] H. Payne, 'Ourselves and the Chinese Church', in *Through Toil and Tribulation*, p. 19.

announced Japan's campaign for a new order in East Asia.[110] Its primary goals were to further Japan's economic and political status but, under slogans such as 'Asia for the Asians', it set about undermining the Western presence, which included attempting to eliminate Western influence within the Chinese church. This came to the surface during the anti-British campaign of July 1939, when Chinese nationals within all the occupied areas were encouraged by the occupiers to demonstrate against the British presence. The demonstrations assumed varying degrees of severity in different areas.

In Shanxi, Chinese Christians were threatened and intimidated at each of the places where BMS missionaries remained. In Taiyuan, Chinese Christian leaders were told that they 'would suffer severely unless they left the British mission'.[111] One Sunday in July, the whole church congregation in Taiyuan was arrested and questioned, many beaten and imprisoned, and sixteen detained and charged with involvement in anti-Japanese guerrilla activities. One of the older evangelists spent several months in prison before being executed.[112] As a result of these and other threatening incidents, BMS missionaries decided that it would be in the interests of their Chinese friends and colleagues if they withdrew altogether from the province, and this they did in August 1939.[113]

In Shandong, missionaries were forced to withdraw temporarily from all contact with churches and church members, and the BMS hospitals in Zhoucun, Qingzhou and Jinan had to close down when death threats were made against Chinese employees. When the foreigners withdrew, church work and church services were allowed to continue. In early September, when the campaign was at its height, Drake wrote to Williamson, indicating his complete confidence in the strength of the Chinese church.

> It is fortunate that with God's leading the Church is a Chinese organisation and in Chinese hands, and that it will carry on whatever happens. It is for us to continue our help as long as possible.[114]

With missionaries disabled by the actions of the Japanese, Drake indicated his belief that the Chinese church had already gained the maturity to survive independently.

At the end of November 1939, Drake reported a great improvement in relationships between missionaries and Japanese authorities in Zhoucun, following the appointment of a new military chief, 'who has already made a courtesy call [...] of a very friendly nature'.[115] By January the next year, it became possible to reopen the mission hospitals, and missionaries were able to

---

[110] Mitter, *China's War*, pp. 205–206.

[111] Williamson, *British Baptists*, p. 164.

[112] Williamson, *British Baptists*, p. 167.

[113] BMSA, CH/22, Secretariat Shansi, Report on the Evacuation of Baptist Mission Stations in Shansi, North China, June–August 1939; CH/22, Secretariat Shansi, Price to Williamson, 18 September 1940.

[114] BMSA, CH/22, Secretariat Shansi, Drake to Williamson, 6 September 1939.

[115] BMSA, CH/22, Secretariat Shansi, Drake to Chesterman, 23 November 1939.

resume their connections with the churches and church schools. Despite the months of closure, it appeared that public confidence in the mission hospitals had not waned, and the Foster Hospital in Zhoucun reported that in 1940 a record number of inpatients were treated.[116]

Experience of the occupation generally was very dependent on the severity of individual military commanders in their dealings with local people and the control they exercised over their staff. This is illustrated by Drake's reference to the appointment of the new military chief in Zhoucun, referred to above. In addition, the different impact of the anti-British campaign on Chinese Christians in Shandong and Shanxi is likely to have been influenced the different relationship between the local church organisations and their missionary colleagues. In Shanxi, foreign missionaries were still closely involved in church leadership and the campaign against the foreigners had severe repercussions for the Chinese church.[117] In contrast, the evident independence of the SBU from foreign control meant that there was less pressure on the Japanese military to clamp down on Christian institutions in Shandong with their Chinese leadership.

In December 1939, the SBU held a conference to review all its recent activities and set out its plans for the future. Zhang sent the BMS a full report of the conference; a report remarkable for its optimism and far-sightedness, given the conditions prevailing in Shandong at the time.[118] Under the devolution scheme reductions had been called for in the numbers of foreign staff working in Shandong, and mission grants to the Chinese church had also been cut. This had resulted in drastic reductions in the numbers of both foreign and Chinese staff engaged in evangelistic work. In view of the urgent need for increased numbers of evangelists, a course for preachers had already taken place in Jinan, which was thought to have been successful.[119] Plans were in hand for a summer training school for preachers and church leaders to be run for four weeks every year for the next four years. Zhang also had plans for an interprovincial Bible school, to give intensive Bible training for twenty students taken from all three provinces where the BMS was active.

> This is regarded as of vital importance to our church in North China. It is envisaged that church work at the close of the war will be making ever increasing demands. In spite of the expense attached to this scheme it is of such importance that it should be carried through.[120]

---

[116] BMSA, CH/65, Annual Report of the Foster Hospital, Chouts'un [Zhoucun], 1940, p. 3.

[117] Mu, Lu, Gao, Liu and Zhang (eds) *Bainian Guangbei*, pp. 34–38. Confirmed in discussion between Audrey Salters and Gao Lingjun (高令俊), Beijing, 15 April 2013.

[118] BMSA, CH/23, Secretariat Shantung, 1939–1946, Zhang to Williamson, 12 January 1940 (trans. R. Edwards, 1940).

[119] BMSA, CH/23, Secretariat Shantung, 1939–1946, Report of Committee Appointed to Prepare Statement on the Effects of the Devolution Scheme in Shantung, 1937.

[120] BMSA, CH/23, Secretariat Shantung, 1939–1946, Zhang to Williamson, 12 January 1940 (trans. R. Edwards, 1940).

However, after three consecutive years of famine, conditions in rural Shandong were desperate, and there was an urgent need for relief funds:

> Our church members are either compelled to leave their homes and travel about as beggars, or else stay at home and endure their hunger. As to their food, it is for the most part husks and woods, and dried leaves etc. If they are able to add a little grain to these things, they reckon themselves among the fortunate ones.[121]

Zhang's letter, which was forwarded by Payne to London, included the comment that he had not asked for help the previous autumn (1939) 'because of the outbreak of the European war and the financial difficulties of the Society of which we are quite aware'. Payne wrote a covering letter to Williamson, in which he reported that Zhang's own brother's children were out begging in spite of the help Zhang had been able to send them from time to time. 'It is deplorable to think that a man like Chang's [Zhang's] brother […] should be reduced to such straits.'[122] Zhang's long-delayed decision to request help from foreign sources had taken place in the context of critically serious conditions in Shandong.

Was Zhang's reference to 'the outbreak of the European war and the financial difficulties of the Society' genuine concern for his European colleagues or merely a sycophantic approach to a powerful benefactor? In the context of Zhang's own assured leadership, and his longstanding relationship with Williamson, it seems much more likely to have been the former. His understanding of the fact that the missionary society's funds were finite suggests both maturity and trust. To outward appearances, the missionary was, by local standards, a very wealthy person. Even in times of war, missionaries lived in large houses, employed servants and ate food that was beyond the reach of most local people, which meant that, despite their comparatively low incomes by European standards (see Table 1, page 28), they continued to be able to maintain a fairly comfortable lifestyle. That Zhang was able to look beyond these conspicuous indicators to underlying factors suggests a generous understanding of his foreign colleagues and the circumstances of the society.

Zhang wrote a further letter a few weeks later, saying that he had decided 'to establish three refuges in the most destitute districts for those families who cannot go out and beg'.[123] From the earliest days of the mission it had been customary for Chinese congregations to depend as much on creative moneymaking schemes as on voluntary gifts from church members. These were just the sorts of initiative William Carey had advocated in the earliest days of the BMS in Bengal. The poverty of most Chinese Christians meant that such schemes were essential. Zhang demonstrated that he was taking initiative to

---

[121] BMSA, CH/23, Secretariat Shantung, 1939–1946, Zhang to Williamson, 12 January 1940.

[122] BMSA, CH/23, Secretariat Shantung, 1939–1946, Payne to Williamson, 12 January 1940.

[123] BMSA, CH/23, Secretariat Shantung, 1939–1946, Zhang to Williamson, 16 March 1940 (trans. Gao Jian (高键), 2014); Payne to Williamson, 16 March 1940.

avoid having to rely on help from abroad: he had appointed a new man to the SBU administrative staff 'to care for the orchard and beef farm, Christian Cooperative, the agricultural work, clerical work, etc.' He had also managed to repay a loan of $500, borrowed from school funds, which had been used to build shops next to the city church that were now being rented for fundraising purposes.[124] His efforts to build up such resources in these difficult times were another indication of his determination to achieve independence from foreign funds.

During the occupation, there was heavy and continuing pressure from the Japanese military to take over any property to which they thought they could make a claim. They were quick to take over many of the Qilu University buildings when parts of the university evacuated to the west at the beginning of the war, and BMS property in Shanxi was seized when missionaries were forced to leave during the anti-British campaign.[125] This made it imperative that property was handed over only when the Chinese church was able actively to use and maintain it, minimising chances of it being opportunistically taken over by the occupiers and lost to the future Chinese church.

Several houses in Zhoucun, which had been built to accommodate foreign missionaries, had fallen vacant during the late 1930s but were still owned by the mission rather than the church. A number of church families had taken refuge in them and on the premises of the mission school at the time of the Japanese invasion in 1937. In the absence of foreigners, the church members sheltering there came to the attention of the Chinese guerrillas, who put church members under pressure to provide them with refuge. At the same time, the Japanese gave signs that they were looking for an opportunity to take over the property themselves.[126] 'I cannot, as you will understand, go into details with regard to guerrilla activities', wrote Payne, but the difficulty had 'led to some anxious times'.[127]

When alternative accommodation was needed for missionary families evacuated from Shanxi following the anti-British campaign of 1939, the BMS decided that some of the Shanxi families should go to Zhoucun. The preferred accommodation for the new arrivals was in the mission houses now occupied by Chinese families. Drake reported to the mission house:

---

[124] BMSA, CH/23, Secretariat Shantung, 1939–1946, Payne to Williamson, 16 March 1940.

[125] BMSA, CH/22, Secretariat Shansi, Report on the Evacuation of Baptist Mission Stations in Shansi, North China, June–August 1939; CH/22, Secretariat Shansi, Price to Williamson, 18 September 1940; CH/63, Phillips to President K.M. Wu, Qilu University, Chengdu, 30 December 1945; CH/23, Secretariat Shantung, 1939–1946, Drake to Consul General, Tsingtao, 28 August 1939; CH/23, Secretariat Shantung, 1939–1946, Drake to Williamson, 13 September 1939.

[126] BMSA, CH/23, Secretariat Shantung, 1939–1946, Payne to Williamson, 5 August and 20 September 1940.

[127] BMSA, CH/23, Secretariat Shantung, 1939–1946, Payne to Williamson 5 August 1940.

> The church leaders have been left with a free hand with the property, and now that more of it is needed to house our Shansi [Shanxi] folk the Chinese resent it…It looks to me that for political reasons (protections, etc.) they wish to have one foreigner, or family, living on the West side, but not a second.[128]

The fact that the BMS staff had loosened their control of the properties, in the interests of providing shelter for church members, meant that the priorities of the foreigners and the Chinese came into conflict.

The two last wartime letters from Zhang that are held in the BMS archive are undated, but were received in London on 6 June and 11 October 1940.[129] In the first, Zhang described the emergency shelters set up in the province using funds from the China International Famine Relief Commission, a local committee for the distribution of international funds, made up of himself and three Chinese colleagues from the SBU, two American Roman Catholic priests and Ronald Still, by that time one of only two BMS staff still in Zhoucun. Zhang was acutely anxious about the effect that the famine conditions were having on the children:

> There is no rainfall so far and there is no hope for the wheat harvest in the north. We don't know how to deal with the hundreds of children…The money is running out. If there is no assistance from other places, they would have no chance to stay alive.[130]

He also described the difficult decisions that had to be made about distributing a limited amount of money between an unlimited number of people in desperate need. One distribution had been restricted to church members only.

> We had no other choices. Even if we had further distributed additional 20,000 yuan, it would still not make a difference. So we decided to carry out the relief in an effective way.[131]

In the later letter, Zhang referred in several places to 'difficulties from outside' having increased. As a result, it had been necessary to cut down on preparation classes for would-be Christians, and there had been great difficulty in maintaining sufficient pastors and evangelists:

> We are short of talent. Male and female preachers and ministers are insufficient. We will cancel three rural preaching teams in the latter half of the year. We have just enough preachers to go round. As for ministers for the congregations, there are six congregations whose preachers are unsuitable. Two congregations need female

---

[128] BMSA, CH/23, Secretariat Shantung, 1939–1946, Drake to Williamson, 7 May 1941.

[129] BMSA, CH/23, Secretariat Shantung, 1939–1946, Zhang to Williamson, received 6 June and 11 October 1940 (trans. Gao Jian, 2014).

[130] BMSA, CH/23, Secretariat Shantung, 1939–1946, Zhang to Williamson, received 6 June 1940.

[131] BMSA, CH/23, Secretariat Shantung, 1939–1946, Zhang to Williamson, received 6 June 1940.

preachers and we don't have any suitable candidates to invite…Even if there were any candidates, we could not recruit them because the cost of living is too high.[132]

Zhang concluded his letter by saying that he wanted to resign as secretary of the SBU, in order to return to his family in Shaanxi, who were in difficulties.

The Baptist archive is almost entirely silent on events in the Chinese church in Shandong from this point until late 1945. Communication under occupation was challenging and ceased altogether following the outbreak of war between the UK and Japan in December 1941. When communications with the BMS were reopened in late 1945, it became possible for those in London to learn something of the experience of their Chinese colleagues, including Zhang Sijing.

Figure 7: Zhang Sijing in 1937 (left) and 1947 (right)[133]

The photographs in Figure 7 illustrate the toll taken on Zhang Sijing by the war years. The contrast between him as he was in early 1937, smiling and assured in his role as a leading figure in the SBU, and the later picture, where his emaciated physique speaks of the privations he had endured in the previous decade, is stark. Williamson met Zhang during his visit to Jinan as part of his China tour in 1945–46, commenting afterwards:

---

[132] BMSA, CH/23, Secretariat Shantung, 1939–1946, Zhang to Williamson, received 11 October 1940.
[133] From private collection of Audrey Salters.

> He [Zhang Sijing] had taken this journey at considerable risk, for he is not in favour with the Communists…He has managed to maintain himself and many of his colleagues in a worthy manner, and has done more than any other single person to keep our Baptist Church in Shantung [Shandong] together, and as actively engaged as possible. We owe a great debt to Chang Ssi Jing [Zhang Sijing] for his courage, loyalty and enterprise.[134]

Missionaries and Chinese Christians in Shandong province all suffered under the occupation, but their relative positions led to significant differences in the way they experienced Japanese rule. Whether these experiences brought them closer in their understanding of each other or forced them further apart is impossible to tell.

Chinese Christians were in constant danger of homelessness, starvation and loss of life. British missionaries also faced danger, injury and hardship, but they had a place in the fabric of international legislation, and the backing of a government with a duty to protect their interests. This fundamental difference in personal vulnerability must have influenced the way they made decisions about the future, the kind of compromises they were willing to accept and the way in which they regarded each other. Even where there was no suspicion of treachery, the vast and evident gap between the concerns and lifestyles of the missionaries and those of their Chinese colleagues during this period are likely to have underlined any sense of inequality in the relationship.

We can only speculate as to how the Chinese Christians and the foreign missionaries regarded each other, and to what extent they understood the constraints under which each was operating. There can be no doubt though that, in the tinderbox conditions brought about by enemy occupation, there was plenty of scope for ill will and misunderstanding. Conversely, there remained close bonds between the missionaries and their Chinese colleagues. Ronald Still, writing in 1946, recalled the challenges as the missionaries left Shandong:

> At the time of our departure, we were virtually the prisoners of the Japanese, and no Chinese could display any friendliness towards us without risking the severe penalties that awaited those who 'collaborated with the enemy'. None the less, in spite of this, during our remaining days in Chouts'un [Zhoucun], we received many touching expressions of friendship and affections from our former colleagus and friends on the staff of the hospital and from embers of the church. They belong to the richest treasures of our memory.[135]

Furthermore, after the war, there was clear evidence that leaders of the Chinese church were ready to resume warm and trusting relationships with British Baptist missionaries (see Chapter Four). This suggests that claims of the

---

[134] H. Raymond Williamson, *The Christian Challenge of the Changing World: Report on a Secretarial Visit to China, India and Ceylon, September 1945 to April 1946* (London: Baptist Missionary Society, 1946) p. 34.
[135] *Through Toil and Tribulation*, p.109.

missionaries' alienation from the leadership in the Shandong church are unjustified.

The other casualty of the period was the plan for the Chinese Baptist churches in Shandong to move towards independence from the mission. The letters exchanged between Zhang Sijing in Shandong and the BMS secretariat in London suggest that Zhang and the society were in agreement in their commitment to devolution at the outset of the war. During the years to 1942, Zhang persisted with his drive towards a church that was self-supporting, self-propagating and self-governing; he continued his efforts to find means to fund the pastoral and evangelical activities of the church and to offer educational and training opportunities to prospective church leaders. The BMS encouraged him in his plans and made contributions towards their implementation. However, the restrictions imposed by the Japanese occupation, the impoverishment of the people resulting from continuing military activity and the terrible consequences of drought and failed harvests in 1938, 1939 and 1941 meant that Zhang was forced on several occasions to plead for foreign help.

There is no evidence in the BMS archives to support Ling's contention that missionaries in Shandong were 'arbiters of doctrine, the source of power, and paymasters of the Chinese Christians', either before or after the war.[136] When Zhang wrote, he did so as an independent leader of the Chinese church, responsible for running the finances of the church, and with the knowledge and authority to make plans for its future. He wrote to Williamson, the China secretary at the mission house, as a sympathetic colleague and appealed to the society not as 'paymaster' but as a body he knew to be concerned for the Chinese people for whom Zhang was responsible, and likely to come to their aid in their time of need. There may be traces of a paternalistic attitude on Williamson's part, but not the imbalance of power in the relationship that Ling asserts, which may reflect different approaches taken by different missionary societies.

---

[136] Ling, *Changing Role*, p. 51.

3. The BMS in Shaanxi, 1937–1945

> 'We recognise that drastic changes in the status of all missionaries in China are inevitable and are already beginning to take place.'[1]

Shaanxi's experience was very different to Shandong's. The province did not fall to the Japanese and was therefore the only place in China where BMS missionaries were able to stay in post throughout the war years, and the only place where foreigners had an unbroken record of work in churches, schools and hospitals. Also, unlike Shandong and Shanxi, where the Baptist church had been founded by the mission, the Baptist church in Shaanxi had been established by Chinese Christians.[2] It was, from the outset, effectively self-supporting, self-propagating and self-governing, until, subsequently, the local church members invited BMS missionaries into the province. By the 1930s, although the long-term goal was independence from foreign support, there was no plan to achieve this in the short term.

Particular political factors coloured developments in the province. A major new element had been introduced into the political scene in China in 1921 with the formation of the Chinese Communist Party (CCP). In late 1935, the Red Army had settled in Shaanxi, and the CCP had established its headquarters there. Some commentators have argued that, before the Communists came to power, the majority of Chinese Christians and foreign missionaries had had no direct contact with Chinese Communists: 'Few knew what to expect when the Communist armies arrived to "liberate" them, but most were apprehensive and many expected the worst.'[3] The BMS archive demonstrates that this was only partially true with regard to missionaries in Shaanxi, who had had direct experience of Communists in the province for several years before and during the war with Japan.

The abrogation in 1943 of the nineteenth-century treaties of Nanjing and Tianjin also had far-reaching implications. The presence of missionaries in China had been dependent on the legal status afforded them by the treaties, and without this they could only remain with the toleration of the Chinese government. While their colleagues in Shandong and Shanxi had been removed from the scene by internment in 1943, BMS missionaries in Shaanxi soon became aware of some of the consequences of the abolition of the treaties, including the shift in Chiang Kai-shek's attitude to the UK as a result of the alliance between China, the

---

[1] BMSA, CH/21, Secretariat Papers, 1938–1946, Minutes of the Shensi Conference held at Sian, 4–8 October 1943.

[2] Williamson, *British Baptists*, pp. 43–44.

[3] Bob Whyte, *Unfinished Encounter: China and Christianity* (London: Collins Fount Paperbacks, 1988), p. 197.

United States and the UK. Other changes in the relationship between the UK and China, brought about by the war, also had an impact on missionaries living there, and began to point to a situation in which foreigners would no longer be able to hold leadership positions.

Although Shaanxi was never captured, Xi'an, along with Chongqing, headquarters of China's displaced Nationalist government in south-west China, was a main target of Japanese aerial bombardment. More than 400 bombing raids on Xi'an caused multiple deaths and injuries, damaged property and disrupted industry. Supply lines were cut, prices for scarce commodities rose and millions of refugees pouring in from the east increased demand on the limited resources. The BMS hospital building, constructed in 1905, was put out of service during air raids in March 1939, and medical work had to be transferred to the former boys' school. The city church and preaching halls and five missionary residences were also badly damaged.[4]

The peculiar confluence of circumstances at work in Shaanxi had an effect both on relationships between missionaries and the Chinese church and secular authorities, and on the way in which missionaries responded to the developing power of the CCP.

The Red Army in Shaanxi

There had been a small Red Army presence, fewer than 10,000 men under the leadership of Liu Zhidan (刘志丹), in northern Shaanxi for some time prior to the arrival of the veterans of the Long March in October 1935, and missionaries were aware of Red Army activity from the early 1930s.[5] The belief that Communism was an ideology incompatible with Christianity, and its history of violence against those who opposed it, formed the basis of initial missionary distrust. Joan Williamson, BMS missionary in Shaanxi from 1923, wrote with characteristic passion describing an attack on Xi'an by the Red Army in August 1926, when the mission compound was thronged with refugees trying to escape the fighting. At two in the morning, Red Army soldiers broke into the compound searching for grain. They returned later in the morning and commandeered the mission's entire food store, including 'all we had prepared for the refugees'.

> I wish some of the people who are always grousing at home could have seen the pathetic sight of the refugees kneeling in the mud and asking the soldiers to leave them some food. If ever I feel inclined to vote 'Red' I shall think of that crowd, as the soldiers were 'Red' and supposed to be the People's Army and the protectors of the common people's rights.[6]

---

[4] Williamson, *British Baptists*, p. 169.
[5] Anthony Garavonte, 'The Long March', *China Quarterly*, No. 22, April–June 1965, pp. 89–124 (p. 113).
[6] BMSA, CH/78, Williamson to friends, 6 December 1926.

George Young, an evangelist with the BMS in Shaanxi from 1924, wrote later that 'people could not be blamed for being scared of the "Reds"', remembering the devastation in Jiangxi province in 1930, when 150,000 people were killed, and more than a million were driven from the province in terror.[7]

In 1932, Fred Russell wrote to mission headquarters, reporting a raid on three villages by armed bandits who carried off several Chinese Christians and held them to ransom. The families concerned had appealed to the local military authorities for help but were told that their men were too busy attempting to ward off Red Army troops who were threatening the provincial capital, and were therefore powerless to do anything about the bandits, who 'were well aware of this situation and, of course, were taking advantage of it'.[8] Already the presence of the Red Army was affecting local conditions. From the missionary point of view, worse was to follow.

In late 1934, a young American couple, John and Betty Stam of the China Inland Mission (CIM), were beheaded by Communist troops in Anhui province, leaving their three-month-old baby daughter orphaned. The story was very widely publicised in missionary circles and left a lasting impression of Communist ruthlessness and antagonism to Christianity.[9] Just as the missionary deaths of 1900 inspired a significant number of young British and American Christians to offer themselves as replacements for the 'Boxer martyrs', so the story of the Stams prompted others in the late 1930s to volunteer for missionary work.

When the main body of the Red Army arrived in Yan'an in late 1935, at the end of its renowned Long March, the BMS immediately felt the impact. Mission premises in Yan'an, including hospital, school and church buildings, were 'forcibly occupied' and 'a good deal of damage was done'.[10] The 200 members of the Baptist church in Yan'an were cut off from the rest of the Baptists in the area and the congregation forced to worship in a cave in a nearby village, to which they transported church furniture, including, rather impressively, a baby organ.[11]

A year later, during what became known as the 'Xi'an incident', Chiang Kai-shek was kidnapped in Xi'an by two of his own generals. Anticipating major disturbances and on the advice of the British and American embassies, seventy-five foreigners, including the majority of the BMS women and children, were evacuated from Shaanxi. The tense political situation was unexpectedly resolved as a result of 'some of the most complex and delicate negotiations in China's

---

[7] Young, *Living Christ*, p. 177.

[8] BMSA, CH/64, Russell to Wilson, 2 December 1934.

[9] Howard Taylor, *The Triumph of John and Betty Stam* (London: China Inland Mission, 1935); Bays, *New History*, p. 123.

[10] BMSA, 145th Annual report for year ending 31 March 1937, p. 18; Williamson, *British Baptists*, p. 150.

[11] Stanley, *History*, pp. 322-23.

modern history', and Chiang agreed to form a united front with the Communists in opposition to Japanese aggression.[12]

In the aftermath of the negotiations, the Communists indicated that they were prepared to modify some of their policies and, in particular, began to adopt a more moderate land reform policy. Rich landlords, who in the past had been killed, were instead subject to fines. The following month, Xi'an was occupied by the Red Army. Jonathan Fenby notes:

> As a sign of the new attitude, the Red Army gave a banquet for local military and civilian officials, north of Xi'an, to which an Italian priest and Protestant missionaries were invited.[13]

Direct archival evidence that BMS missionaries were amongst those invited to the banquet could not be traced, but H. R. Williamson observed that, on the arrival of the Red Army in Shaanxi, 'some interesting contacts were made by our missionaries with Chou-En-Lai [Zhou Enlai]'.[14]

Four BMS men had remained in the province at the time of Chiang's kidnapping, and these had immediate contacts with the Red Army troops. They were 'agreeably surprised' to find that they 'no longer carried out their policy of pillage and murder, but were friendly to the country people and to the church'.[15] Young wrote of his impressions:

> As they settled down in the villages and we came into contact with them, it was clear that the Red soldiers were a well-disciplined body of men who were friendly to foreigners, and who treated the peasants well…They were a keen lot, full of fun and vitality…It was an exhilarating experience to meet the leaders and men and women of the Red Army. I found in them a toughness, a resolution, an abounding energy and buoyancy of spirit.[16]

Elsewhere, Menzies Clow described his interaction with five Communist soldiers who became patients in the BMS hospital:

> All listened very well when I went over to talk to them of Christianity…I found them very willing to discuss religion and keen to learn. They emphasised the point that they now believed in religious freedom.[17]

It is clear from these descriptions that not only did the BMS missionaries have opportunities to engage with the Communist troops in the local area, but they did so on friendly terms. So impressed was Young by his encounters with Communism that, in spring 1939, he wrote enthusiastically to friends at home of

---

[12] Spence, *The Search for Modern China*, p. 423.
[13] Fenby, *Generalissimo*, p. 285.
[14] Williamson, *British Baptists*, pp. 132–33.
[15] BMSA, CH/67, Young to friends, 24 March 1937.
[16] Young, *Living Christ*, pp. 177–78.
[17] BMSA, CH/56, Clow to Chesterman, 19 September 1937.

'the hopeful confidence of the east in contrast to the oppressive and fear-laden atmosphere of European militarism', a surprising comment given that, at the time, China was engaged in all-out battle with Japanese aggressors within its own borders.[18]

BMS missionaries were not alone in forming favourable impressions after early contacts with Communists in Yan'an. The story of the formidable struggles of the survivors of the Long March, and the brave new community they were building in the mountains, spread widely. 'In Communist propaganda, Yan'an became China's "revolutionary holy land", and the border region was promoted as a socially progressive and democratic model for all of China.'[19] In the UK and the United States, a mythology developed around this 'never-never land full of sunshine and bonhomie'.

> The revolutionary enthusiasm was infectious, as Edgar Snow and other journalists reported to the world. The homespun democracy apparent among the CCP leaders was a startling contrast to Chongqing [...] and the superficiality of contact allowed the cultivation of a mythology that captivated liberals abroad.[20]

The positive image of life in Yan'an was not without its critics. Some contemporaries commented on the better food and housing enjoyed by members of the CCP elite, which jarred with its egalitarian ideals, and Ding Ling (丁玲), a left-wing writer who had lived for a while in Yan'an, criticised the CCP's failure to implement its declared commitment to emancipation for women.[21] However, foreigners encountering Communism in Shaanxi in the late 1930s were favourably impressed, and this included some of the missionaries.

Missionaries in Shaanxi were not encouraged to get beyond casual contacts with Red Army personnel. BMS policy had always been to follow 'the policy of His Majesty's Government', which required 'recognition and support of the central Government of the day', and the Nationalist government discouraged relationships with the Communists in the province.[22] In his 1937 annual report for Sanyuan District, Keith Bryan made 'special mention' of Yan'an and referred to the cessation of hostilities and greatly improved conditions. Bryan was keen to revisit the Baptist church members from whom missionaries had been cut off for more than two years. He noted, however, that despite the improved

---

[18] BMSA, CH/67, Young to friends, 20 May 1939.

[19] J. W. Esherick, 'Revolution in a "Feudal Fortress", Yangjiagou, Mizhi County, Shaanxi, 1937-1948', in Chongyi Feng and David S.G. Goodman (eds), *North China at War: The Social Ecology of Revolution, 1937–1945* (Oxford: Rowman and Littlefield, 2000), pp. 59–91 (p. 60).

[20] John K. Fairbank and Merle Goldman, *China: A New History* (Cambridge MA: Harvard University Press, 1998), p. 317.

[21] Christian Hess, 'The Rise of the Chinese Communist Party' in Naomi Standen (ed), *Demystifying China: New Understandings of Chinese History* (Plymouth: Rowman and Littlefield, 2013), pp. 179–186 (p. 183).

[22] FO371/46166 F1690/35/10 Seymour to FO, minute by Hudson, 12 April 1945, cited in Feng, *British Government's China Policy*, p. 19.

conditions, 'negotiations [by the CCP] were still continuing with the Central government in Nanking [Nanjing] and until these had been completed [...] it was considered unwise for a missionary to visit.'[23] William Mudd, writing at much the same time, commented:

> We still have in mind a visit to Yenan [Yan'an]. Journalists pass through on the way there, but we have to be careful to maintain a neutral position between those whose headquarters are in Yenan, and those in Sian [Xi'an].[24]

It is not completely clear from Mudd's reference to 'headquarters' in Yan'an and Xi'an, whether the latter is an oblique reference to the Nationalist authority, or whether he is referring in both instances to Communist authorities. By March 1938, there were Communists in both Yan'an and Xi'an, while the Nationalist government had its administrative headquarters in Chongqing.[25] It would have been in line with BMS policy, however, for Mudd to bow to the authority of the officially recognised government of the whole of China, the Nationalists, while acknowledging a possible exception in the Communist base area in Yan'an.

An attractive opportunity for the BMS doctor Handley Stockley to make contact with the Communist leadership had to be turned down for similar reasons. Stockley had been on the staff of the BMS hospital in Xi'an since 1924 and had a reputation for successful treatment of diseases of the eye. Late in 1941, he was approached by Mao Zedong's personal physician at Yan'an, Dr Fu Lianzhang (傅连璋), a Christian, who invited Stockley to spend a week or two in the Communist headquarters doing ophthalmic work. Reporting the incident to the BMS in London, Russell wrote:

> Dr Stockley and I put the case to an influential official [...] who is in close touch with the Military Governor of Shensi [Shaanxi], and asked him to sound the Governor on the question. The Governor's reaction was most clear and emphatic that we should not go to Yenan.[26]

Later in the letter, Russell referred to 'recent evidence of the sincerity of the Communist welcome to foreign missionaries', giving the impression that, despite the governor's advice, he would have liked Stockley to have been able to respond positively to Dr Fu's invitation. Had he done so, Stockley's name might today be as familiar in the People's Republic of China as that of Norman Bethune (白求恩; *Bái Qiúēn*), a Canadian doctor who served the Communist Eighth Route Army in Shaanxi province from 1938 to November 1939 when he died of septicaemia, contracted while operating on a soldier.

In early 1942, Mao launched the 'Rectification Campaign' in Yan'an with a view to improving CCP discipline and organisation, and consolidating his pre-

---

[23] BMSA, CH/55, Sanyuan District, Annual Report for 1937.
[24] BMSA, CH/62, Mudd to Wilson, 3 March 1938.
[25] Mitter, *China's War*, p. 120.
[26] BMSA, CH/65, Russell to Williamson, 23 October 1941.

eminent position in the party. This produced a 'severe change of mood in Yan'an'. It became much harder for people to enter or leave the region.

> The city was cut off from the outside world not only by enemy blockade, but also by a new hardness of the party line. An earlier atmosphere of openness and collective enterprise gave way to a much more all or nothing environment. Ideas of pluralism and 'new democracy' were replaced by a turn toward party control.[27]

By the end of the war, however, the main deterrent to closer contacts between missionaries and Communists appeared to be the stance taken by the Nationalists. Williamson visited Shaanxi in November 1945, as part of his post-war tour of BMS stations in China, and reported:

> Visitors to the Communist headquarters have said that the leaders are willing to receive missionaries if they go for the welfare of the people, and that they are ready to permit the rebuilding of our church in Yenan [Yan'an] city. However, the Nationalist leaders have discouraged, and practically prohibited, our missionaries from going there, and Nationalist officials in Shensi itself have so far definitely withheld permission for such a venture.[28]

The early reputation of the Red Army had made BMS missionaries in Shaanxi wary of what they might expect from a Communist regime. From 1934, however, first-hand contact with Communist forces had given the missionaries opportunities to modify their views. The evidence from the Baptist archive indicates that missionaries took note of the approachability of the Communists they encountered, and made efforts when they could to interact with them. Nevertheless, BMS policy of remaining loyal to the established Nationalist government, and the missionaries' desire to cooperate with the government where opportunities arose, acted as a barrier to more active cooperation with Communists. By mid-1942, the CCP's own change of policy meant that opportunities for missionaries to forge links with Communists in their neighbourhood were much reduced.

In the two other provinces in which BMS missionaries were involved – Shandong and Shanxi – the Communist presence during the war had taken the form of guerrilla action against the Japanese. Support that missionaries may have privately wanted to give to the Chinese guerrillas in their fight against the Japanese was mixed with apprehension to the destructive effects of guerrilla action in the short term: personal injuries sustained by the guerrillas in carrying out their plans; disruption to everyday life that resulted from successful sabotage operations; and the consequences for innocent civilians of Japanese reprisals. A flavour of the mixed feelings thus generated is reflected in a letter from Gwyneth Still, in Shandong, to her family in England. She explained that she was hoping for rain, because guerrilla action was usually abandoned on wet nights.

---

[27] Mitter, *China's War*, p. 295.
[28] Williamson, *Christian Challenge*, p. 15.

It is pouring with rain now and I think the earth will get sufficiently soaked to guarantee a night's rest [...] I suppose I ought not to feel so pleased but all these affairs are so hopeless. It is tragic how little they do and what big losses they involve.[29]

Any overt indication of association with Chinese guerrillas was carefully avoided by missionaries in occupied Shandong and Shanxi, in order not to jeopardise relationships between the British and Japanese governments. Thus, missionaries there did not have the same opportunities as their colleagues in Shaanxi to form a first-hand impression of Chinese Communism or to develop an understanding of the nature of the movement that was soon to become all important in the future of China. This difference in experience during the war of resistance to Japan may offer a partial explanation for the widely differing accounts of the new regime brought back by British missionaries returning from different parts of China after the founding of the People's Republic in 1949.

BMS Evangelical Work in Shaanxi before and during the War

The early 1930s saw a blossoming of interest in the work of the mission and the local churches in Shaanxi. Missionaries and Baptist church members attributed this to the relatively peaceful political conditions in the province that followed the establishment of the Nationalist Government under Chiang Kai-shek.

In 1930, the Chinese church launched a five-year discipleship campaign that proved 'a remarkable success [...] in reviving the church and winning hundreds of new disciples'.[30] While senior missionaries were involved with church members in this campaign to reach new audiences and lapsed church members, ideas were introduced by a younger generation of missionaries on lines that had proved popular in English industrial towns in the late nineteenth and early twentieth centuries. A young men's group was established in Xi'an, offering a library, reading room, singing class and tennis and ramblers' clubs, along with prayer and Bible study groups. Proposals were also drawn up to open an inn for Christian young men arriving from the coastal towns to work in the city, and a hostel for students from country villages. These proposals echoed exactly the original aims of the Young Men's Christian Association (YMCA) movement; 'to provide low-cost housing in a safe Christian environment for rural young men and women journeying to the cities'.[31] It is likely that YMCA membership had been a significant feature in the early life experience of many of the men serving as missionaries in China in the 1930s. Some of those attending the meetings and classes in Xi'an came simply to acquire English language skills, seen at that time by many Chinese as an avenue 'to study abroad, treaty port employment, or

---

[29] Private collection of Audrey Salters, Still to parents-in-law, 30 May 1938.
[30] BMSA, CH/67, Young to friends, 31 March 1934.
[31] Clyde Binfield, *George Williams and the YMCA: A Study of Victorian Social Attitudes* (London: Heinemann, 1973).

perusal of English literature, political theory, and science'.[32] As the five-year campaign neared its end in 1934, the BMS provincial secretary, Fred Russell, reported that the autumn assembly had been 'the most successful we have ever experienced'.[33]

In the same year, particularly close bonds between BMS missionaries in Shaanxi and the Nationalist leadership were established when Chiang Kai-shek and his wife, Soong Mei-ling (宋美龄), visited Xi'an to promote the New Life Movement (新生活运动; Xin shenghuo yundong), which was a movement initiated by Chiang ostensibly to create a sense of citizenship worthy of the modern Chinese state.[34] It was a regime that claimed to focus on improving national health and standards of personal conduct, and which included on its agenda plans to break the national opium habit. When Soong met with BMS staff, she advocated opening a refuge for female addicts, and volunteered $3,000 towards the necessary equipment. The missionaries had no reason to resist Soong's forceful charisma; she was later described by Joseph Stilwell as a 'clever, brainy woman [...] direct, forceful, energetic, loves power, eats up publicity and flattery'.[35] Clow, one of the missionaries present, records that they 'gladly fell in with her wishes', undertaking to set up and run the refuge under a committee that included the wife of the chairman of the provincial government, Shao Lizi (邵力子), and the wife of the military governor, along with four BMS missionaries.

> Madame Shao is taking a deep interest in the clinic and is concerned about even the smallest details of equipment and management, nothing escapes her notice…Working in cooperation with such energetic and capable Chinese ladies is an interesting experience, and we trust that it will be mutually beneficial.[36]

Although there are other instances of amicable cooperation between mission staff and Chinese provincial and local leadership, in this context Clow's comment reflects the pleasure the missionaries felt at finding themselves accepted, for the moment, into the very heart of local affairs. In this instance, associating with the national government appeared to the missionaries to come with practical benefits.

Following the Shensi Provincial Conference, held in late December 1937, the foreign missionaries held a special, confidential meeting. The purpose of the meeting was to consider a plan whereby the church in Shaanxi 'may eventually

---

[32] Jessie G. Lutz, 'Chinese and Christian Interactions' in R. Gary Tiedemann, *Handbook of Christianity in China, Volume Two: 1800–Present* (Leiden MA: Brill, 2010), pp. 628–39 (p. 628).

[33] BMSA, CH/64, Russell to Wilson, 17 November 1934.

[34] Rana Mitter, 'Classifying Citizens in Nationalist China during World War II, 1937–1941', *Modern Asian Studies*, Vol. 45.2 (2011), p. 249.

[35] Joseph W. Stilwell and Theodore White (eds), *The Stilwell Papers* (New York: MacDonald, 1972), p. 122, cited in Fenby, *Generalissimo*, p. 387.

[36] BMSA, CH/56, Clow, 'Note on Sian Clinic for Opium Addicts', 8 December 1934.

become entirely self-supporting and self-propagating'.[37] At the meeting, many practical points were made to counter the problems that had thus far stood in the way of the Chinese church in Shaanxi achieving independence. Since the church would never be able to afford large numbers of paid leaders, much of the work would have to be structured around the use of trained volunteers. Money raised by church members should be used to maintain the pastorate, and the costs of maintaining church property should be met by income derived from the property. There was agreement that it might be possible to cease BMS funding 'twenty-five years from now' but that the church could not maintain large institutions such as schools and hospitals. If these were to survive, they would have to operate under independent management and generate their own income. The style and nature of church life thus proposed closely resembled the original church planted in Shaanxi by Shandong immigrants before the introduction of large-scale institutional work adopted by the BMS in the early twentieth century. There were immediate implications for school and hospital work, some of which will be discussed later in this chapter. The proposals also anticipated developments necessitated by the intervention of the CCP after the People's Republic of China (PRC) was set up in 1949.

After the onset of the war with Japan, church life continued to flourish. Stockley reported in early 1938 that 'all our Bibles are sold out and it is impossible to get any more'.[38] Many other missionary letters and reports confirmed this account of development and expansion:

> The work goes with a swing just now. Revival has broken out all over the church area, and very encouraging reports come to us from many voluntary preaching bands. This year [1938] has been one of the most successful years for the annual spring preaching and visitation campaign.[39]

> Baptisms […] have doubled, Church contributions have increased considerably, congregations have been much larger, and the spiritual life of the Church has been quickened…We are embarrassed by numbers.[40]

Church work and attendances at church services, meetings and study groups in the Shaanxi churches continued to thrive throughout the years of war. Evangelism in the mission hospitals was also popularly received. Writing in October 1941, Clow declared that 'Never have conditions been more favourable for hospital evangelism. It is a pleasure to take ward services.' The patients took the initiative in suggesting that ward services should be held on Sundays as well as weekdays.[41]

---

[37] BMSA, CH/42, Miscellaneous letters and reports 1933–1951, 'Report of the Discussions of the Sanyuan Station Committee on the Forward Movement in Shensi', undated, but late 1937/early 1938 from context.

[38] BMSA, CH/65, Stockley to Chesterman, 25 February 1938.

[39] BMSA, CH/62, Mudd to Wilson, 3 March 1938.

[40] BMSA, 146th Annual Report for year ending 31 March 1938, pp. 17–18.

[41] BMSA, CH/56, Extract from a letter from Clow to unspecified recipients, circulated from the Mission House, 3 October 1941.

The missionaries' sense that the war had provided them with new opportunities was emphatically confirmed by Dr Margaret Jenkins in an article in which she quoted a Xi'an colleague as saying that the 'doors of opportunity for the Gospel in China have been taken off their hinges'.[42] Several reasons may be put forward for this buoyant interest. In Japanese-occupied China, being associated with missionaries might offer a measure of protection. However, that does not seem to have been the case in Shaanxi. Invading Japanese soldiers might be deterred by British flags denoting a foreign compound, but aerial bombardment did not distinguish so finely, a reality rudely demonstrated by the damage to mission property in Xi'an in early 1939.

There were Christian refugees from other provinces amongst the millions of refugees driven to Shaanxi by the war, and this has been put forward as one of the reasons for the surge in attendance at church meetings and services. The Baptist correspondence refers specifically to several groups of wartime refugees from the Shandong Baptist churches making their appearance and subsequently taking a lead role in church life in Shaanxi, another indication of the strength of the indigenous church in Shandong.[43]

Lary suggests that an important development in China during the 1940s was 'the survival mentality, the idea of looking after oneself at the cost of concern for others':

> It is a mentality borne of extreme poverty and insecurity, when the extended family and broader social connections are either absent, through separation or death, or too demanding in time and money. Each small unit strives only to look after itself in a dog-eat-dog world where you either survive or die.[44]

Some missionaries believed, however, that the stresses of war increased the relevance of the Christian message:

> All around us there are men and women tense, strained, burdened, and bewildered by the hideous cruelty of modern war…To these brothers and sisters in tribulation we come in Christ's name to strengthen their morale and steady their hearts with His message of consolation.[45]

There is research that suggests that personal or community trauma may impel people to examine their belief systems or seek consolation from spiritual sources, although this will not necessarily lead to involvement in organised religion.[46]

---

[42] Margaret Jenkins, 'Letters from Former Students', *Edinburgh Medical Missionary Society Quarterly Paper*, Vol. 20.16, November 1944, p. 166.

[43] Williamson, *British Baptists*, p. 171.

[44] Lary, *The Chinese People at War*, p. 137.

[45] BMSA, CH/67, Young to friends, 30 May 1939.

[46] See for example: Clive D. Field, 'Puzzled People'; S. Bruce and T. Glendinning, 'When was Secularization? Dating the Decline of the British Churches and Locating its Cause', *British Journal of Sociology* 61.1, pp. 107–126 (p. 123); and Currie et al., *Churches and Churchgoers*, p. 123.

Shaanxi missionaries were of the view that Christianity's appeal was enhanced by the exigencies of war.

The conspicuous war work being undertaken by foreign missionaries and Chinese Christians may have been another factor that prompted an interest in Christianity. The very fact that missionaries stayed on in China after the onset of war led some to look more positively on the missionary contribution. An editorial in *The Chinese Recorder* made this point in its issue of March 1939:

> As one businessman remarked, 'What the missionaries have done in staying by to serve the people will do more good for Christianity in China than ten years of preaching.' This same sentiment of appreciation is being received from all parts of the country.[47]

One important piece of Christian war work was the National Christian Service Council for Wounded Soldiers in Transit. This interdenominational and international organisation set up twelve first-aid stations in the provinces of Shaanxi, Henan and Shanxi to provide emergency food, shelter and medical aid to wounded soldiers who, in the absence of transportation or a mobile army medical service, lay helpless in their thousands in villages and along the roadsides in the aftermath of battle.[48] BMS staff, church members, pastors and evangelists were actively involved in the organisation throughout the early part of the war. An article in the *Missionary Herald* reflected a widely expressed, though arguably overly optimistic, view:

> Is it to be wondered at that a Chinese cabinet minister was seen recently studying a Bible because he had been impressed by the fact that the people in China revealing the biggest spirit of sacrifice and service were the Christians?[49]

The apparent upsurge of interest in Christianity in Shaanxi in the 1930s and early 1940s engendered a new sense of optimism in the members of the mission. In his report on his deputation visit to China in early 1946, Raymond Williamson commented that 'probably the church never stood higher in the estimation of the common people of China than it does today.'[50] In time of war, foreign missionaries had played a respected part. Shaanxi missionaries could not be tainted by accusations of collaborating with an enemy occupation, as those in Shandong and Shanxi might have been.

The Educational Work of the Mission

Amongst the most important BMS work in Shaanxi at the time was the work in middle schools. Unlike in Shandong, where schools had been closed due to new regulations, educational work in Shaanxi remained a significant focus, and this

---

[47] *The Chinese Recorder*, Vol. 70.3, March 1939, p. 162.
[48] Young, *Living Christ*, p. 196.
[49] A. K. Bryan, 'In Shensi Today', *Missionary Herald*, January 1939, p. 3.
[50] Williamson, *Christian Challenge*, p. 46.

section examines the place of foreigners within it during the war years. The BMS had opened a boarding school for girls in Shaanxi at Fuyincun in 1892, and a school for boys was opened at the same time.[51] Jennie Beckingsale was principal of the girls' school from 1900 to 1913.[52] She had been one of the first women to study at Somerville College, Oxford (women were not permitted to matriculate at the University of Oxford until 1920), and was a graduate of Trinity College, Dublin.[53] Boarding schools were also opened at Xi'an for both boys and girls, and by the mid-1920s eight BMS higher primary schools and fifty lower primary schools were in operation.

The abolition of the traditional examination system in China in 1905 was the spur to the creation of many new government schools, when for the first time there was a call for the education of girls. Harrison notes, however:

> In practice the new schools were almost entirely for boys…In 1909 girls were less than 2% of the total student body and education for girls remained to a large extent the province of foreign missionaries.[54]

Private schools, including mission schools, became subject to government scrutiny. Paul Cohen, in his comparison of the reforms of the Dowager Empress Cixi (慈禧太后), Yuan Shikai (袁世凱) and Chiang Kai-shek, notes that all three attached importance to the expansion and reform of China's school system, seeing them 'both as an instrument of social control and as a means of fashioning a more patriotic citizenry'.[55] Regulation of both the management of schools and their curricula was an essential element in ensuring that schools conformed to the goals of the national government.

Schools were important to the missionary societies, and the new regulations caused serious debate that has generated a substantial literature.[56] According to Cui, the transfer of control to Chinese headteachers, and predominantly Chinese boards of governors, required by the new regulations did not take place 'as a compulsory action forced upon a reluctant missionary establishment by the new Nationalist Government and a rising tide of Chinese nationalism', as is often portrayed, especially in PRC sources. Primary reasons for conflict between the

---

[51] Williamson, *British Baptists*, p. 55.

[52] J. C. Keyte, *Andrew Young of Shensi: Adventure in Medical Missions* (London: Carey Press, 1924), p. 129.

[53] *Missionary Herald* (August 1913), pp. 257–58.

[54] Harrison, *China*, p. 92.

[55] Cohen, 'Post-Mao Reforms', p. 530.

[56] See, for example, Lutz, *China and the Christian Colleges*; Yip Ka-Che, *Religion, Nationalism and Chinese Students: The Anti-Christian Movement of 1922–27*, (Bellingham WA: Center for East Asian Studies, Western Washington University, 1980); Jessie G. Lutz, *Chinese Politics and Christian Missions: The Anti-Christian Movements of 1920–1928* (Notre Dame, IN: Cross Cultural Publications, Cross Roads Books, 1988); Robert A. Bickers, 'To Serve and Not to Rule: British Protestant Missionaries and Chinese Nationalism, 1928–31', in Robert A. Bickers, and Rosemary Seton, *Missionary Encounters: Sources and Issues* (Richmond, Surrey: Curzon Press, 1996), pp. 211–39.

mission boards and the forces of Chinese nationalism at the time, suggests Cui, were disagreements about the proposed pace of educational devolution, and the right of missionaries to appoint their own successors in leadership positions, rather than government stipulations about the nature of school leadership or curricula. [57] Bickers also argues that, prior to the introduction of national regulations, mission boards understood and widely accepted the necessity of transfering leadership in mission schools to Chinese headteachers.[58]

For a school to be registered, the regulations also required that all Christian teaching must be eliminated from the curriculum in primary schools and made voluntary in higher-level schools. Debate about the appropriateness and nature of religious education within a state education system has been on the agenda of many modernising societies, and it is instructive to be reminded of this in the context of the debate over mission-run schools in China. Widespread furore, for example, preceded the introduction of the 1870 (England) and 1872 (Scotland) Education Acts, including questions about what role the state should play, what sort of curriculum was appropriate and what kind of religious instruction should be given, especially in publicly funded schools.[59] In 1920s China, however, the issue held particular significance. In the context of the growth of Chinese nationalism, the belief that Western missionary institutions constituted a form of imperial exploitation or cultural invasion made the subject particularly inflammatory. [60] This is expressed in an order put out by the Nationalist Government Board of Education to 'all District magistrates and Education Officers' in April 1927:

> Of the Imperialists' methods of encroaching on China those most easy to perceive are the various kinds of oppression in governance and finance; what are most difficult to see are the encroachments of civilisations, e.g. the schools…On the surface these appear to help China and to promote education, but in reality they dope the Chinese people […] to such an extent that in church schools they stop students loving their own country, compel them to believe the doctrine and inflict all kinds of denial of Liberty and equality.[61]

The new requirements in China generated concern within the BMS home leadership. Was it appropriate for the BMS to continue maintaining its own schools and educational institutions if religious teaching was disallowed? C. E. Wilson, BMS Foreign Secretary in London, insisted, 'The schools and colleges which a missionary Society maintains must be *missionary* in the fullest possible sense,' which must include the unashamed purpose of winning converts for

---

[57] Dan Cui, 'British Protestant Educational Activities', pp. 148–49.

[58] Bickers, 'To Serve and Not to Rule', p. 225.

[59] B. J. MacHaffie, 'Old Testament Criticism and the Education of Victorian Children', in Stewart J. Brown and George Newlands, *Scottish Christianity in the Modern World* (Edinburgh: T & T Clark, 2000), pp. 91–118 (p. 92).

[60] Yip, *Religion, Nationalism*, pp. 32–37.

[61] BMSA, CH/63, Nationalist Government Board of Education, Receive-back Education Authority, Special Order No. 537, 3 April 1927 (trans. E. L. Phillips).

Christic.[62] Division over the issue led to the resignation of the distinguished Baptist biblical scholar, H. H. Rowley from Qilu University (Jinan) and from the BMS. He articulated the conservative side of the argument in a letter to the president of Qilu, Li Dianlu (李天祿):

> Either this university stands for a definitely and aggressively Christian purpose, or it does not. If it does, then it seems to me to be the only honest thing to say so clearly and unashamedly, when the Government asks us to define our purpose. If it does not, then it ought to, since it is supported with funds subscribed specifically for aggressive Christian work.[63]

So fundamental was the issue that the BMS sent a special delegation to China in December 1928 to investigate. The delegation found Chinese Christian opinion to be 'unanimous in favouring registration as a means of removing from BMS schools any suspicion of being subversive in their purpose'.[64]

At a conference representative of all China missionaries, held in Taiyuan in May 1929, the view of most missionaries that registration was 'regrettable but to be preferred to closure' prevailed. A recommendation was sent to London to the effect that all BMS middle schools should be registered for a trial period of one year.[65] The China subcommittee approved the recommendation in September, by a vote of twenty-nine to two, and the General Committee accepted the recommendation in October.[66] As a result, BMS schools in Shanxi and Shaanxi applied for and were granted registration. In Shandong, the application to register the boys' and girls' middle schools in Qingzhou was rejected by the provincial education authority on the grounds that religion still appeared on the schools' curricula. The national regulations permitted this, as long as it was on a voluntary basis, and the members of the Shantung [Shandong] Baptist Union (SBU) became confused and distrustful at this refusal. They decided against registration and all Baptist schools in Shandong were closed, a decision that both the SBU and the missionaries soon regretted.[67] We have already seen (in Chapter Two) the struggles of Zhang Sijing to re-establish a middle school in Zhoucun during the years of the war with Japan.

By 1937, the BMS was responsible for fifty elementary schools and two middle schools in Shaanxi, catering for almost 2,000 boys and some 270 girls. Three foreign and 121 Chinese staff members were employed in these schools.[68] This emphasis on educational work was seen as absolutely essential to the

---

[62] *Missionary Herald* (January 1928), p. 7, cited in Stanley, *History*, p.311. Emphasis in original.

[63] BMSA, CH/64, Rowley to Li Dianlu, 7 January 1929.

[64] BMSA, CH/46, Wilson to BMS colleagues, 17 May 1929, cited in Stanley, *History*, p. 313.

[65] Stanley, *History*, p. 313.

[66] BMSA, China Subcommittee Minutes, Vol. 10, 17 September 1929.

[67] BMSA, BMS 138th Annual Report for year ending 31 March 1930, p. 12, cited in Stanley, *History*, p. 314.

[68] BMSA, BMS 146th Annual Report for year ending 31 March 1938, pp. 112-13.

development of the Chinese church within the province, underpinning all hope of providing an educated indigenous leadership in the future. It is reflected in missionary involvement in the enormous efforts made to maintain the work of the Zunde (Tsun Te) Girls' School, Xi'an, (尊德女子学校，西安) during the war years.

As a result of the restructuring of staffing arrangements to reflect stronger Chinese input, by 1937 Joan Williamson was the only foreign missionary assigned on a regular basis to the staff of the Zunde school. It is from her wartime letters and reports that we can acquire some understanding of the struggle in which the school was engaged. In September 1937, just a few weeks after the start of the war against Japan, she wrote in buoyant mood:

> We are quiet, peaceful, busy, excited at times…We are full up with girls, standing room occupied in dormitories, Government grant secure this year, no more trouble so far over our registration, good standing in the city, June leaving exam we got 19 passes out of 20.[69]

Within six months, following the capture by the Japanese of the eastern provinces and the atrocities committed during their seizure of Nanjing, her tone had changed:

> This may be the last letter we can get out for a while as the J[apanese] seem to be getting over the Yellow River…[T]he only hope for women and girls is to fly. Where to?…[F]ood is scarce outside the towns and what province is going to be safe?…Why doesn't some other country DO something? I'm terrified for our girls.[70]

As already described, the war transformed large numbers of the population into refugees and one of the immediate consequences was the movement of people from the eastern provinces to the west. Pupil numbers at schools in western cities like Xi'an were wildly inflated by the influx of refugees from other provinces. Williamson did not provide figures for the years 1938–1941, when the flood of refugees was at its height, but, in her annual reports for 1942 and 1943, she compared the number of pupils from Shaanxi with those from other provinces. During the autumn term of 1943, although more pupils came from Shaanxi than from any other province, these amounted to only just over one third of the girls attending the school. The majority of pupils came from other provinces, predominantly from areas in occupied or partially occupied China; some from up to a thousand miles from Xi'an (see Figure 8).

---

[69] BMSA, CH/78, Williamson to Bowser, 18 September 1937.
[70] BMSA, CH/78, Williamson to Bowser, 16 March 1938.

Figure 8: Provincial origins of Zunde Girls' School pupils, Autumn 1943[71]

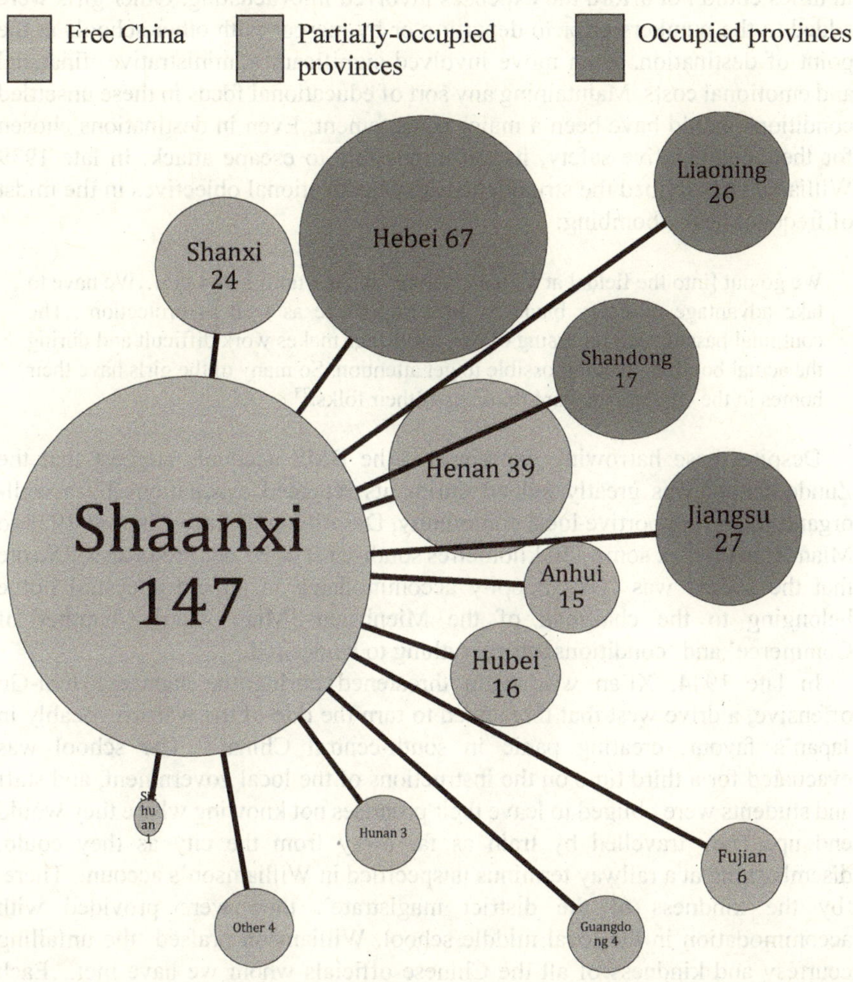

Integrating the members of such a fluctuating and disparate population was no easy task. It was made more difficult by the fact that, over the seven years of the war, the school was evacuated at least four times: in the summers of 1938 and 1939, when Xi'an was suffering from particularly heavy bombing raids; and during 1944 and 1945, when the city was threatened by a new Japanese advance. The school roll fluctuated with each evacuation. Williamson noted with regret that 'One of the sad things about all these moves is that the poorer girls have to

---

[71] Data from BMSA, CH/78, Williamson, Report on Tsun Te Girls' School, January 1944.

be left.'[72] Some pupils were unable to move with the school because their families could not afford the expenses involved in evacuating. Other girls were added to the numbers prior to departure or by merger with other schools at the point of destination. Each move involved significant administrative, financial and emotional costs. Maintaining any sort of educational focus in these unsettled conditions would have been a major achievement. Even in destinations chosen for their comparative safety, it was impossible to escape attack. In late 1939 Williamson described the struggle to pursue educational objectives in the midst of frequent heavy bombing:

> We go out [into the fields] at 6:30 am and remain out until 3 or 4 pm…We have to take advantage of every blade of grass for shade as well as protection…The continual passing and repassing of the aeroplanes makes work difficult and during the actual bombing it is impossible to get attention. So many of the girls have their homes in the city and they are thinking of their folks.[73]

Despite these harrowing experiences, the BMS accounts suggest that the Zunde school was greatly helped during its repeated evacuations by a well-organised and supportive local community. Describing the move in mid-1938 to Mian Xian (勉县), some 350 kilometres south-west of Xi'an, Fred Russell wrote that the school was 'very happily accommodated in an old ancestral home belonging to the chairman of the Mienhsien [Mian Xian] Chamber of Commerce' and 'conditions are everything to be desired.'[74]

In late 1944, Xi'an was again threatened during the Japanese Ichi-Go offensive, a drive west that threatened to turn the tide of the war irrevocably in Japan's favour, creating panic in south-central China.[75] The school was evacuated for a third time on the instructions of the local government, and staff and students were obliged to leave their premises not knowing where they would end up. They travelled by train as far away from the city as they could, disembarking at a railway terminus unspecified in Williamson's account. There, 'by the kindness of the district magistrate', they were provided with accommodation in the local middle school. Williamson praised 'the unfailing courtesy and kindness of all the Chinese officials whom we have met…Each time [we evacuated] we have had to have help and we got it.'[76] This is a significant tribute: it says a lot for the goodwill and competence of the officials involved that they were able to make arrangements for an unexpected party of more than 400 school children with 'unfailing courtesy and kindness' in circumstances where tensions must have been running high on all sides.

Lary argues that the 'innumerable experiences of trauma, instability and chronic anxiety […] produced a morbid fear of chaos [luàn 乱] throughout

---

[72] BMSA, CH/78, Williamson to Bowser, 25 May 1938.

[73] BMSA, CH/78, Williamson, Newsletter No. 11, 17 October 1939.

[74] BMSA, CH/21, Secretariat Papers, 1938–1946, Secretariat letter 18 to Wilson, 21 December 1938.

[75] Mitter, *China's War*, pp. 338–50.

[76] BMSA, CH/78, Williamson to Bowser, received 23 November 1944.

Chinese society.'[77] Williamson's description of cooperation and goodwill suggests that Lary's account of unremitting social dislocation during the war does not altogether reflect the variations across the country.

It is financial problems that dominate Williamson's letters. In May 1939 the school was promised financial support by the government, but a change in management at the Board of Education meant that this support was withdrawn.[78] Williamson uses 'Board of Education' and 'Education Bureau' variously in her letters. It is not always clear whether she is referring to the national Ministry of Education or a provincial authority, but in this instance she appears to refer to the Ministry of Education. By November, the school was again in favour with the government and the ministry promised financial help 'next year', but the situation was already acute. 'We are too small and financially weak to do anything on our own' (June 1939); 'our finance is in a desperate state' (November 1939); 'finance has been a nightmare' (January 1944).[79] 'With all the help the school received during the year from home and local sources, it was still in debt at the end of the year about $50,000' (October 1944).[80]

The substantial costs involved in maintaining school work, the devastating effect of inflation during the war years and the unpredictable attitude of the government towards funding private schools meant that on a number of occasions the survival of the school was at stake. Williamson's letters illustrate the huge financial burden imposed by the commitment of the BMS to institutional work in schools and colleges, making clear the obstacle that this placed in the way of indigenous churches taking on financial responsibility for the work of the mission.

As Figure 9 shows, in 1938 the Chinese government was the major contributor to the school's funds (44%), with the remainder being raised through the BMS contribution (28%) and through fees (28%). By 1942, the school was very largely dependent on fees (45%) for its survival, supplemented by some income from unspecified local sources (16%), while the contributions of both the BMS and the government were less significant (13% and 26% respectively). This does not mean that funding from these sources had been reduced; in fact, the BMS had raised its contribution from $5,606 in 1941 to $20,942 in 1942, and the government from $4,920 to $43,250. Running costs and levels of support had both soared, primarily due to inflation, but the contribution from the government was now significantly greater proportionately than that from the mission. It is also clear how dependent the schools were on secular support and how vulnerable they would have been in its absence.

---

[77] Lary, *The Chinese People at War*, p. 11.
[78] BMSA, CH/78, Williamson to Bowser, 12 June 1939.
[79] BMSA, CH/78, Williamson to Bowser, 12 June 1939; Williamson, Newsletter No. 9, November 1939; Williamson, Tsun Te School Report, January 1944.
[80] BMSA, CH/78, Williamson, Tsun Te School Report, received 23 May 1945.

Figure 9: Sources of funding, Zunde School, 1938-1942[81]

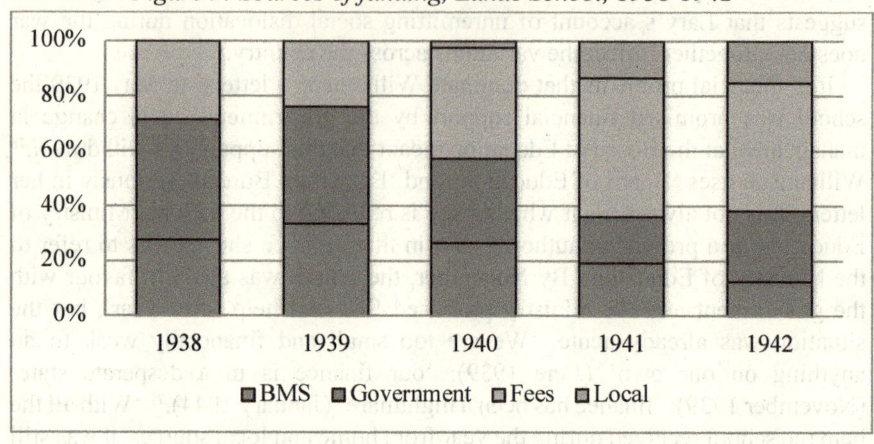

The government's cash grant in 1942 was supplemented by a donation of twelve months' worth of flour for every teacher in the school, a widespread and valuable form of remuneration during this inflationary period in China. Unfortunately, the supplement was not forthcoming in 1943 on the grounds that 'Private schools were started by private bodies and they must find their own funds.'[82] It seems likely that this was an example of the government flexing its muscles in the light of the newly abrogated unequal treaties.

In November 1943, the BMS finance committee agreed to make a special grant of £2,000 (worth almost £117,000 today) to the school to help it over the immediate difficulty, a relatively modest sum but one that reflected the financial difficulties of the society at this point.[83]

The significant reliance on income from fees placed the school in a very vulnerable position. Pupils paid no fees in government schools, and the education authorities fixed the fees charged by private schools. For the first term in 1943, 'they fixed a fee which, if charged, would empty the school.'[84] If the school had places for boys this would not have been a problem, 'as people will pay any money to get their boys into school to avoid military service'. In any case, high fees excluded the very pupils the BMS wanted to admit, including particularly the girls from lower income groups, who would otherwise have no access to education.

For 1942 and 1943, Williamson recorded details of the occupations of parents of school pupils. Figure 10 shows that, in both years, the school was dominated by the children of those working in commerce, government and the military, who were likely to be amongst the better paid, and probably included some of the richest members of the community. The numbers from the professions of

---

[81] BMSA, CH/78, Williamson, Report on Tsun Te Girls' School, 16 February 1943.
[82] BMSA, CH/78, Williamson to Bowser, 16 February 1943.
[83] BMSA, Finance Subcommittee Minutes, Vol. 51, 25 November 1943.
[84] BMSA, CH/78, Williamson to Bowser, 16 February 1943.

teachers and those in medical jobs were relatively low, and in 1942 there were hardly any children from the families of 'workers', though these had increased by 1943. 'Please note' wrote Williamson, using capital letters for emphasis, 'WE TEND TO CATER FOR THE RICH.'[85] From context, it is clear that she was frustrated that the mission school had ended up largely catering for wealthy groups in the community, rather than the more needy and those who were already serving the community such as teachers, doctors and nurses.

Figure 10: Parental occupations of girls attending Zunde School, 1942–1943[86]

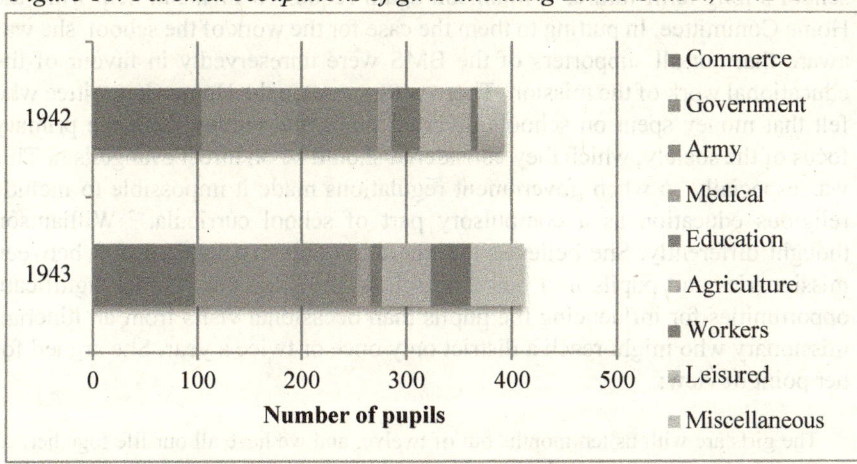

Because the school operated continuously on the very edge of insolvency, it was unable to compete with the salaries paid in government schools and it was difficult to keep good teachers. Some Christian teachers stayed out of loyalty to the school, but many were driven by financial necessity to move to government schools where the pay was better.[87] Even teachers in government schools, like others on fixed salaries and without entrepreneurial connections during this period, were badly affected by inflation. Mitter draws attention to:

> the growing gap between those privileged few who could use connections and the black market [...] and the vast majority who could not. Between the start of the war and the end of 1943 the income of teachers had risen only a fifth as much as the cost of living.[88]

In the spring of 1945, teachers' salaries in government schools were raised, resulting in 'grave difficulties for private schools'. Some missionaries surmised that this was 'a deliberate effort on [the government's] part to eliminate certain

---

[85] BMSA, CH/78, Williamson to Bowser, 16 February 1943.
[86] BMSA, CH/78, Williamson, Report on Tsun Te Girls' School, 16 February 1943.
[87] BMSA, CH/78, Williamson to Bowser, 16 February 1943 and 19 February 1944.
[88] Mitter, *China's War*, p. 277.

private schools'.[89] A decision was made to set up an endowment fund, in order to attempt to secure a long-term future for the school, which was independent both of the BMS and of the local church members. This was in keeping with the moves towards missionary withdrawal, 'surrendering the task', identified at the Sanyuan conference in December 1937.[90] The school began campaigning for a sum of $5 million, asking the provincial governor and the commander of the local military to give it a 'kick start'.[91]

As a contribution towards the endowment fund, and in the interests of the school's long-term future, Williamson again requested financial help from the Home Committee. In putting to them the case for the work of the school, she was aware that not all supporters of the BMS were unreservedly in favour of the educational work of the mission. There were some on the Home Committee who felt that money spent on schools diverted funds and energy from the primary focus of the society, which they considered should be on direct evangelism. This was especially so when government regulations made it impossible to include religious education as a compulsory part of school curricula.[92] Williamson thought differently. She believed that the close and sustained contact between missionaries and pupils in a boarding school provided much more significant opportunities for influencing the pupils than occasional visits from an itinerant missionary who might reach a district only once or twice a year. She argued for her point of view:

> The girls are with us ten months out of twelve, and we have all our life together. Surely this counts more in the long run than visits here and there, paid mebbe [*sic*] twice a year?[93]

A letter from Russell was put before the BMS General Committee in July 1945, asking for backing for the proposed endowment fund. The committee recommended an application to the British United Aid to China Fund, aware that the mission's own resources were already stretched in other directions, and that this was an opportunity for the school to benefit from this currently well-endowed secular fund.[94]

The difficulties in keeping the school open over the whole period of the wars come across clearly in Williamson's passionate and emphatic letters: threatened danger from military activity; the complete absence of a settled routine; fluctuating pupil numbers; strained and unpredictable finances; a struggle to retain competent teachers; and erratic support from government organisations. Williamson's letters were not, however, wholly preoccupied with difficulties:

---

[89] BMSA, CH/69, Curtis to Bowser, 14 December 1945.
[90] BMSA, CH/42, Miscellaneous letters and reports 1933–1951, 'Report of the Discussions of the Sanyuan Station Committee on the Forward Movement in Shensi', undated, but late 1937/early 1938 from context.
[91] BMSA, General Committee Minutes, Vol. 43, 3 July 1945, p. 166.
[92] Stanley, *History*, pp. 312–13.
[93] BMSA, CH/78, Williamson to Bowser, 16 February 1943.
[94] BMSA, General Committee Minutes, Vol. 43, 3 July 1945.

she maintained that the war years brought some benefits, including the opportunity to live in the school rather than with other foreigners in BMS housing. She declared her preference for living with Chinese staff and pupils, and had 'always advocated [this] as the only way to break down certain racial barriers'.

> As a rule it is difficult to carry out as mission houses, large and small are provided for missionaries usually in compounds and somewhat separated from the 'world'. For individuals to alter this and live nearer their friends and comrades in this land creates difficulties and in some cases might mean a breach of loyalty which is a thing to be avoided at all costs.[95]

Despite the independent character that is apparent in her letters, Williamson's emphasis here on the importance of avoiding a breach of loyalty with other missionaries 'at all costs' is a telling comment on the pressures on missionaries to conform to group expectations regardless of personal preferences.[96]

Williamson made clear that she took great pleasure in the company of the girls and from their achievements. She described their contributions to the war effort, the 'street cleaning' that had been 'done specially well by Primary', and the money the pupils raised for charity with their production of Handel's *Messiah*. She celebrated two separate visits the middle school choir made at Christmas and New Year 'to sing to wounded soldiers'.[97] In another letter, written in October 1944, she commented enthusiastically on 'the friendly relation that exists between students and teachers [...] that makes work a pleasure.'[98]

By April 1945, Williamson was on her way back to the UK for furlough. A few months earlier she had expressed the conviction that there was a future for missionaries in China:

> I think there is a great future for our work and we want the best people we can get, educationally, socially and in every way, good mixers who can turn to anything [...] who can rough it and say nothing.[99]

She believed, however, that a new kind of missionary would be needed for this:

> We [who have been here twenty years] are too set in our ways and want things done our way. The new people will have to live with, work with, and under, their excellent Chinese fellow teachers on less than equality for a bit until they have

---

[95] BMSA, CH/78, Williamson to Bowser, 19 February 1944.
[96] Some interesting references appear in Upchurch's often delightfully frank memoirs, *A Prevailing Wind*.
[97] BMSA, CH/78, Williamson to Bowser, January 1944.
[98] BMSA, CH/78, Williamson to Bowser, October 1944, received 23 November 1944.
[99] BMSA, CH/78, Williamson to Bowser, October 1944, received 23 November 1944.

proved themselves worthy of equality, and that is right and the way we want it to work.[100]

Three years earlier, she had thought the need for foreign teachers in schools after the war would be much less, 'and I worked and planned on that'.[101] As she reflected on this on the homeward journey, she had come to believe that 'many more western people will be needed than seemed poss [*sic*] sometime ago'.[102] This was because she thought that the Chinese church leadership had been crushed by war and 'those that remain in the church are war weary…For some time leaders from the west will have to help greatly in the work they themselves thought had passed to their local leaders.' Was this a realistic response to a felt need on the part of the Chinese, or was it the Westerner's sense of being indispensible and a simple reluctance to let go?

When two newly recruited missionaries, Jim and Edna Sutton, first visited the school in early 1946, they were 'shocked' by the condition of the premises.[103] It was operating in the old hospital buildings, which had not been fully repaired since the bombing in 1939. Ceilings were hanging down, windows remained broken, and they described the general condition as 'dilapidated'; conditions that must have discouraged enrolment of children from families who were able to pay substantial fees. Williamson's correspondence reveals the increasing difficulties experienced by the BMS in maintaining satisfactory educational provision in competition with more soundly financed government schools, and the Suttons' observations underline this. It was, however, heartening to see, during Audrey Salters's visit to Xi'an in 2013, that the school was thriving under government administration and in good standing in the local community.

Though the experience in Shaanxi had been different from the experience in the occupied provinces, Williamson believed the war had taken a significant toll on the Chinese church leadership and this had postponed the day when members of the indigenous church could take on the entire responsibility for governing, financing and extending the membership of the church.[104] At the same time, work in the schools was constrained by economic pressures, the necessity of ensuring sufficient income and the pressure to take children from relatively affluent families. This detracted from the original goal of the mission schools, which had been to train up teachers, doctors and nurses to become the church leaders of the future.

---

[100] BMSA, CH/78, Williamson to Bowser, October 1944, received 23 November 1944.
[101] BMSA, CH/78, Williamson to Bowser, 12 June 1945.
[102] BMSA, CH/78, Williamson to Bowser, 23 May 1945.
[103] BMSA, CH/65, Suttons to friends, 30 March 1946.
[104] BMSA, CH/78, Williamson to Bowser, October 1944, received 23 November 1944.

Impact of the War in Europe,
and the British Entry into the War against Japan

Affairs outside China also exerted an influence over the strength and effectiveness of the BMS. China had been at war with Japan for more than two years when the UK declared war on Germany in September 1939. Immediately following the declaration of war, the mission house was faced with enquiries from missionaries wondering whether they should offer themselves for military service, and expressing feelings of sympathy and concern.

> And now the war has come and far greater anxieties fill the minds of us all than anything we have experienced hitherto. It is our turn to be anxious for you in England…Our country is constantly in our thought and prayers, and the cause in which she is engaged in war…The cause is connected with that in which we are engaged, and many of us wish that we could serve in both.[105]

Despite the pacifist views of some individual Baptists, the society did not take any corporate line on the rights and wrongs of military engagement and, like other missionary societies, left such decisions to individual conscience.[106] Initially, however, enquiries from China missionaries both to British consular services in China and to mission headquarters in London were met with negative responses.

Menzies Clow wrote from Xi'an in early September 1939, asking if he would be required to resign from the BMS if he volunteered for war service, and saying he had 'a definite feeling that I have a duty to my country especially as a doctor in wartime'.[107] The reply from Clement Chesterman in London was discouraging:

> I can quite understand your desire to take some share in the present war, as many of us did in the last; if there were a desperate need for medicals in our fighting forces, I would not raise the slightest note of opposition but…

There followed references to the fact that 'several who have offered have not had their offers taken up'.[108] This was consistent with the advice received by Ronald Still in Zhoucun, when he consulted the consul general in Qingdao for advice.

> [The consul general] told me that there was no immediate need for medicals at home, and that the Government was not at present proposing to recall people from

---

[105] BMSA, CH/23, Secretariat Shantung, 1939–1946, Drake to Williamson, 6 September 1939.

[106] See for example, Minute No. 421 of the Medical Advisory Board (MAB), a subcommittee of the Conference of British Missionary Societies (CBMS): CBMSA, Box 506, Plans Regarding Medical Missionary Service in Wartime.

[107] BMSA, CH/56, Clow to Chesterman, 4 September 1939.

[108] BMSA, CH/56, Chesterman to Clow, 30 October 1939.

China, and he gave it as his advice that those who had jobs out here should for the present stick to them.[109]

Two years later, the UK's declaration of war against Japan had an immediate impact on the situation in China. Although Shandong and Shanxi missionaries were interned and unable to enlist, Shaanxi missionaries of an age for military service found themselves within the war zone. In January 1942, Clow responded to a direct appeal from the British military mission in Chongqing to take up a commission in the Royal Army Medical Corps, with which he served until after the war's end. This was despite advice telegraphed to him ('strongly discourage Clow [from] enlist[ing]') from the Home Committee, who were of the view that 'that step might compromise the position of other missionaries in Free China if it ever got known to the Japanese.'[110]

In the autumn of 1943, Bryn Price, BMS missionary in Shaanxi province from 1939, was also asked by the British Military Mission if he would consider undertaking military service. Unlike Clow, who was serving in a job where his skills were in great demand, Price's decision was influenced partly by the fact that he felt himself to be insufficiently employed in his work for BMS. On 1 December 1943 he resigned and enlisted, setting out his reasons in a letter to mission headquarters in February 1944:

> All over the world there were those who were leaving positions in which they were working hard and really achieving something so that they should take their share of responsibility in the war, while I was living in remote Sian [Xi'an] doing less than a full-time job, waiting to enjoy the benefits of a peace that was to be earned through the efforts of others. The more I felt this way, the more intolerable I felt my position to be.[111]

The BMS China subcommittee was not convinced, and expressed its disappointment at his decision.[112]

The BMS was reluctant to lose missionaries to war service, especially medical missionaries who were considered essential if the mission hospitals were to come through the war. Despite the society's clear unwillingness to give its support to the plans of Clow and Price, they both followed their own judgement on the matter, and at the end of the war were reinstated as missionaries in good standing. Although the mission itself depended for survival on the service of individual staff members, it was prepared to accept their decisions where matters of conscience were concerned, even if its own resources were depleted as a result. The correspondence also demonstrates the commitment of individual missionaries to serve their home nation at this time of divided loyalties. Patriotism in its conventional sense continued to be an important aspect of their

---

[109] Private collection of Audrey Salters, Still to parents, 20 September 1939.
[110] BMSA, CH/56, Clow to Clow from the British Military Mission, Chongqing, 25 February 1942.
[111] BMSA, CH/63, Price to Williamson, 11 February 1944.
[112] BMSA, CH/63, Bowser to Price, 19 April 1944.

make-up, despite their commitment to missionary work and their extended periods living abroad.

In all, five missionaries signed up for war service with the British military mission; a sixth served with the British Red Cross Hospital Unit in China.[113] One other BMS missionary was seconded in 1944 to work with the China mission of the United Nations Relief and Rehabilitation Administration (UNRRA) where he was appointed Regional Director for Guangxi province. For each of these men, their knowledge of the Chinese language was an important factor in the way their services were deployed. None were immediately free for demobilisation at the end of hostilities in August 1945 and all were variously involved in rehabilitation and reconstruction work.[114]

The presence of the British and American military in Free China, after the entry of the UK and the USA into the war against Japan, also affected British missionaries working there. The rapid movement of military personnel from Europe to Asia, and back again, gave evidence of a very different lifestyle from that known to the missionaries, who were accustomed to long isolated periods in China. Xi'an was one of the advanced airfields for bombing the Japanese in the occupied zone, and many members of the US and British military missions had been stationed there. Vincent Jasper wrote from Kunming early in the war:

> We are keeping an open house for military and civil officials and not only Chinese. We get army, airforce, Friends Ambulance and students as often as our funds allow. I am in the happy position of being able to do work of national service with the hearty approval of our own church officers – most of whom are more than happy to assist in the work themselves.[115]

Jasper's comment on his satisfaction at being able to contribute to the national efforts combined with his enjoyment of the opportunity to mix with this novel group of Westerners. Elsewhere there are references to social gatherings 'in the house of Mr and Mrs Madge' after Sunday evening services, 'when tea and cakes were supplied'.[116] The special circumstances created by the war seem to have given rise to a sense of fellow feeling between the missionaries and the British business community, only occasionally in evidence in the pre-war era.

Raymond Williamson, arriving in Xi'an by plane for his deputation tour in November 1945, described landing 'on the great airfield [...] where large numbers of American planes were parked'. He captured the atmosphere of change and excitement as he described being introduced to 'the surviving remnant' of the British military mission waiting to leave on the plane by which he had arrived, and meeting several members of the United States Air Force 'about to wind up affairs and leave'. The missionaries were rewarded for past

---

[113] W. S. Flowers, *A Surgeon in China: Extracts from Letters from Dr W. S. Flowers*, (London: Carey Press, undated).
[114] *Through Toil and Tribulation*, pp. 133–78.
[115] BMSA, CH/61 Jasper to Williamson, 27 July 1942.
[116] *Through Toil and Tribulation*, p. 186. Ernest and Edna Madge had joined the BMS as missionaries in Shaanxi in 1935.

hospitality when the Americans departed, leaving them a gift of 'considerable quantities of stores and equipment'.[117]

In these different ways, the Second World War reaffirmed for the missionaries their sense of Britishness, along with an awareness that life in China was coloured by international developments over which they had little control. This would be brought home again when the domestic policy of the CCP was formed in reaction to events on the world stage.

Treaty Revision and International Relationships

As explained in Chapter One, missionaries' experience within China was dependent on the treaties that concluded the opium wars and established the basis of the British presence in China. From the outset, British missionaries had an ambivalent attitude towards them and by the early 1920s their negative effects were generally considered by the missionary societies to outweigh any possible benefits. The anti-British riots that followed the 'May Thirtieth Incident' in Shanghai in 1925 – when Shanghai Municipal Police fired on and killed twelve Chinese demonstrators – prompted British missionary societies to action. On 6 October that year, the standing committee of the conference of British missionary societies (which included both the BMS and the CIM) formulated two resolutions to the effect that those societies approving the resolutions would both welcome the abolition of treaty provisions relating to extraterritoriality, and support the British government in their efforts towards 'comprehensive revision of the existing treaties'.[118] The resolutions were approved at the meeting of the BMS General Committee in November 1925, and supported by most missionaries on the field.[119]

On 11 January 1943, the UK and USA signed new treaties with the Nationalist government, formally relinquishing extraterritoriality. At the time, extravagantly optimistic hopes were attached to the symbolism of the abrogated treaties. For many Chinese the ending of extraterritorial rights served 'as proof of China's acceptance as an equal and sovereign state'.[120] Some Chinese Christians hoped that China's newly independent status on the international scene would prove to be an asset in building 'a genuine Chinese Christian movement'.[121] For missionaries, it was important to throw off the associations between Christianity and imperialism that they believed had undermined the Christian message in the eyes of many Chinese people, and it was expected that the cancellation of extraterritorial rights would go some way towards this. The BMS China subcommittee recorded the new arrangements 'with deep thankfulness', describing them as 'an answer to continual prayers' and expressing to the British

---

[117] Williamson, *Christian Challenge*, pp. 7 and 11.

[118] Williamson, *British Baptists,* pp. 123–25.

[119] BMSA, General Committee Minutes, Vol. 23 November 1925.

[120] Lutz, *China and the Christian Colleges*, p. 421.

[121] Y. C. Tu [Tu Yuqing], 'Profit and Loss in the War', in Chester Miao (ed), *Christian Voices in China* (New York: Friendship Press, 1948), p. 9.

and Chinese governments 'their appreciation and gratitude for this timely and hopeful readjustment of relationships with the Chinese people'.[122]

In a fulsome address to the National Christian Council (NCC) in Chongqing on 18 May 1943, Chiang Kai-shek declared that the 'abolition of unequal treaties has freed the Christian Church from all association with foreign imperialism or aggression'. He went on to speak encouragingly about missionary societies: 'We still need them…Don't feel you are guests. You are comrades working with us to save our people and build a new nation…Let the church identify itself more intimately with the life and needs of the people and cooperate fully with the Government and social welfare agencies and build a heaven in society.'[123] In private, however, Chiang was suspicious of the Allied nations in their negotiations over the treaties, likening them to 'kidnappers', 'hooligans' and 'bullies', dealing with China 'as meat on the chopping board'.[124] He was particularly hostile to Churchill and critical of the British. 'All ambassadors are spies by nature,' he wrote a few months later, 'but the British more than most.'[125] Whether or not Chiang had as low an opinion of British missionaries as he did of British diplomats is unclear, but members of the BMS China subcommittee took his positive words to the NCC at their face value. The minutes record that they received the information about his comments 'with pleasure and satisfaction'.[126]

Bryan, based in the BMS mission station in Sanyuan, prepared a lengthy document at exactly this time on 'The Status of the Missionary in the Chinese Church', which included an historical analysis from the commencement of the China mission to 1943, and ended with predictions for the future. With the proviso that 'the longer one has been in China, the less one feels inclined to predict what the future may be,' he noted that, with the abolition of extraterritoriality,

> The Westerner in China will have quite a different status from formerly. He will come under Chinese laws and regulations, and I foresee a period in which all kinds of new and difficult situations may arise.[127]

He concluded with the comment, 'We must not expect things to return to normal and go smoothly as soon as the war is over'. Earlier in the paper, he had stressed his belief in the autonomy of the Chinese church leaders, and his understanding of the secondary place that missionaries must and should assume, but his use of 'return to normal' here gives an indication that he recognised some missionaries viewed 'normality' as the sheltered life Westerners were able to enjoy in China under the protection of the treaties. For those people, adapting to

---

[122] BMSA, China Subcommittee Minutes, Vol. 11, 12 January 1943.

[123] BMSA, China Subcommittee Minutes, Vol. 11, 1 July 1943.

[124] Chiang Kai-shek diary, 28 February 1943, cited in Mitter, *China's War*, p. 300.

[125] Chiang Kai-shek diary, 19 August 1943, cited in Mitter, *China's War*, p. 301.

[126] BMSA, China Subcommittee Minutes, Vol. 11, 1 July 1943.

[127] BMSA, CH/55, Bryan, 'The Status of the Missionary'.

the practicalities of a less authoritative and more vulnerable position might not be easy.

With the end of extraterritoriality, the location of foreigners within China became the business of the Chinese authorities. At the end of January 1943, Stockley in Xi'an reported with indignation that he had received a visit from the 'Gestapo Police' (宪兵 *Xian Bing*), requiring him to supply details of his name, political and religious affiliations, his family and financial circumstances, his friends, 'thoughts' and 'indulgences' for registration with the civic authority. Stockley recognised immediately that this signalled a change in his status in China, consequent on the abolition of extraterritoriality. He was no longer under the protection of British law and the British government. He must now answer to Chinese authority. Stockley refused to answer the questions, but signed his name across the form, fearing that if he left it blank it would be incorrectly or maliciously completed by a Chinese official.

> This is the first definite act of this regime here to infringe upon my liberty and a very definite Nazi method…Extraterritoriality has been gone less than a month. This is one of the main things Britain and America are fighting against in Germany and Japan, yet these methods are being increasingly employed by the present regime in China…This is one reason why I have expressed before [*sic*], there may be no place for us here in the future.[128]

Joan Williamson's first letter to the mission house after the change was introduced emphasises her sense of the vulnerability of foreign missionaries in the new situation:

> What we have done in the past cuts no ice these days; we are all equal and we cannot say that we have come to do China good or any of the things that might have suited another generation.[129]

Of particular importance to the missionary societies were the implications for their ownership of land and property in China. The original treaties had given foreigners the right to lease land in the treaty ports for residence and trade, and land in the interior of China for the construction of churches and hospitals. The term 'permanent lease' was generally used in foreign contractual agreements before 1943, 'and this term was tantamount to the ownership of the land passing from Chinese to foreign nationals.'[130] Under Chinese land law, land within the boundary of China belonged to all the people of the Chinese Republic. The land law also prohibited Chinese people from transferring or leasing land to foreign nationals 'other than what is permitted by the treaties'.[131] With the abolition of the treaties, any land or property leased by missionary societies was to be handed

---

[128] BMSA, CH/65, Stockley, 30 January 1943.
[129] BMSA, CH/76, Williamson to Bowser, 16 February 1943.
[130] C. Y. W. Meng, 'Foreign Enterprise in Post-War China', *Far Eastern Survey* 12.2 (3 November 1943), pp. 212–219 (p. 216).
[131] Meng, 'Foreign Enterprise in Post-War China'.

over to the Chinese government, constituting a major cause of concern.[132] The society had intended – as it had already done in Shandong – to hand its property over to the Chinese church on devolution, rather than to the government. The fact that the Japanese had seized much mission property in the occupied areas was later to create particular problems in establishing ownership when missionaries returned at the end of the war, expecting to resume possession.

There were other important ways in which relationships between the UK and China were altered during the war years. The collapse of the British Empire in the Far East from December 1941 was a severe blow to British prestige, and a disappointment to Chiang Kai-shek, who had looked for significant support from his newly acquired allies, the UK and the USA. The British loss of both Burma and Hong Kong had immediate practical effects for China, including closure of the Burma Road. The UK's failure in 1942 to respond on favourable terms to a request from China for a major loan further worsened relationships between the two countries, and underlined the contrast with the United States, who had responded generously to a similar request, though, to the chagrin of the Chinese, less generously than to their European allies.[133]

The United States' great wealth, expanded economy and substantial oil reserves ensured that it was a power to be reckoned with. Its gross domestic product constituted roughly one half of the world's total production.[134] As the war advanced, it was clear that the UK had been eclipsed:

> Comparing China's foreign policy in 1943 with her attitude of ten years earlier, nothing is more striking than her dependence on America and acceptance of American leadership. Signs of this meet one at every turn, alike in the cultural, diplomatic, economic, financial and military fields. China looks primarily to America and not to Britain to defeat Japan; to furnish her with materials and sinews of war; and to build up the great new China after the war is won.[135]

The USA did not only dominate politically and materially. British social practices and British culture were dropped. When the war ended, 'Shanghai's developing modernity' was 'much more American in character, and fed by Hollywood'.[136]

Some British missionaries did not find it easy to adjust to this reversal in their relative position in China. In pre-war years, only a very small number of them had worked in the rarified atmosphere of the treaty port cities, and most would not have considered that they had been affected by the artificially inflated importance accorded to them by virtue of their status as Britons. Over many

---

[132] Meng, 'Foreign Enterprise in Post-War China'.
[133] K. C. Chan, 'The Abrogation of British Extraterritoriality in China, 1942–43: A Study in Anglo-American-Chinese Relations', *Modern Asian Studies*, II (1977), pp. 257–91 (pp. 260–64).
[134] Robbins, *The World*, p. 21.
[135] FO371/46211 F4171/186/10, Sir Eric Teichman, Adviser to the British Embassy at Chongqing, cited in Feng, *British Government's China Policy*, p. 22.
[136] Bickers, *Britain in China*, p. 234.

years they had experienced anti-foreign initiatives but they now seemed to be held in open contempt. In August 1945, Fred Russell was in Shaanxi and his wife in England. She wrote telling their old friend Raymond Williamson, Foreign Secretary at mission headquarters, that she had had 'such a depressed letter' from Fred:

> He says he is fit physically […] but mentally he is tired out and sick of it all out there – not least trying for him is the very anti-British feeling in Sian [Xi'an] newspaper articles. 'What is Britain doing to help China?' etc., etc. [*sic*]. This sort of thing worries him much more than most of the others and we have had several years of it.[137]

Russell was nearing sixty and had been in China more than thirty years. It is possible that his depressed mood reflected his recognition of the changed status of foreigners in China, and the fundamental shift in attitudes towards the UK affecting the position of British missionaries. It is also possible that he could see at first hand the great need in post-invasion China and felt powerless, without help from his own government, to do anything to help it.

The BMS in Shaanxi by the End of the War

By the end of the war, new political forces were beginning to make their presence felt across China, and missionaries became aware that China itself was changing. The BMS missionaries in unoccupied China perhaps had a head start in understanding these changes, given the very different challenges they had faced during the war.

In addition to being the first to experience the effects of the abrogation of the treaties and the abolition of extraterritoriality in February 1943, the BMS missionaries in Shaanxi had also had early opportunities for direct contact with local Red Army and CCP leaders. The Shaanxi missionaries had therefore been able to put a human face on the concept of Chinese Communism. The sympathy and admiration that this engendered was in stark contrast to the experience of BMS missionaries based in Shandong and Shanxi, who viewed Communism as an alien ideology that was opposed to Christianity and was therefore to be rejected and resisted rather than accommodated or embraced. Nevertheless, the society's long-established commitment to respecting the national government of the day, at this time the Nationalists, prevented close association even in Shaanxi.

The evangelical work of the BMS in Shaanxi had not been subjected to the crushing blows of enemy occupation and physical devastation that had critically undermined the Chinese church in Shandong during the war. Although some 'war weariness' in the Shaanxi church was identified at the end of the war, the work of the mission there had thrived and its reputation amongst members of the Chinese public appears to have been enhanced. Dependence on foreign missionaries was still a key feature of the Chinese church in Shaanxi, which did

---

[137] BMSA, CH/64/2/2, Russell to Williamson, 10 August 1945.

not appear to have a similar sense of independence as the highly organised SBU. The goal of self-support, though explicit and intact in mission planning in Shaanxi both before and during the war, was not expected to be reached in the immediate future.

There was also a growing awareness, as the Zunde Girls' School illustrated, of the problems created by the high costs of maintaining the institutional work of the BMS and the challenges of running a private institution bound by government regulations, but without the assurance of cooperation or support from the Chinese government. The BMS had invested heavily in school work in Shaanxi and believed that mission schools were essential to the future leadership of the Chinese church, but the war underlined the barrier such institutions placed in the way of self-support. The costs of salaries, equipment and supplies were, for the most part, dependent on factors over which the mission had no control. If they were to survive, therefore, foreign funding or guaranteed Chinese government support was essential.

4. Planning and Recovery, August 1945 to July 1946

> The idea that the work will start up again just where it left off in 1937 or 1939, or any year you like to take, shows a failure to realise the vast changes that have taken place.[1]

As war in Europe ended and the threat from Japan was subdued, the BMS began to assess the new situation. During the previous three years its work in occupied China had been suspended. Missionaries had been scattered; information from China had been scarce and intermittent.

Almost half the workforce had spent the years from 1942 in Japanese internment camps.[2] They had been quartered with hundreds of other civilians of all nationalities and had been deprived of their normal occupations and employment. All internees were holders of British or American passports, but this did not restrict the range of nationalities represented. 'Russians […], who were married to English men but haven't seen them for years […], Chinese, Japanese, Indian, Philippines, Portuguese, French, Swiss, Belgian, Dutch, German, Hungarians, Bulgarians, Rumanians, Poles, Lithuanian, Latvian, Estonian and others, all with British passports.'[3] They had had no contact with family or friends or former colleagues outside the camps, Chinese or Western.

Of the remainder of the Chinese staff, some continued to work in unoccupied China, and the rest had been dispersed to temporary situations around the world. Six were on war service, some held temporary positions in India or as pastors in British churches, one was a translator for the British government in London, and another was attached to the mission to Chinese seamen in Liverpool.[4] For all China missionaries, the war with Japan and the Second World War had brought about fundamental changes in their lives.

Living conditions and individual freedoms in the UK had also changed during the war and were continuing to change. Those who lived there had been affected materially and psychologically, and the consequences of this wartime experience had long-term effects. Political and economic adjustments had been made at government level to accommodate the demands of war, and these impacted all British citizens and the missionary societies.

On the wider international scene, the war had shifted the balance of power between China and the Western nations. Unrest in the British colonies put at risk the stability of the British Empire. More generally, attempts to protect threatened

---

[1] BMSA, CH/58, Flowers to Chesterman, 23 January 1946.
[2] *Through Toil and Tribulation*, pp.10-12.
[3] Private collection of Audrey Salters, Still to family, 20 August 1943 (never posted).
[4] BMSA, China Subcommittee Minutes Vol. 10, 28 September 1944; 16 January and 26 April 1945.

national rights or to salvage damaged economies led to the introduction of restrictions on international trade and shipping and new controls on currency exchange. All these had an impact on the BMS and its work in China in the post-war world.

Preparations for the post-war period had been going on in China since the formation of the optimistically named United Front between the Nationalists and the Communists in early 1937. Long before the Japanese surrender in August 1945, the armies of both sides had an eye for their positions in the aftermath of the war. While Chiang Kai-shek used the surrender ceremonies and victory parades to publicise his role as the leader who had taken his country successfully through the war, Mao Zedong also claimed a place on the national scene. Both joined publicly at the negotiating table with Patrick J. Hurley, the American ambassador, and resolved 'in accordance with justice and reason [...to] build a unified, independent, prosperous and strong new China'.[5] From the outset, however, military manoeuvrings called into question the sincerity of the negotiations. In July 1946, the launch of a general offensive by the Nationalists north of the Yangtze, and the renaming by the Chinese Communist Party (CCP) of their military forces as the People's Liberation Army (PLA), marked turning points. The goal of a negotiated peace was abandoned and the Chinese Civil War of 1946–1949 got under way.[6]

Ling suggests that missionaries were almost uniquely mistaken in the hopes they held out for a political solution to the confrontation between the Guomindang (GMD) and the CCP, and in their continuing expectation that the GMD would retain the upper hand in the government of post-war China. She contends that after 1945 British Protestant missionaries in China badly misjudged the political situation in the country, as well as the mood of the Chinese people.

> Missionaries were optimistic about their future work in China. The underlying assumption was that the Guomindang government would be able to sort out its problems and things would get better...The missionaries did not see any reason to be worried about their future in China.[7]

However, if missionaries were mistaken as Ling suggests, they were not alone in failing to forecast the direction in which events in China would move. Recent historians have argued that the GMD, despite its shortcomings, was in a position of relative strength in the immediate aftermath of the Japanese defeat.[8]

---

[5] W. Morwood, *Duel for the Middle Kingdom: The Struggle between Chiang Kai-shek and Mao Tse-tung for Control of China* (New York: Everest House, 1980), p. 5.

[6] Suzanne Pepper, 'The KMT-CCP Conflict 1945–1949' in John K. Fairbank and Albert Feuerwerker (eds), *The Cambridge History of China, Volume 13: Republican China 1912–1949, Part 2*, (Cambridge: Cambridge University Press, 1986), pp. 723–88 (pp. 758–59).

[7] Ling, *Changing Role*, p. 58.

[8] Westad, *Decisive Encounters*, p. 7.

In retrospect, of course, it seems logical to conclude that during the war years the always tenuous foundations of Chiang Kai-shek's rule had eroded almost beyond hope of repair. But this was wisdom after the fact. At the time, few observers possessed sufficient clairvoyance to predict either the rapidity or the totality of the CCP victory.[9]

In the early post-war months, there were no clear indicators as to the eventual outcome, or to the form any settlement might take. The BMS and its missionaries were subject to various influences as they made decisions about future policy.

Formation of BMS Policy

For the thirty-five Baptist missionaries who had been interned in China, the end of the war with Japan provided their first opportunity to gauge the mood in post-war China. In more than one internment camp, the internees received gestures of friendship from Chinese people living nearby. The editor of the in-house newsletter for the Eastern Area Camp in Shanghai wrote,

> We are full of appreciation for the 'lao pai hsing' (common people) [laobaixing 老百姓] of Shanghai, who themselves were almost ground down to earth with hardships and suffering in the last few terrible years, have already started to contribute to our relief with cigarettes, food, comfort parcels and money.[10]

The magazine went on to record a gift of 'foodstuffs' (11,000 cigarettes and one parcel of sweets) from Major General Y. P. Ling, Commander of the Shanghai District of the Nationalist army, 'as a token of friendship and sympathy of the Chinese army'. The message from the commander conveyed 'sincere greetings to the Allied friends and children. The whole of China rejoices with you today.'[11] In one of the camps outside Shanghai, an internee recorded that they had been visited by local church representatives: 500 boys and girls from the local middle school 'came to greet us bringing banners and presents'. They had had visits from all the local Chinese authorities and had received '$500,000 cash each', a gift from Chiang Kai-shek (although the value of this apparently lavish gift from Chiang is put in perspective by the fact that the Shanghai price for peaches at the time was $35,000 per pound).[12] These gestures gave the impression that many Chinese people felt both warmth and goodwill towards their British allies.

In another camp, Weihsien (now Weifang, 潍坊) internment camp in Shandong, a very different message was delivered when, on a 'chilly gray day in

---

[9] Steven I. Levine, *Anvil of Victory: The Communist Revolution in Manchuria, 1945–1948* (New York: Columbia University Press, 1987), p. 4.

[10] *Camp Chit Chat*, Vol. 1.6, 17 August 1945, Souvenir Edition (Shanghai, 1946), pp. 41-42.

[11] *Camp Chit Chat*, p. 43.

[12] BMSA, CH/66, Smith to Bowser, 8 August 1945; CH/63, Payne to Williamson, 24 August 1945.

mid-September', a British colonel arrived to address the British internees. He told them that most of the small foreign businesses in China had been destroyed; anything that had survived had passed into Chinese hands, and the prospects of recovery or reparations were extremely poor. He drew attention to the consequences of the abolition of extraterritorial rights in January 1943: British residents in China no longer enjoyed special protection; the days of a privileged 'colonial life' in Asia had ended.

> We cannot force you now to leave China [...] but the future here is a bleak one...Our official advice to you is to give up in East Asia...An era has ended, and with it your own past lives. I'm sorry, but these are the facts.[13]

This sombre picture was disturbing. After previous setbacks – the Boxer uprising at the beginning of the century, the anti-Christian movement in the 1920s and the Japanese-orchestrated anti-British campaign of 1939 – missionaries had returned, 'like a flock of birds on a grain field, frightened off by a warning shot or a flapping scarecrow, but soon returning to feed'.[14] The BMS had been planning for some years to bring its work in China to a close. Was this now the time, not to 'give up in East Asia', but to 'surrender its task'? Was the indigenous Chinese church 'able and willing to assume responsibility'?[15]

These first contacts with the wider world made clear to the missionaries that significant changes had taken place. On the one hand, the gestures of friendship offered by local Chinese to ex-internees in Shanghai suggested that they might find themselves in a more welcoming social environment in China than had been the case before internment. On the other hand, the British colonel, one of their own countrymen supposedly familiar with contemporary China, had advised another group of internees that practically, economically and politically things would be much more difficult.

The first letters sent by missionary internees from the liberated camps demonstrate both their understanding that important changes had taken place and their expectation that the society's analysis of the new situation was essential to their own future plans. Ronald Still wrote to his parents that, although most BMS missionaries expected to be repatriated, a small group would be left behind, 'in order to enable the Home Board to keep in close touch with developments in the Chinese Church in the reorganisation that is bound to take place'. He indicated that his own return home could only be determined 'when it has been decided [...] what will be the manner of the new cooperation between the Home Board and the newly organised Chinese Church'.[16] Still was clearly confident that the

---

[13] Langdon Gilkey, *Shantung Compound: The Story of Men and Women Under Pressure* (London: Anthony Blond, 1966), pp. 221–22.
[14] Peter Stursberg, *The Golden Hope: Christians in China* (Toronto: United Church Publishing House, 1987), p. 9.
[15] Tsingchow Conference 1927.
[16] Private collection of Audrey Salters, Still to parents, 25 August 1945.

changes that had taken place would be met by a different approach from the BMS. Another missionary, with more than thirty years' experience of working in China, wrote, 'We long for guidance from you about our future movements'.[17] These missionaries anticipated that the BMS was on the brink of fundamental change – that it might, indeed, be preparing to 'surrender its task' in China – and would not be following blindly on familiar paths.

Several missionaries in unoccupied China had already communicated their thinking about this to the Home Committee. Ernest Madge had written from Xi'an:

> Ways and means of helping the North China church after the war will need a great deal of hard thought, but I personally think that the BMS can never go back to the old role of leaders. We shall need to investigate very carefully the needs of that church, and plan in great detail before we send anyone back there again.[18]

As a formal step in bringing together ideas on future policy in China, a meeting was held in London in June 1945 of all China missionaries, serving and retired, who were currently in the UK and able to attend. Central to the discussion was the statement from the Church of Christ in China (CCC),

> That all questions of reoccupation ought to be considered by them, and that they should have the main voice in deciding whether, when, and under what conditions, work in the present occupied fields should be resumed.[19]

Responsibility for policy decisions about BMS action in post-war China, was in the hands of Raymond Williamson, BMS Foreign Secretary in London.[20] As Bickers has noted, 'a great deal of influence could be wielded by a very few individuals within particular societies', and such was the case with Williamson.[21] Williamson, known to his colleagues throughout his career by his Chinese name 'Wei' (魏礼模 Wei Lima), served in China for almost thirty years. From 1908 he worked in Shanxi but in 1925 moved to Jinan as Dean of Qilu University Extension Department, where he remained until his return to England in 1938.[22] His obituary notice in the *Baptist Yearbook* recorded that he 'was on cordial terms with Chinese officials and with the leaders of Shanxi University', and had been decorated twice by Yan Xishan for his services to education, agriculture and industry.[23] He was popular with missionary colleagues and with Chinese Christians. His departure from China in 1938 to take up office with the mission board in London was regarded as a serious loss by missionaries in the field, who

---

[17] BMSA, CH/63/6, Price to Williamson, 29 August 1945.
[18] BMSA, CH/62/3, Madge to Bowser, 15 April 1944.
[19] BMSA, China Subcommittee Minutes, Vol. 11, 21 June 1945.
[20] BMSA, General Committee Minutes, 29 January 1937.
[21] Bickers, 'Changing British Attitudes', p. 209.
[22] Stanley, *History*, p. 306.
[23] *Baptist Yearbook*, 1967, p. 374.

felt his experience and judgement were needed on the field at such a critical time in Chinese history. Gwyneth Still wrote home:

> The general opinion out here is that he ought to stay on longer. There is no one who can possibly take his place […], no one has the general experience he has, nor the knowledge for the provinces…[P]eople feel that in a situation as serious as this, Dr W[illiamson] ought to be spared longer, but of course it has been settled and is not likely to be altered now.[24]

Nevertheless, Williamson's long experience of living in China, and the working relationships he had developed there, preceded the war years and the cultural changes these had brought. His 1947 book *Teach Yourself Chinese,* one of a series of self-instructional language-learning books published between 1938 and 1973 by the English Universities Press for Hodder and Stoughton, opens with a dialogue that places the reader in a pre-war world, where foreigners expected to have servants, and expected those servants to attend to their practical needs.[25] The scene takes place in a private household somewhere in China. When the doorbell rings and a friend offers to answer the bell, the householder replies, 'No need. I will tell Lung Fu [the servant] to go.'[26] Williamson's confidence in placing this dialogue at the very opening of his book is a telling reflection on the hierarchical nature of social relationships that he took for granted during his years in China and considered would be the experience of the foreign traveller in 1947. This suggests a lack of awareness of the extent of the changes that had taken place since he left. Behaviour that was acceptable practice in foreign and prosperous Chinese households in the 1920s and 1930s was no longer favoured by the mid-1940s. While undoubtedly still wholly committed to serving China's best interests, his time away during such a critical period of the country's development put him at a disadvantage when attempting to analyse the mood and needs post-war.

Williamson's influence on post-war decision-making in London was pivotal. Understanding his thoughts about Chinese attitudes and Chinese politics throws light on BMS decisions in this period. In 1943, in the wake of the treaty revisions, he had published *China Among the Nations*, a reflection on China's early history, philosophy and contemporary standing.[27] Williamson's personal admiration for Chiang Kai-shek comes across strongly in the book, along with his confidence that Chiang would lead his country to peace and stability and to a respected place on the international stage, once the war with Japan ended. Williamson concluded:

---

[24] Private collection of Audrey Salters, Still to parents-in-law, 30 May 1938.

[25] H. R. Williamson, *Teach Yourself Chinese* (London: Hodder and Stoughton, 1947), pp. 30–31.

[26] Guest: Wo ch'ü, k'an I k'an [shih shui]; Householder: Pu yung Wo chiao Lung Fu ch'ü. (Pinyin: Wo qu kan yi kann [shi shui]; Bu yong. Wo jiao Long Fu qu. 我去看一看是谁；不用，我叫龙斧去).

[27] H. R. Williamson, *China Among the Nations* (London: Carey Press, 1943).

China has become democratic. Her feudal age is behind her. She has no territorial ambitions except to secure the return of Manchukuo. She depends not on military might but on moral force to influence the world.

All this should make her an ideal member of future Round Table Conferences. For there, standing four-square against all international injustice and unworthy and compromising attitudes, she will be found conciliatory, reasonable and helpful in unravelling knotty questions of international relationships. Ready to receive, she will be willing to give; making light demands of others she will impose the heaviest demands upon herself.

She is proud, legitimately so, of her long civilisation. But she is ready to learn from others, and adapt herself accordingly.[28]

Members of the BMS London committees with an interest in China were likely to have read Williamson's book and, because of his acknowledged expertise, awaited eagerly the results of his fact-finding tour of China during December 1945 and January 1946, organised to give him an up-to-date picture of circumstances there.

Williamson's report on the tour, published in late 1946, was widely read.[29] With the benefit of hindsight, it is easy to trace in it evidence that Williamson's pre-war experience of China had a strong influence on his perceptions. On arrival in Chongqing, he wrote enthusiastically of meeting 'many government officials, most of them old acquaintances'. Amongst these – along with Yan Xishan, his old ally from Shanxi days – he mentions appreciatively Chen Lifu (陈立夫) and Chen Guofu (陈果夫), who, he writes, 'head up the right-wing faction in the Nationalist government'.[30] In addition, through his personal contacts with the GMD leadership, Williamson was able to secure a letter from 'General Shang Chen [商震; Shang Zhen], the Generalissimo's Chief of Staff' that ensured Williamson safe passage on his travels and proved to be the 'Open Sesame in many a difficult situation'.[31] While clearly influential, all three of these individuals were opposed by a significant body of opinion. Mitter describes the Chen brothers as 'two tough political operators' who would 'push for crackdowns on dissidents and argue that China needed a more regimented society, rather than a more liberal one'.[32] Shang Zhen had been the senior Nationalist general who had been involved in the GMD's deliberate and controversial breach of the Yellow River dykes in June 1938, flooding the surrounding area, killing at least half a million Chinese and creating several million refugees.[33] Williamson, if aware, was undismayed at these men's controversial reputations.

---

[28] Williamson, *China*, p. 125.
[29] Williamson, *Christian Challenge*.
[30] Williamson, *Christian Challenge*, p. 7.
[31] Williamson, *Christian Challenge*, p. 7.
[32] Mitter, *China's War*, p. 53.
[33] Mitter, *China's War*, pp. 159–60; Lary, 'Drowned Earth'.

One particular encounter encouraged Williamson to believe that pre-war trends of cooperation between the missionary societies and the government would be sustained, and even improved. He had a meeting with P. Z. King (金 寶 善 ; Jin Baoshan), Director of the Chinese National Health Administration, which:

> Left no doubt in our minds that in the new medical programme of the Chinese Government, our Mission hospitals will have a recognised and worthy place. We [...] were assured not only that our help would be welcomed in the public health work, but that such help was essential.[34]

This reinforced requests that had already been conveyed by the Chinese Ministry of Foreign Affairs to the British government asking it to facilitate the return of British medical workers to China at the end of the European war.[35]

Williamson attended the National Christian Council (NCC) conference held in Shanghai, 28–31 January 1946. This was the first major post-war Christian conference, attended by delegates who, between them, reflected a broad spread of wartime experience: thirteen Chinese who had spent the war in occupied China; ten Chinese who had experience of both occupied and unoccupied China; up to seventeen Chinese from unoccupied China; and twenty missionaries, eleven of whom had been interned. [36] Williamson's observations at the conference influenced him in forming the conclusions to his report. As regards the political situation, he believed,

> In the not-too-distant future, China will be united under one Government in which all the present political parties will be represented. I consider that Christian influence is strong enough to ensure freedom to propagate our religion in the institutions we organise, and which will need to be recognised by the national Government.[37]

As regards the expectations of the Chinese church, he wrote:

> There is no doubt that the Chinese Church will welcome missionaries and that they need them...But they ask that they shall be as free as possible from 'race-consciousness', ready to 'think things through with the Chinese', and able to convey ideas without any assumption of superiority or desire for any particular status. In a word, they want missionaries who are prepared to be genuine 'colleagues' with their Chinese brethren.[38]

---

[34] Williamson, *Christian Challenge*, p. 11.
[35] FO371/46225, C497434 Ministry of Foreign Affairs to the Chinese Embassy in Great Britain, 3 June 1945.
[36] Williamson, *Christian Challenge*, p. 42.
[37] Williamson, *Christian Challenge*, p. 47.
[38] Williamson, *Christian Challenge*, pp. 47–48.

Williamson clearly foresaw a society where his own collegiate relationships with Zhang Sijing and the Shantung Baptist Union (SBU) in the 1930s would be widely replicated.

He was not alone in anticipating post-war China being a linear extension of its pre-war self. In February 1945, seeing the growing threat from the CCP, the British minister at the Chongqing embassy had been asked by a high-ranking Chinese official what the attitude of the British government would be if China were divided after the war:

> There can only be one answer to such a question. The policy of His Majesty's Government in such an eventuality must be that which it has always followed in the past in a China partitioned by civil war or other causes, namely, recognition and support of the central Government of the day, while at the same time conducting de facto relations through His Majesty's consuls with any regional administration.[39]

Bickers, writing of the revolution of 1911, argues that, in reality, the usual pattern in China was for the British to ally themselves 'behind the force best guaranteeing order and stability'.[40] By mid-1946, it appeared that neither party could be guaranteed to provide either, requiring a different type of decision for the British.

It is likely that Ling was much influenced by the sanguine expectations of Williamson's 1943 book, and by the confident tone of his post-war report, when she described the general mood of optimism amongst missionaries in China in the last months of 1945. 'Most of them believed that the Chinese people wanted them, and thought that their help was important to the future development of the Chinese Church.'[41] She argues that most of the missionaries 'assumed that Christian agencies had overcome anti-foreign prejudice' and 'for these reasons, missionaries seemed to have few doubts that they would be wanted and welcomed'.

The views of other mission workers call into question the validity of such easy generalisations. Rufus Dart had worked in Shanxi since 1925 and was well aware of the 'relationship of friendliness and cooperation between officials and missionaries' that had been considered such a feature of pre-war mission work in the province.[42] On his return to Shanxi after internment, Dart, unlike Williamson, sensed that the situation had changed. Writing via his wife to staff at the mission house, Dart reported:

> Each Chinese Church leader we have heard since liberation stressed the opinion that mishes [*sic*] were needed more than ever, that they will be welcomed [...] but there is a tendency among mishes [*sic*], or there was, to be associated with parties (political) or governments which is not without danger to the church. They [the

---

[39] FO371/46166 F1690/35/10 Seymour to FO, minute by Hudson, 12 April 1945, cited in Feng, *British Government's China Policy*, p. 19.
[40] Bickers, *Scramble for China*, p. 369.
[41] Ling, *Changing Role*, p. 54.
[42] Williamson, *British Baptists*, p. 104.

Chinese church] want us to be more circumspect in our attitude with temporal power.[43]

Factors influencing BMS post-war decision-making included the immediate impressions of interned missionaries, the views of the society's highly respected foreign secretary and his report on his China tour, the voices of those returning to the field and the directions advised by the British government. None pointed clearly to 'surrendering the task'. Several suggested that the task might be redefined, implying a new relationship with the church in China.

Partnership with the Church of Christ in China

There is evidence in the archive that, already during the war, the BMS was open to considering new ways of working with the Chinese church. In February 1940, Victor and Eva Hayward, evacuated from Shanxi province, had been seconded to work with the CCC's Chinese home mission project in Guizhou province.[44] There, Victor Hayward had taught at the Great China University, which had evacuated from Shanghai, had shared in the leadership of the CCC Guizhou committee and had taken part in the Kweizhou [Guizhou] International Relief Association in its massive work with the million refugees escaping the Japanese.

A more significant opportunity to work in partnership with the CCC came in the autumn of 1943, when the director of the CCC Border Service Department (中华 基督教会全国 总会 边疆 服务部; *Zhonghua Jidujiaohui Quanguo Zonghui Bianjiang Fuwubu*) approached the BMS staff in Shaanxi asking that they second a medical missionary to work for them in Xizang province, and a biblically trained missionary to undertake publicity work for them in Chengdu.[45]

The origins of the Border Service movement lay in the relocation of Chiang Kai-shek's government to Chongqing in late 1938. Chiang needed fresh natural resources for the fight against Japan, and his attention was drawn to the border area by the shift of the country's centre of gravity to the west during wartime.[46] He mounted a programme of 'frontier reconstruction' and, from mid-1939, students and young professionals were recruited from the eastern provinces to offer 'service' to the border regions, with the objective of providing educational opportunities, welfare services and a better quality of life to the remote tribes. The programme was initially hugely popular, to the extent that hundreds of students competed each year for the privilege of being selected to take part.[47]

---

[43] BMSA, CH/57, Dart to Chesterman, 26 November 1945.

[44] *Through Toil and Tribulation*, pp. 166–78.

[45] BMSA, CH/21, Secretariat Papers, 1938–1946, Minutes of Shensi Conference held at Sian 4–8 October 1943.

[46] A. Rodriguez, 'Building the Nation, Serving the Frontier: Mobilizing and Reconstructing China's Borderlands During the War of Resistance, 1937–1945', *Modern Asian Studies* 45.2 (2011), pp. 345–76.

[47] Rodriguez, 'Building the Nation', p. 367.

In 1940, Chiang invited the CCC to set up its own branch of Border Service. For the CCC, joining up with the Border Service gave Chinese Christians an opportunity to show themselves as 'a unifying element' within the nation, in contrast to the anti-imperialist narratives that 'traditionally depicted [Christianity] as an alien culture that divided China'.[48] The official guidelines for the new CCC branch, published in 1943, stated:

> This department by using the spirit of service of Christ and the Central party's [GMD's] guiding virtue of transforming the frontier people through education, seeks to engage them in all sorts of service in order to illuminate the frontier brothers' knowledge, their economic toil, improve their livelihood, promote national unity and enrich the nation's strength.[49]

A former professor on the staff of Qilu University, Zhang Bohuai (张伯怀), was appointed its director. Zhang was known to the Baptist community from his work at Qilu, where he was familiarly referred to as WB or Bill Djang. He appears to have had a genial and confident relationship with the foreign missionaries: there is a reference to him hosting a 'dinner party', 'for all English Baptists' in Chengdu in October 1940.[50] Bill Upchurch, BMS missionary in China from 1935 to 1952, described Zhang as 'one of the finest Christians I have ever met and was proud to call my friend'.[51]

Williamson had been engaged in discussion with Zhang about the CCC Border Service from its earliest days. 'I am anxious' wrote Williamson to Fred Russell in Xi'an, 'that we should have our place in these forward movements to the West'.[52] In April 1945 George Young from the BMS in Xi'an, visited 'the North West Border' and reported enthusiastically to the BMS China subcommittee that the Border Service provided 'a great opportunity for evangelistic work'.[53] The subcommittee was 'deeply impressed' by Young's report but decided not to take any action until 'the whole matter of the future policy and scope of work in China' could be considered.[54]

When the matter of assigning staff to work with the Border Service was again considered at the next meeting of the China subcommittee, there was opposition from some of the China missionaries present on the grounds that the society might be spreading itself too thin.[55] They suggested that 'the Society had never yet fully occupied the three provinces in which it worked in the past' and much work needed to be done, particularly in schools and universities in these areas.

---

[48] Rodriguez, 'Building the Nation', p. 364.
[49] Rodriguez, 'Building the Nation', p. 367, quoting Zhonghua Jidujiaohui Bianjiang Fuwubu (Church of Christ in China Border Service Department) *Fuwu Guicheng* (Service Regulations) (1943).
[50] BMSA, CH/71, Hickson to friends, October 1940.
[51] Upchurch, *Prevailing Wind*, p. 183.
[52] BMSA, CH/64, Williamson to Russell, 20 July 1943.
[53] BMSA, China Subcommittee Minutes, Vol. 11, 25 April 1945.
[54] For example: BMSA, China Subcommittee Minutes Vol. 11, 18 January 1944.
[55] BMSA, China Subcommittee Minutes Vol. 11, 21 June 1945.

Despite these concerns, the subcommittee decided to make plans 'for cooperation with the Church of Christ in China in work in the new areas', and, soon after, John Henderson Smith was assigned to the job.[56]

For the BMS, allying itself with the CCC Border Service would mean not just working in a new (and remote) geographical area, but working in a completely different way. Foreign missionaries would be working for a Chinese organisation (the CCC) and they would be working not just on an equal basis with Chinese colleagues, but also under the supervision of Chinese staff. The BMS decision was an indication of its recognition that conditions for missionaries in China would never be quite the same again, and an indication of its full acceptance of the maturity and authority of the CCC. Working with the Border Service mission was a clear break from the BMS's traditional policy of distancing itself from political movements; the CCC Border Service mission was 60% funded by the Chinese Nationalist government.

The minutes of the China subcommittee do not record any discussion about the potential risks involved in aligning the mission so closely with a GMD initiative, and details of the discussion leading up to this positive decision are not included.[57] Zhang's charismatic personality, and his longstanding links with Williamson at Qilu, seem likely to have been important influences. Here was an influential Chinese Christian from the Baptist stable taking the gospel to vast, previously untouched parts of China. He was also working in partnership with the highest authority in the land, the Nationalist leader for whom Williamson had developed a keen admiration. Williamson wrote later: 'We can justifiably feel proud as a Society that one of our Chinese leaders has been chosen for this important pioneering work', showing an understandable delight in what appeared to be the fruits of the society's early labours.[58] Williamson's influence on the meeting and his pre-war associations seem to have swayed the committee decision, despite the reservations of missionaries currently working in China.

The response from the leadership of the CCC to the BMS decision was immediate. H. H. Tsui (Zui), of the general assembly of the CCC, wrote to Williamson commending the decision and recognising the shift in working relationship between missionaries and Chinese:

> The assignment of Western personnel to work under the direction of the General Assembly is a more advanced type of cooperation than has been possible on any large scale in the past, and we hope that this will be the continuation of a fruitful and happy relationship between yourselves and us.[59]

Zhang himself wrote to Williamson thanking the BMS for allocating Smith to work in the Border Service Department, and emphasised 'how grateful we are

---

[56] BMSA, China Subcommittee Minutes Vol. 11, 21 June 1945.
[57] BMSA, China Subcommittee Minutes, Vol. 11, 1 July 1943.
[58] Williamson, *Christian Challenge*, pp. 21–22.
[59] BMSA, CH/66(2), Tsui to Williamson, 21 July 1945.

for this type of relationship with the English Baptist Missionary Society'.[60] Shortly after his arrival, Smith wrote detailing the work to which he had been assigned in Xichang (西昌), Sichuan province, and praising 'this thrilling story of modern missionary enterprise'.[61] Smith recognised and apparently welcomed the reversal of roles between missionaries and Chinese Christians, where the authority lay predominantly in the hands of the Chinese.

A year later, Smith's report was much more negative.[62] There were high levels of disunity, a rapid turnover of staff members and difficulty in recruiting Chinese to work with the service. Smith was particularly concerned about the lack of priority being given to specifically Christian work. No efforts were being made to undertake evangelistic work with the 700,000 ethnic Chinese living in and around Xichang. The Chinese church and the cooperating missions contributed only about $6 million to the $45 million annual budget for the work of the Border Service, and Smith thought that this was one of the reasons that church work was undervalued. His recommendation was, however, for expansion rather than retreat. He advised the appointment of five additional Chinese and two additional Western evangelists, and a Western doctor and nurse, arguing also that for each of the missionaries appointed, a special extra annual allocation of funds should be made to ensure that funds would be available specifically for evangelistic work. Smith believed that the future of the Border Service work rested mainly with the Chinese, but that, because of the widespread disruption in China caused by the impending civil war, 'the years immediately ahead will be the special responsibility of the cooperating missions'.[63]

Smith found that, for him, there were practical difficulties in working in this remote place in such close partnership with Chinese colleagues. He recommended:

That it is a general practice in Forward Movement work for Western Personnel to have food prepared in Western style and that adequate facilities for this be provided on all main stations. Personally I favour such a general ruling on this matter rather than leaving it to individuals to decide. This latter may lead to comparisons being made.[64]

Whether or not to emulate local diet and living styles had been a matter for debate since the earliest days of the missions. For some Westerners, it was difficult to adapt to a diet consisting entirely of Chinese food. In the early years, when missionary compounds provided for very separate lifestyles, flexibility according to personal needs and circumstances was possible and acceptable. Writing in 1888, Alfred Jones's advice to new missionaries read:

---

[60] BMSA, CH/66(2), Zhang to Williamson, 31 July 1945.
[61] BMSA, CH/66(2), Smith to friends, Summer 1945.
[62] BMSA, CH/66(2), Smith, Sikang report, June 1946.
[63] BMSA, CH/66(2), Smith, Sikang report, June 1946.
[64] BMSA, CH/66(2), Smith, Sikang report, June 1946.

> We would of course concede to each most perfect liberty to work conscientiously according to the gift of strength and stamina given to them, recollecting only that the large majority of the old, experienced missionaries would join in pressing upon younger brethren a prudent regard for their strength.[65]

However, Smith was working in the mid-1940s, living alongside Chinese colleagues who were more outspoken than they might have been in times when the treaties were enforced. He believed that lifestyle choices could lead to uncomfortable public comparisons about whether one missionary was better than another. Smith himself was subject to thyroid deficiency, which affected his dietary options, and no doubt he wished to avoid invidious comparisons with other foreigners not affected by such problems.[66] In fact, he resigned from the Border Service in September 1946 because of his difficulties in accessing appropriate drugs for his condition.[67]

Despite the difficulties Smith had experienced in working with the service, the BMS retained its commitment to this CCC initiative.[68] In February 1947, Upchurch was appointed to work among the Lolo tribe in Xichang, where he and his family remained until January 1951.[69] In retrospect, this may have proved misguided, dissipating the society's scarce resources and linking the missionaries clearly to the Nationalist leadership. It was, however, an indication of BMS missionaries' commitment to finding new ways of working with the Chinese church.

Return to the Formerly Occupied Provinces

In the aftermath of the war, the BMS had to make a critical decision as to whether or not work should be reopened in Shandong and Shanxi, where, because of the Japanese occupation, no missionary had been present for three to six years. The decision would ostensibly reflect the basic goal of the mission to 'surrender the task'. So how did the society arrive at its decision?

Immediately following the surrender, both Shandong and Shanxi were engulfed in widespread hostilities (see Figure 11). In all, more than 1,200 battles took place in China between 1945 and 1950 and Shandong and Shanxi were two of the provinces most hard-hit.[70] In Shandong, Nationalist guerrillas had the upper hand until 1943, but by 1945 better internal organisation by the CCP at local level had allowed the Communists to take control.[71] 'By the spring of 1945,

---

[65] BMSA, CH/6, Alfred G. Jones, Hints about Climate, Living and Outfit, etc., Intended for the General Information of Missionaries Proceeding Thither, 1888, p. 8.
[66] BMSA, CH/66/2, Williamson to Smith, 2 October 1946.
[67] BMSA, CH/66/2, Smith to Williamson, 11 September 1946.
[68] BMSA, China Subcommittee Minutes, Vol. 10, 2 July 1946.
[69] Upchurch, *Prevailing Wind*, pp. 183-225.
[70] E. Wilkinson, *Chinese History: A Manual* (Cambridge MA: Harvard University Press, 2000), p. 1022.
[71] Elise A. DeVido, 'The Survival of the Shandong Base Area, 1937–1943' in Feng Chongyi and David S. G. Goodman, *North China at War: The Social Ecology of Revolution, 1937–1945* (Lanham MD and Oxford: Rowland and Littlefield, 2000), pp. 173–88.

almost all of the Shandong countryside had been abandoned [by the Japanese] to Communist control…At the time of the Japanese surrender, Communists claimed control over 92% of the land area.'[72]

Figure 11: Japanese- and Communist-controlled territories, August 1945[73]

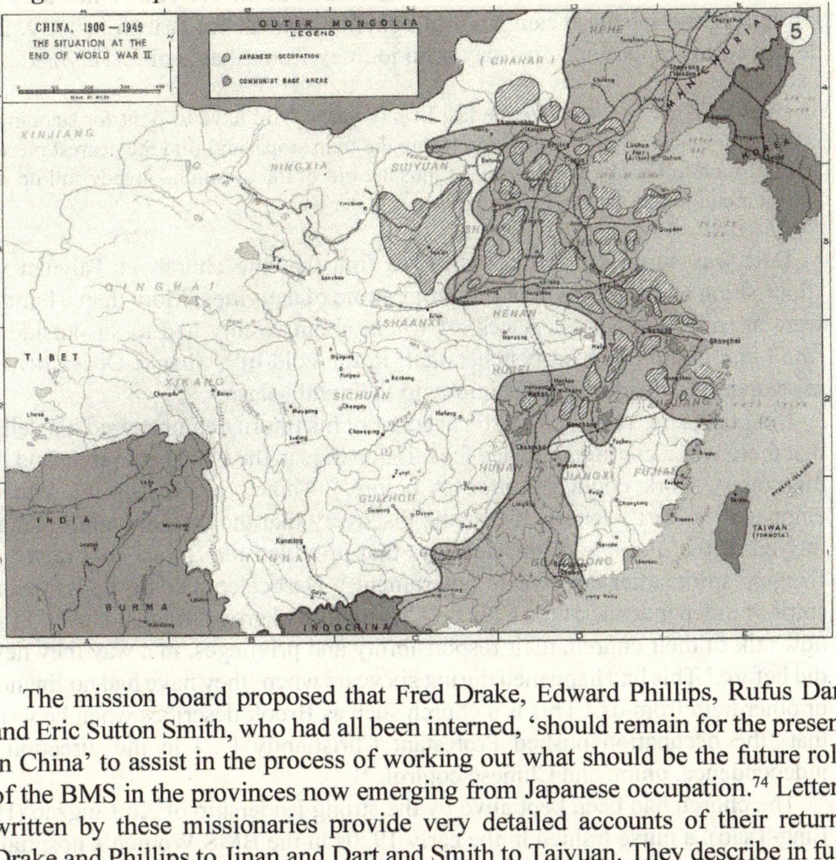

The mission board proposed that Fred Drake, Edward Phillips, Rufus Dart and Eric Sutton Smith, who had all been interned, 'should remain for the present in China' to assist in the process of working out what should be the future role of the BMS in the provinces now emerging from Japanese occupation.[74] Letters written by these missionaries provide very detailed accounts of their return: Drake and Phillips to Jinan and Dart and Smith to Taiyuan. They describe in full the welcome they received, the devastated condition of mission property, their urgent attempts to make good the worst of the damage and their assessments of changes in China that had a bearing on whether or not missionaries were still needed.[75]

---

[72] Konrad Lawson, 'Wartime Atrocities', p. 286.
[73] Source: China Civil War, 1900–1949: Situation at the end of World War II, Department of History, United States Military Academy, https://www.westpoint.edu/academics/academic-departments/history/digital-history-center/atlases/chinese-civil-war [accessed 31 October 2013]. The figure included here is based on an earlier version of this map supplied by Dr Felix Boecking.
[74] BMSA, China Subcommittee Minutes, Vol. 11, 1 November 1945.
[75] The first of the relevant letters are at BMSA, CH/57, Dart to Williamson, 22 December 1945; CH/63, Phillips to President K. M. Wu (吴克明), Qilu University, Chengdu, 30 December 1945; Phillips to friends, 5 January 1946.

Shanxi had been an important CCP base from before the war and, by late 1945, large areas of the province were under Communist control. Taiyuan, the provincial capital, remained nominally Nationalist, under the grip of the provincial governor, Yan Xishan.[76] There, an early priority for the missionaries was to find out what had happened to the church in the six years since they had left during the Japanese campaign of agitation against the British in 1939. Dart described his 'appalling' five-day train journey from Shanghai to Taiyuan:

[W]e have not seen the like the last twenty years. You have to fight for standing room only, and at night must stop where the train stops, and find the nearest piece of ground to lie down and sleep, as inns are out of the question, already full up. I just mention this for your information.[77]

Dart was surprised and delighted to find that the church in Taiyuan was 'flourishing and alive', with a full programme of activities. More than a hundred were attending Sunday services, of whom about twenty had to sit outside the small church building on benches that, in the cold of a Shanxi December, the missionaries considered 'a testimony to their enthusiasm'.[78]

Ling takes the view that Dart's account of his return demonstrated his delight that there was a continuing place for missionaries in the Chinese church, and that missionary work could continue as before.[79] This is not consistent with the emphases in Dart's letters. It was the discovery that the church had grown and thrived in the *absence* of missionaries that provided the 'tonic' that raised his flagging spirits after three years' internment.[80] Dart celebrated his belief that the spirit of independence of the Chinese Christians had grown tremendously. 'They now talk of their church, their responsibility and privileges, in a way they never did before.' This had happened during six years when 'they have had no financial or other help from us.' This is a church such as Brook describes when he writes that 'the occupation pushed Protestant Christianity [...] in the direction of independence, union and Chinese control.'[81]

The church had been kept alive by the strong leadership of Xu Lingzao (Hsu Ling-Tsao), a nurse trained in the early 1920s in the BMS Women's hospital in the city.[82] From 1924 she had been responsible for an orphanage, which she kept open throughout the occupation, and which became the centre of church life. In the last three years of the war, an influx of new members, over half of whom

---

[76] Lyman Van Slyke, 'The Chinese Communist Movement During the Sino-Japanese War 1937–1945', in John K. Fairbank and Albert Feuerwerker (eds), *The Cambridge History of China, Volume 13: Republican China 1912–1949, Part 2* (Cambridge: Cambridge University Press, 1986), pp. 636–39.

[77] BMSA, CH/57, Dart to Williamson, 22 December 1945.

[78] BMSA, CH/57, Dart to Williamson, 22 December 1945.

[79] Ling, *Changing Role*, p. 52.

[80] BMSA, CH/57, Dart to Williamson, 22 December 1945; Dart to friends, 28 March 1946.

[81] Brook, 'Toward Independence', p. 318.

[82] BMSA, CH/57, Dart to Williamson, 22 December 1945.

were 'younger men and women around thirty years and under', had swelled congregational numbers and added a charismatic and emotional dimension with which some of the older members were uncomfortable.[83] In the early months of 1946 a split in the congregation threatened and the newer members opted for a break with the CCC. Individual missionaries judged these developments within the Chinese church differently according to the emphases of their personal beliefs, for there were significant differences of opinion, even within the BMS. Ernest Madge, who joined Dart in Taiyuan early in 1946, looked anxiously at what he described as these 'family squabbles'.[84] Where Dart had seen growing maturity, Madge feared schism.

> The Taiyuan church will be more and more critical of the missionaries who come here, and will demand a large say in the work that they do…With sympathy and patience we know the outlook of this church can be broadened.[85]

These are indicators that in Shanxi, where missionaries had continued to take a dominant role in church affairs up until 1939, the church had indeed grown in their absence as Brook argues.

In Taiyuan, the two hospitals had been an important focus of BMS work. The Japanese military had taken them over during the war, and many valuable buildings had been demolished for street widening.[86] Chinese municipal authorities had moved in after the surrender, and the acute shortage of houses and public buildings made negotiations for repossession of the mission buildings particularly difficult.[87] Missionaries were advised by the provincial authorities that a recent edict from the Chinese government stated that all Japanese property in China must be handed over to the central government as war reparation.

> If the owner of the land wishes to purchase such buildings he may do so, the purchase money to be put to the credit of Japanese reparations. If the owner does not wish to purchase the buildings concerned, then both buildings and site revert to the Central Government who in turn will undertake to compensate the owner for his loss.[88]

As we have seen in Chapter Three, the abolition of extraterritoriality meant that foreigners were now subject to Chinese land and property law. This, coupled with complications arising from Japanese use of much of the property during the war, made establishing ownership fraught.

---

[83] Williamson, *British Baptists*, pp. 165–66; also Hsu Ling Tsao, 'These Little Ones', unpublished booklet, translated from the Chinese, in the private collection of Margaret Wyatt, circulated by E. A. Rossiter, 1946.
[84] BMSA, CH/62/3, Madge to Chesterman, 18 April 1946.
[85] BMSA, CH/62/3, Madge to Williamson, 18 May 1946.
[86] BMSA, CH/57, Dart to Williamson, 22 December 1945.
[87] BMSA, CH/57, Dart to friends, 28 March 1946.
[88] BMSA, CH/62/3, Madge to Williamson, 24 May 1946.

In Shandong, unsettled conditions meant that the small towns changed hands frequently in continuing skirmishes. Zhoucun, headquarters of the SBU and one of the three towns in the province where BMS work had been centred, was captured by the CCP on 28 August 1945 and retaken by the GMD the following month. It remained precariously in GMD hands until retaken on 7 June 1946 by the CCP, only to be recaptured by the GMD on 3 July. Zhoucun changed hands another three times in the remainder of the Civil War.[89] Fred Drake described a visit there in January 1946:

> The Choutsun-Changtien [Zhoucun-Zhangdian (张店)] region is an island held by guerrillas in the interest of the national Government, surrounded by a sea of Communism…The whole town is bristling with arms, and girdled with street fortifications, as this is the last outpost of the Government forces; and one cannot move about the streets after dark without knowing the watchword for the evening.[90]

Jinan, the provincial capital, became 'virtually a besieged city; the railways are still cut; refugees continue to stream into the city from the Communist "liberated areas". There are over one hundred refugee primary school teachers in Tsinan [Jinan] now.'[91]

During the war, church life had been severely disrupted. Church leaders had been impoverished, large numbers of church members had become refugees, and much church and personal property had been damaged or destroyed. However, the returning missionaries were encouraged by the welcome they received on their arrival in Jinan. For Phillips, the moment of return – after three-and-a-half years' internment – to Jinan, the city in which he and his family had made their home since 1928, was personally hugely significant.

> We never had believed in the suggestion of a few that we would not be wanted back again, but we have been surprised and overwhelmed by the sincerity and warmth of our welcome. It was not our practice formerly to shake hands with rickshaw coolies on the streets but it has been quite the right thing on this occasion! From coolies, urchins, street hawkers, through to officials in high positions our welcome has been genuine and very stimulating.[92]

Drake and Phillips noted with pleasure that the south suburb congregation in Jinan was flourishing under the impressive leadership of a young pastor, Sun Shouxin. At the Christmas Day service in December 1945, 'the church was full and many different groups of young people took part.'[93] The congregation had raised sufficient funds over recent years to balance the budget with a little to

---

[89] Zibo City Archives, http://da.zibo.gov.cn/art/2005/5/18/art_358_383969.html accessed 20 October 2011 and 29 November 2023. 中华民国大事记(1939-1949). *Memorabilia of the Republic of China* (1939-1949).
[90] BMSA, CH/57, Drake to Chesterman, 26 February 1946.
[91] BMSA, CH/63, Phillips to friends, 5 May 1946.
[92] BMSA, CH/63, Phillips to friends, 5 May 1946.
[93] BMSA, CH/63, Phillips to friends, 5 January 1946.

spare: a considerable achievement during the war years. Drake and Phillips did not involve themselves in the work of the churches, which they saw as the responsibility of Chinese church leaders, but instead concentrated on the three BMS hospitals in the province and on Qilu University in Jinan, which had been a major focus of missionary work in the province before the war. Phillips took prime responsibility for restoring the university and its buildings, while Drake liaised with the Chinese church leaders Zhang Sijing, Wang Juntang (王均堂) and Jing Yihui about the hospitals and the schools.[94]

Qilu was staffed and financed jointly by eleven missionary societies – British, American and Canadian among others – and was subject to a cumbersome administrative structure.[95] Since November 1937, it had operated on two different sites. When the greater part of the university evacuated to Chengdu in November 1937, fifty faculty members had remained in Jinan and the university hospital had remained open until it was taken over by the Japanese for military purposes in early 1942.

Decision-making was particularly fraught when the staff and student body were physically divided between two sites, almost a thousand miles apart, and were operating for almost eight years under very different conditions and with very different priorities. Like other colleges and universities that had migrated west, Qilu was unable to achieve an early return to its Jinan campus at the end of the war.

Since the departure of the foreigners in August 1942, the main university premises in Jinan had been in use as a Japanese military hospital. By December 1945 the premises were still occupied by about 1,200 Japanese wounded and 600 staff. Following the Japanese surrender, the Whitewright Institute had been taken over by the Provincial Ministry of Military Affairs.[96]

Re-establishing ownership and resuming occupation of university and mission property was laborious and frustrating. There were also more mundane problems with transport. While westward movement away from advancing Japanese troops had taken place on a piecemeal basis at the onset of the invasion, at the end of the war all those who had migrated were eager to return simultaneously and the war-shattered travel network was unequal to the task. It was not until the summer of 1947 that the Qilu programme in Chengdu was discontinued, and the last four teachers and seventy-nine students returned to Jinan.[97]

British businessmen were also frustrated in their attempts to repossess their properties at the end of the war. In June 1946, almost a year after the end of the war, George Kitson, head of the Foreign Office's Far East Department

---

[94] BMSA, CH/63, Phillips to friends, 5 January 1946; CH/57, Drake to Chesterman, 26 February 1946.
[95] Corbett, *Shantung Christian University*, p. 235.
[96] BMSA, CH/63, Phillips to friends, 5 January 1946.
[97] Corbett, *Shantung Christian University*, p. 251. For a detailed account of the difficulties of the post-war return and reorientation of the Christian colleges, see Lutz, *China and the Christian Colleges*, pp. 398–409.

complained that a large proportion of British-owned wharfs and ships had still not been recovered. There was evidence, he suggested, not only of a lack of energy and goodwill on the part of the Chinese authorities, but also of a desire to obstruct, if not confiscate. 'Excuses for non-rendition are often malicious and frivolous.'[98] Geoffrey Wallinger, British Minister at the embassy in Nanjing complained that:

> Widespread lack of respect for property rights and the high-handed action of underlings [...] are one of the more disturbing features of post-war China and have largely contributed to the general atmosphere of pessimism in foreign circles regarding the future in this country.[99]

Phillips's and Drake's disappointment and frustration over the condition of the BMS property and the difficulty of reasserting their ownership were accompanied by anxiety about the enormous costs involved. Letter after letter, from them and from Dart in Taiyuan, contained details of schemes to secure money and materials from relief organisations, and to modify plans to take account of the limited mission resources available.[100]

Drake and Phillips were eager to reopen the university hospital in Jinan. Most of the former hospital staff – including nine doctors and the majority of the nurses – who had worked throughout the war in the Municipal hospital were willing to return when plans were put in place for its reopening. The hospital was gradually re-equipped with help from the British, American and Canadian Red Cross, although help from the United Nations Relief and Rehabilitation Administration (UNRRA) and the Chinese National Relief and Rehabilitation Administration (CNRRA) was slow to materialise. 'I understand', wrote Phillips, 'that CNRRA officials in America and China, of all grades, have been advised of this particular need for months but the farther we go the more remote seems the prospect of help from that quarter.'[101]

As we have seen, the correspondence of the BMS missionaries who remained in Shandong during the occupation is almost entirely silent on the matter of collaboration with the occupiers. A rather different perspective is suggested by Raymond Williamson's visit to Jinan during his China tour, when he did not feel the need to be so circumspect. In the report he wrote on his return home, he noted that the Qilu doctors and nurses who had continued, under the auspices of the local Chinese puppet government, to provide medical services during the occupation were 'regarded by some as collaborators'.

---

[98] FO371/53565 F8984/25/10, 17 June 1946, cited in Feng, *British Government's China Policy*, p. 33.
[99] FO371/53609 F11993/61/10 Wallinger to FO 11 July 1946, cited in Feng, *British Government's China Policy*, p. 34.
[100] BMSA, CH/57, Dart to Chesterman, 19 January 1946; CH/57, Drake to Chesterman, 26 February 1946; CH/58, Flowers to Chesterman, 9 March 1946; CH/63, Phillips to Williamson, 17 March 1946; CH/57, Dart to Williamson, 26 March 1946; CH/62/3, Madge to Chesterman, 26 April 1946.
[101] BMSA, CH/63, Phillips to Williamson, 17 March 1946.

As I see it, but for the steps taken by these graduates of Qilu, multitudes of their fellow countrymen would have gone without medical aid for four years. I leave the problem with you. It is not yet solved in China.[102]

He noted also tensions between those members of Qilu university staff who remained in Jinan and those who left for Free China during the occupation.

The peculiar circumstances attendant on long mutual separation of former colleagues and friends [...] have produced a situation in which mutual suspicions and even hostility readily arise. Those who remained are accused of having collaborated with the enemy, while those who left are regarded as deserters. Between these extremes a great variety of mutually hostile opinion is found.[103]

Nothing is said about such tensions in the very full letters that Drake and Phillips wrote from Jinan. They would certainly have been aware of them, but were probably wary of writing information that might fall into hostile hands. The contrast with Williamson's fuller account, written from the safety of his location back in the UK, illustrates the limitations of relying on correspondence from missionaries in the field as the sole basis for assessing the sensitive realities of the time, or of judging missionary attitudes to them.

It may be that such tensions underlay the hesitation of Chinese nationals to assume leadership roles in the university. Immediately on his return to Jinan in December 1945, Phillips wrote to the university president, Wu Keming (吴克明), then based in Chengdu, pressing Wu to find a Chinese member of staff to lead the university in its post-war recovery in Jinan.

Mr Drake and I would much prefer that one of our Chinese colleagues should head up the takeover, but it seems that at present my colleagues wish to push me forward for that work...I am willing to take the lead here for the time being but I urge you to send your own representative from the West, or, failing that, to appoint one of our Chinese colleagues here to act in that capacity.[104]

No action was taken relating to this request and Phillips felt obliged to continue in the role of acting chair until eventually relieved at the end of 1946.[105]

The BMS also had responsibility for hospitals in Zhoucun and Qingzhou and, in January 1946, Drake and Phillips made a hazardous journey to Zhoucun to assess the situation. During the wartime occupation, the Zhoucun buildings had been used for military purposes and, after the Japanese withdrew, the town had been occupied successively by Communist and Nationalist troops, who used the hospital as a barracks. The missionaries found it 'stripped of every door and window, along with every window and door frame, staircase and floorboard,

---

[102] Williamson, *Christian Challenge*, p. 38.
[103] Williamson, *Christian Challenge*, p. 37.
[104] BMSA, CH/63, Phillips to Wu, 30 December 1945.
[105] BMSA, CH/63, Phillips to Williamson, 6 December 1946.

banisters and verandah rails'.[106] Anything made of wood had been used for fuel by successive detachments of troops. Something of the sense of desolation experienced by the returning missionaries was captured by James Harris, months later, who wrote, 'The shock of seeing our hospital and East side premises in such a state was almost more than I could bear.'[107] Drake and Phillips initiated some basic repairs, and employed gatemen to keep a watch on the property.

It was not only the physical infrastructure that had been damaged. Grievances carried over from the years of the occupation cast a shadow within the Chinese church.[108] The missionaries were advised of a 'local squabble between Chang Suching [Zhang Sijing] and his enemies', which had resulted in 'moves made by recalcitrant local Christians to expropriate the hospital and dispense with foreigners'.[109] The use of the pejorative words 'squabble' and 'recalcitrant' suggests that the missionary who wrote the letter did not attach much importance to the views of those who wanted to 'dispense with foreigners'. There is insufficient archival evidence to explain precisely the nature of the disagreements. The account of Zhang's work in Chapter Two suggests that he had close and congenial relationships with his missionary colleagues. Negative feelings towards the foreigners may have affected the attitudes of other Chinese Christians towards Zhang, and tensions within the Zhoucun Christian community made the mission hospital vulnerable to outside attack.

In early 1946, Qingzhou was in the hands of Communists. Dr Jing, who had been active in the BMS hospital throughout the war, was suffering from stress and had moved temporarily from Qingzhou to Jinan.[110] Williamson describes how Jing was periodically imprisoned by the Japanese during the occupation but 'emerged from captivity during the day to administer the affairs of the hospital and returned to his prison at night'. Staffing levels in Qingzhou had been maintained (including six graduate nurses, ten student nurses, one pharmacist and one business manager) and the fabric of the hospital was in better condition than in Zhoucun. The church, mission school and hospital were being kept together by Wang Juntang, 'an old and faithful steward of the Mission'.[111] Nevertheless, in Dr Jing's absence, the lack of a qualified doctor, Chinese or foreign, left the future of the hospital in doubt.

There are no references in the returned missionaries' letters to the Japanese-imposed Protestant church union that had been initiated at the time the foreign missionaries were removed from the province. Williamson had been in China previously when the very first overtures were made by Japanese pastors to Chinese Christians. He wrote that 'the attempts of the J [*sic*] to unify the Church for the purposes of convenient control had succeeded up to a point' but the

---

[106] BMSA, CH/57, Drake to Chesterman, 26 February 1946.
[107] BMSA, CH/60, Harris to Williamson, 31 October 1946.
[108] BMSA, CH/16, Flowers to Chesterman, 9 March 1946.
[109] BMSA, CH/16, Flowers to Chesterman, 9 March 1946.
[110] BMSA, CH/16, Flowers to Chesterman, 9 March 1946.
[111] Williamson, *Christian Challenge*, p. 35.

Chinese had refused to accept the constitution drawn up by the Japanese and had managed to substitute it with one they had devised themselves.[112]

> The Chinese were suspicious that these overtures were actuated by political motives and in consequence no progress was made in the sphere of Christian fellowship. That I think in general represents the situation here.[113]

It is clear from the letters of these three experienced and energetic missionaries – Dart, Drake and Phillips – that in their first months in post-war China, they focused their efforts on reclaiming and restoring what they could of the mission's institutional work, in particular the hospitals, in which the BMS had invested such substantial amounts of human and material resources, but encountered great practical difficulties. Deciding what to do with these institutions was a major stumbling block in any plans for withdrawal from China. Missionary letters from Shanxi and Shandong also hint at, but do not detail, some fractures in relationships between Chinese Christians that had their origins in the years the foreigners were absent.

Missionaries and Their Families

Another aspect of the missionaries' adjustment to the post-war world was a sense of distance from those at home as a result of their very different wartime experiences. In the UK between 1939 and 1945, newspapers, newsreels and magazines conjured up a powerful sense of the whole nation being part of an intense and shared experience, brought vividly to life in the recurring photographic coverage, and held in the popular memory by phrases like 'finest hour', 'backs to the wall', 'community spirit' and 'people's war'. Missionaries who had neither been in the UK nor engaged personally in the war effort (and particularly the European dimension to it) were largely excluded from the British experience of the war years and could only very partially enter into this important aspect of national identity. This sense of exclusion was magnified many times over for those who had been interned. Langdon Gilkey, who was interned in Weihsien camp in Shandong from 1942 to 1945, captures the disorientating experience:

> A week or so later, on March 11, 1946, I was home…All the familiar sights, sounds, and smells, the well-loved people, the buildings and the streets of the university community were there. Yet inwardly, I was a man from another planet. Everything was absolutely normal – and totally strange. I did not know how to go about finding my way in it.[114]

---

[112] Williamson, *Christian Challenge*, p. 30.
[113] Williamson, *Christian Challenge*, p. 38.
[114] Gilkey, *Shantung Compound*, p. 226.

Gilkey was American and his home was in Chicago, but his experience was comparable to that of British internees returning to the UK. It was not only difficult for them to understand fully what the wartime experience had been like. There are indications that the returning missionaries and their families were made to feel a sense of guilt for not having taken part in the struggle or shared the shortages, difficulties and dangers experienced by those living in the UK throughout the war and who failed to understand the challenges, deprivation and dangers associated with living under occupation or in internment. One former internee was told as a ten-year-old, by a teacher in her school class in late 1949, that her father (who had been interned with his family) had shirked his patriotic duty by remaining in China during the war and failing to sign up for national service.[115]

Fred Russell spent the war years in Shaanxi, separated from his wife and family, subject to bombing, evacuations, shortages and banditry. Yet he felt constrained to conclude his chapter in *Through Toil and Tribulation*, the post-war account of the Baptist missionary experience in China, with words that verge on apology, almost guilt:

> We do not pretend that these difficulties and hardships were comparable with the difficulties and hardships endured in Britain during the bitter war years. But just as people at home proved that they could 'take it' so the missionaries on the field showed the same spirit.[116]

Russell was reflecting here his understanding of the importance of establishing an awareness that the efforts of those at home had been shared by those overseas.

The extensive disruption caused by the war meant that family separations, always a part of missionary life, were more frequent and more prolonged. Fred Drake – himself born in China – and his wife Dora were committed to educating their son in China, but in 1938 war conditions meant that suitable schooling was unavailable.[117] They had been unwilling to send their seven-year-old to boarding school in England, thinking it unfair 'that the whole sacrifice of the divided home, if it had to be divided, should be laid upon the child'.[118] They had therefore decided that Dora would have to stay in the UK when Drake returned to China. By the summer of 1945, Dora had been separated from her husband for seven years. The end of the war raised the prospect of a family reunion but, as we have seen, Drake did not join the other internees on the repatriation ships leaving Shanghai for the UK. Instead, he travelled with Phillips to review conditions in Jinan.

By March 1946, Drake felt his exploratory work in Shandong was at a stage when it could be left to others, and was beginning to think about returning home. At the time, sea passages from China were almost impossible to obtain and a

---

[115] Personal recollection of Audrey Salters.
[116] F. S. Russell, 'Shensi, 1937–1945', in *Through Toil and Tribulation*, p. 186.
[117] BMSA, CH/57, Drake to Wilson, 12 June 1938.
[118] BMSA, CH/57, Drake to Wilson, 12 June 1938.

further long delay seemed inevitable. Sea passages were allocated by the British government and those made available to the missionary societies continued to be scarce between 1945 and 1947. In early 1946, one newly married couple sailed for China on different boats two days apart, which would have meant that they did not see each other for more than six weeks. This led to a protest from the secretary of their home church, who complained that it was 'a great pity that these two young people, so recently married, should have been treated as strangers for the purpose of travelling'.[119] Clement Chesterman replied:

> During the war (and until now) individual societies did not book passages. These were made by the various Government offices to Edinburgh House, the headquarters of the Conference of British Missionary Societies. We then are given our share. Some boats are transport ships and only take men. We have to accept any passage that is offered [to] us or we go down to the bottom of the list for the next allocation.[120]

The only possibility that could prevent further delay in Drake's return was if the BMS would agree to him returning by air. Much to his wife's chagrin, the finance committee refused to allow him to fly home, on the grounds of the extra expense involved and the fact that it would be unfair to other missionaries if one were given such preferential treatment. A very heated correspondence ensued, in which Dora Drake argued passionately that her husband's position was different from that of other missionaries and accused the mission of failure to make proper provision for the very real needs of its staff: 'It is the old state of affairs – the more one considers the Mission, the less he is considered by the Mission.'[121] The committee would not alter its decision. Dora Drake concluded a final indignant letter on a different note:

> It is true that I am very near the end of my tether, but it is also true that much as I want and need Fred, I cannot get clear in my mind how right it is to put family before God's work. Fred himself is in the same quandary.[122]

This letter identified a central dilemma for missionary families. Was it always wrong to put family concerns or personal needs before the work of the mission? Might it be that *sometimes* caring for family *was* God's work?

And what of the impact on the children? As part of the research on which this book is based, oral interviews were conducted with thirteen of the sons and daughters of BMS missionaries who served in China during this period.[123]

---

119 BMSA, CH/56, Deverell to Chesterman, February 1946.
120 BMSA, CH/56, Chesterman to Deverell, 5 March 1946.
121 BMSA, CH/57, Drake, to Chesterman, 7 March 1946.
122 BMSA, CH/57, Drake, to Chesterman, 19 March 1946.
123 For purposes of confidentiality, the views expressed have not been linked to individuals. However, their names are all included, with appreciation, in the acknowledgements. Other relevant information appears in B. Richardson (ed), *Sons of Missionaries: Recollections by Boarders at Eltham College* (Eltham College, 2009).

Between them, they had experienced the many variations of schooling and upbringing open to missionaries for their children. They represented different ages, family structures and family relationships, and a range of different experiences of China. It would be simplistic, without much fuller information and more detailed analysis of a larger sample, to draw conclusions about the impact on children of their parents' missionary work in China and the consequent separations. However, the range of views illustrate that, for many children, these separations had a profound effect. Two of those interviewed, by then in their eighties, remained fiercely bitter about what they saw as their parents' abandonment of them in the interest of their work for the missionary society. Relationships, particularly with their mothers, had become deeply soured. Others who were sent to stay with extended family members, for instance during holidays from boarding school, believed they were unwanted and their presence barely tolerated. Against this, there were also those who spoke with pride of their parents' commitment, or recounted positive experiences stemming from support from siblings or school friends, or described positive and important relationships with guardians in the UK.

Several of the missionaries' children spoke of crying themselves to sleep for days or weeks on arrival at boarding school at the age of seven. This misery was not, of course, confined to missionaries' children, and occurred in an era when it was much more acceptable, even desirable, to send children to boarding school at a young age. Research into the effects on adult men of having been sent away at an early age to boarding school describes a perception of 'woundedness' amongst them, and feelings of having lost 'something very fundamental: trust and innocence, the sense of belonging, a sense of it being all right to be a child and have a childhood'.[124] However, most children at boarding schools were able to reconnect with their families for several weeks each year during the school holidays, while the children of missionaries might not see their parents for years at a time. This, and the fact that use of boarding schools was more common in wealthier groups than the ones from which most missionaries originated, may have compounded the sense of isolation felt by missionaries' children among their boarding school contemporaries.

After the war, missionaries with school-age children could not be certain there would be any appropriate schooling for them in China. Following the opening of the Japanese offensive against the UK and the United States, many teachers and pupils were interned during the war years, and parts of the Chefoo boarding school for missionaries' children were temporarily relocated to India. By late 1945 the future of the school was in doubt.[125] Post-war conditions of scarcity in the UK made it harder for missionaries to find guardians for their children if they left them at home for schooling: housing and feeding additional youngsters, and taking responsibility for their personal support and moral guidance, was not

---

[124] Nick Duffell, *The Making of Them: The British Attitude to Children and the Boarding School System* (London: Lone Arrow, 2000), p. 7.
[125] George Martin, *Chefoo School 1881–1951: A History and Memoir* (Braunton: Merlin Books, 1990).

something to be entered into lightly. This, and the unsettled conditions in China, meant very difficult decisions for missionaries with children.

Almost half (forty-one) of the BMS's China missionaries left the mission between the onset of the war with Japan and the post-war resumption of work in 1945–1946. Seventeen families with school-age or pre-school children were amongst those still prepared to serve. All were faced with a choice regarding arrangements for their children when considering return to China. Five couples returned, leaving their children at boarding school in the immediate post-war period. One other couple took their three pre-school-age children with them when they went back in late 1946, leaving two older children at boarding school in England. Four other families went back with pre-school children. In seven families, the parents decided that the mother would remain in the UK with the children while the father returned to China.[126]

For all of these families, there was no choice that completely met their desire both to maintain some semblance of normal family life and to continue to serve God through the mission. They all had to make compromises of varying degrees of unpalatability. Gwyneth Still responded robustly when Clement Chesterman wrote from the mission house expressing his appreciation of her willingness to allow her husband to return to China alone in 1946, leaving her with three children aged nine, seven and six, all of whom had been interned during the war and only returned to the UK in December 1945:

> Of course I cannot say that I am pleased that Ronald should go back to China without us, but feeling as we do about the need there at present, there seems to be no choice. I know I cannot leave the children yet and it seems quite unsuitable that we should take them out in present circumstances.[127]

Even leaving children approaching adulthood involved considerable sacrifice on the part of the parents and their children. When Handley Stockley and his wife returned to China in 1945 they left behind three children, aged seventeen, fourteen and eleven. The oldest, a son, had left school and was expecting to be called up for military service, but meanwhile was trying to find work. The parents' anxiety for their son's wellbeing, and their sense of helplessness at trying to parent a teenager at such a distance, comes through in their weekly letters to him:

> I wish you would write us oftener. How about once a week? If you are short of money for the 6d, ask Uncle Bernard, for we do want to hear from you.[128]

> If by any misfortune you should find yourself without a definite place to go [...], remember these addresses...If you have to go to any home, be sure to try to have

---

126 Williamson, *British Baptists*, pp. 366–72.
127 BMSA, CH/65, Still to Chesterman, 6 November 1946.
128 Private collection of Dorothy Williamson, Stockley to son, 30 June 1946.

all your rationing cards etc. in proper order before you leave one place and go to the next, it makes so much difference to the lady of the house.[129]

Even for those children who remained at boarding schools, there was a question of where they should stay during school holidays and who should be their local guardians while their parents remained overseas. It had not been unusual in the past for the young children of missionary parents to be sent back to the UK in the care of missionaries other than their parents, and then placed for short-term care with families chosen by members of the mission board, sometimes on the strength only of a church member's verbal recommendation. One concerned missionary wrote in late 1946 about a colleague, 'he is looking forward to coming back to China, but they have three small boys and they do not know what to do with them. I was wondering if Mrs Harris of Rustington would take them?'[130]

The BMS had set up a special subcommittee in 1945 'to consider in all its aspects the care of missionaries' children'.[131] This was prompted by the death in local authority foster care of twelve-year-old Dennis O'Neill. Dennis's death, and the subsequent trial of his foster parents, caused a huge national outcry in early 1945, and for several days was given greater prominence in the pages of *The Times* than even the events of the war.[132] Although there was no direct connection to the mission (Dennis's parents were not missionaries and this was not the reason he was in care), the concerns arising from the case meant that the care of all children living away from their parents was very much in the public eye.

The BMS could scarcely afford to risk a public scandal over arrangements for the children of missionaries. When the special subcommittee eventually reported in 1949, the society's officers 'laid some stress on the fact that the primary responsibility for the care of missionaries' children rested on the parents'.[133] This is the kind of 'double-think' that Manktelow finds again and again in the dealings of the London Missionary Society (LMS) with the first missionaries in the South Seas and in South Africa.[134] The society demanded of its missionary staff that they put themselves in positions in which it was impossible for them to give satisfactory care to their children, while at the same time disowning responsibility for the consequences.[135]

The Curtis Committee – the government committee set up in 1945 in the wake of the Dennis O'Neill inquiry to look into provision for children 'deprived of a normal home life' – was only one of a number of social welfare initiatives

---

[129] Private collection of Dorothy Williamson, Stockley to son, 11 August 1946.

[130] Private Collection of Dorothy Williamson, Stockley to son, 10 November 1946.

[131] BMSA, General Committee Minutes, 3 July 1945.

[132] *The Times*, 6, 9, 13, 14, 15 and 28 February 1945; 16, 17, 19, 20 and 27 March 1945; and 29 May 1945.

[133] BMSA, General Purposes Sub-Committee Minutes, Vol. 3, 13 January 1949.

[134] Manktelow, *Missionary Families*, pp. 99, 112 and 114.

[135] BMSA, General Purposes Subcommittee Minutes, Vol. 3, 13 January 1949.

introduced in the UK at this time.[136] From the early 1940s, promoting the idea of 'a better Britain after the war' was part of government strategy. In July 1940, the war cabinet considered a paper on the proposed social reforms.[137] The Beveridge Report, published in December 1942, became the blueprint for many of the subsequent reforms.[138] Within a remarkably short space of time, a range of new legislation was enacted that established the principle of universal right of access to services, regardless of income, geography, sex, age or occupation. For the first time, the middle classes were included as entitled recipients of sickness and insurance benefits. Stronger central control was a direct consequence of the new legislation. Contributing payments for services, which previously might have been a matter of individual choice, became compulsory.[139]

The new welfare legislation was generally welcomed by the churches because it was 'seen to be identifiably Christian'.[140] The minutes of the BMS committees for the period immediately following the passing of the new statutes suggest that debate centred on the practical consequences: the benefits and costs to the missionary societies as employers, and the possibility that, with the nationalisation of the health service, appeals for cash for the voluntary hospitals 'would probably soon cease' and 'that money might be devoted to missionary purposes'.[141]

One issue that arose was the way in which the 1944 Education Act would affect the two boarding schools that catered specifically for missionaries' children: Walthamstow Hall and Eltham College. The act allowed for independent schools, funded partly by the state and partly through tuition fees, to exist alongside state schools. One quarter of the places in these schools were directly funded by central government, while the remainder attracted fees, some paid by the local education authority and some by private pupils. Walthamstow Hall and Eltham College fit within this administrative framework, being classified as 'direct grant' schools. Prior to the 1944 Act, the children of missionaries paid only £13 per term, whereas other pupils were charged £36 a term, representing a substantial saving over the whole school year, especially where there were two or three children boarding from the same family.[142] Under

---

[136] Brian Watkin, *Documents on Health and Social Services, 1834 to the Present Day* (London, 1975), p. 420.

[137] Ian McLaine, *Ministry of Morale: Home Front Morale and the Ministry of Information in World War II* (London: Allen and Unwin, 1979), p. 103, quoted in Correlli Barnett, *The Audit of War: The Illusion and Reality of Britain as a Great Nation* (London: Macmillan, 1986), pp. 19–20.

[138] The Report of the Interdepartmental Committee on Social Insurance and Allied Services, Cmd 6404, HMSO 1942.

[139] See, for example, Howard Glennerster, 'Social Policy Since the Second World War', in Julian Hills (ed), *The State of Welfare: The Welfare State in Britain since 1974* (Oxford: Clarendon Press, 1990), pp. 12–16.

[140] E. R. Norman, *Church and Society in England, 1770–1970: A Historical Study* (Oxford: Clarendon Press, 1976), p. 375.

[141] BMSA, General Committee Minutes, Vol. 44, 11 September 1946, p. 164.

[142] BMSA, Finance Committee Minutes, Vol. 52, 28 June 1945.

the new administrative arrangements, such preferential treatment for missionaries would not be possible. Minutes of the BMS finance committee in December 1945 report that discussions had taken place between the governors of the two schools and the Ministry of Education to find 'ways and means of assisting missionary parents', but does not specify what kind of 'ways and means' were hoped for or anticipated.[143]

SOS from Shandong

With the workforce depleted and the 1930s decision to withdraw from Shandong by 1942 remaining as established mission policy, why did the BMS continue to deploy missionaries to China from 1946? The answer is because the Chinese church asked them to.

Following the exploratory work of the small group of returning missionaries, in summer 1946 mission headquarters received two letters from Shandong. One letter was from Dr Jing, medical superintendent of the BMS hospital in Qingzhou, who wrote (in English) referring to 'the special circumstances [a discreet reference to the fighting between CCP and GMD troops] which have obtained since the Japanese capitulation', and their destructive effect on staff morale. He went on, 'Our greatest hope is that in the nearest possible future you may be able to send us an English colleague or two to help tide us over this very difficult period.'[144] The other letter was from Zhang Sijing pleading with the BMS to reverse their decision not to allow Henry Payne, already past retirement age, to return to China:

> This destruction is a thousand times more serious than the previous one…We are short of talented people from both East and West. In such a difficult situation, if Pastor Payne came back he would make a very important contribution…In this situation we really need someone to guide and help us.[145]

These two appeals for help from China had an important effect on the BMS.[146] In June, the China staffing subcommittee met to make plans for staffing the work in China. A conference of the CCC was to be held in Shanghai in October and was expected to make a statement of policy regarding the relationship between the CCC and the various societies affiliated to it, but it was considered advisable for the BMS to make some preliminary plans for the immediate future. The meeting concluded that 'at least for the period of the next nine months and without prejudice to the final China set-up, despite the activity of Communists

---

[143] BMSA, Finance Committee Minutes, Vol. 52, 20 December 1945.
[144] BMSA, CH/65 Jing to Chesterman, 6 May 1946.
[145] BMSA, CH/23, Secretariat Shantung, 1939–1946, Zhang to Williamson, original in Chinese, 14 June 1946 (trans. Gao Yan, 1984).
[146] Stanley, *History*, p. 318, citing BMSA, General Committee Minutes, Vol. 25, 3 February and 20 July 1932; Vol. 26, 6 February 1934.

and other difficulties, as many mission stations as possible should be occupied'.[147]

Despite indications of the growing independence of the Chinese church, and the continuing commitment of the BMS to support the Chinese leadership, the terrible destruction of the war years and the continuing turmoil in China had brought about a situation in which the BMS felt unable to hold to its pre-war plan.

As the BMS attempted to make decisions about its future place in China in the autumn of 1945 and the early months of 1946, it was influenced by its leadership in London and by the missionary workforce, both in China and in retirement or on furlough in the UK. Most missionaries who had spent the war in China voiced their awareness that major changes had taken place that necessitated finding new ways to work with the Chinese church. The London leadership was in the hands of a highly respected former China missionary, who, although experienced and knowledgeable about the China scene, had not worked there during the most recent upheavals. In retrospect, it appears that his understanding had not kept pace with the new forces at work in China, and his advice did fully not recognise their importance.

Getting involved with the work of the Border Service was a bold step in finding new ways to engage with Chinese Christians, but it could be said to have proved unwise in the light of the political uncertainties. Returning tentatively to the formerly occupied provinces, missionaries found a warm personal welcome. Missionaries were also confronted by damaged and denuded hospitals and educational institutions, and a shortage of staff to take on professional and leadership roles. Tension was created between the amount of work needed to save the institutions from collapse and the commitments that the BMS had previously made to withdraw support from Shandong.

Conditions in the UK were changing. It was less easy for missionaries to make satisfactory provision for their children. Changed understandings regarding the effects on children of early separation from their parents made earlier expectations regarding the missionary lifestyle seem less and less acceptable. New legislation meant that previous arrangements for missionaries committing to a career for life might need rethinking.

Meanwhile, urgent appeals for help from Zhang Sijing, the respected and resourceful leader of the SBU, and Jing Yihui, the doctor who had sustained BMS medical work in Qingzhou, challenged the society and members of its staff to attempt to take up work once again in 'as many mission stations as possible'.[148]

---

[147] BMSA, China Staffing Subcommittee Minutes, Vol. 11, 6 June 1946.
[148] BMSA, China Staffing Subcommittee Minutes, Vol. 11, 6 June 1946.

5. Civil War, July 1946 to December 1948

> As long as the present situation exists, we shall have to come to the aid of the pastors and the evangelists and church workers who were previously supported by the church. The civil war means that the people are more and more impoverished and pastoral aid is more and more difficult for them…We are slowly and painfully learning the truth of the situation in China and in the church.[1]

After eight years of warfare with Japan, most Chinese people longed, most of all, for the cessation of bloodshed and for a stable government.[2] Instead they were to be plunged into three years of civil war. While the war had begun in the mid-1920s with enmities between Nationalist and Communist forces forged then, the War of Resistance had put internal fighting on hold between 1937 and 1945. The Japanese surrender in 1945 created a power vacuum that both warring factions sought to fill.

The civil war affected the work of the mission and the lives of church members. Military activity, disruptions to the transport network, international and Chinese government attempts at national reconstruction, economic crises and the consequences of inflation all played a part in dictating the options open to the BMS and its missionaries. They also influenced the interaction between missionaries and other players on the scene: the mission board in London, political parties in China, Chinese Christians, members of other missionary societies and their foreign colleagues in China. UK-based supporters of missionary work in China had difficulty understanding the conditions in China, and even the experienced, sympathetic missionaries faced formidable obstacles in understanding the position in which Chinese Christians found themselves at this time. There were difficult decisions to take at both a mission and an individual level.

The Civil War and Its Impact

In the early autumn of 1946, a series of Guomindang (GMD) initiatives in northern China appeared to put the Nationalists militarily in the ascendancy. A leader in *The Times* on 12 September 1946 declared that 'General Chiang Kai-shek has replied to the Communist attacks […] by launching vigorous drives north of the Yangtze […] and the Communists have been unable to resist the Government troops.'[3] On 19 March 1947, the GMD captured the Communist

---

[1] BMSA, CH/54, Allen to Williamson, 26 July 1947.
[2] Westad, *Decisive Encounters*, p. 78.
[3] 'New Moves in China', *The Times*, 12 September 1946, p. 5.

capital Yan'an and Chiang Kai-shek was reported to be 'euphoric'.[4] Ronald Still, based at the time in Shandong, was less confident and wrote home to his father, 'The Government are talking in optimistic terms about clearing up Shantung in the next two or three months. Perhaps they will be right. It will be an unsettled time.'[5] By the end of 1947, however, the Nationalist army, which appeared to have so much in its favour in 1946 and early 1947, was giving ground inexorably to the Communists.[6]

Unlike other modern civil wars, where a high degree of popular participation is a distinguishing feature, the Chinese Civil War was largely fought out between rival armies.[7] There were strategically important, large-scale battles, but when towns and cities changed hands street fighting did not often feature.[8] The common practice was for incoming troops to enter overnight without opposition, the defendants having fled in anticipation of defeat. The war was not even supported in its early stages by strong popular movements. The student movement, which became a powerful influence on the development of the war, and which was denounced by the GMD as 'a creature of the Communist Party', was initially and predominantly an anti-war movement, rather than a movement ideologically in tune with the Chinese Communist Party (CCP).[9] Likewise, the strikes and rice riots, in which members of the general public were also involved, were aimed at practical material gains rather than a calculated attempt to undermine one or the other side of the conflict.[10]

Nevertheless, the population as a whole was fundamentally affected by the war. Conscription by both sides had far-reaching consequences for almost every family, and skirmishes by guerrillas in the countryside made everyday life precarious. Exorbitant taxes were levied to finance military expenditure, and physical contributions to the war effort were exacted in the form of forced labour for building defensive works. Crops were routinely commandeered to feed the military, with the result that hunger and scarcity were widespread. This is the situation that Tom Allen identified when he wrote of the BMS having to come to the aid of church workers, 'who previously were supported by the [Chinese] Church'.[11]

---

[4] Westad, *Decisive Encounters*, p. 151.

[5] Private collection of Audrey Salters, Still to father, 24 March 1947.

[6] See, for example, Jack Belden, *China Shakes the World* (London: Harper, 1949); Lionel M. Chassin, *The Communist Conquest of China: A History of the Civil War, 1945–1949* (London: Wiedenfeld and Nicolson, 1965); Eastman, *Seeds of Destruction*; Pepper, *Civil War in China*; Westad, *Decisive Encounters*; Thomas D. Lutze, *China's Inevitable Revolution: Rethinking America's Loss to the Communists* (Basingstoke: Palgrave Macmillan, 2008); Christopher Lew, *The Third Chinese Revolutionary War: An Analysis of Communist Strategy and Leadership* (London: Routledge, 2009).

[7] Westad, *Decisive Encounters*, p. 69.

[8] Westad, *Decisive Encounters*, p. 1.

[9] Suzanne Pepper, 'The Student Movement and the Chinese Civil War, 1945–49', *The China Quarterly* 48 (October to December 1971), p. 699; Lutz, *China and the Christian Colleges*, pp. 428–33.

[10] See Perry, *Shanghai on Strike*.

[11] BMSA, CH/54, Allen to Williamson, 26 July 1947.

The Communists deliberately allowed Nationalist soldiers to defect and then pressurised defectors to come over to their side, and also periodically impressed on civilian personnel to serve the military.[12] Both sides adopted punitive tactics against ordinary civilians suspected of disloyalty. Brutal methods of enforcing compliance or punishing opposition were common, and missionaries frequently faced the results. Handley Stockley gave many distressing examples from his experience of hospital work in Taiyuan in 1946 and 1947. He described equal ruthlessness on both sides:

> People who come from areas occupied by the Communists to this [pro-Nationalist] city have a very tough time, however innocent their reason for coming…One of our northern Christians was kept in the Provincial headquarters for six weeks, another got out in two weeks – but the latter's hands were double their normal thickness owing to having been beaten with clubs. Nellie, today, had a woman patient beaten from head to feet all down one side by the Communists – so what is there of choice![13]

Chinese Christians and church leaders were considered particularly suspect by the Communists. The pastor of one of the small Baptist churches in northern Shanxi was suspected of Nationalist sympathies and held by the Communists for several months in solitary confinement, before being sent to forced labour in the mines where he was believed later to have been killed.[14] James Harris, on his return to Shandong in 1946, described the fear in the village communities, which endured repeated turnovers between the two sides in 1945, 1946 and 1947:

> I regret that it is not possible to go to the villages and our more distant outposts. It is not that I am afraid to go but the Chinese rightly point out that the people to whom I spoke, and with whom I made contact, would be sure to suffer after I had gone. In the villages no one scarcely dare speak to anyone else.[15]

Wilfred Flowers described the impact of the continuing turnovers in the small towns and villages of Shandong: 'Any who cooperate with the Nationalists are eliminated by the Communists when they take the place, and any who then cooperate with the Communists are liquidated by the Nationalists when they take over.'[16] Mutual suspicion between neighbours put new pressures on Chinese Christians' relationships with foreign missionaries. Anything that made people stand out from the rest of the population put them in danger.

The transport infrastructure had been fundamentally undermined as a consequence of wartime bombing and continued to be the subject of deliberate sabotage by guerrilla forces, both Communist and Nationalist. Stockley wrote, in August 1946, to his teenage son in England:

---

[12] Eastman, *Seeds of Destruction*, p. 164.
[13] Private collection of Dorothy Williams, Stockley to son, 23 October 1947.
[14] Williamson, *British Baptists*, pp. 190–91.
[15] BMSA, CH/60, Harris to friends, 9 November 1946.
[16] BMSA, CH/58, Flowers to Chesterman, 2 December 1947.

> Do you realise that communications in China are very much worse now than they ever were during the war? There is scarcely a single railway that is running even a straight run between any two important towns. All the lines have been ripped up by the Communists.[17]

During the final months of 1945 and throughout 1946, the shattered network was put under huge strain when displaced industrial, commercial and educational institutions began the process of attempting to re-establish themselves in their places of origin, and millions of refugees tried to make their way home. Two years later, when the movement towards Communist victory was beginning to be apparent, a new tide of refugees crammed the transport channels. In November 1948, the British ambassador in Nanjing, anticipating the need to evacuate British personnel, commented on the difficulties of securing transport, 'owing to priority demands of officials and wealthy Chinese fleeing southwards'.[18]

Throughout this period, missionaries were making many journeys to and from the more remote parts of China. There are many examples of tramping from place to place in protracted attempts to find means of transport and authorisation to travel; of harrowing, uncomfortable and dangerous journeys on unmade roads and the shattered remains of bridges and rail tracks; of luggage lost and trucks overturned.[19] Lifts were negotiated from unlikely sources and favours were called in: Connie Allen described her husband getting a lift on a Nationalist army truck when the 96th Army moved its personnel from Jinan to Weifang, 'as Tom knows the secretary of one of the officers'.[20] A few months later, Ronald Still secured the use of a US army jeep to help get around, but access to oil and petrol was problematic. The British manager of the Shell Company in Qingdao had been a fellow internee in Shanghai during the war years and came to Still's rescue with a few barrels of petrol and motor oil. 'We will do our best to help again – but must warn you that our stocks are very short indeed.'[21]

Many missionary accounts of difficult journeys were detailed and graphic, but were undertaken without complaint. Ironically, one of the few murmurs of discontent was from an older missionary who found herself unexpectedly returning from Taiyuan to Xi'an by air: 'I had hoped to go back by cart, ten days, instead we rush back in an hour and a half. It fair takes one's breath away!'[22]

---

[17] Private collection of Dorothy Williams, Stockley to son, 28 August 1946.

[18] *British Documents on Foreign Affairs*, Part IV, Series E: F15541/269/10, Lamb to Bevin, No. 929, 4 November 1948.

[19] See, for example, BMSA CH/62/3, Madge to Williamson, 30 October 1946; CH/54, Bastable to friends, 31 January 1947; CH/60, Harris to Williamson, 27 February 1947; CH/62/3, Madge to Williamson, 1 April 1947; CH/58, Emmott to Williamson, 31 July 1947

[20] BMSA, CH/54, Allen to Williamson, 12 September 1947.

[21] Private collection of Audrey Salters, P. Oliver to Still, 16 January 1948.

[22] Private collection of Dorothy Williams, Stockley to son, 5 January 1947.

Figure 12: Transport challenges[23]

The photographs show Tom Allen (left) in the passenger seat of the Nationalist army truck and (right) one of the many breakdowns of the truck on which Ronald Still hitched a lift to Zhoucun.

Civilian air travel was in its comparatively early days. Military activity forced those who wanted to get around China, including missionaries, to take to the air if they could afford it, since overland travel was usually dangerous and often impossible. In January 1948, the China subcommittee noted:

Certain [BMS] property [in Taiyuan] not at present in use had been let to Chinese Air Organisations and other bodies and special privileges had been secured in connection with plane transport.[24]

The initiative of the Lutheran missionary societies in purchasing their own plane, the *St Paul*, in 1946 proved of great assistance to all missionary societies in facilitating movement during the last years of their presence in China.[25]

University personnel and equipment were flown back from places of refuge in western China, medicine and relief consignments were transported to inland hospitals, missionaries were brought back to their fields and mission executives

---

[23] From the private collections of Peter Nelson (*left*) and Audrey Salters (*right*).
[24] BMSA, China Sub-Committee Minutes, Vol. 11, 20 January 1948.
[25] Jonson, 'Lutheran Missions', p. 109.

were flown to remote places. The extensive operations continued until the close of 1949, when it was no longer possible to fly in China and *St Paul* was sold.[26]

The St Paul 'flew the equivalent of 18.5 times round the world' and 'became a symbol of Lutheran cooperation'.[27] By the early 1950s, when the last missionaries were leaving, air travel was accepted as the most appropriate and efficient way to get around.

Cooperation between missionary societies in the use of the *St Paul* was not the only form of reciprocal help to which the civil war years gave rise. Missionaries from different societies were frequently brought together as they offered or accepted hospitality from each other in the course of broken journeys or enforced stays in unexpected places. There are many references to BMS missionaries having been met, escorted and given hospitality by members of different missionary societies.[28] Whenever possible, the BMS reciprocated. Still undertook a month's medical work in the American Lutheran Mission hospital in Qingdao, 'as some small return […] for their very kind hospitality to me and other members of our mission passing through'.[29] Later in this period, when BMS missionaries were driven from their traditional bases by the Communist presence, many took up work with other missions in other parts of China.[30]

Wartime destruction of mission buildings also brought missionaries and Chinese Christians into more intimate forms of contact. Fred Drake gave an atmospheric description of his first post-war meeting with the three leading members of the Shandong Chinese Baptists, Zhang Sijing, Wang Juntang and Jing Yihui in 'a vacated Japanese house' at Zhoucun.

> We talked far into the night […] but we reached no conclusion. We slept side by side on mats on the floor. In the night I woke and heard them still discussing the same question.[31]

On his return to the bomb-damaged Foster Hospital in Zhoucun after the war, Still shared meals with his former servant, by whom he was welcomed back 'with as much apparent joy as I felt on seeing him'.[32] Missionaries Rufus Dart and Eric Sutton Smith, returning to Taiyuan at the end of 1945, lived for months in the home of the leader of the orphanage, Zhang Hu Shi.

---

[26] Jonson, 'Lutheran Missions', p. 110.

[27] Jonson, 'Lutheran Missions', p. 111.

[28] For example, BMSA, CH/60, Harris to Williamson, 16 July 1946; CH/56, Collins to Williamson, 19 August 1946; CH/54, Bastable to Williamson, 7 February 1947.

[29] BMSA, CH/65, Still to Chesterman, 23 March 1947.

[30] BMSA, CH/54, Bastable to Williamson, 24 July 1948; CH/59, Chesterman to Gunn, 6 August 1948; CH/65, Stockley to Clow, 7 December 1948.

[31] BMSA, CH/57, Drake to Chesterman, 26 February 1946.

[32] Private collection of Audrey Salters, Still, diary entry, 26 December 1946.

> We share a room here and have the use of her [Zhang's] sitting room, and this is
> her expressed wish too. She is feeding us well on Chinese food three times a day,
> and we feel it is right to stay right here.[33]

Such close personal contact between missionaries and Chinese Christians had been unusual before the Japanese invasion. Although there are many examples of missionaries inviting Chinese friends and colleagues to their homes as guests, both for meals and overnight stays, it was rare for foreign and Chinese households to merge in pre-war days. There are two contrasting examples from the early 1940s of missionaries engaging in deliberate experiments in community living with Chinese families, both very different in their attitude and approach. In early 1942, Victor Hayward wrote to his parents of what he called his 'Christian Community Living experiment', living as a family with seven Chinese young people, including a small boy, sharing meals and living expenses according to their means:

> We have learned a great deal from each other, and though naturally everything has
> not come up to our best ideals, we have a very happy life, and the experiment has
> proved immensely worthwhile.[34]

The second occasion, occurring at about the same time, described another missionary couple, who had decided to live together with the family of their 'table boy':

> We have taken on the job of educating, christianising and 'hygienising' [*sic*] this
> family, working out a suitable diet to suit their budget, sending the eldest to school.
> Also trying to teach the mother and younger children the elements of hygiene.
> Chinese children all wear split pants, so that their parents do not have the trouble
> to teach them or train them in matters of hygiene. We are getting rid of the splits in
> the pants.[35]

This second example was the only example of such cultural insensitivity that came to light in the course of extensive exploration of the BMS correspondence for this period. In 1947, Drake wrote expressing his conviction that this couple should not be allowed to return to China.[36]

Post-war reconstruction was a massive task confronting the Chinese government. Despite the well-established historical narrative of incompetence on the part of the Nationalist government, recent work has focused on evidence of substantial efforts that the government made to tackle the task. Refugee relief was an integral and daunting challenge. Mitter points out that the government's efforts in this respect had propaganda value as well as practical and humanitarian importance, since 'the government knew that its treatment of refugees was being

---

[33] BMSA, CH/57, Dart to Williamson, 22 December 1945.
[34] BMSA, CH/60, Hayward to parents, 17 April 1942 .
[35] BMSA, CH/62, [name withheld] to friends, 12 October 1941.
[36] BMSA, CH/57, Drake to Williamson, 14 June 1947.

judged in comparison with the Communists and with the Japanese'.[37] The Development and Relief Committee (DRC, or 赈济委员会; Zhenji weiyuanhui), created in 1937, provided assistance at national level, 'well beyond anything previously seen in China'.[38]

Plans for post-war reconstruction began to be addressed by the Nationalist government in 1940, when the Ministry of Social Affairs was established, with oversight of labour relations, civil society and social policy.[39] Just as Mitter draws attention to the propaganda motives of the GMD in its provision of welfare and relief policies, so Tehyun Ma argues that their social policy initiatives were as much about 'strengthening the nation on the international stage [...] making its government a more viable proposition to support', as they were about 'dealing with questions of industrialisation, urbanisation and labour unrest'.[40] At the international level, the United Nations Relief and Rehabilitation Administration (UNRRA) was formed in 1943 with a view to coordinating aid after the war ended and avoiding the mistakes of the aftermath of the First World War.[41] In China, under pressure from the Nationalist government, it was agreed that legal title to the goods and other donations would pass to the Chinese once they entered China. At that point, a separate organisation, known as the Chinese National Relief and Rehabilitation Administration (CNRRA), would take possession of the supplies, with UNRRA advisers making recommendations.[42]

The national efforts towards reconstruction in China were important to the BMS in two ways. First, any public resources on which they could draw would be invaluable in their own reconstruction efforts. Secondly, working in partnership with others for the good of the whole community was in keeping with the emphasis on the 'social gospel' and the theology of service, which had guided many developments in missionary work during the 1930s and 1940s. One BMS missionary who was seconded to work with UNRRA in Guangxi province gave a positive account of his experience:

> The sum spent directly on relief and rehabilitation in the province was upwards of CNC$2,000,000,000.[43] In addition, in spite of particularly difficult transport conditions, about 10,000 tons of goods were brought in, chiefly food to meet desperate famine needs. Seventy to eighty county and provincial hospitals, and one

---

[37] Mitter, *China's War*, p. 178.

[38] Mitter, *China's War*, p. 178.

[39] Tehyun Ma, 'The Common Aim of the Allied Powers: Social Policy and International Legitimacy in Wartime China, 1940–47', *Journal of Global History* 9 (2014), pp. 254–275 (p. 258).

[40] Ma 'The Common Aim of the Allied Powers', p. 260.

[41] George Woodbridge, *UNRRA: The History of the United Nations Relief and Rehabilitation Administration, Volume 1* (New York: Columbia University Press, 1950), pp. 7–14.

[42] G. H. Kerr, *Formosa Betrayed* (Irvine CA: Taiwan Publishing Company, 1992), Chapter 8.

[43] CNC = Chinese National Currency.

hundred and fifty primary schools, were reconstructed…About 20,000 refugees were given food and shelter.[44]

Seeds, fertilisers, water buffaloes and tractors were also provided to assist in agricultural rehabilitation.[45] Invaluable supplies were made available through the International, British and Canadian Red Cross, and there are references to the fact that hospital work would not have been able to continue at all without such support.[46]

More frequent, however, are the examples of frustration felt by those who were faced with human need on an enormous scale and found themselves unable to access the resources that were available to meet that need. For example, Ernest Madge expressed frustration at the difficulties his colleague, Stockley, was having in getting help with reconstruction efforts at the BMS hospital in Taiyuan.

> We have been having trouble with CNRRA, I'm sorry to say, over help for the hospital. The same trouble has been cropping up all over China, and both the Chinese and the English language press has been severely criticising the whole organisation…There is pressure being brought to bear from some unknown quarter to ensure that only certain groups get help…CNRRA has the power to help any group it sees fit, but just delays every other project…[T]here has been no decision on the whole project which we submitted, while other hospitals in which certain individuals have an interest is [*sic*] getting everything they ask for and at once.[47]

In March 1946, Wilfred Flowers was seconded from the BMS to the British Red Cross and St John War Organisation China Hospital Unit. He wrote home that 'All relief agencies have decided that they can count on UNRRA for nothing but promises and on CNRRA for nothing besides transportation.'[48] Harris complained of receiving

> A typical official letter from CNRRA in response to our appeal on behalf of the Choutsun hospital… It is suggested that 'when the repairs are completed' we should send a further request. By that time I don't think there will be any CNRRA left to whom to appeal.[49]

China's formidable task of aid and reconstruction was further undermined by the fact that, 'in 1946, when the program was well underway, one of the world's worst inflations was in progress.'[50] Between 1937 and 1945, average prices rose

---

[44] *Through Toil and Tribulation*, pp.176-77.
[45] *Through Toil and Tribulation*, pp. 176–77.
[46] BMSA, CH/63, Phillips to friends, 5 May 1946; CH/62/3, Madge to Williamson, 24 May 1946.
[47] BMSA, CH/62/3, Madge to Williamson, 25 July 1946.
[48] BMSA, CH/58, Flowers to Williamson, 14 March 1946.
[49] BMSA, CH/60, Harris to Williamson, 7 November 1946.
[50] Greene, 'UNNRA's Record in China', *Far Eastern Survey* 20.10, pp. 100–102 (p. 101).

2,000-fold.[51] This was the direct result of the GMD policy of printing money to make up the huge deficit between income and expenditure.

In occupied China, the position was complicated further by repeated changes in currency.[52] Each of the three governments that occupied China during this period – Nationalist, Japanese and Communist – issued its own currency, and there were changes even under the same government. The Japanese at first used bank notes from both Korea and Japan; later they issued notes from their central banks in North and Central China and Inner Mongolia. Between 1930 and 1948, the Communists issued approximately thirty local currencies, and used ten different paper currencies in the border regions and 'liberated' areas in 1948. As if this were not already complicated enough, some warlords issued their own currency and at times subsidiary currencies existed within Nationalist areas as well as the main national currency.

The gap between income and expenditure continued after the war and the government continued to deal with the problem by printing more bank notes, leading to soaring prices, labour unrest and increased wage demands, reduction in purchasing power and a contraction in industrial output.[53]

In February 1947, in a desperate attempt to stabilise the economy, wages were frozen and price controls put in place on staple goods, including rice and fuel. The situation did not improve. By the summer, 'people had to carry bundles of $10,000 notes, and traders had to assume that the packets they received had the correct contents'.[54]

The government continued to increase the volume of notes in circulation, which rose from 34 trillion yuan in December 1947 to 250 trillion yuan in June 1948. In the following six weeks it rose to between 600 and 700 trillion yuan.[55]

> Prices […] rose so fast that shopkeepers changed price tags several times a day. On June 25, and again on July 10, prices spurted about 30% during just one working day.[56]

In an attempt to solve the problem in August 1948 the government introduced the Gold Yuan reform. 2 billion notes of new gold yuan were printed. The government demanded that all old notes, the fabi, should be turned in and exchanged for the new currency, along with any privately held gold, silver or foreign currency. In order to promote the success of the new currency, the government simultaneously froze prices and prohibited wage increases. By 31

---

[51] Arthur N. Young, *China's Wartime Finance and Inflation, 1937–1945*, (Cambridge MA: Harvard East Asian Series, 1965), p. 304.
[52] Colin D. Campbell and Gordon C. Tullock, 'Hyperinflation in China, 1937–49' *Journal of Political Economy* 62.3, pp. 236–245 (p. 236).
[53] Pepper, 'The KMT-CCP Conflict 1945–1949'.
[54] Westad, *Decisive Encounters*, p. 89.
[55] Eastman, *Seeds of Destruction*, p. 173.
[56] Eastman, *Seeds of Destruction*, p. 175.

October it was evident that the attempt to curb inflation had failed, and many people had been ruined by the reforms.[57]

Missionaries were seriously affected by these developments. Soaring costs put many of their plans to rebuild mission properties beyond their reach and the continuing uncertainty made planning difficult. Where, and at what date, British allocations were changed into Chinese currency had an instant effect on the funds available to missionaries. Sometimes it was altogether impossible to access funds from abroad.

Colossal increases to the cost of living meant that missionaries had great difficulty making ends meet. Campbell and Tullock dispute 'the usual conclusion' that members of the middle class in post-war China were generally impoverished because they received fixed incomes. Instead, they argue:

> Persons with fixed nominal incomes become extremely rare. The wages of office workers and other employees almost always rose as fast as prices and even discounted anticipated inflation.[58]

Missionaries, paid from London but in local currency, on the basis of regulations last updated in 1939, were amongst that extremely rare group of middle-class workers whose incomes were not adjusted to take account of inflation. The BMS, faced with a £22,000 deficit for the year 1946–1947 (equivalent to more than £1 million in 2023), looked upon any requests for additional expenditure with disfavour.[59] In September 1946, the BMS finance subcommittee had a discussion about rising costs and exchange difficulties, particularly in Shandong, and noted that missionary living expenses in China at that time were 50–70% higher than they had been before the war. There was agreement that 'adjustment of allowances would probably be necessary before long'. The record of the meeting continued, 'The Committee noted this, but recommended no immediate action.'[60]

While overall financial concerns might have driven the finance subcommittee's reluctance to increase expenditure, their decisions were also characterised by a lack of understanding of, or empathy with, the real-world implications for missionary staff and their families and the challenges of currency exchange and rapid inflation. Two months later the finance subcommittee considered a moderately worded recommendation from Edward Phillips, senior BMS missionary in Jinan, that the BMS adopt a more flexible policy with regard to payments to married missionaries in China.[61] Under the existing system, 'the man missionary in the field' was paid his salary in yuan, and the household income – to cover expenditure in both China and the UK –

---

[57] Eastman, *Seeds of Destruction*, pp. 180–93.
[58] Campbell and Tullock, 'Hyperinflation', p. 241.
[59] BMSA, Finance Subcommittee Minutes, Vol. 53, 17 April 1947.
[60] BMSA, Finance Subcommittee Minutes, Vol. 52, 26 September 1946.
[61] BMSA, CH/63, Phillips to Williamson, 'Some notes on Maintenance Allowances, Home and Field', 4 November 1946.

was therefore subject to Chinese inflation, making it harder for the husband to provide a stable income for his family in the UK. Under Phillips's proposal, which was similar to policies already adopted by other missionary societies, the salary would be split into a portion paid in sterling (which would go direct to wives and children in the UK) and a portion paid in yuan, which would go to the missionaries in the field. This would ensure that the families at home were protected from the consequences of inflation in China. The portion paid to wives would be made up of an allowance based on the cost of living, plus a rent allowance. The husband would then be paid a maintenance allowance that could be adjusted according to the actual cost of kitchen expenses, fuel, light, water and wages, plus 45% to cover insurance, postage, toiletries, shoe repairs and other sundry expenses. Phillips suggested that such arrangements would be better adapted to the wildly fluctuating prices in China, noting – by way of illustration for those not directly affected by the current situation – that 'millet costs nearly twenty thousand times its pre-war price in dollars.' Again, the committee 'resolved not to vary the basis of support'.[62]

Changing exchange rates, as well as rising prices, had a significant impact on the missionary budget. Missionaries were dependent on money drawn in sterling for their own living expenses, for paying Chinese pastors, teachers, doctors, manual or domestic workers, and for all the other expenses arising from their work. Often, variations in exchange rates had benefitted foreigners working in China and, to keep on the right side of both the British and Chinese governments, the mission always conducted its financial affairs on the basis of the official government exchange rate. This put them at a serious disadvantage, however, at a time when there was a very large discrepancy between the official rate and the open-market rate, since their living costs were determined by the open-market rate.

In February 1947 Fred Russell wrote to the mission house pointing out that at the time the open-market rate was CNC$54,000 to £1 sterling, while until recently the government bank rate had been CNC$15,000 or $16,000 to £1. Russell requested 'discretionary powers' to deal with the situation. A cabled response authorised 'the Society's financial representatives in China to do the best they could in the emergency'.[63] They were warned, however, that this would probably involve selling drafts on the open market and that, on previous occasions, this had only been possible on the authority of the British ambassador. Despite the rapidly changing situation, the BMS felt obliged to keep very strictly within British government guidelines, while their staff members in China were left to deal with the difficult consequences of the costly delays.

The problem many missionaries faced in necessarily maintaining two homes, one for themselves in China and one for their families in the UK, continued to be a major source of difficulty as the monetary situation in China worsened. Several missionaries wrote, spelling out the difficulties, but the mission board

---

[62] BMSA, Finance Subcommittee Minutes, Vol. 53, 28 November 1946.
[63] BMSA, Finance Subcommittee Minutes, Vol. 53, 27 February 1947.

was reluctant to review its policies or to make exceptions. In October 1946, Hubert Spillett wrote, describing the impossible situation with which his family would be faced if he returned to China. After detailing the allowances for which his wife was eligible and deducting costs for rent and insurance, he pointed out that she would be left with a weekly sum of £4 4s 5d (equivalent to around £61 in 2023) to cover all expenses for herself and two children – an impossible situation he claimed, though one faced by many families of skilled workers at the time.

> I do not see how I myself can work effectively if I am harassed by the thoughts of the difficulties my family is facing…I can only place this matter in your hands and trust that some special assistance may be given us at this time.[64]

The finance committee had that very month increased allowances to missionaries based in India.[65] Nevertheless, the reply to Spillett from Raymond Williamson offered little comfort: 'I fear I cannot offer any more than is done for everybody at this stage…I think, therefore, that you had better plan on that basis.'[66]

Post-war austerity was due to a shortage of goods, not of money to spend.[67] Middle-class incomes had been squeezed and so this group probably felt hardship particularly acutely. To add to the difficulties, the winter of 1946–1947 was one of the most severe in living memory, its effects exacerbated by the national coal shortage. Freezing temperatures, snow and gales lasted from January until early April, and for three weeks in February domestic power supplies were cut daily for three hours in the morning and two hours in the afternoon.[68] Spillett was very conscious of the difficulties his wife and family faced trying to manage on what was seen to be the very small allowance the BMS offered for wives remaining at home. He wrote again, in January 1947, before the worst of the winter, asking that his request be reconsidered, but again he received no satisfaction.[69]

Meanwhile, the end of the war had not brought an end to suffering in China, and BMS missionaries resumed work there feeling that failing to do so would amount to abandoning their Chinese colleagues when they were needed most. Chinese church leaders, who had previously been funded by local church members, were forced to look once more for financial support from abroad.[70] At the same time, funds were urgently required for the reconstruction of mission institutions, and this necessitated close and often frustrating efforts to work with secular and international aid agencies.

---

[64] BMSA, CH/64/7/1, Spillett to Williamson, 7 October 1946.
[65] BMSA, Finance Subcommittee Minutes, Vol. 53, 24 October 1946.
[66] BMSA, CH/64/7/1, Williamson to Spillett, 20 November 1946.
[67] D. Kynaston, *Austerity Britain 1945–51* (London: Bloomsbury, 2008), p. 293.
[68] Catherine K. Schenk, 'Austerity and Boom', in Paul Johnson (ed), *Twentieth Century Britain: Economic, Social, and Cultural Change* (London: Longman, 1994), p. 306.
[69] BMSA, CH64/7/1, Spillett to Williamson, 14 January 1947.
[70] BMSA, CH/54, Allen to Williamson, 26 July 1947.

The Missionaries and Their Chinese Co-workers:
the Case of Wang Juntang[71]

Wang Juntang (Figure 13, *left*) was a prominent figure in the Baptist community in Qingzhou in the 1930s and 1940s. Discussion of his role exemplifies some of the relationships between missionaries and their closest Chinese colleagues during the civil war period. Comparing details of how he was seen by the foreign missionaries and how his activity appears in Communist records raises some interesting questions: on the one hand, how well the foreign missionaries really understood their Chinese colleagues and, on the other, how far historic records are open to reinterpretation.

Figure 13: Wang Juntang (l), Mrs Winifred Emmott and Wang's daughters (r)[72]

Bert Emmott, who describes Wang as 'an old and faithful steward of the Mission', tells us that Wang was educated at the mission school in Qingzhou.[73] At one point he was expelled, apparently because of his rebellious behaviour, but he was reinstated as a result of the pleas of his Christian mother. He went on to have a successful school career and then qualified in law. He served variously as magistrate, secretary to the Young Men's Christian Association (YMCA), instructor in Chinese classics and, later, headteacher at the mission school and business manager at the mission hospital. He was also one of the teachers at the

---

[71] Extracts from this section were published previously, edited by Elisabeth Okasha, as Audrey Salters, 'Portrait of a Twentieth-Century Chinese Christian in Shandong', *Baptist Quarterly*, 2019, pp. 69–81.
[72] From the private collection of Joan Wells, née Emmott. The picture of Wang is not labeled in Mrs Wells's collection, but she is very confident that it is Wang. The other picture identifies its subjects on the back.
[73] BMSA, CH/58, H. A. Emmott, *China Memories*, unpublished memoir.

Bible school for trainee pastors. He was prominent in the work of the Shantung [Shandong] Baptist Union (SBU) and for a while acted as its vice president.

Wang Juntang had a close and long-standing relationship with the BMS missionaries in Shandong, and played an important part in the leadership and maintenance of the institutions founded by them. During this time, he also introduced the foreign missionaries to Chinese culture, the Chinese classics and Chinese art, and demonstrated his belief that Christianity was not incompatible with his national heritage.

The Shandong missionaries held Wang in high regard. Tom Allen, for example, showed his personal regard for Wang by including him among a number of Chinese friends who were guests at his wedding in Jinan in April 1934.[74] In other personal papers it is apparent that when Wang experienced a tragedy in his family life, he was supported by missionary colleagues, who felt his loss keenly. In 1941, his eighteen-year-old daughter (pictured on the right in Figure 13) died of rapid progressive tuberculosis in the BMS hospital in Zhoucun. Gwyneth Still, whose husband had been the doctor in attendance, wrote home:

> I know there are plenty of sad things now, but we all felt this very much…The father [Wang] is such a fine man and makes no complaints. He just went out of his way to express his gratitude for what was done for his daughter.[75]

In February 1946, Wang had been one of the three leading members of the Shandong Baptist community who met with Fred Drake to discuss the role of the mission in Shandong after the war.[76] There are many references to him in missionary correspondence and in the personal memoirs and family letters written by missionaries. As noted above, he features in the unpublished memoirs of Emmott and Allen, as well as in Still's diary and in the published letters of Nancy Bywaters. By piecing together these accounts, and adding other details that appear in official sources, an interesting picture emerges of this man and his relationships with his foreign colleagues, a picture that also throws some light on the Chinese Christian community in Shandong in the troubled period immediately following the end of the Japanese occupation.

The personal regard in which Wang was held by his missionary colleagues is apparent. Writing to his children at boarding school in England, Allen described Wang as:

> a friend of the family, […] a fine type of Chinese Christian, well read in old Chinese literature, and a lover of Chinese painting…He was my teacher, and he used to teach me Chinese customs and ways.[77]

---

[74] Private collection of Margaret Bennett, Allen, letter to Elizabeth.

[75] Private collection of Audrey Salters, Still to parents, 13 May 1941.

[76] BMSA, CH/57, Drake to Chesterman, 26 February 1946.

[77] Private collection of Margaret Bennett, Allen, letters to Elizabeth, Margaret and Phillip 1946–1948.

It is worth noting in passing here the value that Allen placed on familiarising himself with Chinese 'customs and ways'. This appears to have been typical of BMS missionaries in Shandong. Drake, in particular, was respected for his knowledge of Chinese culture and classics, in contrast to the 'arrogant' 'dismissal of Chinese beliefs and the culture' with which missionaries were often charged.[78]

Appreciative descriptions of Wang's central position in the work of the church and support of the foreigners also appear in formal missionary records. In early 1942, when British and American missionaries in Shandong found themselves placed under house arrest by the Japanese and without cash, Wang was one of two Qingzhou Christians who lent substantial sums from their own savings to provide the foreigners with the means of survival. Four years elapsed before it was possible to repay these loans, and meantime there had been multiple currency changes and rampant inflation, which created mathematical puzzles – and ethical dilemmas – for the missionary staff in deciding the most equitable method of repayment. It was not until November 1946 that the Shandong missionaries were able to meet to arrange repayment, when they agreed that the loans should be refunded 'at the rate of exchange prevailing when the money was used'.[79]

On his return to China after the war, Raymond Williamson described Wang's important contribution during the Japanese occupation: 'Mr Wang Chun T'ang [Wang Juntang], an old and faithful steward of the Mission, with characteristic tact and diplomacy managed for a long time to keep the flag flying, through periods of Japanese and Communist occupation.'[80]

However, not all references to Wang were positive. It seems that his strong personality sometimes led to disagreements with other Chinese church leaders. Describing tensions concerning the Qingzhou Bible school in early 1947, there is a reference to discontent among his Chinese colleagues regarding his share in the curriculum. Harris and one other missionary were the only foreigners present at a meeting of the Shandong union executive when the matter was raised. Harris recalled, 'There was strong feeling as to the necessity for the Bible School being moved back [from Qingzhou] to Choutsun [Zhoucun] as soon as possible. I find their [*sic*] is dissatisfaction with the curriculum, especially with the share that Mr Wang Chun T'ang has had in it'.[81] It is not clear whether it was the content or the organisation of the curriculum that gave rise to this dissatisfaction.

The members of the Chinese Baptist church had maintained their work in Qingzhou throughout the Japanese occupation. Despite the intense hostilities between Nationalist and Communist forces immediately afterwards, Wang's leadership skills were instrumental in ensuring that the church, school and hospital, as well as a daily soup kitchen, were in operation when the first foreign missionaries, Bert Emmott and his wife Winifred, returned to Qingzhou at the

---

[78] Bickers, 'Changing British Attitudes', p. 46.
[79] BMSA, CH/57, Minutes of Shantung Conference, 4 November 1946.
[80] Williamson, *Christian Challenge*, p. 35.
[81] BMSA, CH/60, Harris to Williamson, 27 February 1947.

end of 1946. In January 1947, Mrs Emmott fell seriously ill and they called for the help of Nancy Bywaters, newly qualified as a doctor and a recent recruit to the mission, who had arrived in China only a few weeks earlier.[82] Bywaters was in Qingzhou when, on 23 February, the Communists entered under cover of darkness and recaptured the city.[83]

In the weeks that followed, Bywaters had several encounters with Communist soldiers and their civilian leaders as they searched mission premises, looking for billets, inspecting for signs of military involvement, or simply out of curiosity. Her comments reveal the discomfort she felt, as a newcomer to China, at this unaccustomed invasion of her privacy:

> 12 March 1947: I had just finished my bath (luckily) when another troop of soldiers invaded us again and tramped all over the house. When they had satisfied their curiosity most of them departed, but two stayed talking.

> 13 March 1947: On our return from a walk we found the young Communist soldier who visited us yesterday. He had made himself quite at home in our absence and washed his round yellow cap in the kitchen and hung it in the front garden to dry. He talked to Mr Emmott solidly all through dinner, mostly politics apparently.

> 16 March 1947: This afternoon a crowd of forty to fifty soldiers came in and roamed the house and garden, but only for a few minutes.[84]

On 25 April 1947, the missionaries invited one of the Communist leaders in the city, Mr Li, to an evening meal, along with Wang Juntang and two other leading members of the church. It appeared that Wang had first encountered Li when he and other members of the hospital staff had been 'carried off by the Communists' at the end of an earlier period of occupation during 1946 in one of their raids to obtain skilled medical help to treat their wounded.[85] Bywaters noted in her account of the evening:

> But [Wang Juntang] bears [Li] no personal ill-will, though, like all the other Chinese I have met here, he has no room for the Communists as a party. It was interesting to listen to the friendly conversation, knowing what these three Chinese really think about the Communists![86]

Could Bywaters, who had been in China less than five months and at that time spoke virtually no Chinese, truly know 'what these three Chinese really think'? This seems a little improbable, particularly at a time of civil war when political allegiances were sensitive and personal relationships distorted by political and military concerns. It seems likely that she reached this conclusion on the basis of discussions with other missionaries who had been in China for longer; a good

---

[82] G. E. Woods, *Life in China: From the Letters of Nancy Bywaters* (Braunton: Merlin Books, 1992), p. 24.

[83] Zibo City archives: http://www.zbsq.gov.cn/bin/mse.exe accessed 20 October 2011.

[84] Woods, *Life in China*, pp. 33 and 35.

[85] BMSA, China Subcommittee Minutes, Vol. 11, 22 October 1946.

[86] Woods, *Life in China*, p. 44.

example of what Bickers describes as the habitual tendency of the British in China to pick up their knowledge of local conditions not from their own observations, or from the Chinese people themselves, but from the British colleagues who had preceded them.[87]

By 1946, a key objective for many Chinese was to attain peace. Ideological issues had become blurred by regional variations in the performance of the main political parties. 'Several scholars, both Chinese and foreign,' Westad observes, 'have recently negated the nationalism versus socialism debate by describing the purpose of the great majority of peasants as reactive – that is, as aiming at avoiding warfare and surviving its immediate consequences, rather than consciously committing themselves to the revolutionary cause.'[88]

The CCP had a base in Shandong since the early 1930s and large numbers of the local population had been recruited to the Communist guerrilla units during the war against Japan.[89] As in other civil wars, the issues were not simple, personal loyalties were strained, and families and friendships divided. In this context, the friendly interaction between the three Qingzhou Christians and the leader of the local Communist forces could be subject to a wide range of interpretations of which Bywaters and her foreign colleagues were evidently unaware.

The apparently relaxed interaction between the Communist leader Li, the three Qingzhou Christians and the foreign missionaries during their social gathering in late April 1947 belied conditions elsewhere in the province. In west Shandong in early summer, a CCP campaign of 'terror and radical reform' against rich and middle-rank peasants had led to an 'increasingly frenzied atmosphere'. 'In one county, Sanghe, more than one thousand were beaten to death.'[90] By early June, Emmott, then senior missionary in Qingzhou, was greatly exercised as to whether he should move to Jinan, where there was a substantial foreign presence. He stayed, he wrote, with a view to secure ownership of mission property in the face of persistent attempts by the Communists to appropriate it.[91] He enlisted Wang's help in his attempt to prevent its seizure.

> I [...] advanced every reason I could think of (and WCT could think of) but reason is powerless against weapons…Just imagine WCT being unable to advance reasons himself and having to depend on me to express them! But such is the position.[92]

Emmott's informal reference to Wang using only his initials ('WCT' represents the Wade-Giles Romanisation, Wang Chun T'ang) is a measure of the

---

[87] Bickers, 'Changing British Attitudes', p. 72.
[88] Westad, *Decisive Encounters*, p. 5.
[89] For a discussion of the tensions between the indigenous guerrilla units and the main Eighth Route Army troops during the war against Japan, see Elise A. DeVido, 'The Survival of the Shandong Base Area, 1937–1943', pp. 173–88.
[90] Westad, *Decisive Encounters*, p. 133.
[91] BMSA, CH/58, Emmott to Williamson, 18 June 1947.
[92] BMSA, CH/58, Emmott to Williamson, 18 June 1947.

closeness the mission staff felt to their Chinese colleague, who had worked with them over many years. Emmott took Wang's inability to argue the case for the mission as an indication of the obduracy with which they were faced in their dealings with the Communist military. In another letter Emmott mentioned Wang when describing the Communist land reform policy, which was being implemented in the area at the time. He wrote that Wang owned twenty *mu* (around 1.3 hectares) of which eighteen (1 hectare) were taken. '[Wang's] comment, when told of what had happened was "Let them have the lot."'[93] Emmott assumed that here Wang was using irony based on his despair.

Another incident occurred concerning Wang Juntang during the same disturbed period and is recorded in Ronald Still's diary. On 25 June 1947, when the Communists were about to evacuate the town in yet another turnover, 'about thirty to forty Communists surrounded the hospital and carried off nearly the whole of the hospital staff', leaving behind only two male nurses and the hospital evangelist.[94] It is likely that the abduction of the Qingzhou medical staff was connected with a major People's Liberation Army (PLA) offensive in late June under General Liu Bocheng (刘伯承) that resulted in the loss of 80,000 GMD and 10,000 PLA troops, constituting 'a hell of carnage and destruction'.[95] Wang's name heads Still's list of hospital staff thus abducted.

> They were carried westwards into the mountains where the communists are trying to consolidate their power, and the intention no doubt is to try to make them render medical service to their forces. Destination unknown.[96]

Still recorded that he and Drake sent a statement in Chinese to General Y. W. Wang, (王耀武; Wang Yaowu) Commander in Chief of the Nationalist forces operating from Jinan, 'to enlist assistance to clear the fifteen charges of collaboration' and a report to 'the Governor, S. Y. Ho [何思源; He Siyuan]'.[97] In a further urgent effort to rescue the missing staff members, Drake and Still met with the United States colonels at the headquarters of the executive team in Jinan and with Colonel Huang, the Communist member of the team, hoping for American or Communist help in their recovery. Colonel Huang indicated that he himself was 'virtually a prisoner in Jinan', which was then under Nationalist control, and had no means of communication with Communist headquarters at Linyi (黄永胜). 'But,' wrote Still in his diary,

> [Huang] listened very sympathetically to the facts, said that persons would not be maltreated, gave details about Communist commands in the area and promised to

---

[93] BMSA, CH/58, Emmott to Williamson, 3 July 1947.
[94] Private collection of Audrey Salters, Still, diary entry, 25 June 1947.
[95] Westad, *Decisive Encounters*, p. 169.
[96] Private collection of Audrey Salters, Still, diary entry, 25 June 1947.
[97] Private collection of Audrey Salters, Still, diary entry, 3 July 1947. See David D. Buck, *Urban Change in China: Politics and Development in Tsinan, Shantung, 1890–1949* (Madison: University of Wisconsin Press, 1978), p. 195.

send message to Peking to be forwarded to Shantung [Shandong] Communist headquarters at Lin-i [Linyi].[98]

It is not clear from the records how long the group was held but, in his memoir, Emmott describes them as having been 'held in captivity several months'. They eventually returned to their posts in the hospital unharmed.[99]

Communist forces left Qingzhou on 4 August 1947, and Nationalists re-entered the next day. Emmott, who had temporarily relocated to Jinan during the latter part of the Communist occupation, returned on 9 August.[100] All BMS premises were taken over by the incoming Nationalists, who used the mission school buildings as their military headquarters. Wang Juntang was himself living on the school premises and there, wrote Emmott,

> [Wang was] in constant contact with the chief officers. He talks religion with them and has even tackled the General about his vices! The General has a chat with him nearly every day. Wang's learning is an attraction.[101]

Wang clearly showed an impressive capacity to endear himself to those in positions of power, the foreign missionaries, the Communist occupying forces and the GMD leadership.

As already indicated, both parties in the civil war were quick to deal savagely with anyone who appeared to favour their opponents, and Wang's ability to sustain friendly relationships with all sides was surely unusual. Does this reflect his willingness to compromise in the interests of his own or other people's safety, or his skills as a consummate politician?

A new twist to his story emerged forty-five years later, in the history written in 1992 to commemorate the centenary of the Qingzhou hospital. The history acknowledges the hospital's roots in the work of the BMS doctor who led it from its beginnings in 1892 to a fifty-bed hospital with modern theatre and X-ray apparatus in 1928. It makes no mention, however, of Jing Yihui, the Chinese doctor who kept the hospital going, almost single-handedly, through the years of Japanese occupation from 1937 to 1945, and who received much honourable mention in the Baptist archive:

> Imprisoned as he was at times, Dr Ching [Jing] emerged from captivity during the day to administer the affairs of the hospital and returned to his prison at night. He has ministered to Japanese and Communists as well as to the local Chinese population. He has managed to secure the necessary finances from successive and different administrative authorities in the city. The work of Dr Ching and his loyal staff of nurses, is deserving of the highest praise.[102]

---

[98] Private collection of Audrey Salters, Still, diary entry, 5 July 1947.
[99] BMSA, CH/58, Emmott, *China Memories*.
[100] BMSA, CH/58, Emmott to Williamson, 16 August 1947.
[101] BMSA, CH/58, Emmott to Williamson, 16 August 1947.
[102] Williamson, *Christian Challenge*, p. 35.

Another man, who does not appear at all in the Baptist archive, is named as president of the hospital from 1915 to 1946. Wang Juntang is named as president from 1946 to 1947.[103] Under the CCP regime Jing was obliterated from the hospital records, but Wang's name was preserved. Does this mean that Wang's name was one that could be respected in the Communist historiography? And, if so, why?

On 20 September 2011, in response to a general request for information about the history of the hospital, a message was received from Dr Pan Jingnian (潘靖年), assistant president of the modern institution that succeeded the BMS hospital. The message makes reference to Wang's 'abduction' in 1947, but presents it in very different terms to the contemporary missionary accounts:

自 1947 年 7 月王均堂带领部分医务人员随部队转移 [In July 1947 Wang Juntang brought some staff members from the hospital to follow the troops.][104]

Despite Drake and Still's communications on Wang's behalf with the commander of the Nationalist military and with Nationalist Governor He Siyuan, it seems that this did not prevent Wang from being subsequently regarded with favour by the Communist hierarchy.

A much fuller history of the hospital was published in 2012.[105] This time, both Jing and Wang are included.[106] Jing's role as head of the hospital, his specialist skills in ophthalmology and his courage in maintaining the hospital during the Japanese occupation are all recorded. His entry ends by relating that, in 1966, he was 'persecuted to death' but, after the Cultural Revolution, he was 'rehabilitated'.[107] Being 'rehabilitated' in this context means that his reputation was restored to honour, despite the fact that he had been found guilty of being

---

[103] Compilation of Committee Records of Weifang City Yidu Central Hospital (潍坊市益都中心醫院志) 編纂委員會, ed., *Shandong Weifangshi Yidu Zhongxin Yiyuan Zhi (1892–1992)* (山東潍坊市益都中心醫院志(1892-1992)) (Records of Shandong Weifang City Yidu Central Hospital (1892-1992)). (Qingzhou 青州: Privately published, 1992), in unnumbered preliminary pages.

[104] '自 1947 年 7 月王均堂带领部分医务人员随部队转移' *(Si 1947 nian 7 yue Wang Juntang dai ling bu fen yi wu ren yuan sui bu dui zhuan yi)*, emailed message from Pan Jingnian (潘靖年), Assistant President of Yidu Central Hospital to Audrey Salters, in September 2011, (trans. Han Jie, 2011).

[105] Compilation of Committee Records of Weifang City Yidu Central Hospital (潍坊市益都中心醫院志) 編纂委員會, ed., *Weifangshi Yidu Zhongxin Yiyuan Zhi (1882–2012)* (潍坊市益都中心醫院志 (1882)2012)) (Records of Weifang City Yidu Central Hospital (1882–2012)), (Shandong 山東: Renmin Chubanshe 人民出版社, 2012).

[106] Compilation of Committee Records of Weifang City Yidu Central Hospital, p. 795.

[107] Compilation of Committee of Records Weifang City Yidu Central Hospital. The original text reads:
1946 年 6 月, 景以惠應邀去四川西昌專區醫院任院長。1951 年西昌解放後, 任醫院外科主任。1964 年, 任西昌衛校教務主任。1966 年, 受迫害致死。"文化大革命"後, 得以平反昭雪。 (*1946 nian 6 yue, Jing yi hui ying yao qu si chuan xi chang zhuan qu yi yuan ren yuan zhang. 1951 nian xi chang jie fang hou ren yi yuan wai ke zhu ren. 1964 nian, ren xi chang wei xiao jiao wu zhu ren. 1966 nian, shou po hai zhi si wen hua da ge ming hou de yi ping fan zhao xue.*)

'an enemy of the State', and lost his life, either in captivity or during an incident of mass violence, in the Cultural Revolution.

Wang's entry in the 2012 history records, unusually, that he was a Christian (基督教; *ji du jiao*), a detail that does not appear against any other names in the hospital record. It notes his posts within the former BMS school and hospital, without acknowledging the foreign origins of these institutions. It gives particular emphasis to the support he gave to the PLA Eastern China Field Army in June 1946 and again in June 1947, when he is described as having provided accommodation and medical and nursing care for injured PLA soldiers. The history also notes that when the PLA moved out of Qingzhou after the battle of Linqu (临胸) in late July 1947, Wang accompanied the soldiers with a group of hospital staff. [108] This was the event that Still described in his diary as 'kidnapping'. Wang retained his credentials with the CCP after the establishment of the People's Republic of China (PRC): he became the representative of the first provincial People's Congress of Shandong, a member of the city committee of the Chinese People's Political Consultative Conference (CPPCC) of Jinan, and the deputy director of the Shandong provincial committee of the Three-Self Patriotic Movement of the Protestant Church (about which there is more in Chapter Six).

This new information calls for a fresh analysis of some of Wang's earlier behaviour, including his friendly interaction with the Communist Li, when Li was invited to a meal with BMS staff in Qingzhou (pages 163–4). Wang's failure to find words to argue the case for the retention of mission property by the foreigners also assumes possible new meanings. Might the fact that Wang uncharacteristically allowed Emmott to do the talking suggest that he preferred not to be identified as an opponent of Communist goals? And what did Wang really mean when, deprived of his eighteen *mu* of land, he declared, 'Let them have the lot'?[109] Was it irony as Emmott interpreted it, or was he using this occasion to signal his sympathy for the Communist cause?

As the presence of British missionaries was understood to be generally unwelcome to the CCP, Chinese Christians found themselves in a difficult situation. Their future would depend on whatever government took charge of the country at the close of the civil war, while the idealism and emerging competence of the Communists had a strong attraction for anyone looking for peace. It is not unreasonable to suppose that they had won Wang's allegiance, while at the same time he felt no obligation to abandon his foreign friends. Could it be that Wang, despite longstanding relationships with several foreign missionaries, had not felt able to let them know that he had voluntarily taken the hospital staff to work for the PLA? Wang was a Christian, but also Chinese with a commitment to the country and its future that the missionaries, even with the best of intentions, could not share. In this respect, there would always be a gap between missionary and Chinese outlook that could not be bridged. Emmott's daughter, who as a

---

[108] Compilation of Committee Records of Weifang City Yidu Central Hospital.
[109] BMSA, CH/58, Emmott to Williamson, 3 July 1947.

teenager knew Wang and his family, believed with hindsight that 'his chief loyalty would be to his fellow Chinese, and he would do what was needed to care for those in need – which surely is a Christian principle, isn't it?'[110]

Whatever the truth of that incident, there is evidence that Wang did not cut his links with the missionaries. As an apparent token of affection and esteem, when the time came for Still to leave China in late August 1948, Wang presented him with two fine scrolls from his cherished collection of Chinese paintings.[111] And BMS missionaries continued to refer to Wang with warmth and admiration long after they departed from Shandong.[112]

We do not know where the truth lies. Should Pan Jingnian's message and the two published accounts of the history of the hospital be read predominantly as a confirmation of the power of history used as a weapon of the state? Watson writes of 'situations where alternative understandings of the past are tantamount to treason', and the early years of the PRC are known to have created such a situation.[113] Wang's case raises other broad questions about what else of the subtext of the events of these years is missing from the missionary archive and makes clear how much the history of the period is open to reinterpretation.

Rebuilding the Hospital in Xi'an: the Tilehouse Street Gift

At the end of the Second World War, the members of Tilehouse Street Baptist church in Hitchin raised almost £2,700 (equivalent to around £150,000 today), which they decided to give to the BMS in memory of eight members of their congregation who had been killed during the war, and as a thanksgiving for seventy-seven members who had returned safely.[114] Both the church members and the mission board in London felt that such a significant gift should not be absorbed into general funds but should be dedicated to a particular project.[115] One of the church members, Bill Upchurch, was working with the BMS in Shaanxi at the time, and they decided that it would be appropriate to give the money to the BMS hospital in Xi'an, the Jenkins Robertson Memorial Hospital, which had been badly damaged by bombing in 1939.

After the bombing, the hospital had continued to provide outpatient and inpatient services in improvised premises in the suburbs of Xi'an until the end of the war with Japan.[116] Many of the missionaries in Shaanxi left China for furlough immediately after the war, but two missionary doctors remained

---

[110] Personal letter from Joan Wells to Audrey Salters, 24 October 2014.

[111] Personal recollection of Audrey Salters.

[112] See Emmott's memoirs and the letters of T. W. Allen.

[113] Rubie Watson (ed), *Memory, History and Opposition under State Socialism* (Santante: School of American Research Press, 1994) p. 9, cited in Ching Kwan Lee and Guobin Yang (eds), *Re-envisioning the Chinese Revolution: The Politics and Poetics of Collective Memories in Reform China* (Stanford: Stanford University Press, 2007), p. 4.

[114] BMSA, China Subcommittee Minutes, Vol.11, 20 October 1948.

[115] BMSA, CH/21, Secretariat Papers, 1938–1946, Russell to Williamson, 12 December 1943.

[116] *Through Toil and Tribulation*, pp. 179–86.

working in the hospital. Local income had been maintained and, despite inflation, the hospital remained self-supporting and continued offering free treatment to patients who were unable to pay.[117] The departing Americans of the 14th US Air Force, stationed in Xi'an since 1942, had passed on a quantity of valuable drugs, and fresh supplies of hospital linen were purchased with funds contributed by the British Red Cross.[118] By the end of 1946, however, the hospital was having to dig into savings to get through the winter months, and was also experiencing shortages of equipment.[119]

BMS plans for the development of the hospital were held in abeyance until the return of the senior foreign doctor Menzies Clow from war service. The Communist presence in Shaanxi was strong and by November 1947 when Clow returned, Xi'an was cut off from Shanghai except by air or by the circuitous road from Chongqing. On his arrival, Clow promptly sent home a report on the hospital and his plans for it.[120] Income from paying patients had increased by about 8% during the previous year, but the price of wheat had risen sixteen times and the wage bill had risen ten times to roughly £500 monthly (£25,000 today).

> Were it not for very generous grants of drugs and equipment from the Red Cross I do not think we could carry on. As it is we have to sell those drugs to those who can pay to maintain the hospital.[121]

Encouragingly, Clow reported an increase in hospital staff, including graduate doctors and medical students in training. This was in keeping with the recommendations made to Clement Chesterman by P. Z. King, Director of the Chinese National Health Administration, who suggested that mission hospitals should be used as training institutions for doctors, nurses and midwives, and as centres for preventive medicine. 'I can assure you,' King had advised, 'that the health authorities in China will give full support and cooperation to the medical missionaries in carrying out these programmes.'[122]

The Nationalist government had pledged to provide assistance to help restart mission hospitals after the war, and had indicated that it hoped the missionary societies would continue to staff and maintain as many hospitals as before the war (approximately half the total number of hospitals in China at the time).[123] Mitter argues this pledge was driven by the otherwise insuperable gulf between the government's plans for a national system of health care and the almost total

---

[117] BMSA, CH/66, Jenkins Robertson Memorial Hospital, Annual Medical Report, 1946.
[118] BMSA, CH/65, Stockley to friends, April 1946.
[119] BMSA, CH/66, Henderson Smith to Chesterman, 30 December 1946.
[120] BMSA, CH/56, Clow to Williamson, 9 December 1947.
[121] BMSA, CH/56, Clow to Williamson, 9 December 1947.
[122] BMSA, CH/56, Chesterman to Clow, 14 October 1947.
[123] United Nations Organization Archives, New York, S-0528-0053 (China Weekly Reports, 1944–5), cited in Mitter, 'Imperialism', p 65; Yip Ka-Che, *Health and National Reconstruction in Nationalist China: The Development of Modern Health Services 1928–1937* (Ann Arbor MI: Association for Asian Studies, Inc., 1995), p. 54.

absence of financial resources at its disposal in the post-war era.[124] He notes the 'profundity' of Chiang Kai-shek's anti-imperialism, and suggests that

> To propose the delegation of such important elements of a health system to these transnational entities [the Christian missions], whose ultimate control lay beyond the power of a government in Nanjing, was a small but real cession of sovereignty in a nationalist time.[125]

Whatever conflicting influences prompted Chiang's invitation to missionary organisations to cooperate with national health provision, it is clear from the BMS archive that cooperation at an informal level was in place well before the end of the war in 1945. We saw in Chapter Three the involvement of the BMS with Madame Chiang in spearheading the movement to eradicate opium addiction by establishing clinics for addicts in 1934, as part of the New Life Movement.

Nationalist government assistance to mission hospitals in its post-war provision was a source of great encouragement to the missionary societies. Ronald Still was quick to claim the resources on offer when he began devising ways and means to rebuild the war-damaged fabric of the Foster Hospital, Zhoucun.

> I was informed by Dr Han Li-min (a graduate and former staff member of Cheeloo [Qilu] Medical School, and now in the National Health Administration in Nanking) that the Provincial Health Departments had funds available for the repair of Mission hospitals. I therefore made an appeal on behalf of the Foster Hospital to Dr Wang Fu-I, Director of the Shantung [Shandong] P[rovincial] H[ealth] D[epartment]. He told me that he had $400 million at his disposal for the whole Province, of which he had instructions to devote $40 million to Mission Hospitals, and of this sum he has given us $25 million for the Foster Hospital.
>
> Dr Wang (who is also a Cheeloo graduate) is concurrently Medical Director of CNRRA for the Province.[126]

Still's references to these two prominent officials in the National Health Administration who had received their medical education at Qilu University is an indication of the contribution missionary societies had made to the training of Chinese practitioners in Western medicine. Mitter suggests it was China's 'desperate' poverty and a 'lack of funding' that prompted the Nationalist government to turn to missionary societies for help. Another factor, however, was undoubtedly the expertise that the mission hospitals could provide, and the regard in which this expertise was held by many of those in positions of authority in the National Health Administration. In 1947, the use being made of the Jenkins-Robertson Memorial hospital in Xi'an for training purposes is one illustration of this.

---

[124] Mitter, 'Imperialism', pp. 61–65.
[125] Mitter, 'Imperialism', pp. 61 and 65.
[126] BMSA, CH/65, Still to Chesterman, 14 January 1947.

As well as advising the mission board of this important training activity, Clow's letter included the proposal that the hospital should be rebuilt in the city, rather than in its existing position in the suburb. If the hospital remained in the suburb, it would be less attractive to Chinese staff:

> Our Chinese staff are unanimous in wanting to move back…If we are to have a hospital which we can hand over to our Chinese colleagues, it must be in the city.[127]

Clow's comment reflects his expectation that the hospital would be transferred to Chinese management in the not-too-distant future. He went on to say that he considered a hospital staffed predominantly by foreigners 'a retrograde step'. He also argued that a central location would be more convenient for patients, which would ensure that outpatient numbers were maintained. As well as rebuilding the hospital within Xi'an's city walls, Clow was keen to build a new outpatient block, but considered this impossible because of the costs involved and the difficulty in obtaining building materials. The estimated cost for the new inpatient facilities, which included a flour mill, beancurd mill, carpenter's shop and extensive new residential accommodation for staff members, came in at £7,200 (equivalent to around £360,000 today). Clow requested £6,000 from BMS headquarters in London and asked for a cabled response to enable building work to begin immediately.[128]

Getting money into and around China presented problems during this period, but British sterling regulations meant there were also problems getting it out of the UK. In 1948, British missionary societies had been faced with a 25% cut in the amounts they were allowed to send overseas.[129] Clow suggested that the £6,000 might be transferred by arrangement with friends who worked with the Shell company in Xi'an, and that this could be done legally but without sacrificing part of the society's precious allocation of funds to China. The response from London illustrates the importance that the missionary societies placed on working strictly in accordance with British government policy:

> Unfortunately we are all scared of doing something which might eventually turn out to be irregular and would cause not only a scandal but prejudice future relationships with the Treasury. Mr Ernest Brown, who still feels heavy responsibility for our country resting on his shoulders, is very adamant about being quite above board, and he proposes to see the Treasury officials and perhaps Sir Stafford Cripps again…I am awfully sorry about this delay.[130]

Clow responded firmly to the suggestion that the issue should be taken up with the Treasury: 'I think the matter should be dropped. I had no intention of doing anything contrary to the Government's financial policy', and agreed that

---

[127] BMSA, CH/56, Clow to Williamson, 9 December 1947.
[128] BMSA, CH/56, Clow to Williamson, 9 December 1947.
[129] BMSA, Finance Subcommittee Minute Book No. 53, 18 December 1947, and 26 February 1948.
[130] BMSA, CH/56, Chesterman to Clow, 31 March 1948.

any money sent out should come through all the regular official channels.[131] It was considered irresponsible to ignore the advice of the society's treasurer Ernest Brown, whose presence on the BMS General Committee was an indication of the close links the society had with political and social elites. First elected to Parliament in 1923, Brown was 'one of a considerable number of Baptists who have sat in twentieth-century parliaments'.[132] He served as leader of the National Liberal Party during the war years, including as Minister for Health between 1941 and 1943, but lost his seat in the general election of 1945. In addition to his role as treasurer of the BMS – a role he held from 1946 until 1960 – and many other important contributions to the work of the Baptist denomination, he was President of the Baptist Union, 1948–1949.

The Home Committee included a further request in their letter:

> The Building and Equipment Committee […] were interested in the ground plan for the out-patient block. As we have a few professional men on it they wanted an elevation also. I feel this is quite unnecessary, but if we have these Committees then we must display the window dressing to them. If therefore you have time…[133]

The pressures under which Clow was working, and the terrible impact that inflation was having on mission budgets in China, must have meant that this request for 'window dressing' came as an irritant, if not a serious blow. Missionaries were familiar with the concept of 'window dressing'. It was expected that articles for missionary magazines, and talks to church groups by missionaries on deputation, would present their narratives in such a way as to engage the sympathies – and open the purses – of church members in the UK. It was spelt out in the instructions in the BMS manual that each mission station's annual report should contain 'interesting incidents'.[134] It is an indication of the care with which missionaries on the field attended to the views of the church constituency at home, and the wishes of the home committees, that Clow did not demur and promptly complied with the request for elevation plans, which he had drawn up by a local architect.[135]

Clow had raised money for the work on the in-patient unit through a local subscription list, to which the provincial governor contributed CNC$30,000,000 (approximately £30 at the time, or £1,500 today), and a substantial grant was secured from the China Relief Mission of the American State Department. Unfortunately, soaring inflation meant that the original grant from the China Relief Mission, paid in CNC$ and supposed to represent the sum of US$16,000 (nearly £175,000 today), had lost half its value by the time it was received by BMS staff in Xi'an a month later.[136] Meanwhile, when exploring means to

---

[131] BMSA, CH/56, Clow to Williamson, 12 April 1948.
[132] David W. Bebbington, 'Baptist Members of Parliament in the 20th Century', *Baptist Quarterly* 29.2 (April 1981), pp. 252–87.
[133] BMSA, CH/56, Chesterman to Clow, 31 March 1948.
[134] *Manual*, paragraph 46.
[135] BMSA, CH/56, Clow to Williamson, 12 April 1948.
[136] BMSA, CH/56, Clow to Williamson, 12 April 1948.

finance the rebuilding of the inpatient block, Chesterman had written to Clow about the gift from the Tilehouse Street congregation, suggesting that it should be retained 'for something more definite than rehabilitation and removal'.[137] By May it had been agreed that the money should be used for building the new outpatient block, 'but we do not quite see how we can get the £2,500 to you as there is no reply yet from our application to the Treasury for extra capital grants.'[138]

Building work proceeded with despatch: the move to the rebuilt hospital took place early in August 1948, and the new outpatient department was opened a few weeks later. The hospital bed total was now 120, and '[a]s if to meet this need a consignment of actual iron beds, theatre trolleys, enamelware and dressings arrived for us from Chungking on 28 August'.[139] Outpatients in the new unit numbered 900 daily. Free treatment was given regularly to one in three of these patients, who were unable to pay for the services they received.

The successful completion of the new buildings would have been a significant achievement at any time, but was all the more remarkable when the economic situation in China was worsening on a daily basis, and the country seemed to be 'plunging toward utter collapse'.[140] The inflationary spiral reached grotesque levels during the spring and summer months of 1948, the very time the hospital building programme was taking place. The government's introduction of price controls in August 1948, alongside the Gold Yuan reform, made matters worse. In the newly rehabilitated and extended hospital, price controls affected hospital finances very badly, curtailing income without significantly reducing expenditure. As Clow reflected:

> We were very busy at the time and without the controls should have been able to lay aside a balance to carry us over the winter. Not only was this not possible but the large numbers of patients depleted our stock without improving our income.[141]

Meanwhile, the military and political situation was changing rapidly. In February, it was widely reported that a Swedish woman missionary had been beaten to death by Communists in south Shanxi, which underlined the very real dangers for missionaries remaining in China.[142]

The deep-rooted ambivalence of some Chinese Christians towards foreign missions was brought into the open in a challenging article published in April in the new weekly magazine *Tianfeng* (天风), a journal that combined political dogma with articles framing Christianity in terms of Communist ideology. The journal had been founded and was edited by Y. T. Wu (吴耀宗; Wu Yaozong),

---

[137] BMSA, CH/66, Chesterman to Smith, 25 February 1948.
[138] BMSA, CH/56, Chesterman to Clow, 6 May 1948.
[139] BMSA, CH/56, Clow to Williamson, 12 April 1948, 'So we built the Wall: An Account of the Removal of the Sian Hospital, and the Building of the New Outpatient Department', 1948.
[140] Eastman, *Seeds of Destruction*, p. 173.
[141] BMSA, CH/56, Clow to Williamson, 10 November 1948.
[142] BMSA, CH/78, Williamson to Williamson, 23 February 1948.

a leader in the YMCA movement who had received his theological education in the United States.[143] The article 'The Present-Day Tragedy of Christianity' concluded with conciliatory statements about the 'many honourable persons and many noteworthy accomplishments' within the Christian church, and the 'many Christian institutions which serve mankind in the spirit of freedom, equality and love'.[144] Wu's core message, nonetheless, amounted to a 'declaration of war against foreign missions'.[145] Anti-foreign feeling was greatly increased in May 1948 when the United States government undertook to grant $100 million towards the rehabilitation of the Japanese economy (equivalent to around £1.089 billion today).[146]

In mid-July, the British ambassador in Nanjing reported to the foreign secretary that the military situation 'could scarcely be worse'.[147] The autumn of 1948 had seen the most intense fighting of the civil war, the decisive Liaoshen (辽沈) and HuaiHai (淮海) campaigns, which clinched the military superiority of the PLA.[148] Major Nationalist strongholds had been toppled, including Jinan in Shandong and Shenyang in Liaoning. The threat of a Communist takeover intensified. Chinese staff in the Xi'an hospital had begun to leave because of the unsettled conditions and it seemed likely that more would leave if the situation deteriorated. Clow sounded out the remaining senior Chinese doctors for their views on the future management of the hospital in the event of the foreigners leaving.

> There is considerable hesitation on the part of any of them to take responsibility if we all left, and Dr Chang who has always been a standby in the past has definitely said he will not be willing to take over…[A]t the moment the opinion is that if I leave, the institution would break up at once.[149]

When he wrote to London again, Clow had made up his mind to remain as long as possible, whatever the military or political situation. He was determined to keep the hospital going and to do this he felt he had to remain himself:

---

[143] See Francis P. Jones, 'The Christian Church in Communist China', *Far Eastern Survey*, Vol. 24.12, Dec. 1955, pp. 18–188 (p. 187).

[144] Francis P. Jones and Wallace C. Merwin, *Documents of the Three-Self Movement: Source Materials for the Study of the Protestant Church in Communist China* (New York: National Council of the Churches in Christ in the United States of America, 1963), p. 5.

[145] Gao, 'A Christian Leader', in Bays, *Christianity in China*.

[146] Pepper, 'The Student Movement', pp. 721–22.

[147] *British Documents on Foreign Affairs*, Part IV, Series E, Vol. 5, China, January–December 1948: F9833/33/G, Stevenson to Bevin, No. 584, 14 July 1948.

[148] Westad, *Decisive Encounters*, pp. 192–209.

[149] BMSA, CH/56, Clow to Williamson, 10 November 1948.

> My Chinese colleagues are not willing to carry on the hospital through a political
> crisis without any missionary here, and in view of this I have decided to stay here
> through a turnover if it is possible.[150]

The unwillingness of Clow's Chinese colleagues to take on his
responsibilities as medical director of the hospital suggest that it was a role
nobody wanted, possibly because it was considered politically compromising,
possibly because it was a poisoned chalice due to under-resourcing and the
significant challenges of managing amidst security and fiscal crises, and perhaps
also because it was insufficiently remunerated. In these circumstances, Clow felt
it his duty to stay.

The collection in aid of the Xi'an hospital by members of Tilehouse Street
Baptist Church had done well. The minister of the church declared, following a
special Gift Day, that 'never had money come in so readily'.[151] When, nearly two
years later, the time came to send the money to the mission house, Mr Russell,
the church secretary wrote to the Home Committee:

> As a church we feel thankful to God for putting this project into our minds and
> giving us the privilege of carrying it through. Our hearts thrill to the thought that
> we have a share in the beneficent work of the hospital…China has a great place in
> our thoughts and prayers.[152]

A difficulty arose, however, as to how the gift should be memorialised in
China. A key part of the project was to remember the contribution of the
Tilehouse Street Baptists who had died or served in the war, and it seemed
important to the church members that this should be recorded in a tangible way.
They hoped that plaques could be installed both in their own church and in the
new building in China.

Clow's sister, Dr Ellen Clow, who had recently returned from China to take
up the position of China secretary in the mission house, was troubled by this
suggestion:

> I did not think these were days to put up notices in hospitals in China having any
> suggestion of foreign association, as it might endanger the whole hospital and staff
> in any turnover.[153]

With China only months away from the CCP takeover, Ellen Clow recognised
that it might be necessary for mission hospitals to distance themselves from their
Western origins. She commented that Raymond Williamson disagreed with her.
He did not consider it would be problematic to acknowledge publicly the gift of

---

[150] BMSA, CH/56, Clow to Williamson, 30 November 1948.
[151] Minutes of Tilehouse Street Baptist Church, Hitchin, Report on Gift Day,
4 December 1946.
[152] BMSA, CH/56, Russell, Tilehouse Street Church Secretary to Clow,
23 November 1948.
[153] BMSA, CH/56, Clow to Clow, 8 December 1948.

foreign money used to build the new wing. Here, it seems, is another indication that Williamson did not fully appreciate the significant changes that had taken place in China since he had worked there ten years earlier.

It is not clear from the archive just how the matter was taken up with the Tilehouse Street members, but a further letter from the church secretary Mr Russell to Ellen Clow at the mission house makes it clear that they were made aware of the problem and sympathetic to the potential risks:

> It is not necessary for me to say that nothing would be further from our wishes, than to cause our friends at Sian to run the slightest unnecessary risk in times that seem dangerous in all conscience…Obviously wiser to leave this matter to the judgment of those on the spot.[154]

The British Baptists in Tilehouse Street were sincere in declaring that 'China has a great place in our thoughts and prayers.'[155] A deep sense of affection for China had been nurtured by almost a century of missionary letters and visits to the church by missionary speakers on deputation and, occasionally, by Chinese Christians visiting the UK. It would likely have been hard for the church members to understand that a public declaration of these warm feelings could endanger the lives of others, still harder to appreciate the significance of the accusations of imperialism being levelled at the foreign missions. When these warm feelings combined with memories of heroism and sacrifice on the part of those of their own members who had served in the war, the project assumed a particular sensitivity.[156] It was perhaps even harder for British donors to appreciate the emotions that may have been engendered by many years of dependence on gifts from elsewhere.

Their suggestion of leaving the decision 'to the judgment of those on the spot' indicates the church members' willingness to subordinate their wishes to those of their 'friends at Sian', even if they could not fully comprehend them. A plaque was installed in the vestibule of the church in Hitchin (Figure 14) inscribed with the names of those from the congregation who had died and in whose memory 'the church has erected a Tilehouse Street Memorial Wing of the rebuilt hospital in Sianfu [Xi'an], the ancient capital of China.'[157] To this day, the plaque remains on display in the church building.

---

[154] BMSA, CH/56, Russell to Clow, 23 December 1948.
[155] BMSA, CH/56, Russell to Clow, 23 November 1948.
[156] BMSA, CH/56, Russell to Clow, 23 November 1948.
[157] Gladys E. Evans, *Come Wind Come Weather: Chronicles of Tilehouse Street Baptist Church* 1669–1969, (London: Whitefriars Press Ltd,1969) p. 87.

Figure 14: Memorial plaque in Tilehouse Street Church, Hitchin[158]

In Xi'an, during the remaining time when BMS missionaries were involved, the new outpatient building was known as 'the Hitchin Block'.

By 2013, the modern successor of the Xi'an hospital showed no recognition that foreigners had been involved in constructing the building that had predated it within the city walls. There were records, however, of the foreign hospital having operated in the suburbs. It has, perhaps, suited the PRC historiography to link the foreign contribution only to an institution now clearly dead and gone, rather than a thriving modern hospital.

This case study shows it was possible for foreign missionaries to work along with the local Chinese authorities in post-war reconstruction. British supporters of the mission, however, had difficulty appreciating the changed climate of the times. While the Tilehouse Street members continued to regard fellow Christians in China affectionately as brothers, and members of the same Christian family, public expressions of such sentiments might be unwelcome at a time when Chinese links with foreign imperialists were beginning to be regarded with disfavour in China.

Policy with Regard to Mission Work under a Communist Regime

The situation in which missionaries found themselves in Qingzhou, and the experiences of the hospital staff in Xi'an, suggested that, before long, a fundamental matter of principle would have to be addressed both by the society and by each missionary. In the event of a Communist victory, and Communist control of the country, under what circumstances and conditions would the society expect its missionary staff to continue their work, and would they be willing to do so?

---

[158] Photograph by Sam Hallas, Fabric Secretary, Tilehouse Street Baptist Church, Hitchin, 2014.

Central to this issue was the emphasis placed by the Baptist denomination on the fact that there was no hierarchy of membership: 'There are no priests as distinct from people; all alike, in fact, are priests.'[159] Another important principle was that each member should have freedom to obey his own conscience, and be 'protected in doing what he believes his duty against the influence of authority, and majorities, custom, and opinion'.[160] Faced with impending decisions about whether or not to attempt to continue work under a Communist regime, how did the BMS plan to balance its responsibilities as an organisation for its work and the safety of its foreign staff, against the freedom of its individual members to obey their conscience?

At the meeting of the BMS General Committee in September 1946, Fred Russell, home on furlough from China, referred to the fact that Communists were 'in almost complete occupation' in northern China, and 'their attitude to the preaching of the Gospel was believed to be antagonistic.'[161] Russell asked to know the mind of the committee: 'Would they be content with a purely social, educational and medical presentation of the Christian message, or was the Gospel to be preached at all costs?'

One respondent declared that 'the Church must, in all cases, insist on the right of Christian men and women everywhere to worship and witness.' He anticipated that maintaining that principle 'would probably involve the Church in as big a fight as any in which it had ever been engaged'. Henry Cook, presumably engaged at that very time in writing his book on Baptist principles, was also present at the meeting and suggested that 'no concrete policy for China was possible'. Raymond Williamson, apparently expecting a Nationalist victory, concluded the discussion:

> The work in Communist areas must be continued, and, if a political settlement came about, the religious question would probably be settled with it, for the influence of the Christian Church was strong in the Nationalist Government.[162]

However, when it became evident that, contrary to Williamson's expectations, a Communist victory would be the outcome, individual missionaries were faced more urgently with the decision as to whether they would be prepared to work under a Communist regime. There were issues of personal safety involved (whether the missionaries were prepared to risk danger and possible arrest) but there were also matters of conscience. What was the *right,* as opposed to the comfortable or safe, thing to do?

The Home Committee declared in January 1948 that they wished the decision to be taken 'by the missionaries on the spot who were conversant with more factors than the Committee at home' and underlined repeatedly 'that they [the missionaries] should be supported in every case in whatever decision they made

---

[159] Cook, *Baptists*, p. 76.
[160] Dalberg-Acton, *The History of Freedom*, p. 159.
[161] BMSA, General Committee Minutes, Vol. 44, September 1946.
[162] BMSA, General Committee Minutes, Vol. 44, September 1946.

whether to remain or evacuate'.[163] In leaving the decision to the individuals affected, the committee acknowledged the principle of individual conscience while, at the same time, guaranteed the security of official support in whatever decision was taken.

Several letters in the correspondence files of individual missionaries in the BMS archive address the issue. George Young wrote one of his general letters to supporters in March 1948, when the Communists held most of Manchuria, North Korea and much of northern China – with the exception of some large cities and a few railways. A month earlier, British and American consuls had requested their nationals in Central China to evacuate to the coast.[164] 'Now' wrote Young, 'we are facing what is the most difficult question of a missionary – to flee or to stay?'

> It is not simply a question of doing one's duty but of considering the effect of your personal decision on the lives of others…Should we as a mission decide to stay and carry on under a Communist regime, […] we should be cut off from financial support and become a burden and even a danger to our Chinese Christian friends…On the other side […] it would be cowardly to leave the Chinese Church to face this trial alone. I myself feel that I would rather stay…but do the Chinese want me to do this? Would it not be selfish of me to endanger others who would need to support me? Is the day of foreign missionaries ended in China, and has the time come for the Chinese church to face the conflict alone?[165]

Young's final words are interesting. It could be read as showing paternalistic doubt as to whether the Chinese church had the maturity to deal with difficulties. In this context, however, it seems more likely that he felt the urge and the responsibility to stand by fellow Christians in special danger.

At the end of December 1948, when the need for decision became more urgent, the missionaries in Shaanxi took part in a conference at which they discussed the issue fully with their colleagues in the Chinese church. They were unanimously assured by church members that any missionaries who decided to stay would be welcomed and gladly supported by the church members should this be necessary. Keith Bryan described the discussion that followed this assurance:

> One by one we stood up and in true sincerity gave reasons why we felt called of God to go or stay. Then […] each went out of the room […] whilst the remainder of the group discussed the decision we had made and expressed its approval or otherwise. The amazing thing about it all was the sympathy, love and understanding given to each individual case. There was not the least trace of discrimination between those deciding to go or stay, the one thing that concerned us all was to

---

[163] BMSA, China Subcommittee Minutes, Vol. 11, 20 January 1948.
[164] *British Documents on Foreign Affairs*, Part IV, Series E, Vol. 5, China, January–December 1948: F1045/33/10 Stevenson to Bevin No. 44, 19 January 1948.
[165] BMSA, CH/67, Young to friends, 16 March 1948.

know God's will for each individual…It was as right for some to go as for some to stay.[166]

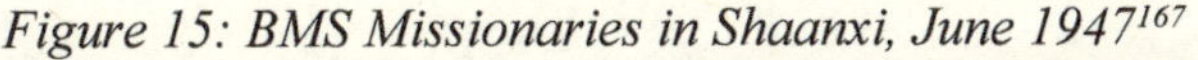

Figure 15: BMS Missionaries in Shaanxi, June 1947[167]

Photo shows (among others): Keith Bryan (seated, far left); Kitty Bryan (seated, second from left); Menzies Clow (back row, sixth from left); Charlotte Mudd (seated, second from right); William Mudd (seated, far right); Fred Russell (seated, centre); Joan Williamson (back row, third from right); George Young (back row, fifth from right).

Of the missionaries then serving in Shaanxi (Figure 15), eleven elected to stay and four to leave.[168] When this was reported to the China subcommittee, its members resolved:

---

[166] BMSA, CH/68, Minutes of the Shensi Synod and Conference, held at Sian 13–14 December 1948.

[167] From the private collection of Elizabeth Jamieson, née Gunn.

[168] BMSA, China Subcommittee Minutes, Vol. 11, 15 January 1949.

To assure all the Shensi missionaries, both those who elected to evacuate in the event of Communist occupation, and those who elected to remain, of their support and their affection and prayers.[169]

This was an important test of the Baptist principle of freedom of conscience. It was also an important illustration of shared decision-making by Chinese and foreign church members. From the last weeks of 1948 until the last of the BMS missionaries left China in 1952, the issues at stake were rehearsed a number of times by the missionaries and by those involved in missionary work in the UK.

Zhang Sijing described conditions in Shandong on the eve of the civil war as 'a thousand times more serious' than during the Japanese occupation.[170] As we have seen, his fears were well founded. It was a time of generalised turmoil and uncertainty, and much personal suffering. Much of the fabric of Chinese society was torn apart. It would have been impossible for missionaries, even if they had wanted to, to continue the roles and routines of pre-war generations.

While Chinese Christians like Wang Juntang were seeking to find a way forward for their country that accommodated both Christian and Communist ideologies, the missionaries' fundamental distrust of Communism coloured their attitude to the Communists they encountered locally, and their Chinese colleagues would have been able to recognise this.

The examples of Wang Juntang and the Tilehouse Street gift provide an insight into the complex relationships between British Baptists in their home churches, the mission board and its members in London, the missionaries working in China and the members of the Chinese Baptist church. They suggest that, even when there was apparent affection on both Chinese and British sides and a genuine wish to understand each other, social and cultural differences put in place significant, perhaps insurmountable, barriers to full understanding. These, along with the tensions and rifts within Chinese society at the time, made complete trust and totally open communication extremely difficult.

Nevertheless, the careful discussion of Shaanxi missionaries with their Chinese colleagues, about whether they should stay or leave, suggests that they continued to be motivated to work together if at all possible.

---

[169] BMSA, China Subcommittee Minutes, Vol. 11, 13 January 1949.
[170] BMSA, CH/23, Secretariat Shantung, 1939–1946, Zhang to Williamson, original in Chinese, 14 June 1946 (trans. Gao Yan, 1984).

6. The BMS in China, 1949–1952

> Things were so much better than we ever dared hope […] and we were carried away in the first three months, as we were meant to be.[1]

So why did the BMS leave China when it did? Did its members believe that the Chinese church was 'able and willing to assume the responsibility' for its own affairs, as had been the goal established at Qingzhou in 1927?[2] We know that there were significant obstacles to achieving this. The Chinese Civil War was making it extremely difficult to keep the churches open in Shandong; Jing Yihui was struggling to maintain medical work in Qingzhou; Menzies Clow had been advised that the Xi'an hospital would break up if he left.[3] Was the BMS surrendering the task as planned, or was it pushed out of China by the Chinese Communist Party (CCP) after the establishment of the People's Republic of China (PRC)?

The standard answer is that there was no place for foreign Christian missionaries in the Communist state. Within this explanation, however, there are a number of alternative emphases. Mitter reiterated the conventional explanation: the missionaries 'were of course expelled from China by the Communists after 1949.'[4] Ling emphasises a different point: the missionary departure was prompted by the realisation that Chinese Christians had rejected them and had requested them to leave.[5] Ashmore argues that they might have stayed on, had they been willing to modify the manner in which they worked and their approach to others. 'It was widespread refusal to adapt, as much as the Communists' hostility, that precipitated the missionary exodus of 1949–1952'.[6] Others point out that it was this very requirement to adapt that led missionaries to choose not to remain: they were not happy with the conditions under which they would have to work within a Communist regime. One BMS missionary declared that 'she [could not] envisage service in Communist China, particularly in view of the inevitable frustration of her desire to preach the gospel.'[7] Other missionaries were heavily influenced by the danger their presence posed to

---

[1] BMSA, CH/56, Clow, 'Points in Favour and Points Against the Present Government', 12 September 1950.
[2] Tsingchow Conference 1927.
[3] BMSA, CH/23, Secretariat Shantung, 1939–1946, Zhang to Williamson, 14 June 1946; CH/56, Clow to Williamson, 10 November 1948.
[4] Mitter, 'Imperialism', p. 65.
[5] Ling, *Changing Role*, p. 181.
[6] Polly Ashmore, 'Quakers and Communists, Partners in Building Utopia?', *Friends Quarterly* 40.1 (February 2012) pp. 16–29 (p. 26).
[7] BMSA, China Subcommittee Minutes, Vol. 12, 24 April 1950.

Chinese Christians. 'The sooner foreign personnel are not around, the easier it will be for church leaders to make a stand on a purely religious basis.'[8]

The gradual steps by which Chinese Protestantism was absorbed into the organisation and control of the PRC are described by Bays,[9] although important questions remain outstanding. How was this process experienced by BMS missionaries? Why have missionary accounts sometimes seemed unsatisfactory. How did the experience of Shaanxi missionaries differ from those in Shandong? And what sort of challenges did the BMS, and its individual missionaries, face as the work in China came to an end?

Shandong was the first of the three provinces in which the BMS worked to fall to the Communists. Zhoucun and Qingzhou, two important centres of BMS activity, had fallen in March 1948, but Jinan and Qingdao had remained in Nationalist hands for a few months longer. The whole of the province, after almost three years of heavy fighting in the country areas, finally fell with the capture of Jinan on 24 September 1948. At that time, Fred Drake was the only member of the BMS in Jinan. The battle for Jinan lasted nine days. At the outset, Nationalist forces had barricaded themselves within the Qilu University campus. The campus was then heavily shelled, first by the Communists and later by the retreating Nationalists. Almost every building was hit, some several times, shattering roofs and windows.[10] In the city itself, two days of running battles on the streets were followed by heavy shelling of railway workshops and factories, leaving much of the city in ruins.[11]

BMS staff evacuated Shanxi in July 1948 when Taiyuan came under siege from the People's Liberation Army (PLA).[12] The PLA tactics employed to such devastating effect in Manchuria were applied to Taiyuan: the city was gradually surrounded and 'became a hunger trap for the KMT [Kuomintang] armies, civilian inhabitants, and refugees. The PLA shut down the food supply [...] and waited.'[13] Although two missionaries returned to Shanxi for a brief period in autumn 1948, the BMS had no presence there after that and, after Taiyuan fell to the Communists, access to news from the province was minimal.

In early 1949, twelve British Baptists remained in Shaanxi. Three British doctors and one missionary nurse were working in the newly reconstructed and enlarged mission hospital in Xi'an; three were engaged in educational work; and five were working as evangelists. Mission work had continued without major disruption, although the city had been under constant threat for almost a year, as Communist guerrilla attacks gradually wore down the Nationalist forces in the

---

[8] BMSA, CH/71, Harrison to Clow, 20 December 1950.

[9] Bays, *New History*, pp. 160–68.

[10] Corbett, *Shantung Christian University*, p. 258.

[11] BMSA, CH/57, Drake to Williamson, 26 October 1948.

[12] BMSA, China Subcommittee Minutes Vol. 12, 24 April 1950.

[13] Anthony Oberschall and Michael Seidman, 'Food Coercion in Revolution and Civil War: Who Wins and How They Do it', *Comparative Studies in Society and History*, Vol. 47.2 (April 2005), pp. 372–401 (p. 399). For a harrowing description of the PLA siege of Chanchun, Manchuria, see Dikötter, *Tragedy*, pp. 3–8.

outlying areas.[14] When, in May 1949, the Communist takeover eventually came, it was as it had been in Beijing: 'systematic, undramatic and bloodless', and 'no violence was called for, because the city was plucked like a piece of ripe fruit.'[15]

By June 1949, only a very small number of BMS missionaries were continuing work in Baptist mission stations in Shandong and Shaanxi, and none remained in Shanxi (Figure 16). Four were still working for the Church of Christ in China (CCC) within the Border Service mission; others had been evacuated to work with the Qilu University staff in Hangzhou; some were working for other missionary societies in other provinces. The remainder were engaged in administrative work for the mission in Shanghai or were waiting for the opportunity to move elsewhere in China or return to the UK.[16]

Figure 16: Location of BMS missionaries in China, June 1949[17]

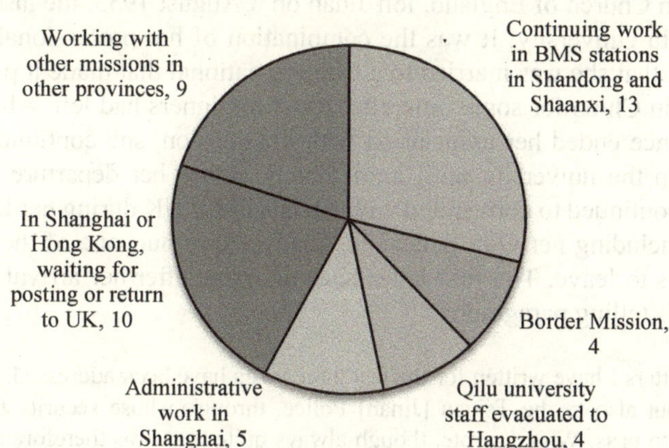

Barriers to Understanding the BMS China Experience

The differing experience of the three provinces in which the BMS had a presence illustrates the various ways in which the Communists came to power in different parts of China. People's expectations of what the future held under the new government were inevitably influenced by these earlier experiences. For Ling, missionaries all over China reached a common view of what to expect, and thereby failed to understand the national mood and political climate during and immediately after the Communist takeover.[18] She argues that missionaries 'deluded themselves', 'made unfounded assumptions', 'misjudged their position, ' naively believed', 'failed to take into account', 'assumed' or 'refused to see'

---

[14] Chassin, *Communist Conquest*, p. 168.
[15] A. Doak Barnett, *China on the Eve of Communist Takeover* (New York: Praeger, 1963), p. 343.
[16] BMSA, China Subcommittee Minutes, Vol. 12, 28 June 1949.
[17] BMSA, China Subcommittee Minutes, Vol. 12, 28 June 1949.
[18] Ling, *Changing Role*.

the real nature of communism.[19] She takes at face value the accusations levelled at missionaries at the time of their departure from China.

For many years a veil of ignorance and uncertainty hung over the understanding in Western churches of what *really* happened in China during the Communist takeover. One important reason for this was the missionaries' self-imposed silence. Fear that restrictions would be placed on missionary activities if any open hostility was shown to Communist activity, or that Chinese Christians would face negative repercussions if their associations with foreign missionaries became known, led missionaries to be very guarded in what they said in their letters. Again and again, the letters contain words along the lines of, 'it is not possible to explain fully in letters', and 'please do not make any reference to matters mentioned in this letter if you are writing to China.'[20]

Margaret Kiesow, a British pharmacist, originally employed by the Presbyterian Church of England, left Jinan on 8 August 1953, the last foreigner to leave Qilu University. It was the combination of her professional expertise and the fact that she was married to a Chinese national that made it possible for her to stay in China for some time after other foreigners had left. Although she had long since ended her association with the mission, she continued to work and teach in the university until immediately before her departure in August 1953. She continued to correspond with friends in the UK during her last months in China, including her Qilu colleague, Gladys Seymour, one of the last BMS missionaries to leave. The first letter Kiesow wrote after her arrival in Europe contains this telling paragraph:

> All the letters I have written for the last three years have been addressed, not only to you, but also to the Tsinan [Jinan] Police, through whose security they had certainly to pass. What I wrote, though always quite true, was therefore only one side – the good side – of the picture. It is important to remember that there is a good side, but to see that side only is wrong.[21]

Kiesow went on to write about the meaning in practice of such phrases as 'freedom of religion', about her experience of campus life under the Communists, and about the impact of Communist controls on her relationships with Chinese students and colleagues in the university. None of this information appears in letters that she wrote while still living in the PRC. The later picture is very different from the earlier one. In a personal letter to Seymour written on arrival in Europe, she gave a glimpse of her real feelings: 'Oh, the relief to be free from fear again!…It was a very lonely life and a very hard one.'[22]

---

[19] Ling, *Changing Role*. Many examples, including those cited from pp. 131, 142 and 143.

[20] BMSA, CH/23, Secretariat Shantung, 1936–1949, Drake to Clow, 7 May 1949; CH/56, Clow to 'Folk', 6 September 1949.

[21] Private collection of David Seymour, Kiesow to friends, 5 November 1953.

[22] Private collection of David Seymour, Kiesow to Gladys Seymour, 11 November 1953.

It was not until much later that the consequences of receiving such restricted information from China began to be appreciated. In 1959, Harold Wickings of St Andrew's College, Selly Oak, wrote to the Conference of British Missionary Societies, suggesting that there was a need for 'an informative book' about China.

> For eight years we have loyally said little about the Chinese church, lest any word of ours might cause trouble for our friends and colleagues in that country. We are surprised that some of the folk in the churches ask odd questions.[23]

The background of violence, distrust and fear pervading much of China during the early years of the Communist takeover is barely mentioned in the missionary correspondence. It comes to life, however, with brilliant economy in a single sentence in Fred Drake's careful seventeen-page report of the work of the English Baptist mission in Shandong for the year 1949:

> It is not possible to describe in detail here the conditions in which the University found itself during the year; but they may be surmised by reference to Luke 10:30.[24]

Drake refers to a passage in the New Testament that reads, 'A man was going down from Jerusalem to Jericho, and he fell among robbers, who stripped him and beat him, and departed, leaving him half-dead.'[25] Even well-trained and well-educated Communist censors were likely to miss this discreet reference.

Taking Drake's report at face value, and failing to pick up the understated reference, might lead a reader to assume, as Ling does, that missionaries were quite unaware of the violent and oppressive behaviour of which the CCP had shown itself capable. Even without this insight, reference to almost any BMS correspondence from China towards the end of 1948 or during the early months of 1949, right up until the last BMS missionaries left in December 1951, suggests that they were not blindly optimistic. Letters from Tom and Connie Allen in Shandong and George Young in Xi'an, written in 1949 within two weeks of each other, both indicate the tentativeness and uncertainty with which they faced the future. The Allens wrote weeks after Jinan had been taken by the Communists. 'We are not as free as we thought…Days are dark…It is impossible to see what will happen we know so little.'[26] Xi'an had not yet fallen when Young wrote to Ellen Clow in the mission house:

> I hear you are a bit pessimistic about the future of Christian missions in China. Well I don't think any of us can say whether there will or will not be a place for Christian

---

[23] CBMSA, Box 392, Folder 22, Wickings to Short, 29 January 1959.
[24] BMSA, CH/23, Secretariat Shantung, 1936–1949, English Baptist Mission, Shantung, Report for the year 1949, Drake, 5 May 1950, p. 14.
[25] Luke 10.30.
[26] BMSA, CH/54, Allens, Newsletter for members of the Shantung Mission, 26 January 1949.

missionary work under the Communist regime. All we can do is try and then we will know.[27]

Missionaries such as Young persevered not because they did not have concerns or questions about the future place of missionaries in China, but because they wanted to go forward with their work while it was possible to do so. Clow, surveying the scene from her vantage point in the UK, was not optimistic: 'I continue to play the part of chief pessimist about openings for missionaries in China in the next five years.'[28]

Another factor in the way of Western understanding of the situation in China, which missionary silence did nothing to dispel, is the way information was deliberately manipulated by the Communist state. Brady uses the example given by the Chinese journalist and former diplomat, Lu Ning, who likened Western analysis of the PRC's foreign affairs to five blind men trying to understand an elephant by each feeling a different part of it: *mangren mo xiang*. Each man only gets one piece of the truth, never the whole picture.

> The reason for this is not, as Lu implies, that foreigners are incapable of understanding China's foreign affairs system, *waishi xitong*, rather it is that the Chinese Government deliberately withholds information about what has always been, and remains, a highly sensitive subject.[29]

The CCP leadership made both its own functionaries and its opponents, whether nations, organisations or individuals, second-guess what they were thinking. This was an important weapon in their armoury of control: when things went wrong, the leadership could deny responsibility or could change direction without admitting error or being tied to previous commitments. Howlett analyses the way that Mao Zedong used this policy to hold off Western governments who were making overtures with regard to recognition. By remaining secretive and keeping his intentions hidden, he could avoid being manipulated. Being 'unknowable' in this way gave him freedom to manoeuvre.[30] Carrying out his terror campaigns, Mao was deliberately vague, 'forcing his underlings to pore over every one of his numerous remarks, speeches and directives for guidance on how to carry out the terror'.[31] Drake recognised this technique in his own experience in working with the party machinery in Shandong:

> We have found that the present government does not like to indicate directly its will to institutions, but likes them to anticipate its will and accommodate themselves

---

[27] BMSA, CH/67, Young to Clow, 7 February 1949. For other examples, see CH/57, Drake to Drake, 21 February 1949; CH/63, Price to Clow, 2 May 1949.
[28] BMSA, CH/56, Clow to Clow, 23 April 1949.
[29] Brady, *Making the Foreign Serve China*, p. xi , citing Lu Ning, *The Dynamics of Foreign-Policy Decision making in China* (Boulder CO: Westview Press, 1997), p. 177.
[30] Howlett, 'Creating a New Shanghai', p. 41.
[31] Dikötter, *Tragedy*, p. 88.

voluntarily to its policy. Those who fail to do this find themselves increasingly involved in difficulties from which it is hard to extricate themselves.[32]

Any attempt to understand this particularly contentious phase of the history of missions in China needs to take account of both these factors – missionaries deliberately withholding information, and the manipulation of information by the CCP – in interpreting evidence and reaching balanced conclusions.

Communists Take Over Xi'an

The acute sense of despondency that overtook the BMS missionaries in Shaanxi at the time of their eventual departure from China can be explained in part by their experiences of the Communist takeover. A dramatic change occurred in the tone of Baptist missionary correspondence from Shaanxi in the summer of 1949. Letters earlier in the year had been characterised by tension and alarms, descriptions of a 'rapidly deteriorating situation', a 'whirlpool of fear' and urgent pleas for cash to be made available for evacuation purposes.[33] In early May, 'the Communists announced that they were very busy in the south and apologised that they would not be able to "liberate" Sian for another two months'.[34] Two weeks later, on 20 May 1949, the Communists took control of Xi'an. It was 'very peaceful [...] very different from what we imagined and a very pleasant difference'.[35] The mood of the missionaries' letters changed. Not only was the foreign community relieved of the threat of being directly caught up in military conflict, but many of its members began to develop a new respect for the conquering army. One missionary, in a letter to mission supporters, went so far as to eulogise the incoming Communist soldiers as 'lean, bronzed and wiry crusaders'.[36] This was too much for a member of BMS headquarters' staff in London, who deleted the phrase before allowing the letter to be circulated.

Over the next six months, admiration for the new regime was apparent particularly in the letters of George Young and Menzies Clow. Describing the commendable manner in which the Communists had conducted themselves, Young exclaimed, 'What a radical change has taken place in Sian [Xi'an]!' He was relieved at the 'friendly attitude of the Communists towards the church', and welcomed the fact that it was now possible to travel freely to the country churches, 'provided we have a pass which is easily obtainable from the police'. On one occasion, Young and two missionary colleagues invited two Communists – one of them 'a high official in the party whom I have known for six years' – to a meal in their home, where they 'enjoyed four hours of frank and friendly discussion' and 'a most stimulating exchange of ideas and experiences'. On an

---

[32] BMSA, CH/23, Secretariat Shantung, 1936–1949, Drake to Clow, 7 May 1949.
[33] BMSA, CH/65, Sutton to Clow, 27 April 1949; CH/59, Gunn to friends, 28 April 1949; CH/59, Gunn to Clow, 1 May 1949.
[34] BMSA, CH/56, Clow to Clow, 16 May 1949.
[35] BMSA, CH/56, Clow to Clow, 29 May 1949.
[36] BMSA, CH/67, Young, Letter to Prayer Partners, 26 August 1949.

almost lyrical note, he wrote, 'Some of our happiest memories this summer are of evenings spent sitting out in courtyards sipping tea and talking with Communist men and women soldiers about all sorts of things...'[37]

As superintendent of the BMS hospital in Xi'an, Clow was particularly concerned with understanding the attitude of the new regime to the work of the hospital. Here, he was greatly reassured:

> The local Government has sent two men recently to make a fairly detailed study of our hospital to improve their own, and they said that this hospital was the best in the city...I get a lot of medical consulting work amongst the senior officers.[38]

> As regards our hospital, one of their political workers said to me, 'We do not tolerate your hospital work, we welcome it and will do all we can to facilitate it.'[39]

Clow went so far as to surmise that the new government may 'have the makings of the best government China has ever known'. He went on to suggest that there was 'no reason why medicals [medical missionaries] should not come out [to China]' and that there was 'plenty of opportunity for [the] technically qualified'. The predominant emphasis in Clow's letters was on the cordial nature of his relationships with the new authorities. 'The police,' he wrote, 'have been especially friendly and we can take such problems as arise to them and discuss them frankly.' He had made 'many new friends', 'many good friends', among the Communist military. He enjoyed meals with Communist officers and commented that Communist students were also 'very friendly'. The military were 'very polite and cooperative', and it was 'a pleasure to look after them' when they came to the hospital for medical care.[40]

Brady's book exploring the management of foreigners in the People's Republic of China, and particularly the chapter on friendship, is instructive when considering the missionaries' exuberant descriptions of their relationships with the new government.[41]

> In the language of the CCP, friendship is political...In Chinese political language, friendship (*youyi* 友谊) has the meaning of a strategic relationship; it does not have the meaning of good or intimate personal relations.[42]

Clow and Young, like many other experienced BMS missionaries, were both good linguists and familiar with Chinese social norms. In their repeated use of the words 'friend' and 'friendly', however, they were almost certainly describing experiences that they considered indicative of warm personal regard between people. There is no suggestion that they saw their friendly interactions with

---

[37] BMSA, CH/67, Young, Letter to Prayer Partners, 26 August 1949.

[38] BMSA, CH/56, M. Clow to E. Clow, 6 August 1949.

[39] BMSA, CH/56, Clow circular letter to 'Folks', 5 September 1949.

[40] BMSA, CH/56, Clow to various recipients, 24 July, 6 August, 6 September, 29 October and 4 December 1949.

[41] Brady, *Making the Foreign Serve China*, pp. 7–66.

[42] Brady, *Making the Foreign Serve China*, p. 7.

members of the new authorities in any other light. It seems likely that they would have considered it cynical if anyone had suggested otherwise.

Brady also describes the strategic principle known as 'treating strangers well in order to win their hearts' (怀柔远人, *huai rou yuanren*).[43] This resonates with details Clow provided of his early interactions with local Communists, including this example of an occasion when he was asked to attend two patients in a military hospital in Xi'an:

> They said my waterproof looked very disreputable (which is quite true) so I told them I am a poor man and they offered to issue me with a set of army padded clothes![44]

Brady identifies another factor that may have affected missionaries' reactions, citing Kaidi Zhan's book, *The Strategies of Politeness in the Chinese Language*:

> Attempts to bring the addressee closer underlie many of the positive politeness strategies of Chinese speakers. Hence often people will say things because they are pleasing, rather than sincere and will focus on finding common points.[45]

In retrospect, and in the light of this kind of analysis, it is tempting to dismiss the missionaries' early reactions as naïve, although, as discussed later, within a few months they had begun to recognise the underlying intention of the CCP to exercise control.

Elsewhere, Brady refers to Zhou Enlai's encouragement to party members to cultivate the 'five diligences' (*wuqin*): diligent eyes, ears, mouth, hands and feet. By 'diligent feet', Zhou means, 'be active, make friends everywhere, don't stay at home waiting for people to come and find you.'[46] It is striking how closely this behaviour reflects the style of the Communists Young described in this extract from one of his letters:

> Communists are all around us – busy purposeful officials, keen Spartan soldiers, enterprising merchant traders, and zealous political workers…They are our neighbours; they sometimes wander into our homes to see how we live; a few come to our churches to hear what we preach; many come to our hospital for medical help; and in all these friendly contacts we and they are finding out that the other fellow is not as bad as he appeared to be from a distance.[47]

---

[43] Brady, *Making the Foreign Serve China*, p. 15.

[44] BMSA, CH/56, Clow to Clow, 4 December 1949.

[45] Kaidi Zhan, *The Strategies of Politeness in the Chinese Language* (Berkeley CA: Institute of Asian Studies, University of California, 1992), p. x, cited in Brady, *Making the Foreign Serve China*, p. 14.

[46] Duan Liancheng, *Duiwai chuanboxue* (textbook for waishi workers), Chinese English bilingual edition, (Beijing: Zhongguo jianshe chubanshe, 1988), p. 59, quoted in Brady, *Making the Foreign Serve China*, p. 51.

[47] BMSA, CH/67, Young, Letter to Prayer Partners, 26 August 1949.

It is possible that the behaviours described above were adopted with the explicit purpose of buying time and misleading potential opponents.

It was not just the foreign missionary community that was the target of the CCP's strategies. Howlett uses CCP records to demonstrate the careful planning and extensive training that CCP cadres were given in anticipation of their entry into new urban areas, and the impact this had on the business community.[48] According to Westad, city entrepreneurs in Tianjin were sent New Year cards by the CCP in anticipation of an early capture of the city, 'wishing them long life and prosperous business…If we should take the city in this new year, do not be alarmed. We shall restore order quickly and welcome your business.'[49] During the takeover of Beijing, the incoming chief of the Military Control Commission, General Ye Jianying, was careful to flatter those from whom he took control by addressing them with self-deprecating words: 'We've been living in the hills…we know much less than you gentlemen about municipal government. Henceforth we must learn from you.'[50] Barnett comments, 'This sort of humility was characteristic of the Communists' line in taking over many organisations.'[51] Even in Beijing, the old leadership was pleasantly surprised by the first official contacts with the new authorities, and 'reacted like a small puppy which, when told to roll over, turns over meekly'.[52]

The CCP approach went further than careful manipulation of social interactions and a few winning words. In her examination of the demise of private-sector charity in Shanghai during the early years of the PRC, Nara Dillon describes the use the new government made of a carefully staged strategy to draw on the resources, organisation and expertise of the elite members of Shanghai's indigenous voluntary sector, before gradually exercising controls and imposing its own agenda.[53] Thus, by a policy of recruiting this powerful and wealthy group, and then attacking its legitimacy, the CCP was able to achieve the lasting institutional change that was its objective.

There were parallels between this approach and the treatment of the missionary hospitals and Chinese Christians.

In Xi'an, the BMS missionaries made a point of communicating and cooperating with the new regime wherever possible. At the same time, the CCP local leadership made use of the professional facilities offered by foreigners at a time when their own provision was comparatively undeveloped. Clow reported that his medical services were in demand by Communist military officers, noting that 'sleeplessness, mental strain and low blood pressure seem to be their chief

---

[48] Howlett, 'Creating a New Shanghai', pp. 71–83.

[49] Westad, *Decisive Encounters*, p. 261.

[50] Barnett, *China on the Eve*, pp. 343–44.

[51] Barnett, *China on the Eve*, pp. 343–44.

[52] Barnett, *China on the Eve*, pp. 343–44.

[53] Nara Dillon, 'New Democracy and the Demise of Private Charity in Shanghai' in Jeremy Brown and Paul G. Pickowicz (eds), *Dilemmas of Victory: The Early Years of the People's Republic of China*, (Cambridge MA: Harvard University Press, 2007), pp. 80–102.

complaints.'[54] He taught medical classes at the government Northwest University, and the hospital staff participated fully in communal activities such as vaccination campaigns, flood relief and work as air wardens. In big civic demonstrations, the hospital regularly sent a medical party, 'in case anyone gets injured or faints'.[55]

Alongside this cooperation with the new regime, normal hospital work continued without interference. Although most hospitals were badly hit by taxes, Clow was able to carry on, thanks to the popularity of the hospital and a good supply of drugs acquired from the Red Cross. He was even able to expand medical work, opening dispensaries in two country districts.[56] He ensured that the BMS hospital in Xi'an complied in every way it could with government requirements. He started a hospital affairs committee with representatives from the whole hospital staff – doctors and nurses, lab technicians, coolies (unskilled labourers) and students. He reported that the first meeting of the committee was 'a great success […], lasted five hours but every minute of it was worthwhile…It carries real weight and [the staff] have developed a sense of responsibility.'[57]

During this period, it seemed that there was scope not just for Christian medical services to be recognised by the new government, but for the activity of the church itself to be incorporated into the national reconstruction efforts. Young wrote that 'They do want the Christian church to come right into this people's movement, to share our resources and work together for a new China.'[58] Young was enthusiastic about the part that Chinese Christians might play in China's national regeneration. He reported that church work carried on without disruption. Unusually close contact with the military authorities took place when one of the church pastors was accidentally knocked off his bicycle and killed by an army lorry. The church pleaded for the release of the accused drivers, and their discharge was celebrated in a 'feast of thanksgiving and reconciliation between church leaders and army officers'.[59]

It seems clear from these accounts that those BMS missionaries who remained in Shaanxi following the turnover believed that there was still work for them within the PRC. This honeymoon period continued into the early months of 1950. Looking back with hindsight in September 1950 on his first impressions, Clow wrote, 'Things were so much better than we ever dared hope (and they still are), and we were carried away in the first three months, as we were meant to be.'[60]

---

[54] BMSA, CH/56, M. Clow to E. Clow, 6 August 1949.
[55] BMSA, CH/56, M. Clow to E. Clow , 24 September and 29 October 1949.
[56] BMSA, CH/56, M. Clow to E. Clow , 24 September 1949.
[57] BMSA, CH/56, M. Clow to E. Clow , 29 October 1949.
[58] BMSA, CH/67, Young, Prayer letter to friends, 26 August 1949.
[59] BMSA, CH/67, Young, Prayer letter to friends, 3 February 1950.
[60] BMSA, CH/56, Clow, 'Points in Favour and Points Against the Present Government', 12 September 1950.

Shandong Churches under the CCP

Unlike Xi'an, the CCP takeover of Jinan in late September 1948 had been hard-fought and violent. Once the Communist victory was confirmed, however, although the tone of the correspondence from BMS missionaries did not match the exuberance of that of their colleagues in Xi'an, a note of optimism became apparent in their letters. In early October, Drake, the only BMS missionary who had remained during the fighting, commented on the 'great courtesy and consideration' being shown by the incoming army and civil authorities. He reported that 'important contacts' were being made with incoming personnel.

> We cannot foretell what changes may take place in the future, [but] we are hopeful that these contacts will have some effect on the course of events, and perhaps lead to better mutual understanding.[61]

These promising conditions were in marked contrast to those that had prevailed during the civil war. For most of the civil war years, the country areas in Shandong had been controlled by Communists, who carried out a campaign against the churches and initiated the first stage of the party's land reform policy. To meet Mao's targets for killings in each locality, the CCP systematically set about turning the villagers against each other. The exact number who perished in the land reform is unknown, but Dikötter estimates between 1.5 and 2 million people were killed between 1947 and 1952.[62]

Christians in Shandong had first-hand knowledge of the ruthlessness with which the CCP implemented its policies. Churches were closed down and church pastors persecuted. Many Christians were left destitute by the fighting, and even the most prosperous church members 'had been reduced to the lowest possible level during the past lean years'. Much church property had been destroyed and, Drake wrote, 'the church members here are therefore looking wistfully to the church at home for some help'.[63]

Encouragement came from an unlikely source when, in September 1948, the CCP authorities in Zhoucun approached the church about reopening the mission hospital.

> The Mayor of Chouts'un has asked repeatedly why the foreign missionaries do not return to Chouts'un, and in particular do not reopen the Foster Hospital, as conditions are quiet and protection is assured.[64]

In response to this enquiry, Zhang Sijing, who had resumed his role as leader of the Shantung [Shandong] Baptist Union (SBU), and Dr Chao, a Chinese

---

[61] BMSA, CH/23, Secretariat Shantung, 1936–1949, Drake to Williamson, 7 October 1948.
[62] Dikötter, *Tragedy*, pp. 65–83.
[63] BMSA, CH/23, Secretariat Shantung, 1936–1949, Drake to Williamson, 26 October 1948.
[64] BMSA, CH/23, Secretariat Shantung, 1936–1949, Drake to Williamson, 26 October 1948.

doctor who had been approached about taking on responsibility for medical work in the Foster Hospital, went to see the chief party secretary and the military commander in Zhoucun. Both the officials expressed 'in very strong terms' the hope that the hospital would open, 'and promised all support in their power, even to the loan of funds for initial expenses'.[65]

This suggested that, at this stage, the Communist authorities were willing to work with the Chinese church leaders and look to the foreign missions for practical help. Just as in Xi'an, the new authorities had enlisted a thriving mission hospital to provide medical services to supplement their own. In Zhoucun, the CCP took initiative in inviting foreigners to resume an apparently abandoned project, offering to work in partnership with them and with Chinese Christians in doing so. This merely replicated the experience of the foreign business community, which, in Shanghai, was essential to preserving civic amenities in the absence of CCP resources.[66] Howlett comments that the British traffic manager of the British Tram Company was approached four times to dissuade him from his plans to return to the UK.[67] It is interesting to note, however, the positive spirit in which the church members prepared to ally themselves with the new government in their efforts towards reconstruction. Here is a reminder of the way Wang Juntang was willing to look for ways of cooperating with the Communist leadership in Qingzhou.

The CCP's invitation came at a time when no BMS medicals were available to take up work in the Foster Hospital. Two experienced missionaries, James Harris and Ronald Still (both pictured with SBU colleagues in Figure 17), had returned to China during 1946 with a view of reopening work in Zhoucun, where Still had previously been medical superintendent of the Foster Hospital. Their movements had been critically restricted by the turbulent military conditions, and they had returned to the UK shortly before the fall of Jinan.

Still had been invited by the Chinese leadership to join the permanent staff at Qilu University Hospital but, before word of the Zhoucun invitation reached the mission house, had reluctantly decided not to return to China in the immediate future, on account of the needs of his young family.[68] He submitted his resignation to the BMS in early 1949.[69] Although two new medical missionaries had been recruited for China since the end of the Second World War, at the beginning of 1949, with limited language skills and little experience of conditions in China, they could not take on the challenge of rebuilding the Foster Hospital at this critical time.[70]

---

[65] BMSA, CH/23, Secretariat Shantung, 1936–1949, Drake to Williamson, 26 October 1948.
[66] Howlett, 'Creating a New Shanghai', pp. 19, 153, etc.
[67] Jonathan J. Howlett, 'The British Boss is Gone and will Never Return: Communists Take Over British Companies in Shanghai, 1945–1954', *Modern Asian Studies*, (2013) Vol. 6, 1960, pp. 1941–1976.
[68] BMSA, China Subcommittee Minutes, Vol. 12, 20 October 1948.
[69] BMSA, China Subcommittee Minutes, Vol. 12, 18 January 1949.
[70] Williamson, *British Baptists*, p. 372.

The hospital was reopened by the Shandong synod at the end of 1948, under the leadership of Dr Chao – 'in ruined buildings and without equipment' but offering out-patient treatment and ten in-patient beds.[71] The staff comprised of Dr Chao, a dispenser, two nurses, two student nurses and four workmen. Initially it was not used as much as had been hoped, and its capacity to survive was therefore in question. In pre-war days it had attracted serious cases from the city and surrounding areas, but now its lack of equipment made it impossible to take on the most difficult cases. The modest services the hospital offered for minor complaints came into competition with the many new dispensaries that were more conveniently located in the city itself, while widespread and chronic poverty meant that many people could not afford treatment even for the most commonplace problems.

Figure 17: SBU Education Committee, June 1947[72]

Photo features (among others): Zhang Sijing (seated, centre), James Harris (seated, far right), the headteacher of Zhoucun school (rear, third from right) and Ronald Still (rear, second from right).

On the non-medical side, there are strong indications that the commitment of the Shandong Baptist church towards self-government and self-propagation was undiminished despite the hardships of the previous ten years. By May 1950,

---

[71] BMSA, CH/23, Secretariat Shantung, 1936–1949, English Baptist Mission, Shantung, Report for the year 1949, Drake, 5 May 1950.
[72] Private collection of Audrey Salters.

when Drake completed his annual report for 1948–1949, he was able to celebrate the fact that the central organisation of the Shandong church had been restored under the leadership of Zhang Sijing as executive secretary, who had resumed his position 'reluctantly at first, but with great energy and prophetic and creative power afterwards'.[73] The total number of pastors and evangelists in the province had been increased from thirty-four in 1949 to forty-five in 1950. Four young men who had joined the ageing group of clergy had emerged as possible church leaders of the future and were working with Zhang at the church headquarters in Zhoucun. After years of disruption and prohibition, nearly every church of the Shandong Baptist synod had been granted freedom to hold services, although this masked underlying practical difficulties. The church property in Qingzhou, for example, had been progressively occupied by government organisations, and the church itself was commandeered every weeknight as a cinema.[74]

The Shandong church leaders made plans for a new organisational structure to replace the 'mission stations' of the past. A 'Christian service centre' was set up in Zhoucun, and three other such centres were planned elsewhere in the province. The idea was to form communities of Christian people, living and working together; centres for 'church leadership, Christian instruction, mutual help in Christian living, training in rural industries, in public health, and in ways of serving the local community'. They were to be 'wholly Chinese in conception and control', but the contribution of foreign missionaries was not ruled out: 'there is no reason why in the future foreign missionaries of the same outlook and simplicity of life should not share in such communal living.'[75] The plan was for the centre to repair and make use of some of the empty and ruined buildings within the Foster Hospital compound for living quarters, workshops, classrooms and offices, and to make use of the vacant ground for growing crops and tending livestock. The crops and livestock would provide both a source of income and an opportunity for the pastors and lay workers to learn practical skills. Graduates of the Bible school in Jinan would spend the first couple of years of their post-graduate service at the centre, working as assistant staff members to support the centre's teaching and community work, while also having the opportunity to continue their training by learning some practical arts as well.

The maturity of the indigenous Shandong Baptists, and their capacity for self-government, is apparent in this Zhoucun initiative, while their wish to remain in association with foreign missionaries is suggested by their invitation to like-minded missionaries to take part. It seems that William Carey's 1796 vision of Christian converts living in community and supported by the labours of their own hands was now to be fulfilled.[76] The emphasis on the new centres being

---

[73] BMSA, CH/23, Secretariat Shantung, 1936–1949, English Baptist Mission, Shantung, Report for the year 1949, Drake, 5 May 1950.

[74] BMSA, CH/23, Secretariat Shantung, 1936–1949, English Baptist Mission, Shantung, Report for the year 1949, Drake, 5 May 1950.

[75] BMSA, CH/23, Secretariat Shantung, 1936–1949, English Baptist Mission, Shantung, Report for the year 1949, Drake, 5 May 1950.

[76] BMSA, IN/13, Carey to Fuller, 16 November 1796, in Stanley, *History*, p. 39.

'wholly Chinese in conception and control' made the social and cultural barriers that had long stood in the way of Carey's vision no longer relevant. At the same time, the Chinese Christians' statement that foreign missionaries were welcome at the invitation of the Chinese was a significant progression from the BMS regulations of 1885 that allowed 'such other Brethren as may be deemed suitable, being recommended by the Missionaries in China' to become full members of the BMS field committees.[77] With a development of this kind in place, the BMS might have been justified in considering their work in Shandong complete and the task successfully surrendered.

By the time Drake wrote his 1949 report, the Zhoucun Christian service centre was in operation, using parts of the former Foster Hospital premises.[78] Thirteen staff were employed, including a warden trained in practical crafts, a carpenter, three students and two workmen. Together, they had already harvested crops of maize (which had helped pay expenses), begun tending Leghorn fowl and purchased both a wool-spinning machine and some beehives, ready to expand the practical work of the community. Four graduates of the Jinan Bible school were about to arrive to begin their postings.

Drake remained in close touch with Zhang Sijing and the mission continued to provide a very modest contribution to church expenses. The total mission grant to China for the year ending 31 March 1950 was £8,337 (just over £365,000 today). This did not include missionaries' salaries and expenses, but covered work in Shaanxi as well as Shandong, including the institutional work of hospitals and schools, and the BMS contribution to Qilu University. Although exchange rates and local prices are not known, it is likely that the amount available for the support of church and pastoral work in the two provinces was extremely modest.[79]

The remaining role for the BMS in Shandong at the time was their work as part of Qilu University. Qilu's two evacuations, first to Chengdu during the Japanese occupation and then to Hangzhou during the civil war battle for Jinan, had left a legacy of rancour within the institution, and had produced tensions between the university and external authorities. Discontinuities in leadership, disagreements over allocation of funds, and discontent with proposals for syllabus reform were all contributory factors. In addition to such ongoing problems, the suspicion of collaboration on the part of those who had remained during the occupation was never completely absent from the minds of those who had left for Free China.[80]

By the end of 1949, the Shandong church had come of age, and was operating with minimal input from BMS personnel. The church's initiatives in pastoral work and evangelism were the outcome of many years of steady growth under

---

[77] BMSA General Committee minutes, 21 January 1885.
[78] BMSA, CH/23, Secretariat Shantung, 1936-1949, English Baptist Mission, Shantung, Report for the year 1949, Drake, 5 May 1950.
[79] BMSA, 158th Annual Report for Year ending 31 March 1950, p. 132.
[80] For a full discussion see Lutz, *China and the Christian Colleges*, pp. 364, 400–1, 407–8 and 454; and Corbett, *Shantung Christian University*, pp. 249–65.

the leadership of the indigenous SBU, with financial support from the BMS in the early years of the Japanese occupation and of the civil war. Efforts to resource the formidable outlay required for the BMS-funded hospitals were less successful, and here the church showed itself ready to work in partnership with local government.

CCP Moves to Control the Chinese Church

Despite the hopes entertained by the BMS missionaries in Shaanxi and Shandong, the period from 1948 saw the CCP assuming control of the Chinese church. Figure 18 sets out the timeline of political change and the responses of church and mission that defined the final stages of the BMS presence in China.

Figure 18: CCP moves leading to the departure of the BMS, 1948-1952

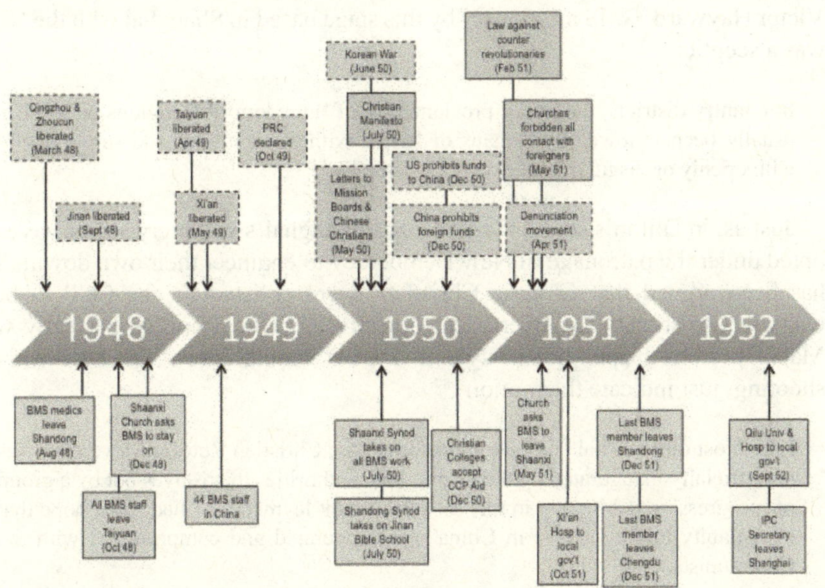

'There is no doubt in my mind', wrote Derk Bodde, then a student in Beijing, in his diary on 26 January 1950, 'that the Communists come here with the bulk of the people on their side.'[81] It is certain that many Chinese Christians were amongst those who welcomed the inauguration of the People's Republic on 1 October 1949. Missionaries and Chinese Christians considered it a positive sign that the first meeting of the new Chinese People's Political Consultative Conference (CPPCC), which convened in September 1949 to discuss the establishment of the new state, included five members of the Protestant church:

---

[81] Derk Bodde, *Peking Diary: A Year of Revolution* (New York: Schumann, 1950), p. 99.

Wu Yaozong, Publications Secretary of the Young Men's Christian Association (YMCA); Dr T. C. Chao, Dean of the Yenching School of Religion and one of six presidents of the World Council of Churches; Cora Deng, General Secretary of the Young Women's Christian Association (YWCA); H. Y. Chang, Editor of the *Christian Farmer* magazine; and Liu Liang-Mao, of the National Committee of the YMCA.[82] These were government nominees, not elected delegates of the National Christian Council (NCC), and all of them had been sympathetic to Communist proposals for ending the civil war and organising a coalition government.[83]

It was this conference that approved the Common Program, effectively the constitution of the PRC until 1954, which guaranteed freedom of religious belief. This was in contrast to the repressive policy of Communists towards Christians in the villages of Shandong during the civil war, when they had been 'bitterly hostile to the Church, and made our pastors one of the main targets of their propaganda. Christians were dubbed "reactionary, feudalistic and capitalistic."'[84] Victor Hayward, BMS missionary by this stage based in Shanghai with the NCC, was a sceptic:

> In country districts, the initial proclamation of 'Freedom of Religious belief' has usually been followed by slogans of 'down with Superstition' and subsequently with openly or disguised attacks on Christianity.[85]

Just as, in Dillon's study, the leaders of Shanghai's voluntary sector were co-opted under the patronage of New Democracy to engineer their own downfall, it has been argued that Chinese Christians were enlisted by the CCP to bend Chinese Christianity to government objectives.[86] This accorded perfectly with Mao's preferred operational style: the CCP should 'draw the bow without shooting, just indicate the motion'.[87]

> Like most other social and cultural reforms, the Christian Reform Movement was not officially inaugurated by the Communist authorities themselves but by a group of 'progressive' Chinese – in this case Protestant laymen who had some hope that Christianity might survive in China if it cooperated and compromised with the Communists.[88]

Following the CPPCC meeting, eighteen leading Chinese Christians – including presidents of Christian Colleges; the general secretaries of the

---

[82] Williamson, *British Baptists*, p. 179.

[83] Lutz, *China and the Christian Colleges*, p. 415.

[84] Williamson, *British Baptists*, p. 186.

[85] BMSA CH/60, Hayward Newsletter 3 to friends, 10 June 1949.

[86] Dillon, 'New Democracy', pp. 80–102.

[87] Mao's report, 'An investigation into the Peasant Movement in Hunan in 1927', in Donald E. MacInnis, *Religious Policy and Practice in Communist China: A Documentary History* (London: Hodder and Staughton, 1972), p. 8.

[88] Hooper, *China Stands Up*, p. 112.

Christian Literature Society (CLS), the Council of Christian Publishers, the Church of Christ in China (CCC), the YMCA and YWCA; and the assistant secretary of the General Synod of the Anglican Communion; as well as 'some well-known Christian laymen' – sent a letter to the home boards of all missionary societies.[89] The letter was critical of the close connection between Chinese church organisations and the UK and the USA, and the consequent implicit association of Chinese Christians with imperialism. In its final section on 'Future Relationships Between the Chinese Christian Church and Missionary Societies', the letter urged that all policy determination and financial administration in church affairs should be turned over to Chinese hands as soon as possible, and urgent steps should be taken towards complete financial independence. The letter went on, however, to say:

> There is nothing in principle which makes the future position of the missionary untenable, or renders his service unnecessary. On the contrary there is a definite challenge to work and serve under adverse circumstances and to bear witness to the ecumenical fellowship.[90]

The insistence that leadership and administrative responsibility of the church should be passed to the Chinese was consistent with accepted BMS policy, and the assurance that there was a continuing role for missionaries was welcome.

Along with the letter addressed to the missionary societies' home boards, the group of CCP-nominated Christians formulated a letter addressed to all Christians in China. This letter commended the Christian contribution to Chinese society in the past, and urged the church 'under the Leadership of the People's Government, to fulfil the responsibilities it bears as a People's Organization, […] energetically pushing forward its pioneering work'.[91] Such an appeal to Christians to lend their support to the vital process of national reconstruction fitted with the widely held aspirations of the period and was well judged to persuade patriotic Christians to comply with government demands. Political education was made compulsory in all organisations by the end of 1949. This increased the pressure on Christians to conform to CCP policy, but was taken up without undue misgiving as indicated by Menzies Clow's response in the BMS hospital in Xi'an.[92]

In May 1950, Premier Zhou Enlai invited a small number of Christian leaders, most of whom 'had a reputation as enthusiastic supporters of the new regime', to Beijing to discuss the future of the Protestant church, the ways in which it could contribute to national reconstruction, and the conditions under which the new government would permit the church to continue to practise and propagate its faith.[93] In Zhou's view, the churches would have no place in the New China

---

89 Williamson, *British Baptists*, p. 179.
90 Jones and Merwin, *Documents of the Three-Self Movement*, p. 17.
91 Jones and Merwin, *Documents of the Three-Self Movement*, p. 10.
92 BMSA CH/10, M. Clow to E. Clow, 29 October 1949.
93 Lutz, *China and the Christian Colleges*, p. 459.

unless they could prove that they were not connected in any way with imperialism. To do this, they must terminate their economic dependence on foreign funding and must sever all other links with foreign missions.[94] A first step must be for responsible church leaders to issue a statement to Chinese Christians. Here, again, the CCP leadership would 'draw the bow' and 'indicate the motion'.[95]

This carefully chosen group of Christian 'supporters of the new regime' responded by producing a document under the official title, 'Direction of Endeavour for Chinese Christianity in the Construction of New China', later better known as the Christian Manifesto.[96] The manifesto was strongly critical of past links between Christianity and imperialism, and called on Chinese Christians to guard against imperialist attempts to destroy the Chinese revolution. It asked them to show their support for the New China by working towards a totally independent Chinese church, free of foreign influence and personnel, and required them to 'carry on anti-imperialistic, anti-feudalistic and anti-bureaucratic-capitalistic education'.[97]

The campaign to obtain signatures to the manifesto marked the unofficial beginning of the Three-Self Patriotic Movement (TSPM).[98] Although the TSPM was not formally approved by the party until 1954, a preparatory council was established following the meeting with Zhou, and those church leaders who had met with him became de facto leaders of the new movement.[99] The 8 May 1951 issue of *Tianfeng*, which had become the official voice of the new leaders, contained a report by Wu Yaozong that dismissed missionary efforts towards self-governance, self-support and self-propagation (自治 自养 自传 *zizhi, ziyang, zizhuan*), such as those made by the BMS, as a 'false Three-Self Movement'.[100] The new movement must be free of all associations with foreigners and independent of foreign financial backing. As such, it would have the support of the new government of China.

CCP hostility towards America, stoked by the United States' post-war support for Chiang Kai-shek and the Guomindang (GMD), was hugely inflamed by the outbreak of the Korean War on 25 June 1950. Any lingering acceptance of the place of foreigners in the PRC ceased. The Christian manifesto was circulated widely just at this time, and its themes resonated with CCP demands to 'hate, curse and despise the imperialists' that formed the bedrock of the 'Resist America, Aid Korea' campaign (抗美援朝 *kang mei yuan chao*). Christians were aware that failing to sign the manifesto was a sure way to draw attention to a lack

---

[94] Hood, *Neither Bang nor Whimper*, pp. 104–5.

[95] Mao's report, 'An investigation into the Peasant Movement in Hunan in 1927', in. MacInnis, *Religious Policy and Practice*, p. 8.

[96] Bays, *New History*, p. 162.

[97] From the summary of the Manifesto by H. Raymond Williamson in *British Baptists*, p. 184. See also Bays, *New History*, pp. 161–62.

[98] Whyte, *Unfinished Encounter*, pp. 217–18.

[99] André Laliberté, 'Religion and the State in China: The Limits of Institutionalization', *Journal of Current Chinese Affairs*, 2011, No. 2, pp. 3–15 (p. 4).

[100] Jones and Merwin, *Documents of the Three-Self Movement*, pp. 34-43.

of patriotism, just at a time when conspicuous demonstrations of national loyalty were called for. One prominent Chinese Christian refused to sign the manifesto, and others were critical of the Marxist tone of the document, but it was eventually signed by more than 417,000 Chinese, almost half the total Protestant church membership.[101]

Prompted by the tone of the manifesto, the members of BMS staff in Shaanxi handed over all responsibility for the work, funds and property of the mission to the Chinese church members. The formal handover took place during the Shaanxi synod meetings of July 1950. Joan Williamson sent home details of the occasion. 'This has been a happy, fruitful and useful year in church life,' she wrote, going on to describe and reflect on the handover:

> This little group [of Chinese Christians] who accepted this trust from the BMS […] were not the mighty, or the strong, or the very wise, but simple people like ourselves. Not a few tears were shed and for a time words were impossible as the business of handing over was transacted. That was because of the happy fellowship which has always existed in this part of China between the sending and the receiving church…From the historical point of view it was a great moment.[102]

Williamson's description of the relinquishment of missionary responsibilities speaks of considerable warmth and of a relationship of mutual trust and respect, which is in stark contrast to Ling's assessment that 'The church and missions were unable to operate on the basis of a relationship of mutual trust and respect.'[103] It was a dignified, formal transaction with apparent agreement on both sides that it was the right thing to do. The Chinese members formally declared that all the Shaanxi missionaries were 'genuine friends of the Chinese people'.[104] The missionaries present welcomed the new arrangement 'with joy as a sign that the goal of all missionary endeavour had been achieved'.[105]

From that point, changes in the international situation worked to bring new pressures to bear. Tensions between China and the United States – further heightened in October 1950 by the entry of the PLA, in the form of Chinese 'volunteers', against the United Nations' forces in the Korean War – led the United States government to forbid the transfer of funds to China.[106] The CCP retaliated by prohibiting any organisation in China from receiving aid from abroad. Christian leaders were told that all Christian institutions receiving money from the United States must be transferred forthwith to government control.[107] The Christian colleges throughout China were forced to abandon any links with the West. Even social contacts between individual Chinese and Westerners might place the Chinese under suspicion, and as a result many Western teachers ceased

---

[101] Whyte, *Unfinished Encounter*, p. 218.
[102] BMSA, CH/78, Williamson to friends, 30 August 1950.
[103] Ling, *Changing Role*, p. 221.
[104] BMSA, CH67, Young to Prayer Partners, 31 July 1950.
[105] Stanley, *History*, p. 330.
[106] Lutz, *China and the Christian Colleges*, p. 461.
[107] Williamson, *British Baptists*, p. 185.

meeting their classes, and missionaries in some places found themselves ostracised by church members who had formerly been friendly.[108]

In February 1951, the CCP issued a new directive: the Campaign to Suppress Counterrevolutionaries, a category that encompassed anyone who had shown themselves to be unsympathetic or opposed to the government, and any individuals or organisations that they were able to connect with imperialism. As a result, following a series of mass rallies during the summer of 1951, many thousands were arrested and executed.

> As the campaign grew in intensity it became brutal and terrifying. For millions of Chinese the violence and humiliation of these days effectively ended any hope that they would be able to live out their lives peacefully under the Communist regime, whatever their past histories might have been.[109]

Brutality combined with intimidation, and the consequences were far-reaching:

> We all felt fear. We stopped speaking even to those with whom we were normally very close…Everybody was denouncing others and was denounced by others. Everybody was living in fear.[110]

A few months later, attacks were orchestrated within churches and church institutions. Denunciation meetings were held in cities throughout China, at which Christians were encouraged to criticise their leaders and fellow members.[111] Delegates from the Baptist church in Xi'an attended meetings with government officials in Beijing. George Young wrote that Christian pastors at these meetings accused their fellows, 'in fiery angry words', 'of being "spies" and "secret servants of imperial power"'.[112] The Shaanxi delegates returned to Xi'an following these meetings. It was almost a year after the BMS had handed over all property and leadership to Chinese Christians, but now the church members met with their missionary colleagues and 'sorrowfully asked us to terminate our work immediately'.

> Since it was no longer possible for us to preach and teach and since our presence was an embarrassment to the Chinese church, we had no option but to apply for our exit permits. These were courteously and speedily given to us by the local authorities.[113]

The last of the BMS missionaries in Shaanxi therefore left China in July 1951.

---

[108] Lutz, *China and the Christian Colleges*, p. 463.
[109] Spence, *The Search for Modern China*, p. 535.
[110] Dikötter, *Tragedy*, pp. 182–83, citing Liu Xiaoyu in Wang Ying, 'Gaizao sixiang: Zhengzhi, lishi yu jiyi' (Reforming Thoughts: Politics, History and Memory, 1949–1953), (PhD dissertation, Beijing: People's University, 2010).
[111] Bays, *New History*, p. 163.
[112] BMSA, CH/67, Young to Prayer Partners, 5 July 1951.
[113] BMSA, CH/67, Young to Prayer Partners, 5 July 1951.

In Shandong, Peter F. Nelson, a pharmacist recruited after the war to work in Jinan, was one of the last to leave in 1951. In his memoir, he recounts details of his last days there, describing the 'constant stream of visits' from staff and students who came to wish him well and thank him for his work in the university.[114] Two or three days before he and his fiancée were due to leave, they had a visit from a group of about thirty students bringing a picture on which they had inscribed a thank-you message signed by all of them. The next day, three of the students returned, this time with the student political cadre, himself a member of Nelson's pharmacy class. They told Nelson that the authorities had expressed strong disapproval of their action and they had been ordered to take the present back.

> The following evening, very late, we had a further visit from the student cadre. He said he had come of his own free will and asked us not to tell anyone else. He apologised for the disappointment we must feel and virtually admitted that he did not approve of the way that the party had acted but he said that at least we knew how much our work for the students had been appreciated.[115]

Glimpses such as this into details of the missionaries' experiences in their last months in China are rare. They provide evidence that the publicised official narrative of alienation between missionaries and Chinese Christians does not tell the full story of the missionary departure.

By November 1951, only two missionaries remained in mainland China: Hubert Spillett in Shanghai and Jim Sutton in Chengdu. Both had applied for exit visas. Sutton's was granted in December 1951 and Spillett's in September 1952.[116] Two others remained in Hong Kong, helping with transit arrangements.

It had become clear during these final months of their work in China that, within the new political dispensation, the time had come for the indigenous church to assume responsibility for the future, and only Chinese Christians could take part in the work.

Departure and Decisions about Subsequent Postings

> We are out of China – that will be good news to many of our anxious friends, but it is a heartbreaking experience for us. Dismantling the old home, saying such a permanent goodbye to beloved friends and fellow workers, stopping the work of preaching the Gospel to the Chinese, leaving the old historic city of Sian, this has all been a shattering experience.[117]

---

[114] Private collection of Peter J. Nelson, unpublished memoir, p. 51.
[115] Private collection of Peter J. Nelson, unpublished memoir, p. 51.
[116] BMSA, China Subcommittee Minutes, Vol. 12, 6 November 1951; Williamson, *British Baptists,* p. 197.
[117] BMSA, CH/67, Young, Prayer letter to friends, 5 July 1951.

The enormous sense of loss that Young expresses in this letter remained with many former China missionaries throughout their lives, as this author[118] observed listening to many conversations between her parents and their former colleagues between 1950 and 1985. Not only had their work been brought to an abrupt end, but they had also been cut off completely from their Chinese friends and colleagues, with whom thereafter no communication was possible for more than thirty years. As the years went by, groups of missionaries circulated amongst themselves compilations of news of former colleagues, in which they were able to include, very rarely, general news from China.[119] It was not until after the death of Mao in 1976 that channels of communication gradually reopened, leading to correspondence between old friends and colleagues, and, eventually, to a number of return visits to China.[120]

Those missionaries who, on leaving China, felt unable to transfer to mission work in another BMS field were faced with acute personal dilemmas about what to do next. Their work experience and work patterns as missionaries had been very different from anything they were likely to experience in the UK. One forty-eight-year-old who had spent more than twenty years in China delayed making the decision to resign for several years. He transferred to Ceylon and eventually wrote to the China secretary about his uncertainty:

At the moment I have merely come to the conclusion that I don't want a pastorate in England. I am not a Denominationalist at all, and my outlook is philosophic rather than dogmatic, and I find this hard to fit into the denominational mould...I really don't know what to do...I need not say how sad we are and how perplexed.[121]

Experience of many years' cooperation with the ecumenical CCC had made this former China missionary keenly aware of his calling primarily as a Christian, rather than as a Baptist. Other adjustments had to be made by medical missionaries returning to the UK, who had to accommodate themselves to the change in structures and opportunities open to them within the newly established National Health Service. One experienced missionary doctor was wary:

I have not yet formed a very favourable opinion of the new Health Service and I am hoping it will be possible to find some work that will not be too closely bound up with red tape.[122]

The BMS itself was faced with logistical problems, trying to make best use of almost eighty missionaries who were on its payroll but not immediately suited

---

[118] Audrey Salters, née Still.

[119] For example, Ingle annual newsletter.

[120] Interview with Peter J. Nelson, Dalgety Bay, 13 May 2010; letters to R. J. Still from private collection of Audrey Salters, including from Gao Xueling, 30 August 1980, Zhou Maozhen, 18 October 1983 and Zhang Yumei, 3 February 1985.

[121] BMSA, CH/54, Allen to Hayward, 23 November 1953.

[122] British Red Cross Archives, JWO/9/2, China Commission, correspondence with Dr Flowers and others, 1946–53, Flowers to Sir Ernest Burdon, 13 September 1949.

to work on any of its other mission fields. For American missionary societies, the primary principle in redeployment was to continue to serve Chinese people wherever possible. It seemed to make sense to capitalise on the missionaries' language skills, familiarity with the cultural background and affection for the Chinese people. Some funds had in the past been specifically set aside for work in China, and a legitimate use had to be made of these. As a result, by the end of 1952, around seventy-five American missionaries from China had been reassigned to Hong Kong, and another 114 to Taiwan, formerly called Formosa. The former director of the Missionary Research Library in New York was concerned that this policy created an unhelpful and inappropriate imbalance between missionaries and indigenous leaders, 'even taking into account the large number of refugees flooding these places'.[123]

The BMS did not follow this route (see Figure 19). Because of its well-developed work and existing infrastructure in India and Ceylon, a majority of missionaries who continued working for the BMS transferred there, while a handful of others were designated to BMS work in Africa and the West Indies. The exodus from China was seen by some in the mission house as 'a providential opportunity to open a new sphere of work'. Latin America offered the prospect of a new and potentially productive BMS field, and one couple was assigned to explore the possibilities for work in Brazil.[124] The Malayan Emergency provided opportunities for those with Chinese language skills, and two former China missionaries resigned from the BMS to take employment with the Colonial Service there.[125] Two others who were able to make continuing use of their fluent Chinese were Drake, who was appointed to the chair of Chinese at the Chinese University of Hong Kong, and Edward Phillips, who took a post with the Foreign Office.[126]

---

[123] Creighton Lacy, 'The Missionary Exodus from China', *Pacific Affairs*, Vol. 28.4 (December 1955), pp. 301–314 (p. 303), citing R. Pierce Beaver.
[124] Stanley, *History*, p. 471.
[125] Upchurch, *Prevailing Wind*, pp. 241–71.
[126] Williamson, *British Baptists*, p. 261; Rosemary Pearson (née Phillips), email to Audrey Salters, 22 October 2014.

Figure 19: Location or Destination of former China missionaries, April 1952[127]

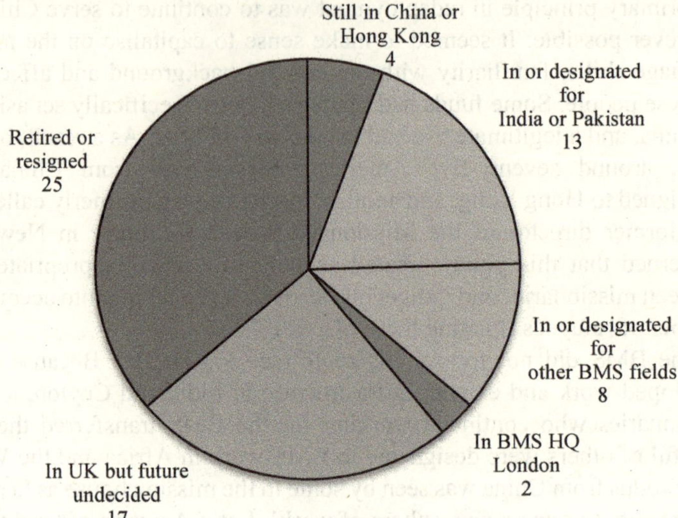

Much information that would have served to provide a fuller picture of the departure of missionaries from China is not available within the missionary archive. We cannot make sense of this final phase of the missionary presence if we do not make allowances for these gaps, and for the pressures under which Chinese Christians were operating.

The BMS missionaries found themselves first greeted with apparent warmth, and then ousted by the CCP, following the formation of the PRC in 1949. This is mirrored in what happened to the foreign business community at the same time. What is different is that the BMS sought to find ways to hand over their work to their Chinese colleagues, rather than aim to get away as soon as they found that their business could no longer be profitable in China. They left behind a well-established Chinese church, striving not primarily to escape from missionary dominance but to find a place for itself in the context of the changed political scene in China.

In Shaanxi, formal agreements were reached, first to transfer leadership and assets from the BMS to the Chinese church, and later for the missionaries to withdraw entirely from China. In Shandong, a decision made by the mission years earlier to 'surrender the task' finally came to fruition: the predominantly Chinese SBU – already set on a path to self-support, self-governance and self-propagation – created mechanisms that it hoped would enable it to survive in the new political climate. Until it proved impossible to do so, the SBU maintained its links with the few remaining Baptist missionaries in the province and drew on the modicum of financial support that the BMS continued to make available.

---

[127] Data from BMSA China Subcommittee Minutes, Vol. 12, 6 April 1952.

The vilification of missionaries that was a feature of the Campaign to Suppress Counterrevolutionaries does not mirror the way Chinese Christians took leave of BMS missionaries at the time of their departure. The Baptist archive shows evidence that relationships between Chinese Christians and missionaries remained cordial, even affectionate, at the time the missionaries left China, and, while there was regret on both sides at their leaving, there was mutual recognition that the time had come for them to go their separate ways.[128]

Nevertheless, the frenzied public repudiation in the PRC of missionaries, and all that they had stood for, was keenly felt and had a profound influence on the development of missions worldwide.[129]

---

[128] BMSA, CH/78, JKW to friends, 30 May 1950; CH/67, Young to Prayer Partners, 5 July 1951.
[129] Stanley, *History*, p. 332.

Conclusions

The Chinese Communists were determined to rid China of the pernicious influences of feudalism and imperialism, and to make Marxism the sole ideological guide for this task…Christian missionary work in China was eliminated shortly after the Communist takeover, and three decades later the native Christian church has virtually disappeared from the People's Republic of China.[1]

Yip, writing in 1980, was correct in his reference to the work of foreign missionaries. Within three years of the Communist takeover, the last Protestant missionaries had left China and, after their departure, were unable to maintain any contact with friends or former colleagues in China.

Yip was not, however, correct regarding the disappearance of the native Chinese Christian church. Bays suggests a figure of 'five to six million Protestants and a very rapid growth rate, in the late 1970s'.[2] Less than ten years later, a 'reasoned estimate' of Protestant Christian numbers stood at 20 million.[3] Subsequent reports from China suggest that numbers have continued to grow substantially. Estimates vary: the government says 24 million; independent estimates agree that this is a vast underestimate. Now a figure of 60 million, once deemed a gross exaggeration, is considered conservative.[4]

Exploring the years 1937 to 1952 in the context of a thriving twenty-first-century Christian church in China introduces a new dynamic to the historical analysis. This was a significant period of transition in the history of Christianity in China, when the Chinese church separated conclusively from its predominantly Western origins; when foreigners left and Chinese Christians sought to find their direction in a changed political environment. These years were not the dying moments of a failed endeavour, but a period of transition and an attempt to bring into being a new organism from the disappearing life of the old. The story of this period of history is told through the lives of individual missionaries and their interactions with Chinese Christians and with secular authorities – Japanese occupiers, the civic administration, the Red Army, Guomindang (GMD), or the Chinese Communist Party (CCP) – as well as with the missionary society in London.

---

[1] Yip, *Religion, Nationalism*, p. 90.

[2] Bays, *New History*, p. 186.

[3] Tiedemann, *Handbook*, p. 815, citing Tony Lambert, 'Counting Christians in China: Who's Right?', *News Network International*, 14 April 1989, pp. 28–36.

[4] Tim Gardam, 'God in China: Christianity and Catholicism', BBC Radio 4 aired on 12 September 2011, at https://www.bbc.co.uk/programmes/b014fblw accessed on 12 March 2014.

These interactions were greatly influenced by the differing political and societal context in each of the provinces studied. They were coloured by the complicated emotions and loyalties generated both by the Japanese occupation of 1937 to 1945, and the Chinese Civil War of 1946 to 1949. During this period, tensions created by the need to find ways to survive within a fractured political environment were added to the existing hurdles in the way of mutual understanding between Chinese people and foreigners. Baptist missionaries associated closely with their Chinese colleagues, but could never enter fully into the needs, hopes and practical considerations that influenced them. There would always be cultural differences, patriotic allegiances and peculiar circumstances that would separate the missionary from the indigenous Christian. The fact that, as far as can be judged from the archival record, BMS missionaries and Chinese Christians kept faith with one another, and continued to work together, is worthy of recognition even though neither party could fully understand the predicaments of the other during the Japanese occupation and the civil war. This has perhaps been insufficiently recognised in the secondary literature.[5]

Missionaries during this period worked often sacrificially to support the Chinese church and enable it to go forward. Most had a deep respect for Chinese culture, Chinese abilities, Chinese intellect. Notwithstanding all of that, they weren't Chinese and could not fully understand the depth of feeling of their colleagues: Chinese nationals, whose homeland had been exploited by the West, invaded and occupied by neighbouring Japan and was engulfed in a bitter civil war. Ultimately, the missionaries had the option of returning home if they chose or needed to. Their Chinese colleagues were already home and needed to make pragmatic choices about the best way to work towards peace and a settled government, something that the People's Republic of China (PRC) promised.[6]

Like all historical accounts, this story reflects both what has been found and what it has not been possible to find. The knowledge of censorship by outside bodies – the Japanese or British military, or the CCP – meant that missionaries withheld from their correspondence much information that would have helped to provide a more complete picture of events in China during these years. Historians of mission and of the CCP have had purposes of their own in compiling their records. The discrepancies between the various accounts of the history of the period demonstrate that much is open to reinterpretation – as the story of Wang Juntang of Qingzhou demonstrates (see Chapter Five).

Some things are, however, clear. By the late 1930s, the Chinese church that the BMS had founded in Shandong was reaching towards the independence that had been the goal of the society from the outset. An organisational structure had been established based on Chinese leadership at both local and provincial levels. In Zhang Sijing the SBU had a leader who was capable of acting independently,

---

⁵ Hood, *Neither Bang nor Whimper*, p. 202; Gao Wangzhi, 'Y. T. Wu: A Christian Leader Under Communism' in Daniel H. Bays, *Christianity in China from the Eighteenth Century to the Presnt*, (Stanford: Stanford University Press, 1996), pp. 338–352 (p. 344).
⁶ Westad, *Decisive Encounters*, p. 5; Bodde, *Peking Diary*, p. 24.

but who also had a strong relationship with BMS missionaries. His relationship with Raymond Williamson, the influential foreign secretary at the mission house in London, was particularly important. The shared desire of the SBU to establish independence from the mission, and the commitment of the society to withdraw from the province, were undermined throughout this period by the impoverishment of the church and the desperate living conditions created by the continuation of war and the Japanese occupation. As a result, the church in Shandong was repeatedly thrown back on the society for material support.

Others have argued that Japanese occupation facilitated the Chinese church breaking free from missionary societies against the wishes of missionaries keen to retain control, and with no real consideration of the real situation in China or the views of their Chinese colleagues.[7] However, those arguments do not stack up against the evidence, at least in respect of the BMS experience. It was poverty and national crisis – not mission control – that prevented the Shandong Baptist church from achieving independence.[8] And it was the urgent request for help from their Chinese colleagues that brought BMS missionaries back to Shandong at the end of the war.

By the mid-1940s, the Chinese Baptist church in Shaanxi had not moved as far towards independence as its counterpart in Shandong. As well as providing financial backing and some leadership to the church, the BMS continued to support and interact with the local community through its institutional provision in the form of schools and hospitals. The work of the Zunde school in Xi'an provided valuable lessons in the necessity of working closely with municipal and provincial lay authorities. These lessons would be necessary to the survival of the school under a Communist regime.

The continued commitment of the BMS to its work in China, so long as this was in keeping with the wishes and needs of the Chinese church, was demonstrated by its persistence in maintaining its workforce there throughout this turbulent and inflationary period. This persistence was accompanied by a recognition that the time had come for a fundamental change in the way the mission organised its work in relation to the Chinese church. It was in recognition of this fundamental change that in June 1945 the BMS China subcommittee recommended the secondment of two of its staff members to work in the GMD-sponsored Border Service Department, under the management of the Church of Christ in China (CCC).

While this initiative showed awareness of important changes in the relationship between church and mission, it also illustrates the fact that senior staff on the Home Committees were not at that time taking sufficient cognisance of changes in the political climate and that there was a divergence in perspectives between home and fieldwork staff. Despite H. R. Williamson's undisputed knowledge of pre-war China and his strong relationship with members of the Nationalist leadership while he was in China during the 1920s and 1930s, his

---

[7] Ling, *Changing Role*, pp. 51 and 53; Brook, 'Toward Independence', p.319.
[8] See for example Ling, *Changing Role*, p. 51.

absence from China during the crucial war years left him distant from the changing political scene and made him slow to recognise the decline in the authority of Chiang Kai-shek and the GMD party that had taken place by the end of the war with Japan.

Both before and after the Communists came to power, Baptist missionaries welcomed opportunities to engage with them at a personal level by inviting them to share meals and engaging them in discussion. The records indicate the wholeheartedness with which the remnant of BMS missionaries who were still in China at the time of the Communist takeover attempted to work in cooperation with the Communist civic authorities. Ling dismisses this as naivety and self-deception, but a convincing alternative interpretation is that they were open to new conditions and willing to embrace change. These are qualities for which missionaries in the past have not always been credited.

The Baptist archive supports the view that relationships between Chinese Christians and BMS missionaries remained cordial, even affectionate, at the time the missionaries left China – and longer-term, when communications could resume post-1976. [9] The archive demonstrates, too, that the missionaries left behind strong Christian communities in both Shaanxi and Shandong and that they had been partners with the Chinese church in building these up. The missionaries' precipitate departure from Shanxi during the siege of Taiyuan leaves the experience of the church there largely unreported in the missionary correspondence in the years that followed. Although the end of the BMS presence in China was neither unplanned nor unwelcome, the public denigration of missionaries that preceded their departure was painful, and the completeness of the enforced break with former friends and colleagues was deeply distressing. The well-publicised criticisms that the missions went hand-in-hand with imperial aggression – which were painfully explored in the retrospective self-analysis of missionaries and missionary societies – owe their origins in no small measure to the Communist-inspired accusations of the first years of the PRC.

On the wider questions about the foreign presence in China, Mitter has written:

> The challenge for the new historiography of China has been to bring the imperial presence into the narrative of Chinese history, avoiding both a black-and-white condemnation of the imperial presence simply as depradation and plunder, and the complacent position that imperialism was essentially a 'helping hand' in bringing China to modernity.[10]

These words about the 'imperial presence' could equally be applied to the missionary presence: both the role of missions within Chinese history and in terms of the role of individual missionaries within mission history. While

---

[9] Interview with Peter J. Nelson, Dalgety Bay, 13 May 2010; letters to R. J. Still from private collection of Audrey Salters, including from Gao Xueling, 30 August 1980, Zhou Maozhen, 18 October 1983 and Zhang Yumei, 3 February 1985.
[10] Mitter, 'Modernity', p. 530.

missionary societies provided the infrastructure and the general directions for the work, the societies' actual achievements were predominantly the work of individual missionaries based in China. Their contributions were shaped by the conditions they were working in, their personal views on what it meant to be part of the endeavour, their personal and familial experiences, and factors in the UK that had a bearing on their work and their well-being.

Personal needs and sensitivities played a part in interactions between British and Chinese colleagues, and between individual missionaries and the home committees. Developments in the UK also shaped the choices and resources open to missionaries and to the BMS as a society. Years of hardship and uncertainty in China (made worse by conditions in the UK), the inability to make satisfactory provision for their families, and anxiety about wider families, and how to fulfil their responsibilities to them, all affected the work of BMS missionaries in China during this period.

The emphasis in recent research on the history of Christianity in China has been on the growth of indigenous Christianity.[11] The BMS archive provides a glimpse of the strong network of indigenous Baptist churches that existed in Shandong in the 1930s and 1940s, formed through the joint efforts of Chinese and foreigners beginning with the arrival of the first Baptist missionaries in the 1860s. Forsyth reports that already by 1910, there were twelve Baptist churches in the province that were self-supporting and able to fund their own Chinese pastors.[12] These snippets of information whet our appetite for learning more about the development of the SBU from the late 1880s. The experience of the Chinese churches during the latter part of the Japanese occupation, when foreigners were absent, is of particular interest and has not been a focus of any substantive Western research to date, with the exception of Brook's.[13]

In this context, it is possible that Chinese documentary evidence that is directly relevant to an understanding of these early church communities is now scarce or currently inaccessible in China. One recent piece of work by a Chinese scholar on the history of the BMS in China relied very heavily on Williamson's *British Baptists*.[14] Archival evidence can, however, be supplemented by archaeological and ethnographic data, as Lee has pointed out. Drawing on physical evidence such as the remnants of old churches, village walls, watch towers and lineage buildings, Lee has sought to reconstruct the social settings within which early Christians operated in Chaozhou (潮州). 'This approach represents a methodological breakthrough by going beyond the writings of

---

[11] For example, Ryan Dunch, *Fuzhou Protestants and the Making of Modern China, 1857–1927* (New Haven, CT: Yale University Press, 2001); Joseph Tse-Hei Lee, *The Bible and the Gun: Christianity in South China, 1860–1900* (London and New York: Routledge, 2003); Bays, *New History*.

[12] Robert C. Forsyth, *Shantung: The Sacred Province of China* (Shanghai: Christian Literature Society, 1912), pp. 189–284.

[13] Bays, *New History*, p. 142; Brook, 'Toward Independence'.

[14] Zhang Daming 張大明, Yingguo Jinlihui zai Hua Huodong Kaocha 英國浸禮會在華活動考察 (*An Investigation of The Baptist Missionary Society's Activities in China*), 1840-1952' (MA Thesis, Shandong University (Shanda 山大), 2010).

Western missionaries and Chinese officials to study the local congregational histories.'[15] Physical and social conditions in the northern provinces in which the BMS worked were very different from those in Guangdong province, where Lee's research was based, but his creative methodology provides some interesting ideas for potential further research. There remain, for example, several church buildings in Shandong that date back to the very early work of the SBU.

Looking ahead from 1952, there is still much that remains unknown, in particular how local Chinese church leaders like Zhang Sijing and Wang Juntang made, or failed to make, the adjustment to the new church order open to Chinese Protestants in the PRC as members of the Three-Self Patriotic Movement (TSPM). How closely did their experience mirror that of those who became high-profile leaders of the TSPM – for example K. H. Ting (丁光训; Ding Guangxun), formerly Anglican Bishop of Zhejiang province – and those who prominently resisted, for example Wang Mingdao (王明道)?[16] Bearing in mind Watson's reference to 'situations where alternative understandings of the past are tantamount to treason', it may still be too early for scholars in the PRC to attempt to open up this sensitive area.[17] But the window of time for collecting first-hand oral evidence from Chinese Christians who lived through this period of history is rapidly closing.

Nevertheless, there remains evidence of the legacy of BMS work in China. Original Baptist church buildings are in regular use by TSPM congregations in Jinan, Qingzhou, Xi'an and Zhoucun, although during the years of the Cultural Revolution they were co-opted for use as canteens, day centres or cinemas. The Guangbei School in Zhoucun (now Zibo No. 6 High School) and the Zunde School in Xi'an (now Xi'an No. 3 High School) have thrived and are held in high regard in their respective communities. The writers of the centennial history of the school in Zhoucun were meticulous in their efforts to do justice to the BMS contribution, to the extent of sending one of their staff to the Angus Library in Oxford to search the primary sources.[18]

Very substantial modern hospitals stand on the sites of all the BMS hospitals. None of the buildings of the former Foster Hospital in Zhoucun remain, but a vast military hospital stands in its place. This is consistent with the immediate post-war developments when, by 1948, it was proving very difficult to maintain a hospital in Zhoucun, run by either church or mission. A statue of Dr Norman Bethune is

---

[15] Lee, *The Bible and the Gun*, p. 169.

[16] See Janice and Philip L. Wickeri (eds), *A Chinese Contribution to Ecumenical Theology: Selected Writings of Bishop K. H. Ting* (Geneva: WCC Publications, 2002); Wickeri, *Reconstructing Christianity*; Bays, *New History*, p. 176; Stephen Wang, *The Long Road to Freedom: The Story of Wang Mingdao*, trans. Ma Ming (Lancaster, 2002); Thomas A. Harvey, *Acquainted with Grief: Wang Mingdao's Stand for the Persecuted Church in China* (Grand Rapids, MI: Bra Press, 2002).

[17] Lee and Yang, *Re-envisioning*, p. 4, citing Rubie Watson (ed), *Memory, History and Opposition under State Socialism* (Santante: School of American Research Press, 1994) p. 9.

[18] Mu, Lu, Gao, Liu and Zhang (eds), *Bainian Guangbei*.

prominent outside the modern hospital, despite Bethune having had no connection with this part of China or this hospital. Mao Zedong's essay *In Memory of Norman Bethune* (紀念白求恩) was required reading in elementary schools in China during the 1960s, and as a result Bethune is widely revered throughout the PRC.[19] The erection of his statue in this location suggests that while the CCP is willing to acknowledge a Western influence, this must be done on terms that are consistent with the party's own historical narrative.

By contrast, the BMS origins of the hospitals in Jinan, Xi'an and Qingzhou are clearly displayed in memorial plaques and early photographs, and are acknowledged in modern accounts of the hospitals' history. The modern specialisms that they advertise have a direct link with the recognised expertise of some of the missionary staff who worked there: Handley Stockley's skills in ophthalmology are echoed in the focus on ophthalmology highlighted in the publicity brochure of Xi'an No. 4 Hospital, the modern successor to the Jenkins-Robertson Memorial Hospital where Stockley had worked; and Gordon King's and Ronald Still's names are both recognised in the history of the nationally prominent Department of Obstetrics at Qilu Medical University in Jinan. King had a prominent part in the academic and practical work of the Qilu University hospital and medical school from his appointment in 1927 to his resignation in 1940 to take up a post as a professor of obstetrics and gynaecology in Hong Kong.[20] Still's work as head of Qilu's Department of Obstetrics and Gynaecology during 1947 and 1948 was honoured in a short film made by Dr Wang Bo (王波), Consultant in Obstetrics and Gynaecology at Qilu Medical University.[21]

There remain associations with the missionary era. Original hospital buildings have been retained in Jinan and Qingzhou. Although in both locations they are completely dwarfed by multi-storey modern additions, they have been maintained to a high standard and are in daily use as administrative offices. In Qingzhou, there is an exhibition of early photographs housed in the present-day nursing college. Niu Jianyi (牛建一), President of the Qingzhou hospital, recalled exploring the old hospital buildings with his friends in the late 1960s and discovering piles of old documents written in English in the basement. What might now be considered a treasure trove for historical research was viewed very differently by the group of nine-year-olds. What impressed them most was the quality of the paper, especially when they discovered it was ideally suited to making paper aeroplanes![22]

---

[19] Gao Yan in conversation with Audrey Salters in Zhoucun, 20 November 2000; interviewed in Jinan 16-19 April 2013.
[20] Williamson, *British Baptists*, p. 247.
[21] Viewed by Audrey Salters in Jinan, 17 April 2013.
[22] Niu Jianyi, President of Yidu Central Hospital (山东益都) in conversation with Audrey Salters, 23 April 2013.

Appendix 1: BMS China Missionaries

This list includes all the BMS missionaries referred to in the text, quoted from or identified in photographs, including the dates of their service in China (including in Hong Kong post-1952). Source: H. Raymond Williamson, *British Baptists*, pp. 363–72.

Allen, Connie (née Greening)	1931–1951
Allen, Thomas W.	1931–1951
Bastable, Albert E.	1945–1950
Bastable, Joyce	1945–1950
Beckingsale, Jennie	1900–1913 (died 1913)
Black, Adam	1923–1951
Bloom, Beryl	1930–1946
Bloom, Dr C. V.	1931–1946
Bryan, A. Keith	1924–1950
Bryan, Kitty	1929–1950
Bywaters, Dr O. Nancy	1946–1952
Clow, Dr Ellen	1928–1948 (transferred to HQ 1948)
Clow, Dr J Menzies	1929–1951
Collins, Edward G.	1944–1952
Collins, Margaret	1944–1952
Dart, Mrs F. E.	1929–1953 (died 1953)
Dart, Rufus H. P.	1925–1954
Drake, Dora	1921–1952
Drake, Frederick S.	1914–1952
Elder, Arthur C.	1940–1953
Elder, Kathleen	1940–1953
Emmott, Amy (née Smurthwaite)	1920–1950
Emmott, Hubert (Bert) A.	1924–1950
Emmott, Winifred F.	1925–1947 (died 1947)
Flowers, Dr Wilfred S.	1928–1949
Flowers, Annie	1929–1949
Glasby, Beulah	1924–1938 (killed 1938)
Greening, A. Ernest	1897–1936
Gunn, W. G. David	1936–1952
Gunn, Winifred	1939–1952
Harris, James S.	1908–1948
Harrison, Vera	1946–1953
Hayward, Eva	1936–1951
Hayward, Victor E. W.	1934–1951 (transferred to HQ 1951)
Jagger, Amy	1939–1950
Jenkins, Dr Margaret W.	1938–1957

Jones, Alfred   1876–1905 (died 1905)
King, Dr Gordon   1927–1940
Lewis, Georgina   1939–1947
Lewis, Dr John Llewellyn   1938–1947
Lewis, Nellie   1909–1948
Light, Arthur Barrington   1939–1946
Light, Constance   1940–1946
Madge, Edna M.   1935–1951
Madge, Ernest G. T.   1935–1951
Manger, Jessie   1908–1938
Mudd, Charlotte   1911–1949
Mudd, William   1909–1949
Nelson, Peter F.   1946–1952
Newton, J. C.   1936–1955
Newton, Marjorie   1938–1955
Pailing, Muriel   1916–1946
Pailing, W. P.   1914–1946
Payne, E. Jessie   1907–1947
Payne, Henry   1905–1947
Phillips, Edward   1924–1951
Phillips, Enid   1927–1951
Price, Brynmor F.   1939–1950
Price, Fred W.   1911–1947
Richard, Timothy   1869–1919
Russell, Frederick S.   1913–1949
Russell, Gertrude   1915–1949
Scott, James Cameron   1929–1951
Scott, Caroline   1931–1951
Seymour, Gladys   1947–1952
Smith, Christina   1924–1947
Smith, Eric Sutton   1939–1952
Smith, John Henderson   1935–1949
Smurthwaite, Amy)   1920–1950
Spillett, Hubert W.   1930–1939 and 1946–1953
Still, Gwyneth M.   1935–1949
Still, Dr Ronald J.   1935–1949
Stockley, Dr Handley G.   1924–1950
Stockley, Jean   1927–1950
Sutton, James (Jim)   1943–1953
Sutton, Edna   1944–1953
Tait, Ruth   1924–1950
Thomas, Margaret   1909–1946
Upchurch, William S. (Bill)   1935–1952
Upchurch, Winifred   1945–1952
Wheal, Alice   1926–1949
Williamson, H. Raymond   1908–1939 (transferred to HQ 1939)
Williamson, Joan K.   1923–1951

Wyatt, Dr Harry G.	1925–1938 (killed 1938)
Young, George A.	1924–1952
Young, Nora	1923–1952

Appendix 2: The BMS in China: A Timeline

This timeline focuses on the key events relating directly to the BMS work in China. Significant wider contextual events are shown in italics, recognising that it is impossible to do justice to the full complexities of Chinese history in a short timeline.

1792	British Missionary Society (BMS) formed, with the first missionary deployed (to Bengal) the following year
1802	BMS established its policy of handing over responsibility to local Christians as soon as possible
1823	Bible translated into Chinese
1839–1842	*First Opium War, culminating in the Treaty of Nanjing, which granted preferential trading status to British merchants in five designated 'treaty ports'*
1856–1860	*Second Opium War, culminating in the Treaty of Tianjin, which significantly expanded trade opportunities for Western powers (including effectively legalising the import of opium) and permitted Christian missionaries to enter China*
1860	First Christian (including BMS) missionaries arrive in China.
1863	BMS mission established in Shandong
1877	BMS mission established in Shanxi, following invitation from the International Famine Relief Commission in Shanghai to support famine relief work in Shanxi
1883	Alfred Jones recommends that BMS missionaries should align their work to existing Chinese culture and norms and enable Chinese Christians to take ownership of the organisations as soon as possible
1885	BMS regulations provide for the appointment of local Chinese representatives on field committees
1889	First BMS hospital established in Shandong (Qingzhou)
1891	BMS mission established in Shaanxi, at the invitation of Chinese Baptist community at Fuyincun
1894–1895	*First Sino-Japanese War, culminating in the Treaty of Shimonoseki, which granted Japan equivalent trade rights to those granted to Western powers following the Opium Wars*
1898–1901	*Boxer Uprising, culminating in the Boxer Protocol Treaty granting reparations to the Western powers and Japan for damages incurred during the uprising*

1900	All BMS Shanxi missionaries killed by Boxers, along with more than 100 Chinese Christians
1905	First BMS hospitals established in Shanxi (Taiyuan) and Shaanxi (Xi'an)
1912	*Establishment of the Republic of China, ending nearly three centuries of Qing dynasty imperial rule in China*
1914–1918	*First World War, with Japan allied to the United Kingdom. As part of the offensive against Germany, Japan seizes German territory in Shandong and occupies it for the remainder of the war. China declares war on Germany in 1917, sending thousands of labourers to work to support the Allied effort in Europe*
1919	*Treaty of Versailles grants sovereignty of Shandong ports and surrounding area to Japan, fuelling anti-foreign and anti-Christian protests and the birth of the 'May Fourth' revolutionary movement*
1922	*Nine-Power Treaty restores sovereignty of Shandong ports and surrounding area to China*
1927	BMS Conference at Qingzhou confirms policy that the society's presence in China should be temporary, with all BMS missionaries in China charged with finding ways of bringing their work to an end
1927–1937	*Chinese Civil War – this initial phase of the civil war is interrupted by the Second Sino-Japanese war (1937–1945)*
1928	*Establishment of the Nationalist state by the Guomindang party (GMD), led by Chiang Kai-Shek*
1929	*Chiang Kai-Shek's conversion to Christianity*
1932	BMS announcement of decision to withdraw from Shandong by 1942 (later extended to 1947)
1934	Substantial BMS property transfer to Shandong Baptist Union (SBU) in Zhoucun as part of devolution process
1935	*Red Army arrives in Shaanxi (Yan'an) at the end of the Long March*
1937	BMS conference at Sanyuan to discuss plans for the Shaanxi church to become self-sufficient
1937–1945	*Second, Sino-Japanese War (or War of Resistance). Both Shandong and Shanxi were occupied from 1937*
1939	BMS missionaries evacuated from Shanxi following Japanese-inspired anti-British campaigns
1939-1945	*Second World War against Germany (1939–1945) and Japan (1941 1945)*
1940	Shantung Baptist Union requests additional support from BMS

1941	Mission staff in Shandong placed under house arrest
1942	BMS institutions in Shandong and other occupied territories close, and foreigners transferred to Shanghai for internment
1943	*Abrogation of the unequal treaties*
1945	Return of BMS missionaries to Shandong and Shanxi following the end of both the Second Sino-Japanese War and the Second World War
1946	Following requests for help from Zhang Sijing and Jing Yihui in Shandong, BMS resolves that as many mission stations as possible should be occupied, notwithstanding the ongoing plan to devolve responsibility as soon as practicable, and deploys missionaries accordingly
1946–1949	*Resumption of Chinese Civil War*
1948	BMS medics leave Shandong and all BMS missionaries leave Shanxi
1949	*Founding of the People's Republic of China (PRC)*
1950	CCP's 'Christian Manifesto' published, together with letters sent to mission boards and Chinese Christians, encouraging missions to turn over property to Chinese hands as soon as possible and calling on Chinese Christians to work towards an independent Chinese church
1950	All remaining BMS property in Shaanxi handed over to Chinese church
1951	All remaining BMS missionaries leave Shandong and Shaanxi, following Chinese Christians being forbidden contact with foreigners and the Campaign to Suppress Counter-revolutionaries
1952	Last BMS missionary leaves mainland China

Bibliography

Primary Sources

Archival Collections

Baptist Missionary Society Archives (BMSA), Angus Library, Regent's Park College, Oxford

CH/5   Miscellaneous correspondence from Alfred G. Jones (primarily to Alfred Henry Baynes) 1868-1885.

CH/6   Miscellaneous papers by Alfred. G. Jones, 1879–1886.

CH/11 H. Raymond Williamson, Miscellaneous correspondence and papers, 1939–1951.

CH/18 Interprovincial papers and correspondence, 1943–1949.

CH/21 Secretariat papers, 1938–1946.

CH/22 Secretariat Shansi.

CH/23 Secretariat Shantung, 1930–1949.

CH/24 Secretariat Shensi.

CH/27 Miscellaneous correspondence from China, 1939-1946.

CH/42 Miscellaneous letters and reports, 1933–1951.

CH/43 Miscellaneous reports and impact of religion, 1947–1954.

CH/44 British United Aid to China, 1942–1950; correspondence re internment; Church of Christ in China, 1940–1946; National Christian Council of China, 1938–1939.

CH/45 Jessie Payne and Nellie Lewis, 'Unbroken China – Some Account of the Church and Mission in Shantung and Shansi during the Japanese Occupation, 1937–1945'.

CH/54–CH/78 Correspondence files of C. Allen, T. W. Allen, A. E. Bastable, J. Bastable, J. I. Bell, A. K. Bryan, K. Bryan, O. N. Bywaters, E. Clow, J. M. Clow, E. G. Collins, M. Collins, D. Curtis, F. E. Dart, R. H. P. Dart, D. Drake, F. S. Drake, A. C. Elder, K. Elder, A. Emmott, H. A. Emmott, W. F. Emmott, W. S. Flowers, A. E. Greening, W. G. D. Gunn, W. Gunn, J. S. Harris, V. Harrison, V. E. W. Hayward, G. M. Hickson, L. M. Ingle, A. Jagger, V. J. Jasper, M. W. Jenkins, P. Jenkins, G. King, E. M. Madge, E. G.T . Madge, J. Manger, C. Mudd, J. M. Mudd, W. Mudd, P. F. Nelson, E. J. Payne, H. Payne, Ed. Phillips, En. Phillips, B. F. Price, F. W. Price, F. S. Russell, G. Russell, J. C. Scott, G. Seymour, C. Smith, E. S. Smith, J. H. Smith, H. W. Spillett, G. M. Still, R. J. Still, H. G. Stockley, J. Stockley, J. Sutton, E. Sutton, R. Tait, M. Thomas, W. S. Upchurch, W. Upchurch, C. Waddington, J. Watson, H. R. Williamson, J. K. Williamson, H. G. Wyatt, G. A. Young and N. Young.

CH/58 *China Memories*, unpublished memoir of Hubert (Bert) Emmott.

H96/97 Details of Missionary Staff 1900–1949.

Minutes of China, Finance, General Purposes, Staffing and Women's Subcommittees.

Minutes of General Committee, Volume 25 (1927) and Volumes 26–50 (1934–1952).

Periodical Accounts Relative to the Baptist Missionary Society, 'Form of Agreement'.

British Red Cross Museum and Archives, 44 Moorfields, London
JWO/1/1/11 Chairman's meeting minutes, 1943–1944 and correspondence, memoranda and reports regarding relief assistance in China.
JWO/2/1/14 Subcommittee minute book, 1944–1947, including papers regarding relief activities in China.
JWO/9/2 China Commission, correspondence with Dr Wilfred Flowers and others, 1946–1953.

Conference of British Missionary Societies Archives (CBMSA), School of Oriental and African Studies (SOAS), London.
Box 7 (S7), Finance, 1949–1954.
Box 333, Far Eastern Committee minutes and circulars, 1950–1953.
Box 349, NCC [National Christian Council].
Box 361, China Mission Reports.
Box 380, Mission personnel in wartime.
Box 387, China: Messages, Prayers for China
Box 390, China: Redeployment of Men and Resources .
Box 392, China: Church under Communism .
Box 506, Plans Regarding Medical Missionary Service in Wartime.

Council for World Mission Archives (CWMA), SOAS, London
68 Reports: Annual report for 1948.
69 CH/2 Annual report for 1951.
229 CH/15 Central China District Committee Minutes, 1950.

National Archives, Kew, London
FO233/263/C613770 Safety of missionaries in China, 1937.
FO371 Foreign Office General Correspondence (Political):
FO371/46125 Relief and rehabilitation of the British community in occupied China: relief for internees in Far East.
FO371/46126 Re-entry and repatriation of allied and neutral nationals to and from China 1944–1945.
FO371/46225 Reoccupation of British owned property in China 1945–1946.
FO371/53608-53610 Reoccupation of British properties: taking over of enemy assets by the Chinese government;
FO371/63407-63411 return of British-owned properties illegally occupied by Chinese individuals or institutions.

FO371/69527-69550 Political situation in China, possible evacuation of British
   Subjects, 1948.
FO371/75734-75778 Events leading to formation of a communist government
   of the People's Republic of China, 1949.
FO371/83535 Restriction on churches and missionaries in China, 1950.
FO371/92330-92334 Situation of foreign nationals in China, 1951.
FO371/92361 Chinese takeover of foreign schools and universities, 1951.
FO371/92368 Attitude of Chinese Government to Christian church, 1951.
FO916/1325 Welfare of missionaries in China, 1943–1944.
FO917 Embassy and Consular Archives, China.

National Library of Scotland, Edinburgh
Acc 9663/2, Acc 9663/4 Diaries of Ruth Tait.

Tilehouse Street Baptist Church, Hitchin
Minutes of Tilehouse Street Baptist Church, Hitchin, November 1947.

Private Collections

Allen family papers, private collection of Margaret Bennett, Ludlow.
Emmott family papers, private collection of Joan Wells, Woodhall Spa.
Greening photographs, private collection of Celly Rowe, Leeds.
Gunn family papers, private collection of Elizabeth Jamieson, London.
Peter J. Nelson, unpublished memoir, private collection of Nelson family,
   Dalgety Bay.
Gladys Seymour letters, private collection of David Seymour, London.
Still family papers, private collection of Audrey Salters, St Andrews.
Stockley letters, private collection of Dorothy Williams, Wareham.
Zao Xu Ling (Hsu Ling Tsao), 'These little Ones', unpublished booklet,
   translated from the Chinese, in the private collection of Margaret Wyatt,
   Upper Bucklebury.

Interviews and Personal Contacts

In the UK:
Ball, Sally (née Price), emails May, 20 July 2011; interviewed in Caerphilly 13
   June 2011.
Bennett, Margaret (née Allen), Ludlow, correspondence received 26 January
   2011; interviewed in London, 22 June 2011.
Clow, William, Haverfordwest, email received 23 September 2011; telephone
   conversations, 6, 8, 13 November 2013.
Dart, Peter, interviewed in Bristol, 7 October 2011.
Fifer, Elisabeth (née Allen), Desford, telephone conversation, 28 January 2011.
Flowers, Ian, correspondence received, 20 May, 15 and 28 June 2010; email 7
   February 2012.
Harrison, Vera, Accrington, correspondence received 8, 24 April 2010;
   telephone conversation, 18 April 2010.

Hingley, Ruth (née Wyatt), interviewed in Upper Buckleberry, 15 November
   2013.
Hollingworth, Rosemary (née Still), interviewed in London, 23 November
   2013.
Hollingworth, Brian, in conversation with Audrey Salters, Edinburgh, 30 July
   2012.
Houghton, Jean (née Clow), telephone conversation, 7 November 2013;
   correspondence received, 7 November 2013.
Jamieson, Elizabeth Eleanore (née Gunn), interviewed in London, 29
   November 2011.
Littlewood, Margaret, (née Craig), Edinburgh, email 22 August 2010.
Nelson, Peter J., correspondence received, 8 April 2010; interviewed in
   Dalgety Bay, 13 May and 22 June 2010.
Pearson, Rosemary (née Phillips), interviewed in Cheltenham, 19 June 2011,
   email 20 October 2014.
Qinghong Li (李庆洪), interviewed by Clare Salters in London, 25 August
   2023 and email correspondence received 30 October 2023.
Redfern, Carol (née Bastable), Wellingborough, email 6 April 2010.
Seymour, David, correspondence received 19 April 2010, 17 and 30 March
   2013; interviewed in London, 4 March 2013.
Smith, Jean Shipton (née Light), Cleator Moor, correspondence received, 14
   April 2010.
Smyly, William, Bedford, correspondence received 10 August 2010.
Wells, Joan (née Emmott), Woodhall Spa, telephone conversation 20 October
   2014; correspondence received 13, 18, 22 October 2014.
Williamson, Dorothy (née Stockley), interviewed in Wareham, 3 May 2010.
Wyatt, Margaret, interviewed in Upper Bucklebury, 15 November 2013.

In China:
Gao Dawei (高大卫), interviewed in Jinan, 16 April 2013.
Gao Lingjun (高令俊), interviewed in Beijing, 15 April 2013.
Gao Yan (高艳), interviewed in Jinan, 16, 17, 18 April 2013.
Guo Jisheng (郭济生), interviewed in Zhoucun, 17 April 2013, and in Jinan, 18
   April 2013.
Hou Xinguo (侯新国), Head of International Office, Qilu University Hospital,
   interviewed in Jinan, 16 April 2013.
Hu Weiqing (胡卫请), Professor, Department of History, Shandong University,
   interviewed in Jinan, 16 April 2013.
Kong Beihua (孔北华), Vice President of Qilu University Hospital,
   interviewed in Jinan, 16 April 2013.
Liu Tianlu (刘天禄), Professor, Department of History, Shandong University,
   interviewed in Jinan, 16 April 2013.
Niu Jianyi (牛建一), President of Yidu Central Hospital, Qingzhou,
   interviewed in Qingzhou, 23 April 2013.

Pan Jingnian (潘靖年), Assistant President of Yidu Central Hospital, correspondence received 21 September 2011.

Wang Bo (王波), professor of Obstetrics and Gynaecology, Qilu University Hospital, interviewed in Jinan, 16 April 2013.

Xie Xiaoming (解晓明), President of Xi'an No. 4 Hospital, interviewed in Xi'an, 28 April 2013.

Published Collections of Primary Documents

British Documents on Foreign Affairs, Part IV, Series E, Vol. 1 Far Eastern Affairs January–June 1946; and Vol. 5, China January–December 1948.

Centenary History of the Guangbei School, Zhoucun, 百年光被, 周村, 2007.

Compilation Committee of Records of Weifang City Yidu Central Hospital 《潍坊市益都中心醫院志》編纂委員會, ed., *Shandong Weifangshi Yidu Zhongxin Yiyuan Zhi (1892-1992)* 《山東潍坊市益都中心醫院志(1892-1992) 》 (Records of Shandong Weifang City Yidu Central Hospital (1892-1992))。Qingzhou 青州: Privately published, 1992.

Compilation of Committee Records of Weifang City Yidu Central Hospital, 《潍坊市益都中心醫院志》編纂委員會, ed., *Weifangshi Yidu Zhongxin Yiyuan Zhi (1882-2012)* 《潍坊市益都中心醫院志 (1882-2012) 》 (Records of Weifang City Yidu Central Hospital (1882–2012)), (Shandong 山東: Renmin Chubanshe 人民出版社, 2012).

Jones, Francis P. and Wallace C. Merwin, *Documents of the Three-Self Movement: source materials for the study of the Protestant church in Communist China* (New York: National Council of the Churches of Christ in the United States of America, 1963).

Mu Feng 牟峰, Lu Chengliang 呂承良, Gao Xilu 高希祿, Liu Yuwah 劉玉華, and Zhang Jun 張軍, Eds. 2005 *Bainian Guangbei: Shandong Sheng Zibo Diliu Zhongxue 1897–2005* (百年光被: 山東省淄博第六中學 1897-2005) (*A Hundred Years of the Sixth Middle School in Zibo, Shandong Province, 1897–2005*), Shandong 山東: Privately published.

Salters, Audrey, Ed. 2007 *Bound With Love: Letters Home from China 1935–1945*. St Andrews: Agequod Press.

Wickeri, Janice and Philip L. Wickeri, Eds. 2002 *A Chinese Contribution to Ecumenical Theology: Selected Writings of Bishop K. H. Ting*. Geneva: WCC Publications.

Wickert, E. (ed) 2000 *The Good Man of Nanking: The Diaries of John Rabe*. Trans. J. E. Woods. New York: A. A. Knopf.

Woods, G. E. 1992 *Life in China: From the Letters of Nancy Bywaters*. Braunton: Merlin Books.

World Mission Council. 2012 *Proposed Deliverance to the General Assembly of the Church of Scotland.*

Newspapers and Periodicals

British Weekly, 1935–1953

China Christian Yearbook, 1910–1939

The Chinese Recorder, 1867–1941
The Manchester Guardian, 1944–1952
Missionary Herald, 1900–1954
The Times, 1792–1952

Published Memoirs

Bodde, Derk, 1950. *Peking Diary: A Year of Revolution*. New York: Schuman.

Cook, Faith, 2004. *Troubled Journey, A Missionary Childhood in War-Torn China*. Edinburgh: The Banner of Truth Trust.

de Jaegher, Raymond J. and Irene Corbally Kuhn, 1952 *The Enemy Within: An Eyewitness Account of the Communist Conquest of China*. Bombay: St Paul Publications.

Gilkey, Langdon, 1966. *Shantung Compound: The Story of Men and Women Under Pressure*. London: Anthony Blond.

Kiesow, E. Margaret, 1954. *China, the Challenge*. London: Overseas Mission Committee of Presbyterian Church of England.

Kuhn, Irene Corbally, 1958. *Green Leaf in Drought: The Story of the Escape of the Last C. I. M. Missionaries from Communist China*. London: Lutterworth Press.

Lyall, Leslie, 1961. *Come Wind, Come Weather*. London: Hodder and Stoughton.

Marshall, James F. 1986. *Whereon the Wild Thyme Blows: Some Memoirs of Service with the Hong Kong Bank*. Grayshott, Surrey: Token Publishing Ltd.

Martin, George, 1990. *Chefoo School 1881–1951: A History and Memoir*. Braunton: Merlin Books.

Melby, John, 1969. *The Mandate of Heaven: Record of a Civil War, China 1945–49*. London: Chatto & Windus.

Menon, K. P. S., 1972. *Twilight in China*. Bombay: Bharatiya Vidya Bhavan.

Munro, John, 1990. *Beyond the Moon Gate, A China Odyssey, 1938–1950*. Vancouver: Douglas & McIntyre.

Richardson, B. (ed), 2009. *Sons of Missionaries, Recollections by Boarders at Eltham College*. Eltham: School for the Sons of Missionaries.

Scott, George A., 1947. *In Whose Hands? A Story of Internment in China*. London: China Inland Mission.

Thomas, William H. E., 1956. *Vanished China: Far Eastern Banking Memories*. London: Thorsons.

Upchurch, William S., 2007. *A Prevailing Wind*. Peterborough.

Contemporary Publications

Baptist Missionary Society, 1939
Manual of the Baptist Missionary Society for India, Ceylon, China, Congo and the West Indies, revised edition. London: Carey Press.

Belden, Jack, 1949
China Shakes the World. London: Harper.

Burt, E. W., 1916
  'China's Second Revolution.' *Missionary Herald*, September 1916, pp. 197–200.
Burt, E. W., 1937
  After Sixty Years: The Story of the Church Founded by the Baptist Missionary Society in North China. London: Carey Press.
Burt, E. W., 1944
  Alfred George Jones: Layman, Pioneer Missionary and Theologian. London: Carey Press – Brief Biographies of Leading Laymen, No.8.
Cable, A. Mildred, 1917
  Fulfilment of a Dream of Pastor Hsi's: The Story of the Work in Hwochow. London: Morgan and Scott, China Inland Mission.
Cartwright, F. T., 1949
  'Protestant Missions in Communist China.' *Far Eastern Survey*, Vol.18 (26), pp. 301–305.
Cook, Henry, 1947
  The Why of our Faith, 3rd Edition. London: Carey Kingsgate Press.
Cook, Henry, 1947
  What Baptists Stand For. London: Carey Kingsgate Press.
Copland, E. B. (ed), 1949
  Christians Under the Communist State, supplement to June 1949 issue of *The Church*, a magazine in English published occasionally by the General Assembly of the Church of Christ in China, Shanghai, printed by South China Morning Post Ltd, Hong Kong.
Dalberg-Acton, J. E. E., 1907
  The History of Freedom and Other Essays. London: Macmillan.
Flowers, Wilfred S., undated
  A Surgeon in China. Extracts from Letters from Dr W. S. Flowers. London: Carey Press.
Forsyth, Robert C., 1912
  Shantung: The Sacred Province of China. Shanghai: Christian Literature Society.
Fullerton, W. Y. and C. E. Wilson. 1910
  New China: A Story of Modern Travel. London: Morgan and Scott Ltd.
Galbraith, Winifred, 1941
  In China Now. New York: W. Morrow & Company.
Gibson, J. C. 1901
  Mission Problems and Mission Methods in South China: Lectures on Evangelistic Theology. Edinburgh and London: Oliphant, Anderson and Ferrier.
Greene, K. R. C. 1951
  'UNRRA's Record in China', *Far Eastern Survey*, 20.10, pp. 100–102.
Ingle, A. C. and R. F. Moorshead, 1920
  The Challenge of China: Being the Report of a Deputation Sent Out to Visit the China Mission Fields of the BMS, 1919–1920. London: Carey Press.

Jenkins, Margaret, 1944
  'Letters from Former Students', *Edinburgh Medical Missionary Society Quarterly Paper*, 20.16, p. 166.
Johnston, R. F., 1911
  A Chinese appeal to Christendom concerning Christian Missions. London: G. P. Putnam's Sons.
Jones, Alfred G., 1883
  North China English Baptist Mission: Our Past and Present Principles and Policy in China. London: Baptist Missionary Society.
Jones, Alfred G., 1888
  Hints about Climate, Living and Outfit, etc., Intended for the General Information of Missionaries Proceeding Thither. London: Baptist Missionary Society.
Keyte, J. C. 1913
  The Passing of the Dragon: The Story of the Shensi Revolution and Relief Expedition. London: Hodder and Stoughton.
Keyte, J. C. 1924
  Andrew Young of Shensi: Adventure in Medical Missions. London: Carey Press.
Latourette, K. S. 1929
  A History of Christian Missions in China. London: Society for Promoting Christian Knowledge.
MacGillivray, Donald, 1907
  A Century of Protestant Missions in China 1807–1907: Being the Centenary Conference Historical Volume. Shanghai: American Presbyterian Mission Press.
Meng, C. Y. W., 1943
  'Foreign Enterprise in Post-War China', *Far Eastern Survey* 12.2 (3 November 1943), pp. 212–219.
Miao, Chester (ed), 1948
  Christian Voices in China. New York: Friendship Press.
Payne, Ernest A., 1939
  Harry Wyatt of Shansi, 1895–1938. London: Carey Press.
Taylor, Howard, 1904
  Pastor Hsi of North China: One of China's Christians. London: Morgan & Scott.
Taylor, Howard, 1935
  The Triumph of John and Betty Stam. London: China Inland Mission.
Taylor, J. H. 1884
  China: Its Spiritual Need and Claims, 5th edition. London: James Nisbet & Co.
Tu, Y. C. [Tu Yuqing]. 1948
  'Profit and Loss in the War'. In *Christian Voices in China*. Ed. C. Miao. New York: Friendship Press, pp. 7–13.

Young, George A., 1947
  The Living Christ in Modern China. London: Carey-Kingsgate.
White, Theodore H. and Annalee W. Jacoby, 1947
  Thunder Out of China. [An account of the war in China with maps.]
  London: Victor Gollancz.
Williamson, H. Raymond. 1943
  China Among the Nations. London: Carey Press.
Williamson, H. Raymond. 1946
  *The Christian Challenge of the Changing World, Report on a Secretarial
  Visit to China, India and Ceylon, September 1945 to April 1946.* London:
  Baptist Missionary Society.
Williamson, H. R., 1947
  Teach Yourself Chinese. London: Hodder and Stoughton.
Unknown author. 1943
  Zhonghua Jidujiaohui Bianjiang Fuwubu (Church of Christ in China Border
  Service Department) *Fuwu Guicheng* (Service Regulations).
Various., 17 August 1946
  Camp Chit Chat, Vol. 1.6, Souvenir edition. Shanghai: The Voice
  Publishing Company.
Various. 1947
  *Through Toil and Tribulation, Missionary Experiences in China During the
  War of 1937–1945.* London: Carey Press.
Various. 1947.
  Proceedings of the Social Welfare Conference, March 24–28, 1947, New
  Asia Hotel, Shanghai, sponsored by Chinese National Relief and
  Rehabilitation Administration and United Nations Relief and Rehabilitation
  Administration.

Secondary Sources

Published Works

A Christian Missionary. 1952.
  'First thoughts on the Debacle of Christian Missions in China.' *African
  Affairs* 51.202, pp. 33–41.
Ashmore, Polly. 2012
  'Quakers and Communists, Partners in Building Utopia?' *Friends Quarterly*
  40.1, pp. 16–29.
Austin, Alvyn. 2007
  *China's Millions: The China Inland Mission and Late Qing Society, 1832–
  1905.* Cambridge: W. B. Eerdmans.
Barnett, A. Doak. 1963
  China on the Eve of Communist Takeover. New York: Praeger.
Barnett, Correlli. 1986
  The Audit of War: The Illusion and Reality of Britain as a Great Nation.
  London: Macmillan.

Barrett, David P. and Lawrence N. Shyu. 2001
  China in the Anti-Japanese War, 1937–1945: Politics, Culture, and Society.
  New York, Oxford: Peter Lang.
Barrett, David P. and Lawrence N. Shyu, Eds. 2001.
  Chinese Collaboration with Japan, 1932–1945: The Limits of
  Accommodation. Stanford CA: Stanford University Press.
Bays, Daniel H. 1996
  Christianity in China from the Eighteenth Century to the Present. Stanford
  CA: Stanford University Press.
Bays, Daniel H. 2012
  A New History of Christianity in China. Chichester, West Sussex: Wiley-
  Blackwell.
Bebbington, David W. 1981
  'Baptist members of Parliament in the 20th Century.' *Baptist Quarterly*,
  29.2, pp. 252–287.
Bebbington, David W. 2010
  The Nonconformist Conscience: Chapel and Politics, 1870–1914. London:
  Routledge.
Bickers, Robert A. 1996
  'To Serve and not to Rule'. In *Missionary Encounters: Sources and Issues.*
  Eds. Robert A. Bickers and Rosemary Seton. Richmond, Surrey: Curzon
  Press, pp. 211–239.
Bickers, Robert A. 1999
  Britain in China: Community, Culture and Colonialism 1900–1949.
  Manchester: Manchester University Press.
Bickers, Robert A. 2003
  Empire Made Me: An Englishman Adrift in Shanghai. London: Allen Lane.
Bickers, Robert A. 2012
  The Scramble for China: Foreign Devils in the Qing Empire, 1832–1914.
  London: Allen Lane, 2012.
Bickers, Robert A. and Christian Henriot, Eds. 2000
  New Frontiers: Imperialism's New Communities in East Asia, 1842–1953.
  Manchester: Manchester University Press.
Bickers, Robert A. and Rosemary Seton, Eds. 1996
  Missionary Encounters: Sources and Issues. Richmond, Surrey: Curzon
  Press.
Binfield, Clyde. 1973
  George Williams and the YMCA: A Study of Victorian Social Attitudes.
  London: Heinemann.
Boecking, Felix. 2013
  'Republican China under the Nationalists, ca. 1925–1945'. In *Demystifying*
  China, New Understandings of Chinese History. Ed. Naomi Standen.
  Lanham, MD: Rowman and Littlefield, pp. 171–178.
Bohr, P. R. 1972
  Famine in China and the Missionary: Timothy Richard as Relief
  Administrator and Advocate of National Reform, 1876–1884. Cambridge
  MA: East Asian Research Center, Harvard University.

Bowden, Sue. 1994
'The New Consumerism'. In *Twentieth Century Britain: Economic, Social, and Cultural Change*. Ed. Paul Johnson. London and New York: Longman, pp. 244–262.
Boyle, John H. 1972
China and Japan at War, 1935–1945: The Politics of Collaboration. Stanford CA: Stanford University Press.
Brady, Anne-Marie. 2003
Making the Foreign Serve China: Managing Foreigners in the People's Republic. Lanham MD: Rowman and Littlefield.
Brierley, Peter. 1988
'Religion'. In *British Social Trends Since 1900*. Ed. A. H. Halsey. Basingstoke: Macmillan Press, pp. 518–560.
Brook, Timothy. 1996
'Toward Independence, Christianity in China under the Japanese Occupation, 1937-1945'. In *Christianity in China, from the Eighteenth Century to the Present*. Ed. D. H. Bays. Stanford CA: Stanford University Press, pp. 317–337.
Brook, Timothy, 2005
Collaboration: Japanese Agents and Local Elites in Wartime China. Cambridge MA: Harvard University Press.
Brook, Timothy. 2012
'Hesitating before the Judgment of History.' *Journal of Asian Studies* 71.1, pp. 103-114.
Brown, Callum G. and Michael Snape, Eds. 2010
Secularisation in the Christian World (Farnham, Surrey and Burlington, Vermont: Ashgate Publishers.
Brown, Jeremy and Paul G. Pickowicz. 2007
Dilemmas of Victory: The Early Years of the People's Republic of China Cambridge, Mass., London: Harvard University Press.
Brown, S. J. and George Newlands. 2000
Scottish Christianity in the Modern World. Edinburgh: T & T Clark.
Bruce, S. and T. Glendinning. 2010
'When was Secularization? Dating the Decline of the British Churches and Locating its Cause.' *British Journal of Sociology* 61.1, pp. 107–126.
Buck, David D. 1978.
Urban Change in China: Politics and Development in Tsinan, Shantung, 1890–1949. Madison: University of Wisconsin Press.
Campbell, Colin D. and Gordon C. Tullock 1954
'Hyperinflation in China, 1937–49.' *Journal of Political Economy* 62.3, pp. 236–245.
Cavalcanti, H. B. 2005
'Human Agency in Mission Work: Missionary Styles and their Political Consequences.' *Sociology of Religion* 66.4, pp. 381–398.
Chan, K. C. 1977
'The Abrogation of British Extraterritoriality in China, 1942–43: A Study in

Anglo-American-Chinese Relations.' *Modern Asian Studies* 11.2, pp. 257–291.

Chang, Iris. 1998
The Rape of Nanking: The Hidden Holocaust of World War II. London: Penguin.

Charbonnier, Jean-Pierre. 2007
Christians in China A.D 600 to 2000. Trans. M. N. L. Couve de Murville. San Francisco: Ignatius Press.

Chassin, Lionel M. 1966
The Communist Conquest of China: A History of the Civil War, 1945–49. London: Weidenfeld and Nicolson.

Cleall, E. 2012
Missionary Discourses of Difference: Negotiating Otherness in the British Empire, 1840–1900. London: Palgrave Macmillan.

Clegg, Arthur. 1989
Aid China, 1937–1949: A Memoir of a Forgotten Campaign. Beijing: New World Press.

Cohen, Paul A. 1984
Discovering History in China: American Historical Writing on the Recent Chinese Past. New York, Guildford: Columbia University Press.

Cohen, Paul A. 1988
'The Post-Mao Reforms in Historical Perspective.' *Journal of Asian Studies* 47.3, pp. 518–540.

Cohen, Paul. A. 2003
'Reflections on a Watershed Date: The 1949 Divide in Chinese History'. In *Twentieth-Century China: New Approaches*. Ed. Jeffrey N. Wasserstrom. London, pp. 27–36.

Comaroff, Jean and John Comaroff. 1991
Of Revelation and Revolution: Christianity, Colonialism and Consciousness in South Africa. Chicago: University of Chicago Press.

Constantine, L. 1952
'The Gospel to Communists.' *International Review of Mission* 41, pp. 202–215.

Coote, Robert T. 1991
'A Boon or a Drag? How North American Evangelical Missionaries Experience Home Furloughs.' *International Bulletin of Missionary Research* 15.1, pp. 17–23.

Corbett, C. H. 1955
Shantung Christian University (Cheeloo). New York: United Board for Christian Colleges in China.

Cox, Jeffrey. 2008
The British Missionary Enterprise Since 1700. New York, London: Routledge.

Cui, Dan.. 2001
'British Protestant Educational Activities and the Nationalization of Chinese Education In the 1920s'. In *Education, Culture and Identity in Twentieth-*

Century China. Eds. G. Peterson, R. Hayhoe, and Y. Lu. Ann Arbor MI: University of Michigan Press, pp. 137–159.

Currie, Robert, Alan Gilbert and Lee Horsley. 1977
Churches and Churchgoers: Patterns of Church Growth in the British Isles Since 1700. Oxford: Clarendon Press.

DeVido, Elise. A. 2000
'The Ssurvival of the Shandong Base Area, 1937–1943'. In *North China at War: The Social Ecology of Revolution, 1937–1945*. Eds. C. Feng and D. S. G. Goodman. Lanham MD and Oxford: Rowman and Littlefield, pp. 173–188.

Dewey, P. E. 1997
War and Progress, Britain 1914–1945. London and New York: Longman.

Dikötter, Frank. 2013
The Tragedy of Liberation: A History of the Chinese Revolution, 1945–59. London: Bloomsbury.

Dillon, Nara. 2007
'New Democracy and the Demise of Private Charity in Shanghai'. In *Dilemmas of Victory: The Early Years of the People's Republic of China*. Eds. Jeremy Brown and Paul G Pickowicz. Cambridge MA and London: Harvard University Press, London, pp. 80–102.

Du, Zhongyuan. 1998
Return Our Rivers and Mountains: The Collected Essays of Du Zhongyuan. Shanghai.

Duan, Liancheng. 1998
Duiwai chuanboxue, (textbook for waishi workers), Chinese English bilingual edition, Beijing: Zhongguo jianshe chubanshe.

Duffell, Nick. 2000
The Making of Them: The British Attitude to Children and the Boarding School System. London: Lone Arrow.

Dunch, Ryan. 2001
Fuzhou Protestants and the Making of Modern China, 1857–1927. New Haven, CT: Yale University Press.

Dunch, Ryan. 2002
'Beyond Cultural Imperialism: Cultural Theory, Christian Missions and Global Modernity' *History and Theory* 41.3, pp. 301–325.

Dunch, Ryan. 2009
'Science, Religion and the Classics in Christian Higher Education to 1920'. In *China's Christian Colleges: Cross-Cultural Connections, 1900–1950*. Eds D. H. Bays and E. Widmer. Stanford CA: Stanford University Press, pp. 57–82.

Duus, Peter, Raymond Myers and Mark Peattie, Eds. 1989
The Japanese Informal Empire in China, 1895–1937. Princeton MJ: Princeton University Press.

Eastman, Lloyd. 1974
The Abortive Revolution: China Under Nationalist Rule, 1927–1937. Cambridge MA: Harvard University Press.

Eastman Lloyd. 1984
    Seeds of Destruction: Nationalist China in War and Revolution, 1937–1949.
    Stanford CA: Stanford University Press.
Erh, Deke and Tess Johnston. 1998
    Hallowed Halls: Protestant Colleges in Old China. Hong Kong: Old China
    Hands Press.
Esherick, J. W. 2000
    'Revolution in a "Feudal Fortress", Yangjiagou, Mizhi County, Shaanxi,
    1937–1948'. In *North China at War: The Social Ecology of Revolution,
    1937–1945*. Eds. Feng Chongyi and David S. G. Goodman. Oxford:
    Rowman and Littlefield pp. 59–91.
Evans, Gladys E. 1969
    *Come Wind, Come Weather: Chronicles of Tilehouse Street Baptist Church
    1669–1969*. London: Whitefriars Press Ltd.
Fairbank, John K. Ed. 1978
    *The Cambridge History of China, Volume 10: Late Ch'ing 1800-1911, Part
    1*. Cambridge: Cambridge University Press.
Fairbank, John K. and Kwang-Ching Liu Eds. 1980
    *The Cambridge History of China, Volume 11: Late Ch'ing 1800-1911, Part
    2*. Cambridge: Cambridge University Press.
Fairbank, John K. Ed. 1983
    *The Cambridge History of China, Volume 12: Republican China 1912-1949,
    Part 1*. Cambridge: Cambridge University Press.
Fairbank, John K. and Albert Feuerwerker Eds. 1986
    *The Cambridge History of China, Volume 13: Republican China 1912–
    1949, Part 2*. Cambridge: Cambridge University Press.
Fairbank, John K. and Merle Goldman. 1998
    China: A New History. Cambridge MA: Belknap Press of Harvard
    University Press.
Fenby, Jonathan. 2003
    Generalissimo: Chiang Kai-shek and the China he Lost. London: Free
    Press.
Fenby, Jonathan. 2009
    *The Penguin History of Modern China: The Fall and Rise of a Great Power,
    1850–2009*. London: Penguin.
Feng Chongyi and David S. G. Goodman. 2000
    North China at War: The Social Ecology of Revolution, 1937–45. Lanham
    MD and Oxford: Rowman and Littlefield.
Feng, Zhong-ping. 1994
    The British Government's China Policy 1945–1950. Keele: Keele
    University Press.
Field, Clive D. 2008
    'Puzzled People Revisited: Religious Believing and Belonging in Wartime
    Britain, 1939–45.' *Twentieth Century British History* 19.4, pp. 446–479.
Fogel, Joshua A. 2000
    The Nanjing Massacre In History and Historiography. Berkeley, London:
    University of California Press.

Fu, Poshek. 1993
  Passivity, Resistance and Collaboration: Intellectual Choices in Occupied Shanghai, 1937–1945. Stanford CA: Stanford University Press.
Gao Wangzhi. 1996
  'Y. T. Wu: A Christian Leader Uunder Communism'. In *Christianity in China from the Eighteenth Century to the Present.* Ed. D. H. Bays. Stanford: Stanford University Press, pp. 338–352.
Gao Xingzu. 1985
  Rijun qin Hua baoxing: Nanjing datusha (*Japanese Army Atrocities During its Occupation of China: The Nanjing Massacre*). Shanghai: Shanghai Renmin Chubanshe.
Garavonte, Anthony. 1965
  'The Long March.' *China Quarterly*, No. 22, pp. 89–124.
Gilbert, Alan D. 1976
  Religion and Society in Industrial England: Church, Chapel and Social Change, 1740–1914. London: Longman.
Gilbert, Alan D. 1980
  The Making of Post Christian Britain: A History of Secularization of Modern Society. London, New York: Longman.
Glennerster, Howard. 1990
  'Social Policy Since the Second World War'. In *The State of Welfare: The Welfare State in Britain since 1974.* Ed. J. Hills. Oxford: Clarendon Press, pp. 12–16.
Goodall, Norman. 1964
  Christian Missions and Social Ferment. London: Epworth Press.
Halsey A. H., Ed. 1988
  British Social Trends Since 1900. Basingstoke: Macmillan Press.
Hannah, B. 1975
  'Shanghai: The Last of the Good Old Days.' *Asian Affairs* 2.3, pp. 179–191.
Harris, Paul W. 1999
  Nothing but Christ: Rufus Anderson and the Ideology of Protestant Foreign Missions. Oxford, Oxford University Press.
Harrison, Henrietta. 2001
  China: Inventing the Nation. London and New York: Arnold with Oxford University Press.
Harrison, Henrietta. 2013
  The Missionary's Curse and Other Tales from a Chinese Catholic Village. Berkeley, UC Press.
Harvey, Thomas A. 2002
  Acquainted with Grief: Wang Mingdao's Stand for the Persecuted Church in China. Grand Rapids MI: Brazos Press.
Hayward, Victor E. W. 1955
  'Ears to Hear': Lessons from the China Mission. London: Edinburgh House Press.
Hayward, Victor E. W. 1974
  Christians and China. Belfast: Christian Journals Ltd.

Hedlund, R. E. 1981
  *Roots of the Great Debate in Mission: Mission in Historical and
  Theological Perspective.* Madras: Evangelical Literature Service.
Hennessy, P. 2006
  Never Again, Britain 1945–51. London: Cape.
Henriot, Christian and Wen-Hsin Yeh. 2004
  In the Shadow of the Rising Sun: Shanghai Under Japanese Occupation.
  Cambridge: Cambridge University Press.
Hess, Christian. 2013
  'The Rise of the Chinese Communist Party'. In *Demystifying China: New
  Understandings of Chinese History.* Ed. Naomi Standen. Plymouth MD:
  Rowman and Littlefield, pp. 179–186.
Hills, Julian, Ed. 1990
  The State of Welfare: The Welfare State in Britain since 1974. Oxford:
  Clarendon Press.
Hood, George A. 1986
  *Mission Accomplished?: The English Presbyterian Mission in Lingtung,
  South China.* Frankfurt am Main, Bern, New York: Verlag Peter Lang.
Hood, George A. 1991
  Neither Bang Nor Whimper: The End of a Missionary Era in China.
  Singapore: The Presbyterian Church in Singapore.
Hooper, Beverley. 1986
  China Stands Up: Ending the Western Presence, 1948–1950. Sydney,
  London: Allen and Unwin.
Howlett, Jonathan J. 2013
  'The British Boss is Gone and will Never Return: Communists Take Over
  British Companies in Shanghai, 1945–1954.' *Modern Asian Studies* 47.6,
  pp. 1941–1976.
Huang, Philip C. C. 1985
  The Peasant Economy and Social Change in North China. Stanford CA:
  Stanford University Press.
Huang, Philip C. C. 1990
  *The Peasant Family and Rural Development in the Yangzi Delta, 1350–
  1988.* Stanford CA: Stanford University Press.
Jones, Francis P. 1955
  'The Christian Church in Communist China.' *Far Eastern Survey* 24.12, pp.
  184–188.
Kerr, G. H. 1992
  Formosa Betrayed. Irvine CA: Taiwan Publishing Company.
King, F. H. H. 1987
  *History of the Hong Kong and Shanghai Banking Corporation Vol. IV: The
  Hong Kong Bank in the Period of Development and Nationalism 1941–
  1984.* Cambridge: Cambridge University Press.
Kirby, William C. 1984
  Germany and Republican China. Stanford CA: Stanford University Press.
Klein, T. 2002
  'Anti-Imperialism at Grassroots: Christianity and the Chinese Revolution In

Northeast Guangdong, 1919–1930'. In *The Chinese Revolution in the 1920s: Between Triumph and Disaster*. Eds. R. Felber, A. M. Grigoriev, M. Leutner and M. L. Titarenko. London: Routledge, pp. 289–306.

Kynaston, D. 2008
Austerity Britain 1945–51. London: Bloomsbury.

Lacy, Creighton. 1955
'The Missionary Exodus from China.' *Pacific Affairs* 28.4, pp. 301–314.

Lai, S. X., 2011
A Springboard to Victory: Shandong Province and Chinese Communist Military and Financial Strength, 1937–45. Leiden: Brill.

Laliberte, André. 2011
'Religion and the State in China: The Limits of Institutionalization.' *Journal of Current Chinese Affairs*, 2011.2, pp. 3–15.

Lambert, Tony. 1989
'Counting Christians in China: Who's Right?' *News Network International*, 14 April 1989, pp. 28–36.

Lary, Diana. 2001
'Drowned Earth: The Strategic Breaching of the Yellow River Dyke, 1938.' *War in History* 8.2, pp. 191–207.

Lary, Diana. 2010
The Chinese People at War: Human Suffering and Social Transformation, 1937–1945. New York: Cambridge University Press.

Lary, Diana and Stephen R. MacKinnon, Eds. 2001
Scars of War: The Impact of Warfare on Modern China. Vancouver: University of British Columbia Press.

Lee, Bradford. 1973
Britain and the Sino-Japanese War, 1937–1939: A Study in the Dilemmas of British Decline. Stanford and London: Stanford University Press and Oxford University Press.

Lee, Ching Kwan and Guobin Yang, Eds. 2007
Re-envisioning the Chinese Revolution: The Politics and Poetics of Collective Memories in Reform China. Washington DC: Woodrow Wilson Center Press.

Lee, Joseph Tse-Hei. 2003
The Bible and the Gun: Christianity in South China, 1860-1900. London and New York: Routledge.

Levine, Steven I. 1987
Anvil of Victory: The Communist Revolution in Manchuria, 1945–1948. New York: Columbia University Press.

Lew, Christopher. 2009
The Third Chinese Revolutionary War: An Analysis of Communist Strategy and Leadership. London: Routledge.

Liao, Guangsheng. 1986
Antiforeignism and Modernization in China, 1860–1980. Hong Kong: Chinese University Press.

Ling, Oi Ki. 1999
The Changing Role of the British Protestant Missionaries in China, 1945–1952. London: Associated University Presses.

Lo, Jiu-jung. 2001
'Survival as Justification for Collaboration, 1937–1945'. In *Chinese Collaboration with Japan, 1932–1945: The Limits of Accomodation*. Eds. D. P. Barrett and L. N. Shyu. Stanford CA: Stanford University Press, pp. 116–132.

Lodwick, Kathleen. 2010
'Missionaries and Opium'. In *Handbook of Christianity in China, Volume Two: 1800–Present*. Ed. R. Gary Tiedemann. Leiden MA: Brill, pp. 354–360.

Lu Ning 1977
The Dynamics of Foreign-Policy Decision Making in China. Boulder CO: Westview Press.

Lucas, A. 1982
Chinese Medical Modernization: Comparative Policy and Continuities, 1930s–1980s. New York: Praeger.

Lutz, Jessie G. 1971
China and the Christian Colleges, 1850–1950. Ithaca and London: Cornell University Press.

Lutz, Jessie. G. 2010
'Chinese and Christian Interactions'. In *Handbook of Christianity in China, Volume Two: 1800–Present*. Ed. R. Gary Tiedemann. Leiden MA: Brill, pp. 628–639.

Lutz, Jessie G. 1988
Chinese Politics and Christian Missions: The Anti-Christian Movements of 1920–1928. Notre Dame IN: Cross Cultural Publications, Cross Roads Books.

Lutze, Thomas D. 2008
China's Inevitable Revolution: Rethinking America's Loss to the Communists. Basingstoke: Palgrave Macmillan.

Ma, Tehyun 2014
'"The common aim of the Allied Powers": Social Policy and International Legitimacy in Wartime China, 1940–47.' *Journal of Global History* 9, pp. 254–275.

MacFarquhar R. and John K. Fairbank (Eds.), 1987
The Cambridge History of China, Volume 14: The People's Republic, Part 1: The Emergence of Revolutionary China, 1949–1965. Cambridge: Cambridge University Press.

MacFarquhar, R. and John K. Fairbank (Eds.), 1991
The Cambridge History of China, Volume 15: The People's Republic, Part 2: Revolutions within the Chinese Revolution, 1966–1982. Cambridge: Cambridge University Press.

MacHaffie, B. J. 2000
'Old Testament Criticism and the Education of Victorian Children'. In

Scottish Christianity in the Modern World. Eds. Stewart J. Brown and
George Newlands. Edinburgh: T & T Clark, pp. 91–118.

MacInnis, Donald E. 1972
Religious Policy and Practice in Communist China: A Documentary History
London: Hodder and Stoughton.

MacKinnon, Stephen R. 2001
'Refugee Flight at the outset of the Anti-Japanese War'. In *Scars of War:
The Impact of Warfare on Modern China*. Eds. Diana Lary and Stephen R.
MacKinnon. Vancouver: University of British Columbia Press, pp. 118–
134.

MacKinnon, Stephen R., Diana Lary and Ezra F. Vogel (Eds.). 2007
China at War: Regions of China, 1937–1945. Stanford CA: Stanford
University Press.

MacKinnon, Stephen R. and Robert Capa. 2008
Wuhan 1938: War, Refugees and the Making of Modern China. Berkeley
CA: University of California Press.

McLaine, Ian. 1979
*Ministry of Morale: Home Front Morale and the Ministry of Information in
World War II*. London: Allen and Unwin.

MacMillan, Margaret. 2001
Paris 1919: Six Months that Changed the World. London, John Murray.

Manktelow, Emily. 2013
*Missionary Families: Race, Gender and Generation on the Spiritual
Frontier*. Manchester: Manchester University Press.

Marwick, A. 1976
The Home Front, The British and the Second World War. London: Thames
and Hudson.

Maughan, Stephen. 1996
'"Mighty England do Good": The Major English Denominations and
Organisation for the Support of Foreign Missions in the 19th Century'. In
Missionary Encounters: Sources and Issues. Eds. Robert A. Bickers and
Rosemary Seton. Richmond, Surrey: Curzon Press pp. 11–37.

Mitter, Rana. 2004
A Bitter Revolution: China's Struggle with the Modern World. Oxford:
Oxford University Press.

Mitter, Rana. 2005
'Modernity, Internationalization, and War in the History of Modern China.'
The Historical Journal 48.2, pp. 523–543.

Mitter, Rana. 2008
Modern China: A Very Short Introduction. Oxford: Oxford University Press.

Mitter Rana. 2011
'Classifying Citizens in Nationalist China during World War II, 1937–1941.'
Modern Asian Studies, Vol. 45.2, p. 243-75.

Mitter, Rana. 2013
China's War with Japan, 1937–1945: The Struggle for Survival. London:
Allen Lane.

Mitter, Rana. 2013
  'Imperialism, Transnationalism, and the Reconstruction of Post-War China:
  UNRRA in China, 1944–7.' *Past and Present*, Supplement 8, pp. 51–69.
Morwood, W. 1980
  *Duel for the Middle Kingdom: The Struggle Between Chiang Kai-shek and
  Mao Tse-tung for Control of China.* New York: Everest House.
Norman, E. R. 1976
  Church and Society in England, 1770–1970: A Historical Study. Oxford:
  Clarendon Press.
Oberschall, Anthony and Michael Seidman. 2005
  'Food Coercion in Revolution and Civil War: Who Wins and How They Do
  it.' *Comparative Studies in Society and History* 47.2, pp. 372–402.
Paton, D. M. 1953
  Christian Missions and the Judgment of God. London: SCM Press.
Peattie, Mark. 1989
  'Japanese Treaty Port Settlements in China, 1895-1937'. In *The Japanese
  Informal Empire in China, 1895–1937.* Eds. Peter Duus, Raymond Myers
  and Mark Peattie. Princeton MJ: Princeton University Press, pp. 166–205.
Pepper, Suzanne. 1971
  'The Student Movement and the Chinese Civil War, 1945-19', *The China
  Quarterly* 48 (October to December 1971), pp. 698-735.
Pepper, Suzanne. 1986
  'The KMT-CCP Conflict 1945-1949'. In *The Cambridge History of China,
  Volume 13: Republican China 1912–1949, Part 2.* Eds. John. K. Fairbank
  and Albert Feuerwerker. Cambridge: Cambridge University Press, pp. 723–
  788.
Pepper, Suzanne. 1999
  Civil War in China: The Political Struggle 1945–1949. Lanham MD and
  Oxford: Rowman and Littlefield.
Perry, Elizabeth J. 1993
  Shanghai on Strike: The Politics of Chinese Labor. Stanford CA: Stanford
  University Press.
Peterson, G., R. Hayhoe and Y. L. Lu. 2001
  Education, Culture and Identity in 20th century China. Ann Arbor MI:
  University of Michigan Press.
Porter, A. 1997
  '"Cultural Imperialism" and Protestant Missionary Enterprise, 1780–1914.'
  Journal of Imperial and Commonwealth History 25.3, pp. 367–391.
Porter, Brian E. 1967
  *Britain and the Rise of Communist China: A Study of British Attitudes,
  1945–1954.* London: Oxford University Press.
Prochaska, F. K. 1978
  'Little Vessels: Children in the Nineteenth-Century English Missionary
  Movement.' *Journal of Imperial and Commonwealth History* 6.2, pp. 103–
  112.
Rodriguez, A. 2011
  'Building the Nation, Serving the Frontier: Mobilizing and Reconstructing

China's Borderlands During the War of Resistance, 1937–1945.' *Modern Asian Studies* 45.2, pp. 345–376.

Routh, Guy. 1980
Occupation and Pay in Great Britain 1906–79. London: Macmillan.

Saich, T., Hans J. Van de Ven, and D. E. Apter, Eds. *New Perspectives on the Chinese Communist Revolution.* Armonk NY and London: M. E. Sharpe.

Salters, Audrey. 2020
'Portrait of a Twentieth-Century Christian in Shandong.' *Baptist Quarterly* 51.2 pp. 69–81.

Schenk, Catherine K. 1994
Britain and the Sterling Area: From Devaluation to Convertibility in the 1950s. London: Routledge.

Schenk, Catherine K. 1994
'Austerity and Boom'. In *Twentieth Century Britain*: *Economic, Social, and Cultural Change*. Ed. Paul Johnson. London: Routledge, p. 306.

Seton, Rosemary. 1996
'Open Doors for Female Labourers'. In *Missionary Encounters: Sources and Issues*. Eds. Robert A. Bickers and Rosemary Seton. Richmond, Surrey: Curzon Press pp. 50–69.

Seton, Rosemary. 2013
Western Daughters in Eastern Lands: British Missionary Women in Asia. Santa Barbara CA: Praeger.

Shin, Michael D. 2012
'Yi Kwang-su: The Collaborator as Modernist against Modernity.' *Journal of Asian Studies* 71.1, pp. 115–120.

Skeats, H. S. and C. S. Miall. 1891
History of the Free Churches of England, 1688–1891: From the Reformation to 1851. London: Alexander & Shepheard.

Smith, M. 2000
Britain and 1940: History, Myth and Popular Memory. London and New York: Routledge.

Spence, Jonathan D. 1990
The Search for Modern China. New York and London: Norton.

Spurling, Hilary. 2011
Burying the Bones. London: Profile.

Standen, Naomi, Ed. 2013
Demystifying China: New Understandings of Chinese History (Lanham MD: Rowman and Littlefield.

Stanley, Brian. 1990
The Bible and the Flag: Protestant Missions and British Imperialism in the Nineteenth and Twentieth Centuries. Leicester: Apollos.

Stanley, Brian. 1992
The History of the Baptist Missionary Society, 1792–1992. Edinburgh: T & T Clark.

Stanley, Brian. 1998
'The Legacy of Robert Arthington.' *International Bulletin of Missionary Research* 22.4, pp. 166–71.

Stanley, Brian. 2008
    'The Church of the Three Selves: A Perspective from the World Missionary
    Conference, Edinburgh, 1910.' *Journal of Imperial and Commonwealth
    History* 36.3, pp. 435–451.
Stanley, Brian. 2009
    The World Missionary Conference, Edinburgh 1910. Grand Rapids MI and
    Cambridge: William B. Eerdmans.
Stevenson, J. 1984
    British Society, 1914–45. Harmondsworth: Penguin.
Stilwell, Joseph W. and Theodore White, Eds. 1972
    The Stilwell Papers. New York: MacDonald.
Stursberg, Peter. 1987
    The Golden Hope: Christians in China. Toronto: United Church Publishing
    House.
Tiedemann, R. Gary. 2009
    *Reference Guide to Christian Missionary Societies in China: From the
    Sixteenth to the Twentieth Centuries.* Armonk NY: M. E. Sharpe.
Tiedemann, R. Gary, Ed. 2010
    Handbook of Christianity in China, Volume Two: 1800–Present. Leiden
    MA: Brill.
Treat, John W. 2012
    'Choosing to Collaborate: Yi Kwang-su and the Moral Subject in Colonial
    Korea.' *Journal of Asian Studies* 71.1, pp. 81–102.
Unschuld, P. U. 1985
    Medicine in China: A History of Ideas. Berkeley: University of California
    Press.
van de Ven, Hans J. 2003
    War and Nationalism in China, 1925–1945. London: Routledge.
Van Slyke, Lyman. 1986
    'The Chinese Communist Movement During the Sino-Japanese War 1937–
    1945'. In *The Cambridge History of China, Volume 13: Republican China
    1912–1949, Part 2.* Eds. John. K. Fairbank and Albert. Feuerwerker.
    Cambridge: Cambridge University Press, pp. 609-722.
Wakabayashi, Bob Tadashi, Ed. 2007
    The Nanking Atrocity 1937–8: Complicating the Picture. New York and
    Oxford: Berghahn Books.
Wakeman, F. 2004
    'Shanghai Smuggling'. In *In the Shadow of the Rising Sun: Shanghai Under
    Japanese Occupation.* Eds. Christian Henriot and Wen-Hsin Yeh.
    Cambridge: Cambridge University Press, pp. 116–156.
Walls, A. 1996
    The Missionary Movement in Christian History. NY and Edinburgh: Orbis
    Books and T & T Clark.
Wang, Stephen. 2002
    The Long Road to Freedom: The Story of Wang Mingdao. Trans. Ma Ming.
    Lancaster: Sovereign World.

Warren, Max. 1960
   Challenge and Response: Six Studies in Missionary Opportunity. London: SPCK.
Warren, Max. 1967
   Social History and Christian Mission. London: SCM Press.
Wasserstrom, Jeffrey N. 1991
   Student Protest in Twentieth-Century China: The View from Shanghai. Stanford CA: Stanford University Press.
Wasserstrom, Jeffrey N, Ed. 2003
   Twentieth-Century China: New Approaches. London: Routledge.
Watson, Rubie, Ed. 1994
   Memory, History and Opposition under State Socialism. Santante: School of American Research Press.
Wemheuer, Felix. 2014
   'The Chinese Revolution and "Liberation": Whose Tragedy?' *The China Quarterly* 219 (September 2014), pp. 849–863.
West, R. 2000
   The Meaning of Treason. London: Reprint Society.
Westad, Odd Arne. 2003
   Decisive Encounters: The Chinese Civil War, 1946–1950. Stanford CA: Stanford University Press.
Westad, Odd Arne. 2012
   Restless Empire: China and the World Since 1750. London: Bodley Head.
Whyte, Bob. 1988
   Unfinished Encounter: China and Christianity. London: Collins Fount Paperbacks.
Wickeri, Philip L. 1988
   Seeking the Common Ground: Protestant Christianity, the Three-Self Movement, and China's United Front. Maryknoll NY: Orbis Books.
Wickeri, Philip L. 2007
   Reconstructing Christianity in China: K. H. Ting and the Chinese Church. Maryknoll NY: Orbis Books.
Wilkinson, A. 1978
   The Church of England and the First World War. London: SPCK.
Wilkinson, E. 2000
   Chinese History: A Manual. Cambridge MA: Harvard University Press.
Wilkinson, Mark F. 2000
   'The Shanghai American Community, 1937–1949'. In *New Frontiers: Imperialism's New Communities in East Asia 1842–1953* Eds. R. Bickers and C. Henriot. Manchester: Manchester University Press, pp. 231–249.
Williams, C. Peter. 1990
   The Ideal of the Self-Governing Church: A Study of Victorian Missionary Strategy. Leiden MA: Brill.
Williamson, H. Raymond. 1957
   British Baptists in China, 1845–1952. London: Carey Kingsgate Press.

Woodbridge, George. 1950
  UNRRA: The History of the United Nations Relief and Rehabilitation Administration, Volume 1. New York: Columbia University Press.
Wyman, Judith. 2000
  'Foreigners or Outsiders? Westerners and Chinese Christians in Chongqing 1870s–1900'. In *New Frontiers: Imperialism's New Communities in East Asia, 1842–1953.* Eds. Robert A. Bickers and Christian Henriot. Manchester: Manchester University Press, pp. 75–87.
Xi, Lian. 2010
  Redeemed by Fire: The Rise of Popular Christianity in Modern China. New Haven CT and London: Yale University Press.
Yip Ka-Che. 1980
  Religion, Nationalism and Chinese Students: The Anti-Christian Movement of 1922-27. Bellingham WA: Center for East Asian Studies, West Washington University.
Yip Ka-Che. 1995
  Health and National Reconstruction in Nationalist China: The Development of Modern Health Services, 1928-1937. Ann Arbor MI: Association for Asian Studies.
Young, Arthur N. 1965
  China's Wartime Finance and Inflation, 1937–1945 (Cambridge MA: Harvard East Asian Series.
Zarrow, P. 2005
  China in War and Revolution, 1895–1949. London, New York: Routledge.
Zhan, Kaidi. 1992
  The Strategies of Politeness in the Chinese Language. Berkeley CA: Institute of Asian Studies, University of California.
Zhang Kaiyaun, Ed. 2001
  Eyewitnesses to Massacre: American Missionaries Bear Witness to Atrocities in Nanjing. New York: M. E. Sharpe.
Zhao, P. 1995
  Waishi gaishuo (Outline of foreign affairs). Shanghai: Shanghai shehui kexue chubanshe.

Unpublished works

Bickers, Robert A. 1992
  'Changing British Attitudes to China and the Chinese, 1928–1931'. PhD thesis. School of Oriental and African Studies, University of London.
Chatterton, J. M. 2010
  'Protestant Medical Missionary Experience during the War in China 1937–1945: The Case of Hubei Province'. PhD thesis. University of London.
Cliff, N. H. 1995
  'A History of the Protestant Movement and Shandong Province, 1859–1951'. PhD thesis. University of Birmingham.

Howlett, Jonathan J., 2012
   'Creating a New Shanghai: The End of the British Presence in China (1949–57)'. PhD thesis. Bristol University.
Jonson, Jonas. 1972
   'Lutheran Missions in a Time of Revolution: The China Experience 1944–51'. Doctoral thesis. Uppsala University.
Lacy, Creighton, 1953
   'Protestant Missions in Communist China'. PhD thesis. Yale University.
Ladds, C. 2008
   'Empire Careers: The Foreign Staff of the Chinese Customs Service, 1854–1949'. PhD thesis. University of Bristol.
Lawson, Konrad. 2012
   'Wartime Atrocities and the Politics of Treason in the Ruins of the Japanese Empire, 1937–1953'. PhD thesis. Harvard University.
Lee, Sophia, 2011
   'Yenching University and the Japanese Occupation, 1937–1941'. Unpublished paper. California State University.
Wang Ying. 2010
   '*Gaizao sixiang: Zhengzhi, lishi yu jiyi*' (Reforming Thoughts: Politics, History and Memory, 1949–1953). PhD thesis. Beijing: People's University.
Watson, Rubie E. 1996
   'The Foreign Office and Policy-Making in China 1945–1950: Anglo-American Relations and the Recognition of Communist China'. PhD thesis. Institute for International Studies, University of Leeds.
Zhang Daming. 張大明. 2010
   'Yingguo Jinlihui zai Hua Huodong Kaocha 英國浸禮會在華活動考察 (An Investigation of The Baptist Missionary Society's Activities in China), 1840–1952'. MA thesis. Shandong University (Shanda 山大).

Websites

Gardam, Tim (2011) 'God in China: Christianity and Catholicism', BBC Radio 4 aired on 12 September 2011, at
   https://www.bbc.co.uk/programmes/b014fblw accessed on 12 March 2014.
Daily Mail financial website, historic inflation calculator, accessed 5 and 19 November and 1 December 2014 and 3 January 2015,
   www.thisismoney.co.uk/money/bills/article-1633409/Historic-inflation-calculator-value-money-changed-1900.html.
Internet Archive, 'The Challenge of China: being the report of a deputation sent out to visit the China mission fields of the B.M.S., 1919-20', accessed 12 March 2014
   www.archive.org/details/cu31924022920999.
Stories about an English missionary in Zhoucun 英国传教士在周村 (*Yingguo chuan jiao shi zai zhou cun*) from 山东往事 (*Shandong wang shi*) section by 齐鲁网 (*Qilu wang*) of 山东网络台 (*Shandong wang luo tai*) (v.iqilu.com), accessed 10 September 2013,

First Part: （上 shang) http://v.iqilu.com/2013/09/09/3941353.shtml
Second Part: (下 xia) http://v.iqilu.com/2013/09/10/3941889.shtml.
United States Military Academy, Department of History website, accessed 31
    October 2013,
    www.westpoint.edu/history/SiteAssets/SitePages/Chinese%20Civil%20War
    /ChineseCivilWar05.gif.
Zibo City Archives, accessed 20 October 2011 and 29 November 2023
http://da.zibo.gov.cn/art/2005/5/18/art_358_383969.html.

Index

Allen, Connie, 150, 187, 219

Allen, Tom, 52, 148, 150–51, 161, 187, 219

American Presbyterian Mission Board, 4

Anderson, Herbert, 34

Anhui province, 54, 83, 97

anti-British campaigns
  pre-occupation, 45, 108
  under occupation, 51, 66, 73, 74, 76, 118

anti-Christian movement, 44, 118, 224

anti-foreign movement, 1, 44, 112, 175

Arthington bequest, 31, 32, 43

Ashmore, Polly, 183

Baptist Missionary Society (BMS), 1, 19–21, 24–25, 29–31, 39, 43
  China, 3, 21, 37–48, *See also* Shaanxi, Shandong *and* Shanxi provinces
    handover, 1–4, 45–48, 70–73, *See also* three-self principles
    political views, 62, 108–10, 178–81
    property, 41, 46, 76–77, 110–11, 131–34, 151
    staffing, 46–47, 106–7, 125–26, 144, 181, 205–8, 213
    finances, 1, 31–34, 45, 47, 71, 157
    missionary pay etc, 27–29, 144

Baptist principles, 22–24, 179, 180–81

Barnett, Doak, 192

Barrett, David, 7

Bastable, Albert, 219

Bastable, Joyce, 219

Bays, Daniel, 13, 21, 184, 211

Beckingsale, Jennie, 93, 219

Beijing, 53, 67, 192, 201, 204

Bethune, Norman, 86, 216–17

Bickers, Robert, 5, 8, 9, 94, 119, 123, 164

Binzhou, 40, 70

Black, Adam, 52, 219

Bloom, Beryl, 52, 219

Bloom, C. V., 52, 219

Border Service. *See* Church of Christ in China

Bowser, Eleanor, 25, 26

Boxer Protocol. *See* Treaties

Boxer uprising, 41, 67, 83, 118, 223

Brady, Anne-Marie, 9, 188, 190–91

British Government
  consular advice (China), 60, 61–62, 66, 85, 105–6, 180
  diplomacy (China), 21, 108, 111, 122, 123, 133–34
  diplomacy (Japan), 58, 60, 88
  military mission (China), 106–8

British United Aid to China Fund, 102

Brook, Timothy, 13, 49, 56

Brown, Ernest, 173

Brown, Jeremy, 8

Bryan, Keith, 85, 109–10, 180–81, 219

Bryan, Kitty, 181, 219

Buck, Pearl, 4

Burma, 111

Bywaters, Nancy, 161, 163–64, 219

Campaign Against Counter-Revolutionaries, 204, 209

Campbell, Colin, 157

Carey, William, 19–20, 22, 75, 197

Cavalcanti, H. B., 4

censorship of mail, 49–50, 135, 186, 187, 212

Ch'ing-Chou-fu. *See* Qingzhou

Chang, H. Y., 200

Chang, Iris, 52

Chao, Dr, 194, 196
Chao, T. C., 200
Chaozhou, 215
Chatterton, Jocelyn, 9, 57, 63
Cheeloo. *See* Qilu
Chefoo boarding school, 29, 140
Chen Guofu, 121
Chen Lifu, 121
Chengdu, 198, 205
Chesterman, Clement, 25, 28, 105, 139,
    174
Chiang Kai-shek, 54, 89, 116, 148, 171,
    214
    and Christianity, 3, 109, 117, 125
    kidnap, 83
    views on British government, 81, 109,
    111
China Inland Mission, 29, 31, 83
China Relief Mission (US State
    Department), 173
China, People's Republic of (founded
    1949), 183–209, 225
China, Republic of (founded 1912), 43,
    224
Chinese Baptist church, 39, 41, 46, 68–
    80, 88, *See also* Shantung Baptist
    Union *and* three-self principles
    and BMS, 4, 30, 42, 81, 144–45, 148
    establishment, 37–42, 42, 81
Chinese Christians, 21, 41, 56–57, 160–
    69
    and Communist authorities, 86, 149,
    162–69, 199–205
    and missionaries, 11, 136, 200, 214
    persecution/execution, 41, 42, 45, 51,
    73, 83, 149, 167, 194, 204
Chinese Communist Party (CCP). *See*
    Communist authorities
Chinese National Relief and
    Rehabilitation Administration, 134,
    154–55, 171
Chinese People's Political Consultative
    Conference, 168, 199
Chinese Recorder (The), 14, 31, 33, 92
Chongqing, 82, 86, 106, 109, 123
Choutsun. *See* Zhoucun

Christian Farmer magazine, 200
Christian Literature Society, 201
Christian Manifesto, 201–3
Church of Christ in China, 119, 131, 201
    Border Service, 124–28, 145, 185,
    213
Civil War, 116, 147–82, 224, *See also*
    Communist authorities *and*
    Nationalist authorities
Clow, Ellen, 25, 176–77, 187–88, 219
Clow, Menzies, 9, 90, 181, 183, 193, 219
    and Communist authorities, 84, 189–
    92, 192–93
    and Nationalist authorities, 89
    reconstruction of Jenkins Robertson
    Memorial Hospital, 170, 172–76
    war service, 105, 106–7
Cohen, Paul, 7, 93
Collins, Edward, 219
Collins, Margaret, 219
Columbia Country Club, 51
Communist authorities, 16, 50, 81, 183–
    209, 188–89, 203
    and Chinese church, 10, 149, 162–69,
    199–205
    and missionaries, 112, 189–93, 194–
    96, 214, 217
    Civil War, 147–49, 175
    land reforms, 165, 194
    Shaanxi, 82–88, 170, 189–93
    Shandong, 128–30, 165, 194
    War of Resistance, 84, 116
Cook, Henry, 179
Council of Christian Publishers, 201
Cripps, Sir Stafford, 172
Cui, Dan, 93
currency and exchange rate issues, 116,
    155–59, 162, 172, 174
Curtis Committee, 142

Dai Xian, 63
Dart, F. E., 52, 219
Dart, Rufus, 52, 123, 129–31, 134, 137,
    152, 219
Deng, Cora, 200
Dennis O'Neill inquiry, 142

Development and Relief Committee, 154
Dikötter, Frank, 8
Dillon, Nara, 192, 200
Ding Guangxun, 216
Ding Ling, 85
Djang, Bill. *See* Zhang Bohuai
Drake, Dora, 138–39, 219
Drake, Fred, 129, 161–62, 165, 197, 207,
    219
    reporting on Civil War, 132–37, 184,
        187, 194
    travel home from China, 138–39
    working with Zhang Sijing, 71–74,
        152–53, 198
Du Zhongyuan, 54

Eastern Area internment camp
    (Shanghai), 117
Eastman, Lloyd, 6
Eden, Anthony, 61
education and schools, 10, 40, 44, 72,
    92–104, 124, 125, 150, *See also*
    Guangbei School *and* Zunde School
Elder, Arthur, 219
Elder, Kathleen, 219
Eltham College, 36, 143–44
Emmott, Amy. *See* Smurthwaite, Amy
Emmott, Hubert (Bert), 64, 160, 162–65,
    166, 168, 219
Emmott, Winifred, 161, 163, 219
exchange rates. *See* currency and
    exchange rate issues

famine, 41–42, 75, 77, 154
Fenby, Jonathan, 84
Field, Clive, 13
flooding, 54, 70–71, 121
Flowers, Annie, 219
Flowers, Wilfred, 62, 149, 155, 219
Formosa. *See* Taiwan
Forsyth, Robert, 215
Foster Hospital (Zhoucun), 43, 57, 70,
    152, 161, 216
    closures, 66, 73–74, 135–36
    reconstruction (1945-48), 171, 194–
        98

Fu Lianzhang, 86
Fujian province, 97
Fuller, Andrew, 23
Fullerton, W. Y., 39
Fuyincun, 42

Gao Xingzu, 61
Gao Yan, 16
Gilkey, Langdon, 137
Glasby, Beulah, 60, 219
Gold Yuan Reform, 156, 174
Gospel Village. *See* Fuyincun
Greening, Ernest, 40, 68, 219
Guangbei School (Zhoucun), 17, 72, 216
Guangdong province, 97, 216
Guangxi province, 107, 154
Guizhou province, 124
Gunn, David, 219
Gunn, Winifred, 219
Guomindang (GMD). *See* Nationalist
    authorities

Han Fuju, 53
Han Jie, 16
Hangzhou, 185, 198
Hankou, 62, 70
Harris, James, 136, 149, 155, 162, 195–
    96, 219
Harrison, Henrietta, 59, 93
Harrison, Vera, 219
Hayward, Eva, 124, 219
Hayward, Victor, 25, 34, 124, 200, 219
He Siyuan, 165, 167
Hebei province, 97
Henan province, 54, 92, 97
Henriot, Christian, 9
Hong Kong, 59, 111, 205, 207
Hood, George, 12
Hooper, Beverley, 9
Howlett, Jonathan, 9, 188, 192, 195
HuaiHai campaign, 175
Huang He (Yellow River), 44, 54, 70, 121
Huang, Colonel, 165
Hubei province, 9, 97
Hunan province, 97
Hurley, Patrick, 116

Ichi-Go offensive, 98
inflation, 99–101, 155–58, 162, 170,
    173–74
Ingle, A. C., 39
International Famine Relief Committee,
    77
internment, 51–52, 115, 117–18, 137,
    140

Jagger, Amy, 52, 219
Japan, 45, 57–59, *See also* Sino-Japanese
    Wars
Jasper, Vincent, 107
Jenkins Robertson Memorial Hospital
    (Xi'an), 30, 44, 183, 184, 190, 193,
    201
    BMS legacy, 216–17
    evacuation (1939), 82
    reconstruction (1945-48), 169–78
Jenkins, Margaret, 91, 219
Jiang Jieshi. *See* Chiang Kai-shek
Jiangsu province, 54, 97
Jiangxi province, 83
Jin Baoshan (P. Z. King), 122, 170
Jinan, 16, 65, 72, 74, 119, 205, 216–17,
    See also Qilu University, Hospital
    and Medical School
    Civil War, 132, 164–66, 175, 184,
        187, 194
    Japanese occupation, 53, 64–65, 67
    reconstruction, 129, 132–37
Jing Yihui, 69, 133, 136, 144, 152, 166–
    68
Jones, Alfred, 3, 37–39, 41, 127, 220

Kiesow, Margaret, 186
King, Gordon, 217, 220
King, P. Z.. *See* Jin Baoshan
Kitson, George, 133
Konoye, Fumimaro, 72
Korean War, 202, 203
Kuomintang (KMT). *See* Nationalist
    authorities

Lary, Diana, 7, 53, 54, 91, 98

Laughton, Richard, 22, 37
Lee, Joseph, 215
Lewis, Georgina, 52, 220
Lewis, John, 52, 220
Lewis, Nellie, 67, 220
Li Dianlu, 95
Li Jianwu, 56
Lian Xi, 13
Liaoning province, 97, 175
Liaoshen campaign, 175
Light, Arthur Barrington, 52, 220
Light, Constance, 52, 220
Ling, Oiki, 5, 12, 49, 80, 116, 123, 130,
    183, 185, 187, 203, 214
Ling, Y. P., 117
Lingdong, 12
Linyi, 165
Liu Bocheng, 165
Liu Liang-Mao, 200
London Missionary Society, 27, 57, 142
Long March, 82, 83, 85
Lu Ning, 188
Lutz, Jessie, 11

Ma, Tehyun, 154
Mackinnon, Stephen, 7, 53
Madge, Edna, 107, 220
Madge, Ernest, 107, 119, 131, 155, 220
Malayan Emergency, 207
Manger, Jessie, 58, 220
Manktelow, Emily, 27, 142
Mao Zedong, 116, 188, 194, 200, 206,
    217
    Rectification Campaign, 86
Marshman, Joseph, 20, 22
Maughan, Stephen, 25
May Fourth Movement, 45, 224
May Thirtieth incident, 45, 108
medicine and healthcare, 43, 122, 134,
    151, 183, 197
    BMS hospitals. *See* Foster Hospital,
        Jenkins Robertson Memorial
        Hospital and Qilu University,
        Hospital and Medical School
    BMS legacy, 217
    Communist policy, 190–93, 194–95

Nationalist policy, 89, 170–71
  war-time, 61, 66, 92, 133, 163, 168
  women's healthcare, 40, 44, 89, 217
Meng Lo San, 66
Miall, C. S., 23
Mian Xian, 98
missionaries, 4–5, 24, 35–37, 57–68,
  205–8
  and Communist authorities, 82–88,
    112, 163–64, 189–93, 192, 214
  and Japanese authorities, 60, 62–64,
    64–65, 66–67
  and Nationalist authorities, 89, 128
  family life, 15, 28–29, 137–44
  killed, 41, 60, 83, 174, 224
  terms and conditions, 27–29, 33, 75,
    157
  war work, 91–92, 105–7
Missionary Herald, 14, 92
Mitter, Rana, 7, 10, 54, 153, 154, 170,
  171, 183, 214
Moorshead, R. F., 39
Moss, George, 62
Mudd, Charlotte, 181, 220
Mudd, William, 86, 181, 220

Nanjing, 3, 70, 86, 134, 150, 171, 175
  (Treaty of). *See* Treaties
  military activity, 52, 61, 96
Nanking. *See* Nanjing
National Christian Council, 33–34, 109,
  122, 200
National Christian Service Council for
  Wounded Soldiers in Transit, 92
National Health Administration, 122,
  170, 171
National Health Service (UK), 206
Nationalist authorities, 3, 8, 50, 82, 213
  and Chinese church. *See* Church of
    Christ in China Border Service
  and missionaries, 85–87, 88, 117,
    121, 170–71
  Civil War, 128–30, 132, 147–49,
    165–67, 175, 184–85
  education reforms, 93–94
  inflationary fiscal policy, 156

reconstruction, 154–55
  War of Resistance, 54–55, 70, 84, 116
Nelson, Peter, 16, 205, 220
New Life Movement, 89, 171
Newton, J. C., 52, 220
Newton, Marjorie, 52, 220
Niu Jianyi, 217

opium, 21–22, 43, 89
Opium Wars, 223

Pailing, Muriel, 52, 220
Pailing, W. P., 52, 220
Pan Jingnian, 167, 169
Payne, Henry, 52, 70, 75, 76, 144, 220
Payne, Jessie, 220
Peichen. *See* Binzhou
People's Liberation Army (PLA). *See*
  Communist authorities
Pepper, Suzanne, 7
Phillips, Edward, 26, 52, 64–65, 129,
  132–37, 157–58, 207, 220
Phillips, Enid, 52, 220
Pickowicz, Paul, 8
Poshek Fu, 55
Price, Bryn, 106–7, 220
Price, Fred, 52, 60, 67, 220

Qilu University, Hospital and Medical
  School (Jinan), 30, 43, 95, 186, 195,
  198, 205
  BMS legacy, 171, 217
  Civil War, 184, 185
  Japanese occupation, 73, 76
  reconstruction, 133–35
Qing Empire, 42, 43
Qingdao, 45, 58, 60, 66, 152, 184
Qingzhou, 39, 43, 69, 95, 166, 197
  BMS conference (1927), 3
  BMS legacy, 216–17
  Civil War, 135, 144, 160–69, 184
  Japanese occupation, 63, 73

Rabe, John, 61
reconstruction, 129–34, 154–55, 169–78
Rectification Campaign, 86

Red Cross, 134, 155, 170, 193
refugees, 70, 82, 207
    Civil War, 132, 150, 153–55, 184
    Japanese occupation, 53–54, 64, 82,
        91, 96, 124
    Yellow River diversion, 54, 121
rice riots, 148
Richard, Timothy, 3, 37, 41, 220
Roberts, John, 57
Rowley, H. H., 95
Russell, Fred, 112, 138, 179, 181, 220
    reports from Shaanxi, 83, 86, 89, 98,
        158
Russell, Gertrude, 220

Sanyuan, 44, 85, 102, 109
Scott, Caroline, 220
Scott, James Cameron, 52, 220
Seymour, Gladys, 186, 220
Shaanxi province, 46–47, 78, 124, 180,
        198, *See also* Fuyincun, Sanyuan,
    Yan'an *and* Xi'an
    BMS handover (1950-51), 203–4
    Civil War, 184–85, 189–93
    establishing BMS mission, 3, 42–44
    Free China, 5–6, 49, 81–113
Shandong province, 43, 95, 97, 157,
        194–99, *See also* Jinan, Qingdao,
    Qingzhou *and* Zhoucun
    'Shandong Problem', 45
    BMS handover plans, 45–48
    BMS institutions closed (1942), 51
    BMS return (1945), 132–36
    BMS withdrawal (1951), 16, 205
    Civil War, 112, 128, 148, 149, 160–
        69, 184–85
    establishing BMS mission, 3–6
    Japanese occupation, 5–6, 49–80
    Shantung Baptist Union, 24, 39, 46,
        95, 123, 208, 215–16
        photograph, 196
        under Japanese occupation, 68–80
Shang Zhen, 121
Shanghai, 29, 61, 111, 122, 144, 192,
    195
    BMS mission, 185, 200, 205

internment of missionaries, 51–52,
        117–18, 150
    massacre (1925), 45, 108
    repatriation of British citizens, 59,
        138
Shansi. *See* Shanxi
Shantung. *See* Shandong
Shanxi province, 3, 43, 47, 86, 92, 95,
        97, 119, *See also* Taiyuan
    BMS evacuation (1939), 51, 73, 76,
        214
    BMS evacuation (1948), 184–85
    BMS return (1945), 123, 128–31
    Civil War, 112, 128, 149, 174
    establishing BMS mission, 41–42
    Japanese occupation, 5–6, 49, 67, 74
    missionaries killed, 39, 41, 174
Shao Lizi, 89
Shell company, 172
Shell Company, 150
Shensi. *See* Shaanxi
Shenyang, 175
Shimonoseki (Treaty of). *See* Treaties
Shyu, Lawrence, 7
Sian. *See* Xi'an
Sianfu. *See* Xi'an
Sichuan province, 42, 97, 127
Sino-Japanese Wars
    First, 57–59, 223–25, *See also*
        Treaties
    Second, 1, 3, 51–52, 124, 224
        and Second World War, 105–8
        military attacks, 53, 61, 82, 87–88,
            96–98, 107
        occupation, 4, 5–6, 17, 41, 49–80,
            136
Skeats, H. S., 23
Smith, Caroline, 52
Smith, Christina, 63–64, 220
Smith, Eric Sutton, 52, 129, 152, 220
Smith, John Henderson, 126–28, 220
Smurthwaite, Amy, 52, 219, 220
Soong Mei-ling, 89
Spillett, Hubert, 158–59, 205, 220
St Paul plane, 151
Stam, John and Betty (execution), 83

Stanley, Brian, 2, 10, 21, 34
Steane, Edward, 22
Still, Audrey (Salters), 52
Still, Gwyneth, 52, 60, 87, 120, 141, 161, 220
Still, Ronald, 105–6, 118, 150–51, 169, 195–96, 220
  in occupied Zhoucun, 57, 66, 77, 79
  legacy, 217
  photograph, 52, 196
  reconstruction during Civil War, 148, 152, 165, 171
Stilwell, Joseph, 89
Stockley, Handley, 1, 110, 141–42, 149, 220
  invitation to operate on Mao, 86
  legacy, 216–17
  resource concerns, 28, 30, 90, 155
Stockley, Jean, 220
Stuart, John Leighton, 67
student movement, 45, 148, 190, 205
Sun Shouxin, 132
Sutton, Edna, 104, 220
Sutton, Jim, 104, 205, 220

Tait, Ruth, 220
Taiwan, 207
Taiyuan, 41, 43, 155, 184
  BMS conference (1929), 95
  Civil War, 129–31, 149
  Japanese occupation, 54, 60, 64, 73
taxation, 148, 193
Thomas, Margaret, 52, 220
Three-Self Patriotic Movement (TSPM), 168, 202, 216
three-self principles, 2, 20, 22
  Shaanxi, 42, 47–48, 81, 89–92, 113, 170
  Shandong, 38–40, 41, 47–48, 69, 80, 196–98, 208, 215
  Shanxi, 41, 47–48
Tian Xuelin, 64
Tianfeng, 174, 202
Tianjin (Treaty of). *See* Treaties
Tilehouse Street gift to Xi'an, 169–78
Ting, K. H.. *See* Ding Guangxun

travel
  inside China, 70, 130, 132, 133, 149–52, 154, 189
  to/from China, 29, 107, 138
Treaties, 21–22, 45, 58, 59, 223
  abrogation, 81–82, 108–12, 120, 225
  link to opium trade, 21–22
Tsinan. *See* Jinan
Tsingchow. *See* Qingzhou, *See* Qingzhou
Tsun Te School. *See* Zunde School
Tulloch, Gordon, 157

Unequal Treaties. *See* Treaties
United Nations Relief and Rehabilitation Administration, 107, 134, 154–55
Upchurch, William (Bill), 32, 125, 128, 169, 220
Upchurch, Winifred, 220

Versailles (Treaty of). *See* Treaties

Wallinger, Geoffrey, 134
Walthamstow Hall, 36, 143–44
Wang Bo, 217
Wang Fu-I, 171
Wang Juntang, 133, 136, 152, 160–69, 195, 216
Wang Mingdao, 216
Wang Tongzhao, 56
Wang Yaowu, 165
War of Resistance. *See* Sino-Japanese Wars
war reparations, 131
Ward, William, 20–22
Watson, Rubie, 216
Weifang, 117
Weihsien internment camp, 117, 137
welfare reform (UK), 142–44
Westad, Odd Arne, 7, 8, 164, 192
Wheal, Alice, 52, 220
Whitewright Institute, 64–65, 67, 133
Wickeri, Philip, 13
Wickings, Harold, 187
Williamson, Joan, 35, 82, 95–104, 110, 181, 203, 220

Williamson, Raymond (H. R.), 10, 39,
    67, 84, 220
    as BMS Foreign Secretary (1939-48),
        25, 71–72, 159, 176, 179, 213
        China visit (1945-46), 87, 92, 107,
            119–24, 134
        communications with Zhang
            Sijing and Jing Yihui, 69, 78,
            125–26
    as BMS missionary, 25, 42, 119, 136
Wilson, C. E., 1, 39, 94
workers' strikes, 45, 148
World Congress of Baptists (Atlanta,
    Georgia, 1939), 23
World Council of Churches, 200
World Missionary Conference
    (Edinburgh, 1910), 2, 34
World War (First), 45, 58, 154, 224
World War (Second), 51, 61, 75, 78,
    105–8, 169, 224
Wu Keming, 135
Wu Yaozong, 174, 200, 202
Wuxi, 57
Wyatt, Harry, 5, 36, 60, 63, 64, 221
Wyman, Judith, 42

Xi'an, 88–91, 93, 110, 192, 216–17, *See
    also* Jenkins Robertson Memorial
    Hospital *and* Zunde School
    BMS handover plans, 204
    Civil War, 65, 82–85, 86, 187, 189
    War with Japan, 97, 107–8
Xi'an No. 3 High School. *See* Zunde
    School
Xi'an No. 4 Hospital. *See* Jenkins
    Robertson Memorial Hospital
Xichang, 127, 128
Xizang province, 124
Xu Lingzao, 130

Yan Xishan, 41, 119, 121, 130

Yan'an, 83, 85–87, 148
Yanjing Daxue, 67
Yantai, 29
Ye Jianying, 192
Yellow River. *See* Huang He
Yenching School of Religion, 200
Yip, Ka-Che, 211
Young Men's Christian Association
    (YMCA), 88, 160, 175, 200, 201
Young Women's Christian Association
    (YWCA), 200, 201
Young, George, 181, 205–6, 221
    reports from Shaanxi (1924-45), 83,
        84–85, 125
    reports from Shaanxi (1946-51), 180,
        187–88, 189–92, 193, 204
Young, Nora, 221
Yuan Shikai, 93

Zhan, Kaidi, 191
Zhang Bohuai, 125–27
Zhang Hu Shi, 152
Zhang Sijing, 123, 125, 126, 136
    as leader of SBU, 30, 68–80, 197,
        212, 216
    partnership with BMS, 46, 133, 144,
        152, 194, 198
    photograph, 69, 78, 196
Zhou Enlai, 84, 191, 201
Zhou Fohai, 56
Zhoucun, 46, 70, 76–77, 132, 152, 216–
    17, *See also* Foster Hospital *and*
    Guangbei School
    Christian Service Centre, 20, 197–98
    Civil War, 184
    Japanese occupation, 62, 70
Zhouping, 43
Zibo No. 6 High School. *See* Guangbei
    School
Zui, H. H., 126
Zunde School (Xi'an), 95–104, 213, 216